TOMB RAIDER™

TOMB RAIDER™

OMNIBUS

VOLUME 1

TOMB RAIDER: THE BEGINNING

Script **RHIANNA PRATCHETT**
Pencils **ANDREA MUTTI, NICOLÁS DANIEL SELMA**
Inks **JUAN GEDEON, PIERLUIGI BALDASSINI**
Colors **MICHAEL ATIYEH**
Letters **MICHAEL HEISLER**

TOMB RAIDER ISSUES #1–#6

Script **GAIL SIMONE**
Pencils **NICOLÁS DANIEL SELMA**
Inks **JUAN GEDEON**
Colors **MICHAEL ATIYEH**
Letters **MICHAEL HEISLER**

TOMB RAIDER ISSUES #7–#9

Script **RHIANNA PRATCHETT** and **GAIL SIMONE**
Pencils **DERLIS SANTACRUZ**
Inks **ANDY OWENS**
Colors **MICHAEL ATIYEH**
Letters **MICHAEL HEISLER**

TOMB RAIDER ISSUES #10–#12

Script **RHIANNA PRATCHETT** and **GAIL SIMONE**
Pencils **NICOLÁS DANIEL SELMA**
Inks **JUAN GEDEON**
Colors **MICHAEL ATIYEH**
Letters **MICHAEL HEISLER**

TOMB RAIDER ISSUES #13–#18

Script **RHIANNA PRATCHETT**
Pencils **DERLIS SANTACRUZ**
Inks **ANDY OWENS**
Colors **MICHAEL ATIYEH**
Letters **MICHAEL HEISLER**

DARK HORSE BOOKS

PUBLISHER
MIKE RICHARDSON

EDITOR
MEGAN WALKER

ASSISTANT EDITOR
JOSHUA ENGLEDOW

ORIGINAL SERIES EDITOR
DAVE MARSHALL

ORIGINAL SERIES ASSISTANT EDITORS
SHANTEL LAROCQUE, ROXY POLK, IAN TUCKER, and AARON WALKER

DESIGNER
SKYLER WEISSENFLUH

DIGITAL ART TECHNICIAN
SAMANTHA HUMMER

This volume collects issues #1 through #18 of the Dark Horse Comics series *Tomb Raider*, originally printed in 2014, as well as a bonus prequel issue to Crystal Dynamics' 2013 *Tomb Raider*, entitled *Tomb Raider: The Beginning*.

Published by Dark Horse Books
A division of Dark Horse Comics LLC
10956 SE Main Street, Milwaukie, OR 97222

DarkHorse.com
TombRaider.com

Facebook.com/DarkHorseComics
Twitter.com/DarkHorseComics

Advertising Sales: (503) 905-2315
Comic Shop Locator Service: comicshoplocator.com

First Edition: July 2019 | ISBN 978-1-50671-421-9 | Digital ISBN 978-1-50671-423-3

10 9 8 7 6 5 4 3 2 1
Printed in China

Library of Congress Cataloging-in-Publication Data

Names: Pratchett, Rhianna, author. | Mutti, Andrea, 1973- penciller. | Gedeon, Juan, inker. | Atiyeh, Michael, colourist. | Heisler, Michael, letterer.
Title: Tomb Raider omnibus.
Description: First edition. | Milwaukie, OR : Dark Horse Books, 2019- | v. 1: script: Rhianna Pratchett [and others] ; pencils: Andrea Mutti [and others] ; inks: Juan Gedeon [and others] ; colors: Michael Atiyeh ; lettering: Michael Heisler. | v. 1: "This volume collects issues #1 through #18 of the Dark Horse Comics series Tomb Raider, originally printed in 2014, as well as a bonus prequel issue to Crystal Dynamics' 2013 Tomb Raider, entitled Tomb Raider: The Beginning."
Identifiers: LCCN 2019005953 | ISBN 9781506714219 (v. 1)
Subjects: LCSH: Comic books, strips, etc.
Classification: LCC PN6728.T6625 T69 2019 | DDC 741.5/973--dc23
LC record available at https://lccn.loc.gov/2019005953

TABLE OF CONTENTS

Whitman's World
BEST Documentary Series

IT'S TOM.
COME!
Dr. James Whitman
KNOCK KNOCK

HOW'S MY FAVORITE CLIENT?
IF I SEE HIM, I'LL ASK. I HOPE THAT'S A CHAI LATTE.
SO THE NETWORK TELLS ME SEASON TWO'S FIGURES ARE DOING OKAY.

ER, SHELLY, COULD YOU GIVE US A FEW MINUTES, PLEASE?
IT'S SHELBY.
OH, OF COURSE. OF COURSE!

JUST OKAY?
OKAY IS GOOD.
NO, GOOD IS GOOD.
SLAM

DON'T PANIC. THEY'VE COMMISSIONED A THIRD SEASON. YOU'RE STILL GOLDEN.

AH, THE NEW CREW!

LOOKS LIKE THEY COULD FIND A BAR, A BROTHEL, OR A BURGER. NOT SO SURE THEY COULD FIND THE LOST KINGDOM OF, WHERE WAS IT? YAMI...
YAMATAI.
RIGHT. STILL, BET THEY'VE GOT SOME STORIES.
I'M TAKING A UNIT DOWN TO THEIR BOAT TOMORROW. START ON THE INTERVIEWS.

AN EX-COP. SEEMS A BIT EXCESSIVE FOR AN ARCHAEOLOGICAL EXPEDITION.
Joslyn Reyes
I KNOW. BUT CAPTAIN ROTH INSISTED HE PICK HIS OWN PEOPLE.

LARA CROFT. CROFT... *CROFT.* WHERE HAVE I HEARD THAT NAME BEFORE?
Lara Croft

NOW *SHE* IS SOMEONE I WOULDN'T MIND GETTING LOST WITH.

ENDURANCE
THE ENDURANCE. THIS IS IT.

THAT'S WHAT SELLING YOUR SOUL LOOKS LIKE.
SURPRISED IT WAS WORTH SO MUCH.

GOOD TO MEET YOU, CAPTAIN.
CALL ME ROTH. THIS IS ANGUS GRIMALDI, MY HELMSMAN.

AND THIS IS LARA CROFT, ONE OF OUR DECKHANDS.
IT'S AN HONOR. I'VE WATCHED ALL YOUR SHOWS. I STUDIED ASIAN ARCHAEOLOGY AT COLLEGE.
DID YOU, NOW? WELL, ALWAYS GOOD TO MEET A FAN.
I'D VERY MUCH LIKE TO GET STARTED ON THE INTERVIEWS, ROTH.

OH MY GOD! IT'S AN ALEXA!

SAM! DON'T DISTURB THEM.

I HAVE TO. IT'S SO BEAUTIFUL.

IT'S AN ARRI ALEXA, ISN'T IT?
YES, THE PLUS.
I'VE GOT THE ORIGINAL. DIGITAL'S THE ONLY WAY TO GO, ISN'T IT?
COUGH
LET'S NOT LOSE THE LIGHT!
SORRY, SHE'S A CAMERA NUT.

DR. WHITMAN, THIS IS MY FRIEND, SAMANTHA NISHIMURA. WE WENT TO COLLEGE TOGETHER.
I'M NOT ONE OF THE CREW. I'M JUST KEEPING LARA COMPANY AND TOPPING UP MY TAN.

AIN'T NO POWDER'S GONNA HELP *OUR* FACES, LASS.
THEN PERHAPS I CAN TAKE YOUR DRINK?
NOPE. THE BRU STAYS WITH ME.

WE'D RATHER YOU DIDN'T DRINK ON CAMERA.
NOT BREW. BRU! IRN-BRU. FINEST DRINK IN SCOTLAND. FINEST DRINK IN *THE WORLD!*
OH, JUST LET HIM HAVE IT. WE HAVE TO START!

I'M HERE WITH CAPTAIN CONRAD ROTH, OF THE *ENDURANCE*. AND HIS HELMSMAN, MR. ANGUS GRIMALDI.
GRIM.
MR. GRIM.
SO, I BELIEVE YOU GENTLEMEN HAVE BEEN GOING ON EXPEDITIONS TOGETHER FOR OVER TWENTY YEARS?

WHAT HE DOESN'T KNOW ABOUT SHIPS ISN'T WORTH KNOWING.
IF IT'S WET, I CAN SAIL ON IT.
TELL US ABOUT ONE OF YOUR ADVENTURES.
12.36 F5.0 (42.7)k

REMEMBER SOMALIA, ANGUS?
AYE.
52.86 F5.0 (42.7)k

"A COUPLE OF YEARS BACK, WE WERE DOING A BIT OF BUSINESS IN SOMALIA.
"ACTUALLY, IT WAS MORE LIKE RECLAIMING A CLIENT'S PERSONAL PROPERTY.
"LET'S JUST SAY THE NATIVES WEREN'T FRIENDLY."
DAFT BASTARDS! AIN'T GOT NOTHING ON ME MA.
PITY YOUR MA AIN'T HERE THEN.
THINK THEY'LL KILL US.
PROBABLY.
WISH THEY'D HURRY UP THEN. IT'S ALL THIS FANNYING ABOUT I CAN'T STAND.

YOU SAW THE HORSE, RIGHT?

YEAH, IN THAT SIDE OFFICE. ALONG WITH YOUR PISTOLS. BUYER MUST'VE NOT SHOWN UP YET.

DAMN IT, ANGUS. I'M NOT GOING OUT LIKE THIS.

THERE'S A JEEP OUTSIDE. UNGUARDED.

WE JUST NEED SOMETHING SHARP TO CUT THESE BINDINGS.

I CAN HELP THERE. WHEN THEY KNOCKED ME DOWN, I MANAGED TO SECURE US A LITTLE BIT OF...

PTEW

SO THEN WE ESCAPED, GOT THE HORSE BACK, STOLE THE JEEP, NARROWLY ESCAPED BEING SHOT, STABBED, AND CUT UP WITH A MACHETE.
I'D RATE IT A SEVEN POINT DAY.
MAYBE SEVEN POINT FIVE.

ER, SHOULD THAT BE HAPPENING?
SHIT! IT'S COMING FROM THE ENGINE ROOM.
HOW THE HELL HAVE YOU BEEN KEEPING THIS THING AFLOAT FOR SO LONG?

CAN YOU FIX HER?
UNLIKELY. EVEN IF I COULD, IT WOULD TAKE WEEKS.
WE DON'T HAVE WEEKS! WE'RE ON A SCHEDULE HERE!
YOU'D BETTER PRAY FOR A MIRACLE THEN.

OR PHONE ONE.
SHE WON'T BE HAPPY.

BIT OF A SITUATION. CAN YOU COME A FEW DAYS EARLY?
YOU *KNOW* I'M LOOKING AFTER ALISHA.
WE NEED YOU.
...
OKAY, OKAY. I NEED YOU, REYES.
I'LL BE THERE TOMORROW.

I'M SORRY, BABY. I KNOW YOU HAD A WHOLE THING PLANNED FOR US.
IT'S OKAY.
ENDURANCE

UNCLE ROTH! LARA!

ALISHA! YOU'VE GROWN.
DUH! IT'S BEEN A YEAR!
IS SHE MAD?

YEAH. BUT WORK'LL CALM HER DOWN.

THANKS FOR COMING EARLY, REYES. THE ENGINE'S DIED ON US. I WAS HOPING YOU COULD COAX IT BACK TO LIFE.
MOM CAN FIX ANYTHING.
IT COULDN'T WAIT UNTIL ALISHA'S SUMMER VACATION WAS OVER?

WE'RE ON A TIGHT SCHEDULE. T.V. MONEY'S GOOD, BUT THEY DON'T LIKE BEING JERKED AROUND.
NEITHER DO I.

COME ON, LET'S GET YOU SOME BREAKFAST.

LET'S GET HER WHILE SHE'S FRESH.

JOSLYN REYES, I PRESUME?
YUP. MR. T.V., I PRESUME?

I'D LOVE TO INTERVIEW YOU.
I'M BUSY.

I PROMISE WE WON'T TAKE UP TOO MUCH TIME.
GO ON THEN. GET IT OVER WITH.

WHY DON'T YOU TELL ME WHY AN EX-COP ENDED UP BEING A MECHANIC?
SMART GUY LIKE YOU...I'M BETTING YOU KNOW THE ANSWER TO THAT ALREADY.
WELL, I KNOW YOU QUIT THE N.Y.P.D. OVER A GANG SHOOTING. SOMETHING TO DO WITH YOUR PARTNER.

LET ME TELL YOU SOMETHING...
26.76 F8.0 (43.8)K

"HE WAS ONE OF THE BEST ON THE FORCE. TAUGHT ME EVERYTHING HE KNEW ABOUT BEING A GOOD COP.

"AFTER A FEW YEARS ON THE JOB, WE GOT CAUGHT IN A DRUG DEN SHOOTOUT. HIS WEAPON MUST'VE JAMMED. THEY GUNNED HIM DOWN LIKE HE WAS NOTHING.

"I PROMISED HIS FAMILY THAT I'D MAKE IT RIGHT.
POLICE
9-1-1

"BUT DRUG MONEY BUYS GOOD LAWYERS. THE BASTARDS GOT AWAY WITH IT.

"I COULDN'T TAKE THAT. SO I QUIT. BUT I'D MADE A PROMISE.

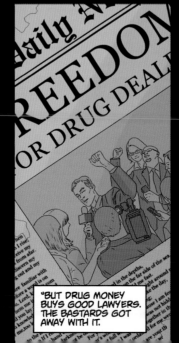

"AND I KEPT IT.

"BUT I STILL HAD BILLS TO PAY, SO I MOVED IN WITH MY SISTER.
"AND WENT TO WORK IN MY BROTHER'S GARAGE.
GT
"THE WORK CALMED ME.
"I GUESS YOU COULD SAY I HAD A KNACK WITH MACHINES.
"THEY'RE LESS COMPLICATED THAN PEOPLE.

"CERTAINLY LESS COMPLICATED THAN A CONRAD ROTH.
"I MET HIM DOWN AT A BAR I USED TO DRINK AT AFTER WORK.
"IT HAD BEEN A TOUGH DAY. I WAS MISSING THE FORCE."
YOU'VE HAD ENOUGH!
FILL IT UP, DAMN IT! IF I CAN'T FIND THEM, I'LL FORGET THEM!
"SOME GUY WAS MAKING A FUSS. HE'D BEEN DRINKING ALL DAY AND THEY'D CUT HIM OFF. HE WASN'T HAPPY. KEPT TALKING ABOUT HIS MISSING FRIENDS AND HOW HE SHOULD'VE FOUND THEM BY NOW.
"I WASN'T IN THE MOOD FOR OTHER PEOPLE'S BULLSHIT.
THWAK
"SO I SORTED IT.

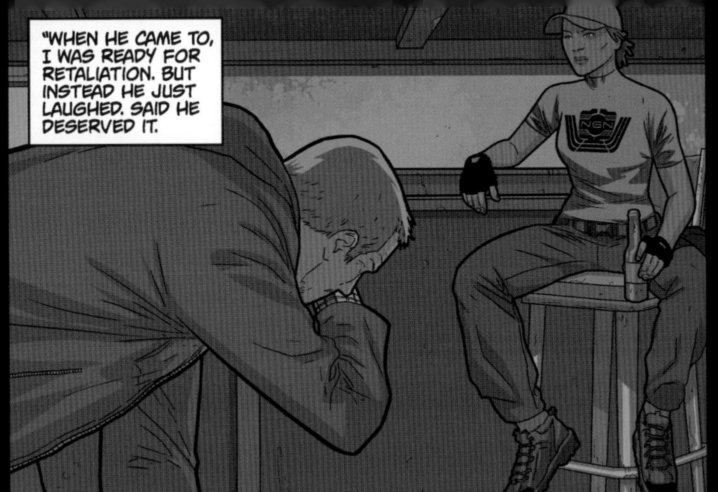
"WHEN HE CAME TO, I WAS READY FOR RETALIATION. BUT INSTEAD HE JUST LAUGHED. SAID HE DESERVED IT.

"WE TALKED, AND THEN HE OFFERED ME A JOB. THIS JOB."

SO HE SAW POTENTIAL IN YOU?
PERHAPS. ROTH HAS AN INSTINCT ABOUT PEOPLE. CAN'T SAY I AGREE WITH HIM EVERY TIME, BUT THE MAN TRUSTS HIS GUT.

AND WHAT ABOUT ALISHA? HAS SHE EVER COME ON AN EXPEDITION?
NO. I NORMALLY KEEP HER AWAY FROM ALL THAT. MY SISTER LOOKS AFTER HER WHEN I'M AWAY.
WHAT ABOUT HER FATHER?

HE WASN'T READY TO BE A PARENT.

THERE'S A CALL FOR YOU, DOCTOR. A THOMAS GOLDMAN.
I'LL BE RIGHT THERE.

JAPAN
NORTH PACIFIC OCEAN
JAMES! HOW'S IT GOING DOWN THERE?
THIS BUNCH'LL MAKE FOR GREAT T.V.
ER, THAT'S WHAT I WAS RINGING ABOUT.
WHAT IS IT?
BEST Documentary Series

THE FINAL FIGURES ARE IN FOR SEASON TWO OF *WHITMAN'S WORLD*. THEY'RE NOT GOOD.
WHEN YOU SAY NOT GOOD...
I MEAN BAD. ***REALLY*** BAD.
SHIT. SHIT. I SAID AZTEC RUINS WERE A MISTAKE!

THERE'S NO EASY WAY TO PUT THIS, BUT THE NETWORK'S PULLING THE FUNDING FOR SEASON THREE.

IT'S OVER.

WE'LL SEE YOU IN A FEW DAYS.

WHAT'S HE TALKING ABOUT?
I DON'T KNOW. JUST KEEP WALKING.

ARE YOU SURE EVERYTHING'S OKAY, DR. WHITMAN?

OH, OF COURSE. THE NETWORK JUST NEEDED THEM ELSEWHERE FOR A WHILE. THEY'LL BE BACK.
OKAY. BUT IF YOU NEED ANY HELP WHILST YOUR ASSISTANT IS AWAY, JUST LET ME KNOW.
I APPRECIATE THE OFFER, LARA. BUT I'M SURE I'LL BE FINE.

THOMAS! TELL ME YOU'VE BEEN BUSY WITH CONVINCING THE NETWORK TO REINVEST IN *WHITMAN'S WORLD?*

YOU KNOW WHAT THE NETWORK'S LIKE. IT'S ALL ABOUT RATINGS WITH THEM.
BUT IT'S THE SEARCH FOR **YAMATAI**...THE LOST KINGDOM. IT COULD BE A GOLD MINE!

IT'S ARCHAEOLOGY LIVE! FOLLOW THE ADVENTURES AS THEY HAPPEN!
YOU KNOW *I* LOVE THE CONCEPT.

THIS IS GOING TO HAPPEN, TOM. EVEN IF I HAVE TO FUND IT MYSELF.
YOU MEAN SHEILA ACTUALLY LEFT YOU WITH SOMETHING AFTER THE DIVORCE?

LOOK, JUST TRY TO GET THEM TO RECONSIDER. **PLEASE.** I **NEED** THIS.
I'LL TRY.

IT'S JAMES. MY CODE'S NOT WORKING.

THAT'S BECAUSE I CHANGED IT!
JUST LET ME IN!

WHAT THE HELL ARE YOU DOING, SHEILA?
SELLING YOUR OLD STUFF.
OLD STUFF? THEY'RE ANTIQUES!
WHATEVER!

ARE YOU LEAVING ME ANYTHING?
YOU'RE NOT BEING REASONABLE.
YOU GET THE HOUSE, WHEN I'M THROUGH WITH IT. I GET THE BANK ACCOUNT AND THE REST!

OH, NOT THE CHINESE ARMOIRE!

THOMAS TOLD ME ABOUT THE NETWORK CANCELLING YOUR SHOW. I THOUGHT I'D BETTER TAKE WHAT'S OWED TO ME WHILE YOU'VE STILL GOT IT!
LOOK. LET ME SELL THEM FOR US. I'LL GET A MUCH BETTER PRICE.
DO YOU REALLY THINK I'D TRUST YOU AFTER WHAT YOU DID? SHE WAS 24!
22 -- BUT IT DOESN'T MATTER --

CRASH

THOMAS, THOSE PIECES THE LONDON MUSEUM SENT US FOR SEASON THREE, HAVE THEY GONE BACK YET?
I'VE GOT THEM HERE. THEY'LL HAVE TO GO BACK SOON THOUGH.
THEN GET THEM READY FOR ME.

IT'S
BEST I DON'T
KNOW WHAT YOU
WANT THESE FOR,
ISN'T IT?

SO WHO
ARE THESE
GUYS?

FU, LU,
AND SHOU. THE
CHINESE GODS OF
GOOD FORTUNE,
PROSPERITY, AND
LONGEVITY.
MY
LOCAL CHINESE
RESTAURANT HAS
SOMETHING
SIMILAR.

THERE'RE
VERSIONS IN
EVERY HOME IN
CHINA. BUT THESE
BOYS DATE BACK
CENTURIES.
IF THESE
DON'T GET BACK TO
THE MUSEUM, WE'RE
GOING TO BE IN SOME
SERIOUS SHIT.
DELAY IT
AS LONG AS
YOU CAN.

WORSE COMES
TO WORST, JUST TELL
THE MUSEUM THAT I'M
DELIVERING THEM BACK
PERSONALLY.

FERGUS? IT'S ME. GREEN DOOR, RIGHT?

RIGHT. LOOK, YOU NEED TO BE CAREFUL WITH THIS GUY.
YOU WANTED A QUICK BUYER. I GOT YOU ONE. BUT HE'S... UNPREDICTABLE.

I DON'T HAVE A CHOICE. I'LL GIVE YOU YOUR CUT AFTER THE SALE.
BUZZ

ER, I'M HERE TO SEE MR HONG.
GO IN.

YOU'RE LATE.

SHOW THEM TO ME.

DISCOLORATION IS SUSPECT. PRICKLING IS TOO EVEN.
ER, MAYBE IF YOU TOOK YOUR SHADES OFF...

THAT WON'T BE NECESSARY, DR. WHITMAN. BUT I WILL NEED TO TAKE THIS AWAY FOR FURTHER EXAMINATION.
I'M AFRAID I CAN'T LET YOU DO THAT.
CHENG, COULD YOU HELP THE DOCTOR WITH HIS HEARING, PLEASE?

I CAN ASSURE YOU. THOSE ARE GENUINE AND WELL WORTH THE AGREED PRICE.
SORRY. REALLY LIKE YOUR SHOW.

SMACK

紅寶石大酒

THWAK

BLAM

ARRRRRHHH!

BLAM

UGGH!
KRSH

PLEASE. NO MORE HITTING!
DR. WHITMAN.
...YES?

QUICK, LET'S GET OUT OF HERE.
OH GOD... THERE GOES THE FUNDING.

THAT'S MY VAN!

BLAM

KRSH

I'M JONAH MAIAVA. ROTH SENT ME. HE THOUGHT YOU MIGHT BE GETTING YOURSELF INTO TROUBLE.
WHO ARE YOU?
ROTH KNEW.
HE PRETTY MUCH KNOWS EVERYTHING THAT HAPPENS ON HIS SHIP.
BLAM

THANK YOU FOR WHAT YOU DID BACK THERE.
YOU'RE WELCOME, MAN. WE'RE ALL PART OF THE SAME CREW.
I'D BETTER GO AND TALK TO ROTH.
HE'S OUT AT THE MOMENT. COME ON, GIVE ME A HAND.

IS THIS FOR THE SHIP?
YUP. I'M THE COOK AND GENERAL DOGSBODY. JUST ARRIVED TODAY.

WE'D BETTER GET THAT SEEN TO.
IT'S JUST A GRAZE. I'VE HAD WORSE.

HEY, GUYS. I'M GOING TO SEE MY FOLKS FOR A BIT, AND DROP ALISHA AT THE AIRPORT. I'LL BE BACK FOR THE BIG LAUNCH.
TAKE CARE OF YOURSELVES, YOU TWO.

YOU HAVE TO FIND A WAY, JAMES. YOU *HAVE* TO.

HOW ARE YOU DOING?

I'VE BEEN BETTER.
WHY DIDN'T YOU TELL US THE NETWORK HAD PULLED THE FUNDING?
I WAS HOPING I COULD FIND THE FUNDING SOME OTHER WAY.

MY AGENT IS STILL TRYING TO CONVINCE THE NETWORK TO RECONSIDER. IF THEY DON'T, THEY'RE IDIOTS! THE SEARCH FOR YAMATAI, IT COULD BE...
GROUND-BREAKING!
EXACTLY!

IT'S OUT THERE SOMEWHERE.
IF THE SPIRITS MEAN FOR US TO FIND IT, THEN WE WILL.
I DON'T THINK SPIRITS HAVE ANYTHING TO DO WITH IT, JONAH.

LARA, MY LITTLE BIRD. YOU'VE GOT TO LISTEN TO YOUR HEART SOMETIMES.
YOU'RE STARTING TO SOUND LIKE DAD. AT LEAST AT THE END.

WAIT A MINUTE. WAS YOUR FATHER RICHARD CROFT, THE ARCHAEOLOGIST?
YES.
I THOUGHT I RECOGNIZED THE NAME.
I'M SORRY ABOUT WHAT HAPPENED.
THANK YOU.

I USED TO WANT TO BE LIKE HIM. BUT HE SPENT MORE TIME CHASING DREAMS THAN FACTS.
YAMATAI IS NO DREAM. IT'S OUT THERE.
I KNOW. IT HAS TO BE.
WE **WILL** GET FUNDED. I'M EVEN PREPARED TO INVEST MY **OWN** MONEY IN THIS VENTURE.
YOU DON'T SEE THAT VERY OFTEN.

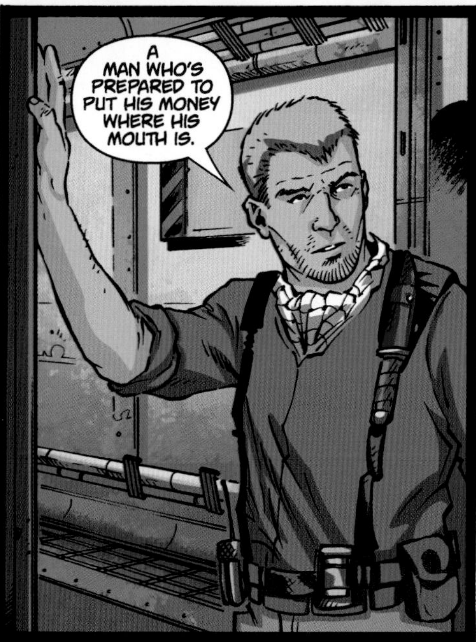
A MAN WHO'S PREPARED TO PUT HIS MONEY WHERE HIS MOUTH IS.

UNFORTUNATELY, THE DIVORCE DIDN'T LEAVE ME WITH QUITE AS MUCH AS I'D HOPED.
MY AGENT'S STILL WORKING ON THE NETWORK. THEY MIGHT RECONSIDER.
WELL...NOT THAT WE DON'T APPRECIATE YOUR EFFORTS IN TRYING TO SECURE MORE, BUT WHERE DOES THAT LEAVE US?

AND WHAT HAPPENS IF THEY DON'T?

I CAN PUT UP HALF THE MONEY. BUT THAT'S STRETCHING IT. I'M STILL WITHOUT A CAMERAMAN OR A RESEARCHER.

I COULD BE YOUR RESEARCHER. I'VE DONE IT BEFORE, AND I USED TO GO ON DIGS WITH MY PARENTS.

THAT WOULD SOLVE ONE PROBLEM. BUT RESEARCH IS NO GOOD WITHOUT FUNDING.

GET OUT ON DECK, ROTH. IT'S ALEX!

WHAT'S HE DOING HERE?

SKREECH

GOOD TO SEE YOU TOO, BIG MAN.

YOU'VE GOTTA GIVE A GUY SANCTUARY, ROTH. THEY'VE FINALLY FOUND ME!

SO WHAT HAVE YOU DONE THIS TIME...AND HURRY UP, THERE'S A MATCH ON.

YOU KNOW HOW CERTAIN GOVERNMENT BODIES HAVE BEEN COVERING UP CERTAIN ACTIVITIES THAT CERTAIN PEOPLE ARE KEEN TO EXPOSE...

WELL...I MAY HAVE...JUST A LITTLE BIT, HACKED INTO CERTAIN DATABASES THAT SAID GOVERNMENT BODIES GET QUITE ANTSY ABOUT PEOPLE SEEING.
AND NOW?

NOW HE'S ON THE RUN.
L.C.'S GOT IT! AND I WAS IN THE MIDDLE OF WORKING ON SOME GROUNDBREAKING SOFTWARE TOO.
AND YOU THOUGHT YOU'D RUN HERE?
Esc

I THINK I'VE LOST THEM. BESIDES, I HEARD YOU WERE STARTING AN EXPEDITION. THOUGHT YOU MIGHT BE ABLE TO USE MY...SKILLS.
COME ON, ROTH. WE COULD USE HIM, COULDN'T WE?
Esc

AS LONG AS YOU KEEP HIM OUT OF MY WAY.
HEY, WHERE'S THE LOVE, REYES?
Esc

THE EXPEDITION'S EXPERIENCING A FEW FUNDING ISSUES.
TEMPORARILY!

GOT IT, ROTH!
YOU JOIN US TODAY FOR SHEFFIELD UNITED VERSUS TRANMERE ROVERS.
YOU KNOW I'M USEFUL, ROTH. SERIOUSLY. I'LL DO IT FOR FREE.
THE LAD MUST BE DESPERATE.

IF WE GET PAID, YOU'LL GET PAID.
SO I'M IN?
YES. GET SET UP.
Esc

AND THERE'S THE KICK OFF!
COME ON, YOU BLADES!

OFF YOU GO. FLY, MY PRETTY, FLY!
KNOCK KNOCK
WHO IS IT?
DR. WHITMAN.
COME IN.
YOU'RE THE T.V. GUY, RIGHT?
RIGHT.
SO WHERE'S YOUR CREW? CAMERAS? A HOT GIRL TO POWDER MY FACE?
IT'S JUST ME FOR NOW, I'M AFRAID.
SO, JIMMY WHITMAN. YOU BEING ALL BY YOUR LONESOME WOULDN'T HAVE ANYTHING TO DO WITH THE NETWORK PULLING YOUR FUNDING?
OR MAYBE IT'S THE DIVORCE?
HOW DO YOU KNOW ABOUT ALL THAT?

IT'S AMAZING WHAT YOU CAN DO WITH THE INTERNET AND FIFTEEN YEARS OF HACKING EXPERIENCE.

WELL YES, IT IS TRUE THAT THE NETWORK CHANGED THEIR MIND ABOUT FUNDING SEASON THREE.
I'M HOPING MY AGENT CAN MAKE THEM RECONSIDER.
SO WHAT EXACTLY ARE WE DOING HERE THEN?
Esc

BUT YOU DON'T THINK THEY WILL, DO YOU? THAT'S WHY YOU'VE BEEN GOING TO SUCH ***EXTREME*** LENGTHS TO TRY AND FUND THIS YOURSELF.
Esc

THE INTERNET TOLD YOU ***THAT?***

NO. JONAH DID.
COME ON, LET'S GET SOME AIR. I NEED TO LET A PIECE OF SOFTWARE RUN.

ONE THING'S FOR SURE. THE SECRET OF YAMATAI WON'T BE IN ANY BOOK. THERE ARE PEOPLE THAT MAKE SURE CERTAIN SHIT DOESN'T GET WRITTEN DOWN.
AT LEAST NOT IN BOOKS.
WHAT DO YOU MEAN?

IT'S OBVIOUS, ISN'T IT? YAMATAI'S A COVER-UP BY THE JAPANESE GOVERNMENT.

IT'S PROBABLY FULL OF ALL KINDS OF STUFF THEY DON'T WANT US FINDING OUT ABOUT.
WELL, YOU ALWAYS SAID THAT *WE'VE* GOT LOTS OF STUFF WE DON'T WANT *THEM* FINDING OUT ABOUT.
YEAH, SURE. BUT THEIR STUFF IS PROBABLY *MUCH* COOLER.

I'D ASK FOR MY BOOK BACK, BUT I THINK YOU COULD USE THE EDUCATION.
IF WE FIND YAMATAI AND IT'S FULL OF KILLER ROBOTS AND GENETIC MUTATIONS, I CALLED IT.
OF COURSE, WE NEED TO GET OUT OF PORT FIRST.
Esc

I MAY KNOW A WAY WE CAN KICK UP A BIT OF EXTRA FUNDING.
MEET ME IN MY CABIN. AND DITCH THE TAPE RECORDER.

BEFORE I LEFT, I WAS WORKING ON A PIECE OF SOFTWARE THAT COULD HACK GAMBLING SITES. TURN THE TABLES IN MY FAVOR.
I DON'T LIKE THE SOUND OF THAT.
IT'S A FACELESS CRIME, L.C.

I'VE BEEN TESTING IT OUT OVER THE LAST COUPLE OF HOURS. LOOK, IT'S ALREADY RAKED IN TWO GRAND!
AND IT'S UNDETECTABLE?
99.9%!

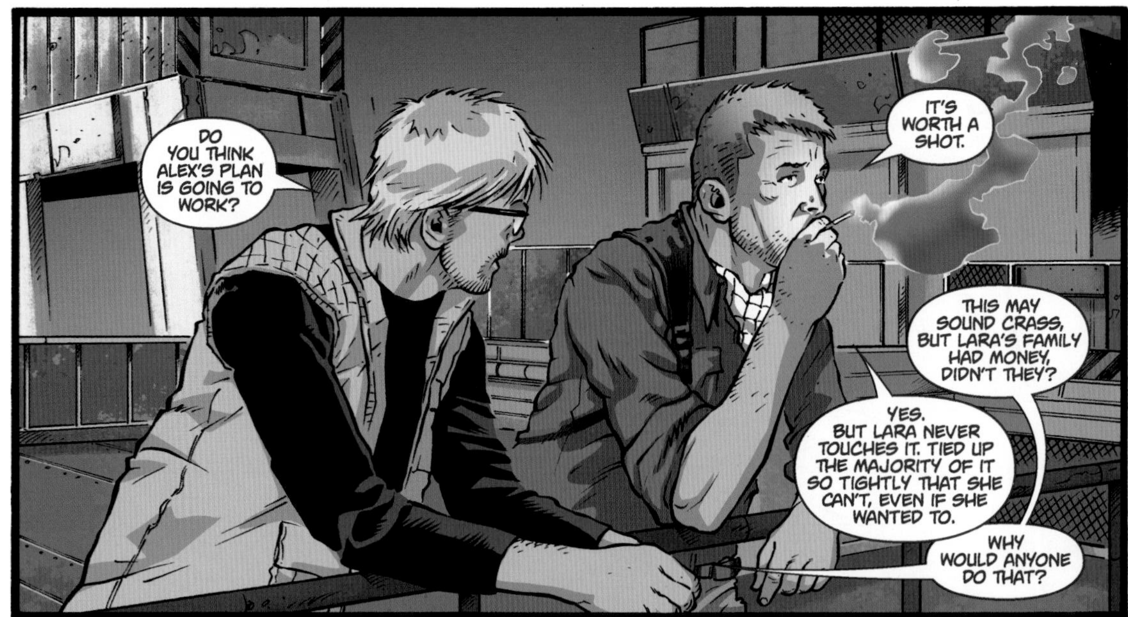
DO YOU THINK ALEX'S PLAN IS GOING TO WORK?
IT'S WORTH A SHOT.
THIS MAY SOUND CRASS, BUT LARA'S FAMILY HAD MONEY, DIDN'T THEY?
YES. BUT LARA NEVER TOUCHES IT. TIED UP THE MAJORITY OF IT SO TIGHTLY THAT SHE CAN'T, EVEN IF SHE WANTED TO.
WHY WOULD ANYONE DO THAT?

BECAUSE SHE WANTS TO MAKE HER OWN WAY. ON HER TERMS.
LOOK OUT!
ESC

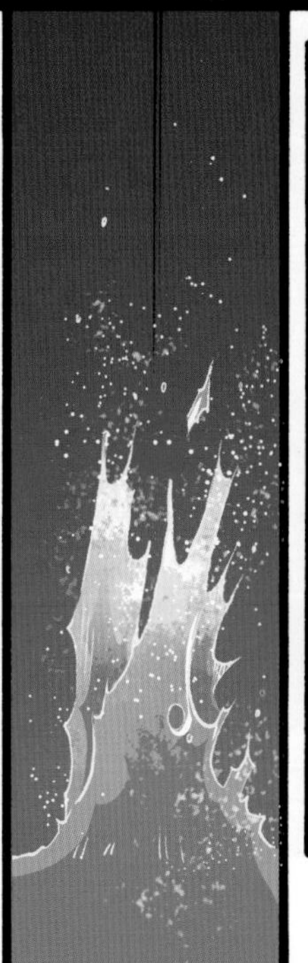

WHAT HAPPENED?
THE 0.1%.
ESC

SAM. IT'S LARA.
HEY, SWEETIE. YOU ALL READY TO GO?
NO. THE FUNDING'S FALLEN THROUGH.
YOU'RE KIDDING?

NO. BUT WHITMAN STILL WANTS TO MAKE THE DOCUMENTARY. HE'S PUTTING HIS OWN MONEY INTO IT. BUT IT'S NOT ENOUGH.

I KNOW YOUR UNCLE'S FINANCED ROTH BEFORE.
WANT ME TO TALK TO HIM? HE'LL WANT A BIG SLICE OF WHAT WE FIND THOUGH.
I DON'T THINK THAT'LL BE A PROBLEM.

THEN LET'S MAKE THIS HAPPEN!
THANKS, SAM.

HE SAID YES!

YOU DON'T KNOW WHAT THIS MEANS, SAM.

IT GETS BETTER...I'M COMING WITH YOU!

I'LL TAKE THAT. IT'S MY BABY.

EVERYONE'S HAVING BREAKFAST. LET'S TELL THEM.

MY AGENT SAYS THE NETWORK WON'T BUDGE. THERE'LL BE NO FUNDING.

THEN WE MIGHT AS WELL JUST PACK UP OUR BAGS AND GO.

NOT UNTIL YOU'VE HEARD SAM OUT.

HEY, MY MORNING'S LOOKING UP!
I'D QUIT THAT ATTITUDE NOW, IF I WERE YOU, ALEX. OR IT'S GOING TO BE A VERY LONG TRIP!

LARA LET ME KNOW THE SCORE. I SPOKE TO MY UNCLE. HE'S PREPARED TO COVER THE REST OF THE FUNDING.
THAT'S INCREDIBLE.
I KNOW YOUR UNCLE. WHAT'S HIS PRICE?

60% OF THE SALE PRICE OF ANYTHING YOU BRING BACK.
YEAH. THAT SOUNDS LIKE HIM. THE BASTARD ALWAYS DRIVES A HARD BARGAIN.
CLICK

ANYTHING ELSE WE SHOULD KNOW?
THERE IS ONE OTHER CONDITION.
YOU NEED A NEW CAMERA-PERSON.
YOU'RE RIGHT. THE NETWORK PAID FOR THE LAST ONE.

WELL, NOW YOU'VE GOT ONE.

I STUDIED CINEMATOGRAPHY AT COLLEGE. I'VE FILMED IN THE ARCTIC, THE CONGO, AND, THE RED DESERT.
I CAN DO THIS.

SO WE'RE ON, RIGHT? WE'RE *FINALLY* GOING TO LEAVE?
THANK GOD. I HATE BEING THIS CLOSE TO LAND.

DO YOU THINK THERE'S ENOUGH FOR A NEW LAPTOP? MY HANDS FEEL WEIRD WITHOUT ONE.
MORE THAN ENOUGH.

OKAY THEN. LET'S GET THIS SHOW ON THE ROAD.

I BETTER GET SOME MORE SUPPLIES IN.
BACON AND EGGS WOULD BE GOOD. TOAST'S NO KIND OF BREAKFAST.
WHAT SHOULD I DO, DR. WHITMAN?
NOUGAT PILLOWS

I NEED YOU TO PICK UP A FEW BOOKS FROM MY OFFICE.
OKAY.
TAKE MY DRIVER. I'M GOING TO START FILMING.

THE SOUTH MIGHT BE WARMER, BUT THERE'S LESS CHANCE OF PIRATES IF WE GO VIA NORWAY.
THEN WE BETTER MAKE SURE WE'VE GOT THE RIGHT PERMITS.
ALEX, CAN YOU ***HURRY*** THEM ALONG?

BY HURRY, YOU MEAN...?
JUST MAKE THEM HAPPEN.
ON IT. RIGHT AFTER THIS SCREEN IS FIXED.

YOUR LAPTOP'S HERE, ALEX.
AWESOME!
THE ENGINE'S AS GOOD AS SHE'LL EVER BE.
THANKS, REYES. WE'LL SET SAIL IN A COUPLE OF HOURS.

ANYTHING YOU'D LIKE TO SAY TO ALISHA, REYES? I'LL SEND IT ON TO HER.
BE GOOD FOR AUNTIE UNA WHILE I'M AWAY. KEEP PRACTICING YOUR PIANO. I LOVE YOU, BABY.

ARE YOU READY FOR YOUR CLOSE-UP, MISS CROFT?

DON'T BE SILLY, SAM. I'M NOT IMPORTANT.

YOU WILL BE. ONE DAY. I *KNOW* IT.
MAYBE ONE DAY WE'LL BOTH BE.

I CAN'T BELIEVE WE'RE DOING THIS.
I KNOW. IT'S INCREDIBLE. IT'S GOING TO CHANGE OUR LIVES.

THE BEGINNING.

THEY'RE COMING.

BUDDA BUDDA BUDDA
BUDDA BUDDA BUDDA

CHUK
CHOK
CHOK
GOD!

CHUFT
CHUFT
CHUFT

SHE'S *HERE*. THE GIRL IS *HERE*.
SHE HAS NOWHERE TO *RUN*.

RRRRRRRRRKKK

CHOKKK

HELLO, LARA.

RO... ***ROTH?***

BUT...BUT I ***SAW*** YOU DIE, CONRAD!

DIDN'T I ALWAYS SAY I'D COME BACK FOR YOU, LARA?

DIDN'T I PROMISE?

HERE I AM.

I'VE COME BACK FOR YOU.

YOU'RE NOT ROTH!
CHUK

LARA.
YOU'RE BEING UNREASONABLE.
Esc

WE JUST WANT YOU TO STAY.

WITH US.

FOREVER.

AND EVER.

AND
EVER.

GOD!

Every slumber, a new nightmare.
I keep thinking people will read each new entry and say, "There. That's the night Lara Croft's mind broke."

OH, ROTH.
I MISS YOU.
"That was the night that the guilt and the memories got to be too much."
I suppose there should be a record.

Of the island.
Of YAMATAI.

Lara Croft. 21 years old. One of the few survivors of the shipwrecked ENDURANCE. ROTH's ship.
Maybe it wasn't such a brilliant idea to name it after Shackleton's doomed Arctic exploring vessel, sunk under the ice, 1915.

It was my idea to search Dragon's Triangle. Mine.

We found Yamatai. But we lost most everything else.

Our ship.

Most of our friends.

ROTH & GRIM.

SAM & DR. WHITMAN

JONAH

Maybe even our sanity.

So few of us made it home, and we're ALL struggling.
Everything we saw, every horrid thing we experienced?
Happened because of ME.
LARAAAAAA!
SAM?
SAM!

SAM!
ARE YOU OKAY?
WHAT HAPPENED?
WHAT? NO.
'M FINE.

I WAS JUST...JUST SLEEPWALKING. I'M FINE.
I'M MAKING YOU SOME TEA.
AND A BISCUIT?
DEFINITELY A BISCUIT.

SAM, YOUR ARM.
HUH?
OH. YEAH, FELL AGAINST THE WARDROBE.
DON'T LOOK SO AGHAST, LARA.

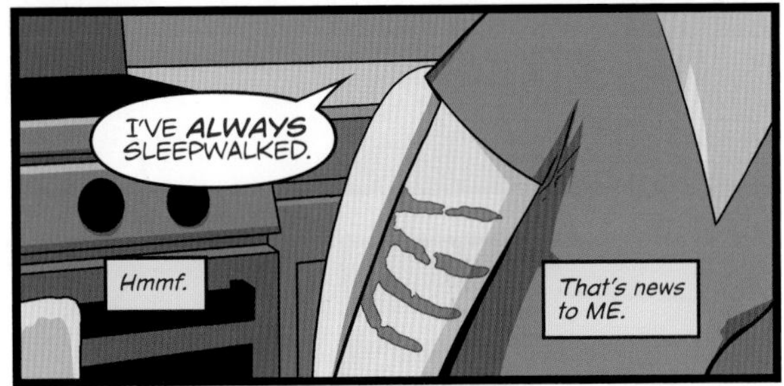
I'VE ALWAYS SLEEPWALKED.
Hmmf.
That's news to ME.

I'M GOING TO ASK YOU A QUESTION, SAM.
ARE YOU HAVING NIGHTMARES?
ABOUT THE ISLAND?
Jaffa Cakes

THAT'S RIDICULOUS.
WHY WOULD I HAVE DREAMS ABOUT THAT AWFUL PLACE?
UGH. NEVER.
She's lying. ALL of us who made it out have had the dreams.
WE'VE BEEN MATES FOR YEARS.
WHY ARE YOU LYING TO ME, SAM?

I SHOULD GET BACK TO BED. WE'RE STARTING THE DOCUMENTARY ON FISSURE GAS LEAKS IN THE MORNING.
SAM. PLEASE.
WE HAVE TO **TALK.**

LARA, STOP IT. I'M **TIRED.**
QUIT BEING SO **WEIRD.**
SAM...!

BZZZT BZZZT BZZZT

HELLO?
LARA. PLEASE. YOU HAVE TO COME. RIGHT NOW.
RIGHT THIS **MINUTE.**
JONAH?
I **NEED** YOU. WE **ALL** DO. AND LARA...?

...BRING SOME **SUN-BLOCK.**
And I'll go, just like that.
Because it was my idea.
And that makes me RESPONSIBLE.

Devil's Rest. Lowest precipitation in North America.
In a few thousand years, it'll be swallowed by the Grand Canyon.
There's no life, no greenery. The only water is blocked by a massive dam system God knows how many kilometers away.
WELL, SEE, YOU'RE A SMART ONE, THAT'S PLAIN.

Why on earth would Jonah, a Maori man who loves green things and the sea more than anyone I've ever known...
...deliberately make his way HERE?
MMM?

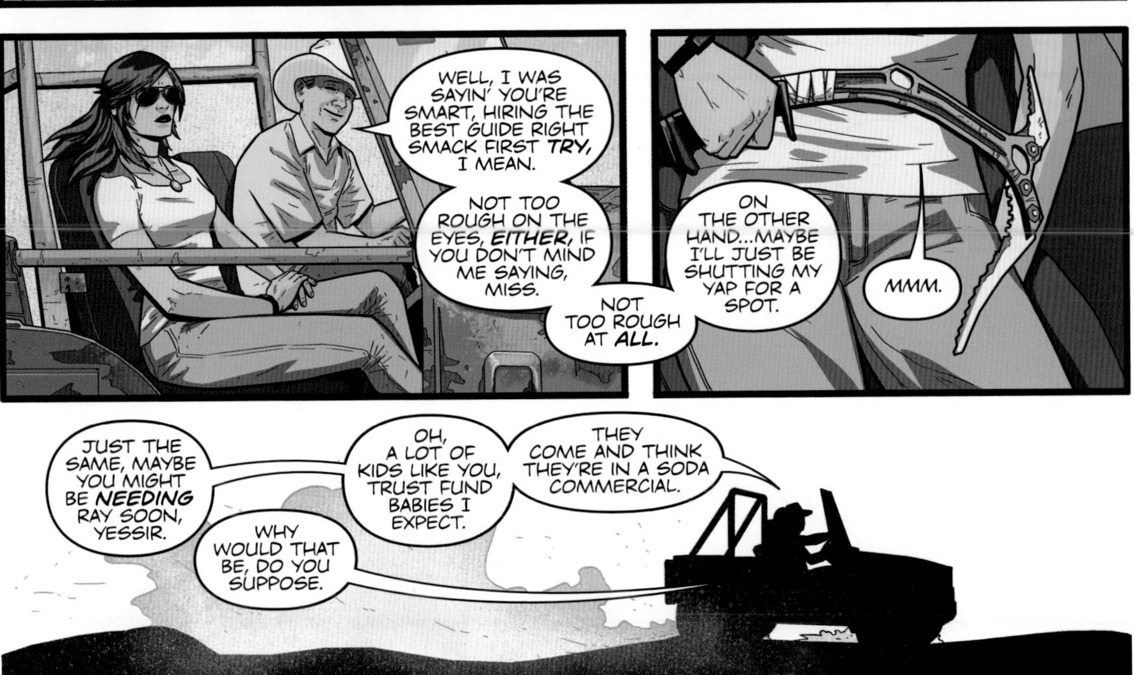
WELL, I WAS SAYIN' YOU'RE SMART, HIRING THE BEST GUIDE RIGHT SMACK FIRST **TRY,** I MEAN.
NOT TOO ROUGH ON THE EYES, **EITHER,** IF YOU DON'T MIND ME SAYING, MISS.
NOT TOO ROUGH AT **ALL.**
ON THE OTHER HAND...MAYBE I'LL JUST BE SHUTTING MY YAP FOR A SPOT.
MMM.
JUST THE SAME, MAYBE YOU MIGHT BE **NEEDING** RAY SOON, YESSIR.
WHY WOULD THAT BE, DO YOU SUPPOSE.
OH, A LOT OF KIDS LIKE YOU, TRUST FUND BABIES I EXPECT.
THEY COME AND THINK THEY'RE IN A SODA COMMERCIAL.

THEY COME AND TRY TO CLIMB THE SPIRES.
THEY'RE HALF-DEAD. BROKEN LEGS, BROKEN ARMS. BROKEN SENSE, I SAY.
SURE ENOUGH, WHEN I COME BACK TO GET 'EM?

THEN MAYBE OL' RAY DON'T SEEM SO UNWELCOME, IS ALL I'M SAYING.
Well, America...
I can't say much for the company so far.
But no one else from the Endurance dies, if I can help it.

I'm coming, Jonah.
WELL.
A PARCHED THROAT AND A SORE RUMP LATER, HERE WE ARE, MISS.

IF YOU LEAVE BEFORE WE'RE DONE...
...I'LL FIND YOU.
AW, RAY'S BROUGHT A FRIEND, MISS. YOU HAVE YOUR LITTLE CHAT.

KNOCK KNOCK
JONAH?
JONAH, IT'S LARA. LET ME IN.

JONAH?

JONAH? IT'S ME.
IT'S LARA.

Can't help but worry.
On the Endurance, Jonah loved everyone.
This quiet is... unsettling.
It feels like an omen.

WHAT ON EARTH?

Jonah's pou pou, his ancestor.
Why in God's name is everything in a clear plastic bag?
Did he become a germophobe since Yamatai?

DON'T **MOVE.**
DON'T YOU EVEN **MOVE!**
He's...he's gone mad.

JONAH.
KIA ORA, MY FRIEND. IT'S ME. IT'S **LARA.**

DON'T **LIE TO ME!**
YOU THINK YOU CAN **TRICK** ME?
I **KNOW** WHO YOU ARE!

JONAH, I DON'T KNOW WHAT YOU'RE SAYING.
YOU CALLED ME. I CAME TO **HELP.**
On the Endurance, *he was the kindest of us. The sanest.*

I can't do it. I can't hurt him.
PLEASE.
WHAT IS GOING **ON** HERE?

YOU KNOW THE STORY OF JONAH, SWALLOWED BY THE WHALE?
I THINK...
I THINK I AM THAT JONAH.

DON'T ACT LIKE YOU DON'T **KNOW.**

JONAH. PLEASE.
HELP ME **UNDERSTAND.**

THEY FOLLOWED US FROM THE ISLAND.
THEY'RE **COMING** FOR US.

JONAH.
THE SOLARII... THEY'RE **GONE.**
NO ONE'S GOING TO **HURT** YOU.

YOU DON'T UNDERSTAND. WE EACH...WE EACH **TOOK** SOMETHING FROM THERE.
A PIECE OF HIS **HOUSE.**
KA, LARA. BEWARE OF **KA.**

IT WAS GOLD, LARA. ALL THE PIECES WERE **GOLD.**
WELL, WELL, WELL.
ISN'T **THAT** INTERESTING.

HUH.
WELL, THIS IS DOWNRIGHT BECOMING A BIT OF AN ODD DUCK DAY.

THERE ARE FOUR GUARDIANS. FOUR, FOUR OF EVERYTHING.
FOUR CALAMITIES. FOUR PIECES TO BUILD HIS HOUSE.
THE CIRCLE HAS TO BE BROKEN.
NO. NO.
JONAH, I DON'T UNDERSTAND. IS...IS SOMEONE TRYING TO KILL US?

SOMEONE'S TRYING TO KILL EVERYONE.

DEAR GOD IN HEAVEN.

I CAN'T KILL YOU, LARA.
THIS IS THE ONLY WAY.
JONAH!
DON'T!

AN ODD DUCK DAY, INDEED.

He's too strong. He's too STRONG.
I can't STOP him.
WE HAVE TO STOP THEM. WE HAVE TO STOP THEM!

AAAAAA...KK

Good LORD.
What is HAPPENING?
UHGH.

OH, NO.

CHUK
THUK
CHUK

How could this...
...this is IMPOSSIBLE.

"HE WILL HAVE HIS HOUSE
WALL, FLOOR, ROOF, AND DOOR
AND EACH SHALL HAVE A GUARDIAN
AND EACH SHALL BEAR A CALAMITY."

IT'S JAMMED. I CAN'T GET THE... THE DOOR. JONAH.
HELP ME!
LARA.
IT'S OKAY.

I'LL BE OKAY.

YOU NEED TO GO.

TAKE THIS AND GO, LARA.

I'M NOT GOING TO LEAVE YOU!

I'M NOT GIVING YOU A CHOICE.
AROHA MAI.
NO. NO!

I'M SORRY.
JONAH.
DON'T DO THIS!

JONAH!
I CAN'T... THERE'S NOWHERE TO GO TO!

OH, NO.

GUFHH

BEWARE THE FOUR GUARDIANS, LARA.

Rushing water and a leap of faith.

Didn't I just DREAM this a few hours ago?

Jonah. Please. Get OUT.

Hurry. Hurry, before it...

...smashes to pieces.

JONAAAAAAAAAAH.

Oh.
Oh, Jonah.

The sun.
The sun's coming out.

Too late.
The sun's too late.
DAMN IT ALL TO HELL.

Careful, Lara.
So CAREFUL.
ENDURANCE
PLYMOUTH

Coast LOOKS clear...
It'll be under lock and key, for certain.
And guarded WELL, no doubt.
WELL.
LOOK WHO'S HERE.
I... UM.
I WAS JUST LOOKING FOR--
--THESE SWEET THINGS, AM I RIGHT, MY LITTLE BIRD?
DON'T YOU KNOW JONAH'S GOT YOU COVERED?
I STOCKED A CASE. HIDDEN AWAY SPECIAL.
I KIND OF ADORE YOU RIGHT NOW.
I KNOW.

That was just six weeks ago.
We almost both drowned THEN, too, just a few hours later.
JONAH!

Searching for the legendary lost kingdom of Yamatai, in the Dragon's Triangle.
He...watched over me.
He was my FRIEND.

And now there's a FLOOD where there hasn't been one since the glaciers cut the mountains into spires and canyons thousands of YEARS ago.

And I've LOST him.

NO.

I'm COMING, Jonah.

It's impossible.
Devil's Rest, lowest precipitation on the entire CONTINENT.

Suddenly, it's like a prehistoric ocean.
And Jonah...

...it's like he KNEW it was coming.
Beware of KA, he said.
He's not...
He's gone.

I'm SORRY, Jonah.

Jonah's pou pou. The carving of his ancestors.
He...he said he's the last of his line.

Damn it.

I made a promise.

No one else from the Endurance DIES.

His TRAILER.

Jonah's TRAILER!

Jonah said he thought he might be THE Jonah, the one that got swallowed by a whale.

Please.
Please let my friend be alive.

The water. It's hit a CANYON.

It'll pull us right OVER.

JONAH!

WAKE UP!

CAN'T... HANG ON.

Well, crap.

AH, AH, AH, PRETTY LITTLE DUMPLIN'.
DON'T WORRY.
What in the world...?

OL' RAY'S GOT YOU.
LOOKS LIKE I GOT **EXTRA** LUCKY TODAY, DIDN'T I?
It's that creepy GUIDE.
I thought CERTAIN he was dead.

NO YOUNG BRIT GIRLS JUMPIN' IN THE CHURN TO SAVE **RAY,** HUH?
PUT YOUR LITTLE HOG CHUCKER **DOWN,** MISS, IF YOU PLEASE.
LET ME TELL YOU WHAT I HEARD.

"NOT THAT OL' RAY WAS **EAVESDROPPIN',** MIND YOU.
"COULDN'T **HELP** BUT OVERHEAR SOME **INTRIGUING** WORDS."
IT WAS GOLD, LARA. ALL THE PIECES WERE **GOLD.**

WHAT DO YOU WANT?
I TOLD YOU, MISS.
PEOPLE GO MISSIN' HERE ALL THE TIME.
HIKERS, CLIMBERS, TOURISTS. SOMETIMES, EVEN CUTIES LIKE YOURSELF.

AND THEN, LITTLE PRETTYPANTS?
SO I GUESS WHAT I WANT IS FOR YOU TO HAND ME THAT BOX YOUR FAT FRIEND WAS HOLDING SO TIGHTLY.

YOU'RE GOING TO JUMP OFF THE EDGE OF THIS CLIFF FOR ME, THERE'S A GOOD GIRL. NO ONE EVER COMES HERE, YOU WON'T BE FOUND FOR DECADES.
GIVE ME THE BOX.
...
SCREW YOU.
RAY.

WELL, I ADMIT THAT'S A VERY TEMPTING OFFER, MISS.
BUT OL' RAY HAS DEBTS, YOU SEE.

SO I THINK I'LL JUST SHOOT YOU BOTH IN THE GODDAMN HEAD AND GET THE BOX FOR MYSELF. HOW'S THAT SOUND FOR A LAUGH?
SAY GOOD NIGHT.
TOURIST.

WHAT THE HELL?

LEV...
LEAVE HER 'LONE.

OKAY, BIG MAN. YOU WANT TO DIE SO BAD?
YOU GO FIRST.

He'll do it. I know it.
RAY.

GO TO HELL.
WH...
WAIT. NO.

NO.
NO.

NOOOOOOOOOO!

He was going to kill us both.
Keep telling yourself that, Lara.
JONAH. JONAH.
LITTLE...
BIRD.

I'M SORRY.
I WAS TRYING TO PROTECT... EVERYONE.
I'M GOING TO FIND A WAY TO GET YOU OUT OF HERE, JONAH.
LET ME DO THE PROTECTING THIS TIME, ALL RIGHT?

TAKE THE BOX, LARA. WATCH OUT FOR...
KA. YOU HAVE TO WATCH OUT FOR. YOU.
He's raving. Not making any sense.

Huh. A piece of his trailer... with writing on it?
MOBY DICK
MOTORCOACHES AND TRAILERS

MOBY DICK
MOTORCOACHES AND TRAILERS

Three days later, I'm at Trinity College, in Dublin.
Home of Ireland's greatest national treasure, the Book of Kells, the illuminated manuscript of the New Testament. Created by Columban monks, somewhere around the year 800.
Takes my breath away every time I see it.
It's also home to the place I love best in all the world.

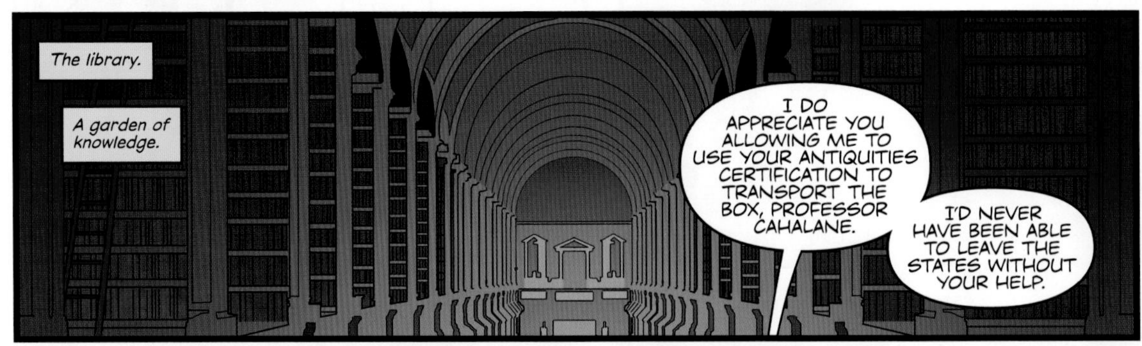

The library.
A garden of knowledge.
I DO APPRECIATE YOU ALLOWING ME TO USE YOUR ANTIQUITIES CERTIFICATION TO TRANSPORT THE BOX, PROFESSOR CAHALANE.
I'D NEVER HAVE BEEN ABLE TO LEAVE THE STATES WITHOUT YOUR HELP.

I DID IT FOR YOUR FATHER, LARA.
I MUST CONFESS, I CAN'T IMAGINE HE'D BE ALL THAT DELIGHTED TO HEAR THAT YOU'D BEEN GALLIVANTING ABOUT RISKING YOUR **LIFE** LIKE THIS.
HOW IS YOUR FRIEND?

NOT WELL...WE WERE FOUND BY A NEWS HELICOPTER, OF ALL THINGS.
HE'S STILL IN THE HOSPITAL UNDER OBSERVATION. HE DOESN'T REMEMBER ANY OF IT, SOMEHOW.
IT TURNS OUT A **DAM** HAD BURST. IT WASN'T THE WRATH OF GOD AT **ALL**.

ARE YOU SO **CERTAIN** OF THAT?
I'LL PRAY FOR HIM, LARA.
THAT'S KIND OF YOU, PROFESSOR.
I'M SURE HE'D APPRECIATE THAT.

WELL? YOU'VE COME THIS FAR.
SHOW ME WHAT'S IN THE **BOX,** GIRL.
I trust this man... He was my father's dearest friend.
But I suddenly feel reluctant to show him what I've found.

Is it simply possessiveness? Or an OMEN?
GREAT GOD IN HEAVEN.
LARA, WHAT HAVE YOU DONE?

THIS FIRST. I KNOW IT'S AN ANTEFIX...THE ENDPIECE OF A ROOF TO A ROYAL HOUSE, CORRECT? AND THERE'S AN INSCRIPTION ON THE UNDERSIDE.
YES, IT'S IN AFGHAN.
IT'S AN INVOCATION OF SOME KIND. OR A PROPHECY?

"HE WILL HAVE HIS HOUSE WALL, FLOOR, ROOF, AND DOOR AND EACH SHALL HAVE A GUARDIAN AND EACH SHALL BEAR A CALAMITY."
JONAH said something like this.
I thought he was feverish!

NOW THIS PIECE...

...THIS IS THE REALLY DANGEROUS ONE!

YOU KNOW WHAT IS EXPECTED OF YOU.

IT IS MY HIGHEST HONOR.

PRAISE BE TO YAMATAI.
THEN IT IS TIME FOR YOU TO REMAKE YOURSELF AND DO WHAT MUST BE DONE.

MY DAUGHTER.

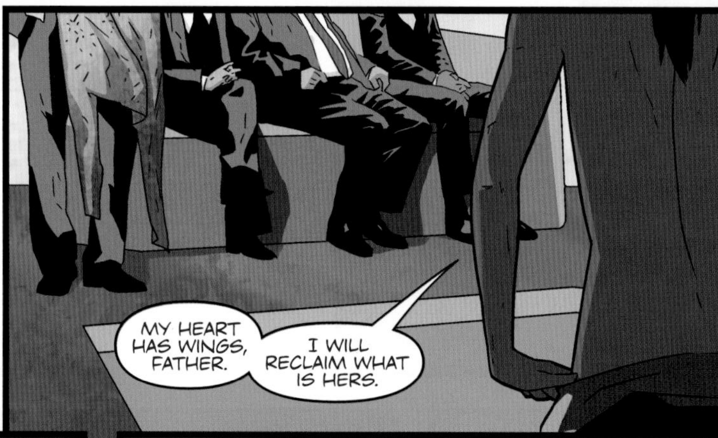
MY HEART HAS WINGS, FATHER.
I WILL RECLAIM WHAT IS HERS.

"I KNOW YOU WILL, DAUGHTER. BLOOD CALLS TO BLOOD."
IT'S ALSO FROM AFGHANISTAN, BUT IT SHOWS GREEK INFLUENCE.

IT'S A MAKARA, PART WOMAN, PART CROCODILE, PART ELEPHANT.
THE EXACT MIRROR IMAGE OF THIS PIECE IS TOURING THE WORLD AS PART OF A TRAVELING MUSEUM EXHIBIT.
AH.

SHE'S A GUARDIAN.
OR AN INSTRUMENT OF **REVENGE.**
LARA, YOU HAVE TO ANNOUNCE THIS FIND. IT DOESN'T BELONG TO YOU.

OH. DAMN.
MY PHONE.
ARE YOU **INSANE?**
YOU CAN'T ANSWER PHONE CALLS IN **HERE.**
BZZZT BZZZT BZZZT

PROFESSOR, I HAVE TO TAKE THIS.
GET **OUT,** THEN.

GO BEFORE THEY KICK **ME** OUT **WITH** YOU!
Incoming call
Reyes
SEND
OK
CLR

CROFT?
I NEED TO TALK TO YOU. YOU...WE'RE **ALL** IN DANGER.
YOU, ME, SAM, **EVERYONE.**

JOSLIN? I DON'T UNDERSTAND. WHERE ARE YOU?
I'M IN BELFAST, N.I. I CAN BE AT THE SPIRE IN TWO AND A HALF HOURS. CAN YOU BE THERE?
WELL, IF IT'S THAT URGENT, LET ME COME TO **YOU.**

NO.
I DON'T WANT YOU ANYWHERE **NEAR** MY DAUGHTER.
NOT EVEN THE SAME **POSTAL** CODE, IF I CAN HELP IT.

I WASN'T SURE YOU'D COME.
THAT MAKES TWO OF US. FANCY A PINT?
MORE THAN YOU'LL EVER KNOW.

I KNOW WHAT HAPPENED TO JONAH.
HOW --
DO YOU HAVE THE PIECES?
I HAVE THE ANTEFIX, REYES. THE PROFESSOR BEGGED TO STUDY THE MAKARA.
NO

I HAVE TO SHOW YOU SOMETHING, LARA.
I'M DOING THIS TO WARN YOU OFF.
TO SAVE YOUR LIFE. BECAUSE ROTH CARED ABOUT YOU, YOU UNDER-STAND?

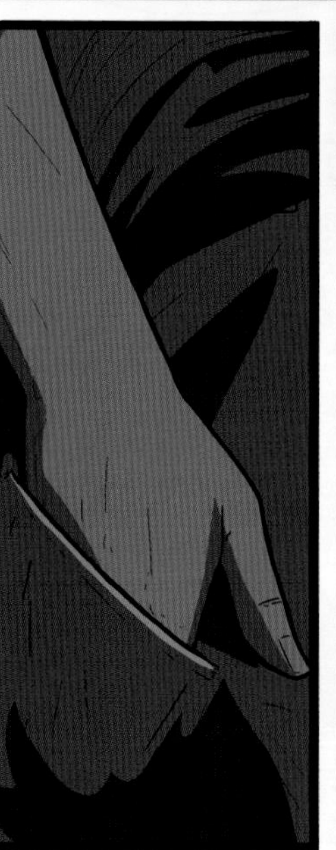

YOU SEE...
I HAVE AN ARTIFACT, TOO.

I LOOKED IT UP. IT'S PART OF A BEAM, ACROSS THE BOTTOM OF AN ANCIENT CHINESE DOORWAY. A *MEN KAN*, I THINK IT'S CALLED.
BUT NOT EVEN THE FORBIDDEN *CITY* HAS THEM IN SOLID *GOLD.*

JOSLIN, I DON'T UNDERSTAND. HOW DID YOU EVEN *GET* THESE?
SAM, JONAH AND I...WHEN WE WERE IMPRISONED, THEY SHOWED US A TROVE. THE SOLARII.
WE EACH TOOK A PIECE...FOUR IN TOTAL.

DON'T YOU JUDGE ME, LARA CROFT.
I HAVE WORKED MY ENTIRE LIFE, AND CAN BARELY KEEP A ROOF OVER MY DAUGHTER'S *HEAD.*
AND THE GOLD WAS JUST...JUST *THERE.* LIKE IT WAS *CALLING* US.

ONLY...
...I THINK IT'S MESSING WITH US, LARA. SOMETHING *BAD* FROM THE *ISLAND* CAME BACK *WITH* US IN THE GOLD.
I THINK SOMETHING *TERRIBLE* IS GOING TO HAPPEN.

YOU SAID YOU'D EACH TAKEN A SINGLE GOLDEN PIECE.
BUT YOU SAID THERE WERE *FOUR.*
THAT'S CORRECT.

"BECAUSE YOU TOOK ONE, TOO, LARA.
"IT WAS YOUR IDEA."
THAT'S IMPOSSIBLE.
YOU SAID ALL THE TREASURE HAD LONG SINCE BEEN LOST.
YOU SAID WE DESERVED IT FOR OUR ORDEAL.
YOU WEREN'T YOURSELF, LARA.
YOU'D... YOU'D KILLED. YOU WERE RACKED WITH FATIGUE AND PAIN AND GUILT.
Is it, is it POSSIBLE, what she's saying?
I was near insane by the end.
Could my mind be PROTECTING me from what REALLY happened?

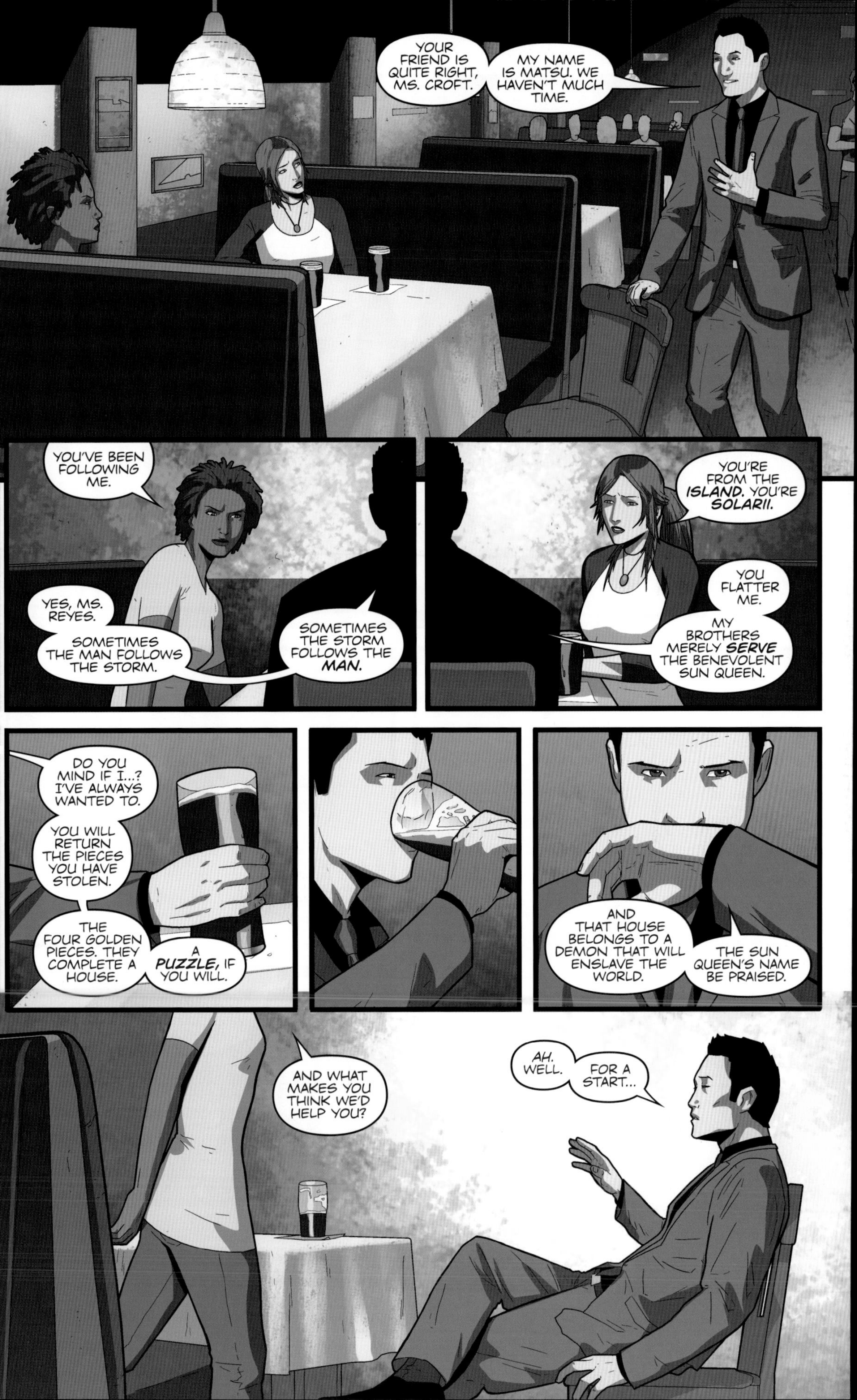

YOUR FRIEND IS QUITE RIGHT, MS. CROFT.
MY NAME IS MATSU. WE HAVEN'T MUCH TIME.
YOU'VE BEEN FOLLOWING ME.
YES, MS. REYES.
SOMETIMES THE MAN FOLLOWS THE STORM.
SOMETIMES THE STORM FOLLOWS THE ***MAN.***
YOU'RE FROM THE ***ISLAND.*** YOU'RE ***SOLARII.***
YOU FLATTER ME.
MY BROTHERS MERELY ***SERVE*** THE BENEVOLENT SUN QUEEN.
DO YOU MIND IF I...? I'VE ALWAYS WANTED TO.
YOU WILL RETURN THE PIECES YOU HAVE STOLEN.
THE FOUR GOLDEN PIECES. THEY COMPLETE A HOUSE.
A ***PUZZLE,*** IF YOU WILL.
AND THAT HOUSE BELONGS TO A DEMON THAT WILL ENSLAVE THE WORLD.
THE SUN QUEEN'S NAME BE PRAISED.

AND WHAT MAKES YOU THINK WE'D HELP YOU?
AH. WELL.
FOR A START...

...WE HAVE YOUR DAUGHTER, MS. REYES.

WHEN THE SOVIETS INVADED AFGHANISTAN IN THE LATE SEVENTIES, CURATORS OF THE NATIONAL MUSEUM IN KABUL RISKED THEIR LIVES TO HIDE THEIR CULTURAL ARTIFACTS FROM PLUNDER.

THIS PIECE **MUST** HAVE COME FROM THAT COLLECTION.

BUT HOW DID A YOUNG MAORI MAN IN THE UNITED STATES GET HOLD OF IT?

"I WILL RECLAIM WHAT IS HERS."
"I KNOW YOU WILL, DAUGHTER. BLOOD CALLS TO BLOOD."
"BLOOD CALLS TO BLOOD."

NEW YORK CITY, TEN YEARS BEFORE THE STORM.
...othy's
Authentic Irish PUB
...AND SO, THIS IDIOT WHO HIRED ME, HE'S ON THE SOUTH FACE, SAME LINE AS ME, AIR STARTS GETTING THIN, RIGHT?
AND HE KEEPS STOPPING TO TAKE, I SWEAR, PHOTOS OF HIMSELF ON HIS CELL PHONE.
Roth told me how they met, almost ten years ago.
It was hardly an AUSPICIOUS serendipity.
15,000 FEET ON A SHEER ROCK-FACE, AND IT'S SNOWING.
AND THIS RICH FOOL SAYS TO ME, "HEY, ROTH! HOWSABOUT YOU HOLD MY PHONE AND TAKE A SHOT OF ME FROM BELOW?"
AN' I THINK FOR A MOMENT, RIGHT?
AND I SAY, "HEY, YOU BLEEDING FOOL, HOWSABOUT I CUT THE LINE WHEN YOU FALL AND YOU CAN TAKE A PICTURE OF MY ARSE ON THE WAY DOWN?"
HAHAHA!
NOTHING?
JUST LIKE A YANK, NO SENSE OF HUMOR AT ALL.
ANOTHER ROUND FOR MY FRIENDS, THEN.

YOU DIDN'T BRING ANY FRIENDS, MISTER. AND WE AIN'T SERVIN' YOU NO MORE BOOZE.
YOU'VE HAD ENOUGH.
Roth said he was drinking to forget.

Didn't even know what he was doing...what he was SAYING.
FILL IT UP, DAMN IT!
IF I CAN'T FIND THEM, I'LL FORGET THEM!

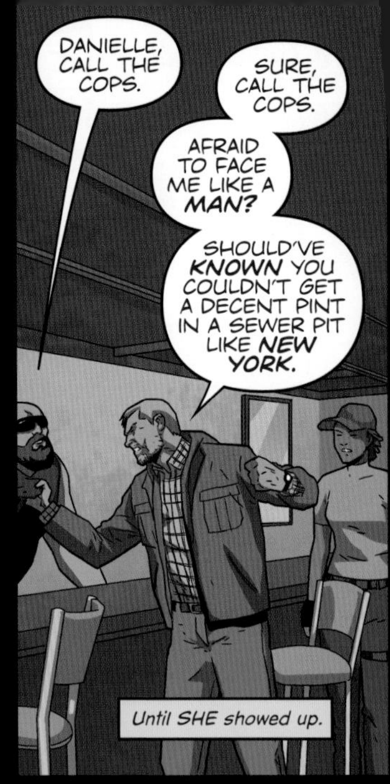

DANIELLE, CALL THE COPS.
SURE, CALL THE COPS.
AFRAID TO FACE ME LIKE A MAN?
SHOULD'VE KNOWN YOU COULDN'T GET A DECENT PINT IN A SEWER PIT LIKE NEW YORK.
Until SHE showed up.

AT LEAST IN NEW YORK, WE KNOW HOW TO DRINK QUIET.

Roth always said she had a hook like a SLEDGE.

SOMETIME LATER...
WELL, HEY THERE, SUNSHINE.
MAYBE THE PINTS HERE'RE A LITTLE MORE POTENT THAN YOU THOUGHT, HUH?

IF YOU'RE PLANNING ON SUING ME...I DON'T HAVE ANYTHING TO TAKE.
IF YOU'RE GONNA GET ME ARRESTED, I WAS A COP TILL I QUIT A WHILE BACK.
STILL GOT FRIENDS ON THE JOB. MIGHT NOT GO WELL FOR YOU.

SUCKER PUNCH.
IF YOU SAY SO.
YOU GONNA CAUSE ME GRIEF, MR. ANGRY DRINKER?

FOR PUNCHING ME FOR ACTING LIKE A JACKASS?
I WAS THINKING MORE ALONG THE LINES OF OFFERING YOU A JOB.

CHIEF OF SECURITY SOUND GOOD TO YOU?
I was always a little jealous of how tight they were, how close.
And then I lost him, on the island.
I was sure she and I would never speak again.

But now this man, this cold-eyed man...he's from a sick cult that worships the Solarii.
And he just threatened to kill Reyes's daughter, Alisha, if I don't give him the artifact I took from the island.
He means it. I can see it.
The problem is, I can't remember ANY of that.
BUT...
I DON'T **KNOW** WHERE MY PIECE IS. I DON'T EVEN KNOW **WHAT** IT IS!
I MUST SAY, THAT IS **MOST** UNFORTUNATE.
THE COUNTDOWN WILL CONTINUE, HOWEVER.
FIVE.
FOUR.
THREE.

LARA.
I KNOW WE NEVER REALLY... CONNECTED.
PLEASE. SHE'S MY DAUGHTER.

VERY TOUCHING.
TWO.
ONE.

I have no idea what to do.
So I try the old fallback plan.
Lie through my TEETH.
WAIT. WAIT.
OKAY.
IT'S AT MY FATHER'S HOUSE IN LONDON.

I DON'T BELIEVE YOU, MS. CROFT.
SHOOT THE GIRL, GENTLEMEN.

AND THEN EVERYONE ELSE IN THE BAR, PLEASE.

NO!

MOMMY.

SHOTS.
We have an ALLY.
OUR ENEMY IS HERE.
SECURE THE AREA!
SOMEONE CALL THE GARDA!
JOSLIN, WE HAVE TO GO.

RUN. TAKE THEM AND GET SOMEWHERE CROWDED, **NOW.**
I'LL HOLD THEM OFF, IF I CAN. **GO.**
...
WHO **ARE** YOU?

Something FAMILIAR about this guy.
But--
BLLAMM
I'M A FRIEND. SORT OF.
GO!

ONE DAY BEFORE THE STORM
Truth to tell, I was always a little TERRIFIED of her.
YOU TELL HER.
NO, YOU TELL HER.
ENDURANCE
PLYMOUTH
SOMETHING ON YOUR MINDS, LADIES?
UM. JOSL... UH. MS. REYES?
LARA HAS SOMETHING TO SAY.
OH, THANKS SO MUCH, SAM.
WELL, IT'S JUST THAT... ANGUS SAYS YOU DIDN'T THINK THIS EXPEDITION TO FIND YAMATAI WAS A GOOD IDEA.
HE... USED MORE COLORFUL LANGUAGE, ACTUALLY.
SO I GUESS I JUST WANTED TO SAY THANK YOU.
FOR BELIEVING IN ME ENOUGH TO GO THROUGH THE DRAGON'S TRIANGLE TO LOOK FOR THE ISLAND.

I DON'T BELIEVE IN YOU, LARA.
YOU'RE RISKING ALL OF OUR LIVES FOR A FAIRY TALE.
A KID'S DREAM.

I'M HERE FOR MY DAUGHTER'S FUTURE, FOR THE PAYCHECK.
AND BECAUSE ROTH **ASKED** ME.
JUST SO YOU KNOW.

IF I WERE YOU, I'D GO MAKE SURE ALL THE FILM GEAR WAS PROPERLY STOWED. ANGUS SAYS THERE'S SOME BAD AIR CURRENTS COMING.
IT'S PROBABLY NOTHING.
LADIES.

WOW.
SHE REALLY DOESN'T **HOLD BACK,** DOES SHE?
WHO KNOWS-- MAYBE SHE'S RIGHT.
I HEARD SHE USED TO BE A COP.

REALLY?
WELL, I HEARD SHE USED TO LIVE UNDER A BRIDGE AND EAT **CHILDREN.**
THAT DOES SOUND PLAUSIBLE.

WAIT, WAIT. I **ALSO** HEARD THAT SHE WAS STALIN'S SWAGGER COACH!
SAM...
SHUT UP, GOOFUS.

And then the world split open.
Those air currents?
Turned out to be something after all.
The Endurance didn't live up to its name.
And we all should have died.
Most of us DID.
But she and I, we survived, out of a tiny handful.

I want to believe there was a REASON.
ARE THEY FOLLOWING?
I DON'T... WAIT.
DAMN IT.

WHAT IS IT?
SAM.
SHE'S THE ONLY ONE OF US UNACCOUNTED FOR.

I'm barely out of my teens and I've lost everyone I care about: my father, my mother, Roth...
Everyone except the person I love most in the world.
SAM.
YOU'VE REACHED ME, SAM NISHIMURA, AND I'M EITHER OFF SHOOTING AN AWARD-WINNING DOCUMENTARY OR PASSED OUT DRUNK. YOU KNOW WHAT TO DO!
SAM. IT'S ME.
YOU HAVE TO HIDE, SAM. GET OUT OF THE HOUSE NOW AND FIND SOMEWHERE SAFE. SOME-WHERE LOUD. GO.

LARA.
THEY'RE COMING.

THEY'RE COMING!

YOU'VE REACHED ME, SAM NISHIMURA, AND I'M EITHER OFF SHOOTING AN AWARD-WINNING DOCUMENTARY OR PASSED OUT DRUNK. YOU KNOW WHAT TO DO!

KEYS, KEYS, KEYS.

HEY, BABE, YOU HOME?

I GOT THIS **AMAZING** VINTAGE FOOTAGE OF DOWNTOWN DURING THE BOMBING... HARD TO **BELIEVE** THIS ACTUALLY **HAPPENED** RIGHT HERE IN...

AND YOU BELONG TO US NOW.

TEMPLE BAR
TEMPLE BAR
COME ON. WE CAN GET LOST IN THE TEMPLE BAR AREA.
HURRY.

WHICH WAY? WHICH WAY?
I HAVEN'T BEEN HERE IN AGES...LET ME THINK!

LOOK OUT!
BLAMM
GUN!

MOM!

LARA. STOP.
WHAT? THERE ARE **ARMED MEN** RIGHT **BEHIND** US.
DUBLIN SWEETS

LARA.
WHICH WAY ARE YOU GOING?

WELL, I DON'T KNOW. RIGHT, I GUESS?
WHY?

BECAUSE THE TWO OF **US** ARE GOING **LEFT.**
I'M SORRY, LARA.
BOTH YOUR PARENTS. THE ENDURANCE. **ROTH.**
BAD NEWS SEEMS TO FOLLOW YOU.

I'M SORRY.
I HAVE TO GET MY BABY AWAY FROM YOU.
Well.
That actually STUNG.
AS I WAS GOING OVER THE CORK AND KERRY MOUNTAINS
I SAW CAPTAIN FARRELL, AND HIS MONEY HE WAS COUNTING

Who knows. Maybe Reyes is RIGHT about me.
I FIRST PRODUCED MY PISTOL, AND THEN PRODUCED MY RAPIER.
I SAID STAND AND DELIVER, OR THE DEVIL HE MAY TAKE YE.
MUSHA RIN DO-RUN DO DO-RUN DA
WHACK FOL DE DADDY-O, WHACK FOL DE DADDY-O

Lord knows, misery HAS seemed to make me its mate.
THERE'S WHISKEY IN THE JAR-O.
HANG ON A SECOND.
GUHK.
HEY!
SORRY.
SORRY!
I counted at least three more on the way after us.
The difference between now and the pub is...
Now, Lara Croft is ARMED.

OKAY, HOLD UP, BABY. LET ME... LET ME GET MY BEARINGS.
...
THAT WAS MEAN.
WHAT?

LARA LOST HER PARENTS. SHE LOVED MR. ROTH, TOO.
WHAT YOU SAID.
IT WAS MEAN.

Think, Lara.
I can't have a crossfire with all these DUBLINERS around.
All they want is a good TIME.

Oh.
Sh...

GET BACK.
I'M WARNING YOU.

NGH.
WE HAVE YOUR FRIEND, MISS NISHIMURA, MISS CROFT.
SOON, SHE WILL BE BEYOND YOUR REACH FOREVER.
SAM.

YOU WILL **NEVER** SEE HER AGAIN.
No.
DAMN it.

NO!

UHNGN!

He's lying.

He's GOT to be lying.

But if not...

...then heaven help the Solarii.
MISS CROFT. PLEASE LOWER YOUR WEAPON.
IF YOU GIVE US THE LOCATION OF THE LAST ARTIFACT, I PROMISE YOU A QUICK, PAINLESS END.
NO MORE OF YOUR LOVED ONES NEED TO SUFFER.
Damn.
Damn damn DAMN.

HEY!
YOU CELTICS LOT!
Green and white!
Angus told me a lot of local fans support his home team here on game days.
Here goes absolutely NOTHING.

THIS GOBSHITE EEJIT RIGHT HERE IS A POXY ABERDEEN SUPPORTER!
Okay, so I am terrible at fake Irish SLANG.

THAT RIGHT, SON?
YOU WITH FECKIN' ABERDEEN, SON?
I CAN SEE YOU'RE BUSY.
EXCUSE ME, WON'T YOU?

Someday, I really must learn to appreciate the intricacies of FOOTBALL.

FORGIVE ME, MISS CROFT.
THWACK

THIS ISN'T HOW WE WHO WORSHIP THE SUN QUEEN PREFER TO CONDUCT OURSELVES, I PROMISE.

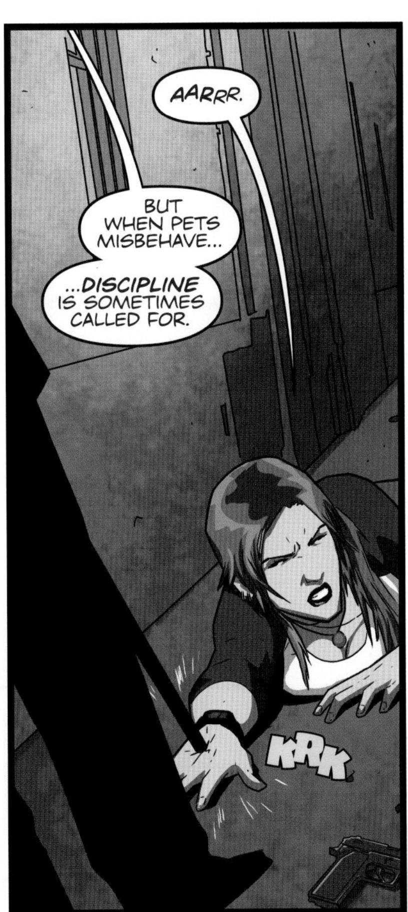
AARRR.
BUT WHEN PETS MISBEHAVE...
...DISCIPLINE IS SOMETIMES CALLED FOR.
KRK

GO. TO. HELL.
THAT'S SORT OF THE PLAN, TO BE HONEST, MISS CROFT.
WHEN WE HAVE THE ARTIFACTS BACK AND ASSEMBLED.
EVERYONE GOES TO HELL.

YOU'VE BEEN A CLEVER RABBIT.
BUT YOUR TIME IS OVER.
WHERE IS THE ARTIFACT?

I DON'T KNOW.
I BELIEVE YOU.
PITY. SAY GOODBYE TO THE WORLD, MISS CROFT.
HEY, BUDDY.

LEAVE MY PAIN-IN-THE-ASS FRIEND **ALONE.**

REYES.

GUH.

Hook like a bleeding SLEDGE!

YOU ALL RIGHT?

DEFINE "ALL RIGHT."

DON'T THANK ME. THANK MISS MANNERS, HERE.

THANK YOU.

REYES. THEY HAVE SAM. SHE'S MY ONLY REAL FRIEND.

SHE'S... SHE'S ALL I HAVE.

LISTEN.

The one bit of good news...
Jonah woke up.
ROCK CANYON MEDICAL CENTER
I'M IN, LITTLE BIRD. OF COURSE I'M IN.
AMBULANCE
In more than one sense, apparently.

YOU SURE, JONAH? WHAT DO THE DOCTORS SAY?
THEY SAY I HAD A "DELUSIONARY EPISODE."
THEY'RE DOCTORS.
THEY LIKE TO LABEL THINGS.

I MEAN THE COMA, JONAH. YOU HAD A CONCUSSION, REMEMBER?
VAGUELY.
LOOK, I DON'T WANT TO GO BACK TO THE ISLAND ANY MORE THAN YOU DO.

BUT THEY GOT SAM. I'M GOING.
MR. MAIAVA.
I AM GOING TO HAVE TO INSIST YOU GO BACK TO YOUR ROOM, SIR.

DO YOU HAVE SOME LEGAL RIGHT TO MAKE ME STAY, NURSE?
WELL, NO, BUT --
WELL, THEN I AM CHECKING OUT IMMEDIATELY, ALL RIGHT?
AND IF IT'S NOT TOO MUCH TROUBLE...

...COULD I POSSIBLY GET SOME PANTS?

I'M ON MY WAY TO SEE PROFESSOR CAHALANE, JONAH.
REYES GOT A BOAT, SAILING OUT OF INCHEON.
He doesn't remember the things he said, the premonitions.
Someone put them in his mind, somehow.

BE...BE CAREFUL, ALL RIGHT? THESE PEOPLE ARE STILL OUT THERE.
TRINITY COLLEGE, MISS.

The professor was a friend of my father's, and acts a bit like an overprotective uncle, sometimes.
I had him researching the little makara statue that Jonah found.
Hopefully, he'll have answers.

But no.
No answers this side of the afterlife.
The Solarii worshipers.
SCENE DO NOT CROSS
CRIME SCENE
CRIME SCENE DO NOT CROSS
CRIME SCENE

They GOT to him.

And those bastards have SAM.
MISS NISHIMURA.
YOU ARE AWAKE.

WHAT DO YOU WANT FROM ME?
IT IS BUT NOTHING, MISS NISHIMURA.
WE MERELY WANT YOU TO SLEEP PEACEFULLY.
AND LET YOUR TRUE NATURE TAKE ITS COURSE.

MY QUEEN.
OH.
YOU'RE ONE OF **THEM.**
THE **SOLARII.**

NO.
WE MERELY **SERVE** THE SOLARII, IN THEIR GREATNESS AND WISDOM.
BUT WE ARE NOT WITHOUT CERTAIN... GIFTS.

MESMERISM, YOU MIGHT CALL IT. HYPNOSIS. DECEPTION.
WE DON'T WISH TO RESURRECT THE SUN QUEEN, MISS. NOT TRULY.
WE HAVE A **DIFFERENT** REBIRTH IN MIND.

HAHAHA!
WHY DO YOU LAUGH, CHILD, WHEN YOUR OBLIVION IS AT HAND?

BECAUSE, YOU WELL-DRESSED IDIOT...
...MY FRIEND WILL COME FOR ME.
EVEN WITH AN OCEAN BETWEEN US?
DOESN'T MATTER.

YOU WILL BE TAUGHT TO HOLD YOUR INSOLENCE, MISS.
YOU WILL BE TAUGHT TO RESPECT THOSE WHO WORSHIP THE SOLARII.
SLAPPP

THE SOLARII, RIGHT. I REMEMBER THEM.
UNLIKE YOU, THEY ACTUALLY WERE SCARY.

UNTIL LARA KILLED THEM ALL, I MEAN.

Three hours later, we're at the flat Sam and I share. Shared.
I'm afraid to look.
But there's something here I NEED.

OH. OH, LARA, I'M SO SORRY.
THANK YOU.
What are you supposed to say, when someone has done THIS to your entire life?

YOU SAID YOU DIDN'T REMEMBER THAT YOU'D *TAKEN* AN ARTIFACT...?
I DON'T.
BUT I KNOW WHERE I'D HAVE PUT IT IF I *HAD.*
AND WE MAY NEED IT FOR RANSOM.

A PIECE OF A WALL CARVING, A FRIEZE, BUT IN GOLD.
THE *ERGASTANAI* WEAVERS, ATHENS. HUNG IN THE PARTHENON.
I SWEAR, I DON'T REMEMBER TAKING THIS FROM THE ISLAND.

I PROMISED MYSELF I'D SEE YOU HOME, FOR ROTH'S SAKE, LARA.
BUT I CAN'T GO WITH YOU BACK TO THAT HELL. I CAN'T.
I KNOW, JOSLIN.
I HELPED YOU CHARTER A TRAWLER. THAT'S ALL I CAN DO.
I HAVE TO THINK ABOUT MY BABY.

LARA. STAY HOME. SHE'S...SHE'S GONE.
I'VE LOST EVERYONE WHO TRULY CARES ABOUT ME, RECENTLY.
I HAVE ONE FRIEND WHO LOVES ME. WHO UNDERSTANDS ME.

WHAT CHOICE DO I HAVE?

DON'T YOU GIVE ME THAT LOOK, YOUNG LADY.
WHAT LOOK?
I'M NOT MAKING A LOOK.

SIGH
I GUESS I'M GOING, THEN.

YOU BRING MY MOM **BACK,** LARA.
I WILL.
I **PROMISE.**

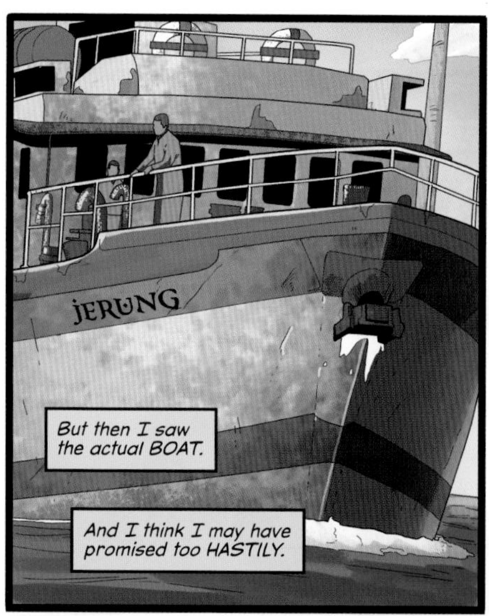

JERUNG
But then I saw the actual BOAT.
And I think I may have promised too HASTILY.

It's the Jerung, a fishing trawler, registered to Malta, though not a single person on it has ever set foot there.
The flag of convenience is a well-known maritime maneuver.
Makes it harder to place BLAME when things go BAD, though. Harder to trace when the cargo isn't exactly fresh FISH.
And that's VERY MUCH SO intentional.

And it seems with Jonah...
...the reunion takes a while to END.
AW, I JUST MISSED YA, LITTLE BIRD!
JONAH, YOU CAN QUIT HUGGING ME NOW.

THE WEATHER'S COOPERATING THE ENTIRE WAY, JOSLIN.
GLAD TO HEAR IT, NUR. GOOD TO SEE YOU.
Reyes assures me that Captain Hussein will protect us with his life, if need be.

The crew is all Malaysian...They seem very friendly, but a bit amused by my presence.
JADI ITULAH SANG PUTERI YANG NAK MENGEJAR HANTU?
AKU TAK KISAH BENDA MENGARUT APA YANG DIA NAK KEJAR, JANJI KITA DIBAYAR.
AKU TAK KISAH DIA NAK KEJAR HANTU KE, TOYOL KE, LANGSUIR KE, TU DIA PUNYA PASAL. JANJI KITA DIBAYAR!

WE'LL FIND HER. I PROMISE. SHE'S ON THE ISLAND, I KNOW IT.

YES.

WE WILL.

Or die TRYING.

I TRUST IN YOU, JONAH.

I TRUST IN **ALL** OF US.

WELL. I DID DO A LITTLE HEDGING MY BETS.
COME LOOK.
STATE OF THE ART LIFE RAFTS, AND IMMERSION SURVIVAL SUITS.

NICE. BUT WHAT'S IN THE CASE YOU KEEP CARRYING EVERYWHERE YOU GO, LADY CROFT?
YOU'RE NOT THE ONLY ONE WITH CONNECTIONS, REYES.
LISTEN, I'M EXHAUSTED FROM THE FLIGHT.
I'M GOING TO TAKE A SHORT SLUMBER, SHALL I?

NIGHT, YOU TWO.
TAKE CARE.
I don't say what I'm really thinking.
"Keep an eye out for STORMS."

THE ISLAND.
NO ONE WANTS TO SAY ITS NAME.
NOT EVEN ME.

Yamatai.

LARA.

SAM?
HOW DID YOU --
I DIDN'T, LARA.
YOU'RE DREAMING.

WHY ARE YOU CRYING?
BECAUSE YOU'RE GOING TO DIE, LARA.
I KNOW YOU'VE COME TO SAVE ME. YOU CAN'T.
AND YOU'RE GOING TO DIE TRYING.

YOU'RE THE MOST IMPORTANT PERSON IN THE WORLD TO ME.
YOU HAVE TO GO **BACK**, LARA. **FORGET** ABOUT ME.
SAM.
SAM.

GO BACK, LARA CROFT.

The NIGHTMARES are back, apparently.
GAH.
Why does my room smell like petrol?

Not petrol.
ACCELERANT.

We're on fire.
DAMN!

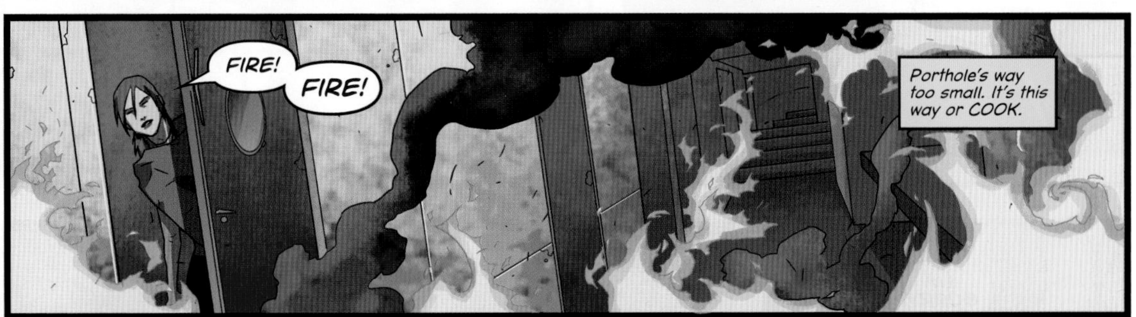
FIRE!
FIRE!
Porthole's way too small. It's this way or COOK.

MISS CROFT!
THE SHIP IS COMPROMISED.
GIVE ME YOUR HAND!

GLSH
CAPTAIN!

YOU BASTARD.

I'M SORRY.
I'M SO SORRY.

SPLT
GLLG.

They're burning the RAFTS.

We are AGES from the shipping lanes, and WAY off our registered course.
We'll DROWN before rescue.

UNG.
I need some COVER.
Get to my GEAR.

The sailors haven't even seen what's going ON yet.

JONAH!
REYES!
Oh, God, please don't be...

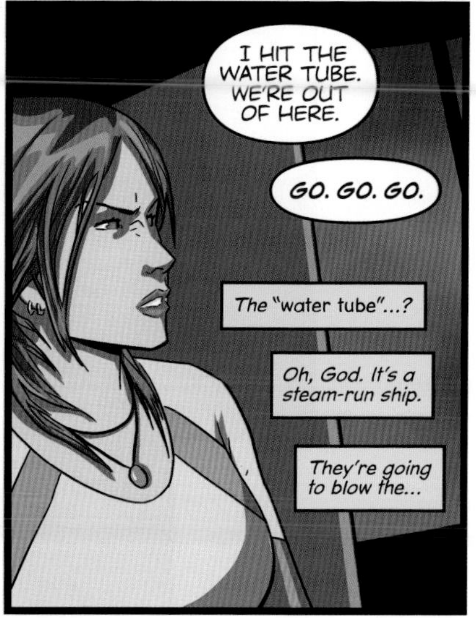
I HIT THE WATER TUBE. WE'RE OUT OF HERE.
GO. GO. GO.
The "water tube"...?
Oh, God. It's a steam-run ship.
They're going to blow the...

...boiler.

EH.

Daylight.
And rain.

No wreckage. No fuel slick.
I've been drifting for hours.
Did I get in the raft on my own?
I don't remember ANYTHING.

COME ON, GUYS. JUST...JUST A SIGN.
I did try. I used the raft's survival kit glasses, scanned the horizon for hours.
Nothing.

No PEOPLE anyway.
But hours of aimless drifting somehow managed to bring me where I least wanted, but most NEEDED, to go.
NO ONE WANTS TO SAY ITS NAME.
NOT EVEN ME.

YAMATAI.

SNK

ENDURANCE
CARGO SUPPLIES
(TIE-DOWNS, CABLE BOLTS)

The one place in the world I never wanted to see again.

Where I lost my friends.
Alex. Grim. Roth.

Where I lost my INNOCENCE.

But there's a difference this time.
KLIKK

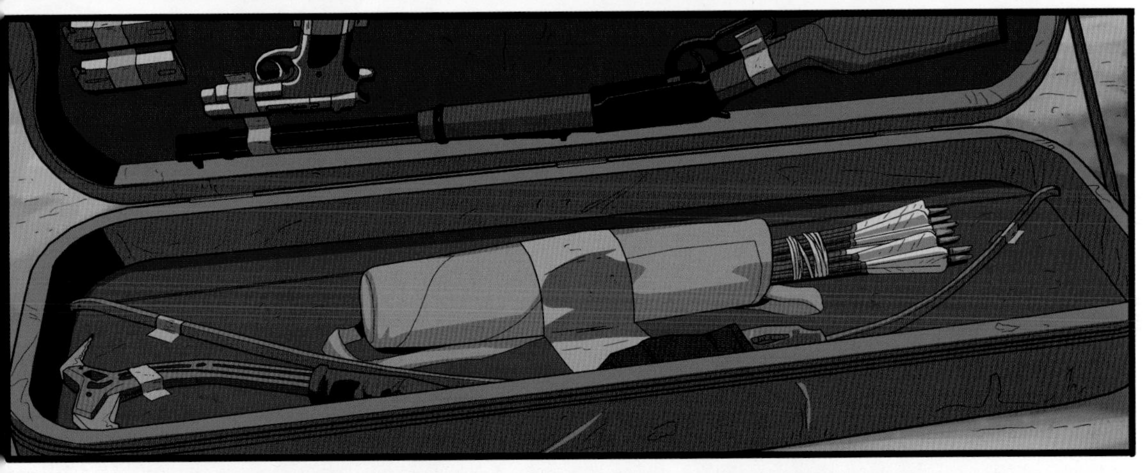

THIS time, I came PREPARED.
I'm COMING, Sam.

FOUR YEARS AGO, UNIVERSITY COLLEGE LONDON
By all logic, by everything I understood about people...
...we should never have worked, Sam and me.
MIND IF I SHOOT YOU?

MM-FFOOF FEE?
YOUR PICTURE, SILLY.
I was the posh London girl, trying not to show it, and she was the gregarious Yank who drew attention wherever she went.
I was studious, where she was creative.

I was shy, where she was bold.
WHAT? NO, NO, THANK YOU. I DON'T --
-- I DON'T LIKE TO HAVE MY PICTURE TAKEN, PLEASE.

And where I thought mostly of the past, she dealt exclusively in the now.
HMM.
MAKE YOU A DEAL.
GIVE ME ONE OF THOSE AND I'LL PUT THE CAMERA AWAY. FOR NOW.

I'M SAM, SAM NISHIMURA.
WANNA GO DANCING?
If you ask me how we became inseparable, I couldn't begin to tell you.

I just know we DID.
BULGARIA

I was always dragging her somewhere ancient and dusty, and she was always dragging me somewhere loud and colorful.

3 DAYS OF RAIN IN CHINA :(

But because we were together, we'd end up both having fun, anyway.

TWININGS
Jaffa Cakes
TRAVEL ESSENTIALS :)

only a night

I WILL TEACH YOU TO DANCE, LARA CROFT!!!
We needed each other, somehow.
Sometimes, it's just like that. Two people who should never even have met become friends forever.
SOUTH FACE OF KILIMANJARO
Until heaven falls.
MY FUNNY FACE :D
Sometimes, it's just like that.

Until I dragged her along looking for THIS godforsaken place.
YAMATAI.
I'M COMING, SAM.
I'LL FIND YOU.
I PROMISE, I'LL FIND YOU.

BUT...
...WHERE ARE YOU, MIGHT BE THE PERTINENT QUESTION.
She just wanted to make a documentary.
But a band of zealots known as the SOLARII, led by the madman MATHIAS, captured her.
For HIMIKO, the first and last QUEEN of this island.

No wind. No rain.
ARE YOU TRULY GONE, SUN QUEEN?
They felt Sam was a "Daughter of the Sun."
That her body could host the return of Himiko.

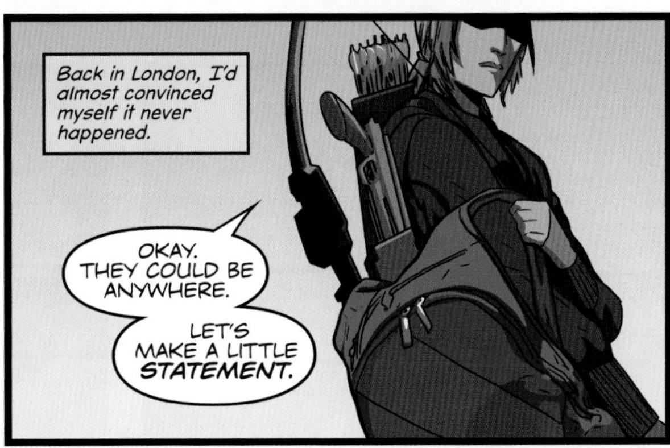
Back in London, I'd almost convinced myself it never happened.
OKAY. THEY COULD BE ANYWHERE.
LET'S MAKE A LITTLE STATEMENT.

YOU WHO WORSHIP THE SOLARII!
I KNOW YOU HEAR ME!
I HAVE WHAT YOU WANT.

I HAVE THE ARTIFACTS!
When we left the island before, Reyes, Jonah, Sam, and I...
...we each took a golden artifact, from a different era and continent.
Or so I was TOLD.

Priceless pieces of various noble houses, from China to Afghanistan.
Only, I don't remember DOING it.
YOU GIVE ME SAM, UNHARMED.
AND YOU CAN HAVE THE BAG.
IF NOT...

...I WILL THROW IT INTO THE SEA!
I'LL DO IT, I SWEAR I WILL!

DID YOU HEAR THAT, MATSU-SAMA?
SHE HAS THE ARTIFACTS.

YES.
"HE WILL HAVE HIS HOUSE WALL, FLOOR, ROOF, AND DOOR AND EACH SHALL HAVE A GUARDIAN AND EACH SHALL BEAR A CALAMITY."
PLEASE.

PLEASE.

MMM?
HAVE YOU SOMETHING TO SAY, MISS NISHIMURA?
PLEASE. DON'T HURT HER.
I WILL...I'LL DO YOUR RITUAL. I'LL LET HIMIKO INHABIT ME, IF THAT'S WHAT YOU WANT.
JUST DON'T HURT HER.
WELL.
MY DEAR MISS NISHIMURA. **SAM.**

NO DEAL.
MY PEOPLE DO NOT WORSHIP THE SUN QUEEN.

BUT...I THOUGHT YOU SOLARII...
MY PEOPLE ARE NOT **WORTHY** OF THAT AUGUST NAME.
WE DO NOT SEEK TO RESURRECT HIMIKO.
WE SEEK TO RAISE HER ONLY TRUE **DISCIPLE.**

"WE SEEK TO BRING BACK **MATHIAS.**"

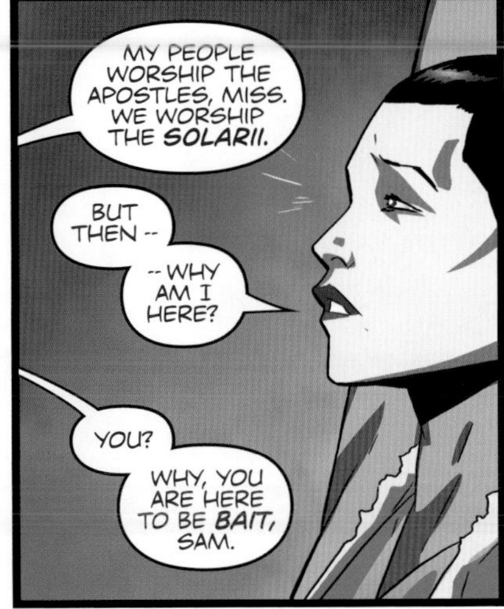

MY PEOPLE WORSHIP THE APOSTLES, MISS. WE WORSHIP THE **SOLARII.**
BUT THEN --
-- WHY AM I HERE?
YOU?
WHY, YOU ARE HERE TO BE **BAIT,** SAM.

YOUR FRIEND, MISS.
LARA CROFT.
SHE'LL COME RIGHT TO THE KILLING FLOOR FOR YOU, DON'T YOU SEE THAT?
NO. NO.

"OH, YES. WE STILL NEED BLOOD FOR OUR SACRIFICE.
"BUT IT HAS TO BE HER BLOOD, IN THE TEMPLE WHERE SHE MURDERED OUR SAVIOR.

"WE DON'T EVEN HAVE TO BRING HER HERE.
"SHE'LL COME IN AND BEG TO GIVE HERSELF UP TO US.
"FOR YOU, MISS NISHIMURA."

IT'S ALL PART OF A PROPHECY, YOU SEE? THIS WAS FORETOLD.
THERE ARE FOUR ARTIFACTS. AND FOUR GUARDIANS.
AND FOUR CALAMITIES...ALL MUST PRESENT THEMSELVES TO BRING BACK THE ONE, TRUE DISCIPLE.

"THE FOUR ARTIFACTS YOU KNOW.

"I AM THE FIRST OF THE GUARDIANS."

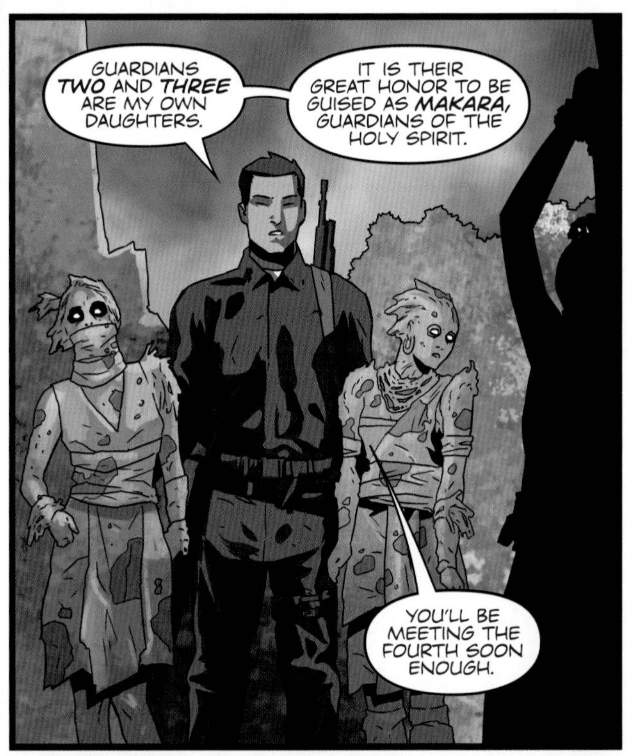

GUARDIANS TWO AND THREE ARE MY OWN DAUGHTERS.
IT IS THEIR GREAT HONOR TO BE GUISED AS MAKARA, GUARDIANS OF THE HOLY SPIRIT.
YOU'LL BE MEETING THE FOURTH SOON ENOUGH.

MY PEOPLE, WE ARE EXPERTS IN STAGECRAFT. LIES, DECEPTION, AND MESMERISM, SAM.
WE LACK THE TRUE MAGIC THAT ONLY MATHIAS UNDERSTOOD.

THAT'S WHY HE IS OUR SAVIOR.
YOU'RE MAD.
OH. OH, YES.
ALL POINTS, ALL POINTS. SHE'S COMING.

YOU MAY INCAPACITATE HER. YOU MAY CRIPPLE HER. YOU ARE **NOT** TO USE LETHAL FORCE.

GOT IT, MATSU-SAMA. ALL GLORY TO MATHIAS.

ALL HAIL, ALL HAIL.

..."How did a privileged British schoolgirl...

"...get to be so good at KILLING?"

GUHK

GAAKKKGH!

Was it the island...

...or was it something INSIDE?

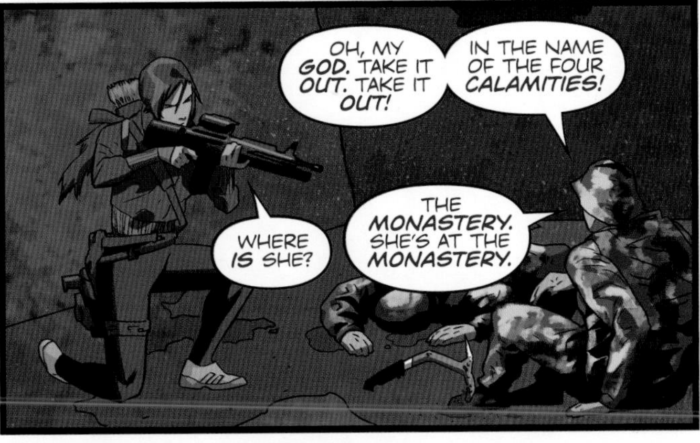
OH, MY GOD. TAKE IT OUT. TAKE IT OUT!
IN THE NAME OF THE FOUR CALAMITIES!
WHERE IS SHE?
THE MONASTERY. SHE'S AT THE MONASTERY.

THANK YOU.
BLAMM

WHAT WAS THAT SHOT?
RED TEAM CHECKPOINT TWO ISN'T ANSWERING OUR HAILING, MATSU-SAMA.
WE PRESUME SHE GOT TO THEM.
WELL.
MAYBE THIS WHOLE BLOOD SACRIFICE THING ISN'T THE BEST PLAN IN THE WORLD AFTER ALL, HUH?
"MATSU-SAMA."
That thing the soldier said, like the prophecy that Jonah yelled at me, in his trailer, during the flooding.
I remember it. Persian, from the Silk Road.
The era of Herodotus, I think.
"THERE SHALL BE FOUR CALAMITIES."
Supposedly, a great event happens when the elements mix.
Water swallows the earth, fire burns the seas.
Armageddon, basically.
Why does that sound so familiar?
OH.
THERE SHE IS.

IT'S THE ENDURANCE.
Where dear, strange, brilliant Alex gave his life to save mine.
Alex. Roth. Grim.
They all died to save us.
Esc
Esc

Wait. The calamities.
"WATER SWALLOWS THE EARTH."
When the desert FLOODED at Jonah's trailer.
It hadn't rained there in a hundred YEARS!
"Fire burns the seas."
The petrol on the water when the JERUNG exploded.
The calamities are FOLLOWING ME.
THE THIRD CALAMITY. WHAT WAS THAT ONE SUPPOSED TO BE?
OH, NO.
"EARTH PUMMELS THE SKY."
GROUNDSLIDE.

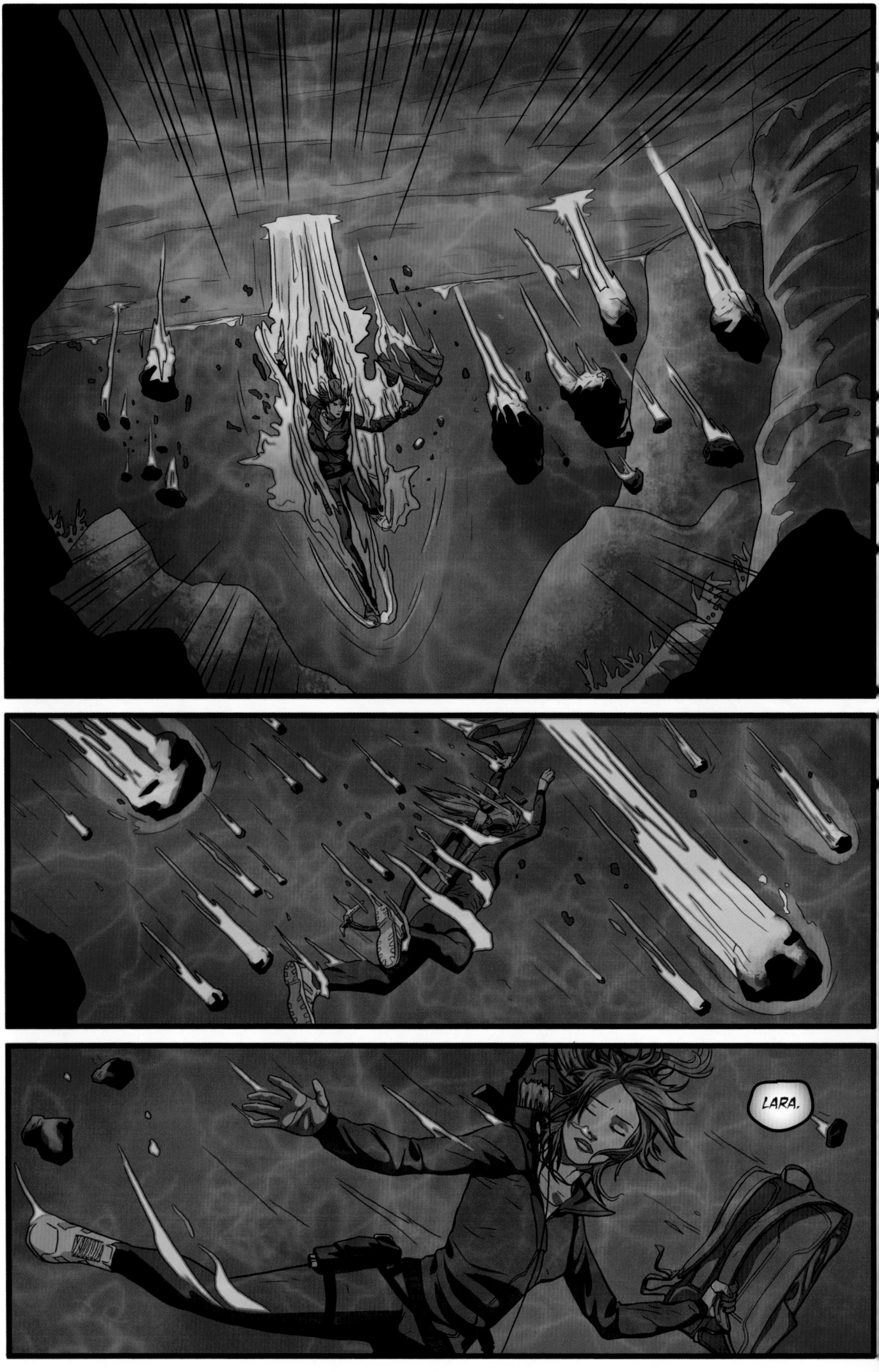

LARA.

LARA.

ALEX?

HELLO, LARA.

I MUST LOOK A FRIGHT.

GO, LARA.
WAKE UP.
IF YOU DREAM ON YAMATAI, YOU DIE!

BEWARE THE FOURTH GUARDIAN, LARA!

OKAY. IT'S OKAY, LARA.
I GOT YOU.

I GOT YOU.

To dream on Yamatai is to die.
I must be dreaming, then.
LARA?

WHO...?
YOU HAD ME WORRIED THERE, MISS CROFT.
YOU SWALLOWED A LOT OF WATER.
KIND OF A TOUGH BIRD, AREN'T YOU?
I'M DANNY, BY THE WAY.

I DIDN'T TAKE YOUR WEAPONS, LARA. THEY'RE DRYING BY THE FIRE.
YOU.
YOU'RE THE MAN FROM THE PUB IN DUBLIN.

"YOU HELPED US ESCAPE MATSU AND THE CULTISTS."

I DID.
I USED TO WORK FOR YOUR FATHER, LARA.
I WAS FOLLOWING YOU. HELP ME UP?

ARE YOU INJURED?
NOTHING WORTH MENTIONING.
YOUR FATHER KNEW WHAT A THREAT THESE PEOPLE WERE, LARA.

BUT HIMIKO IS **GONE**. I **SAW** HER FADE AWAY.
THESE PEOPLE WANT TO RESURRECT MATHIAS, NOT THE SUN QUEEN, MISS CROFT.
AND BELIEVE ME, MATHIAS WILL FIND A **WAY** TO HIMIKO.

I CAME TO STOP THESE PEOPLE. AND YOU WERE THE BEST CHANCE OF DOING THAT.
DO YOU HAVE THE ARTIFACTS?

Well.
He did save my life. TWICE.
YES.
I --

SHH.
QUIET!

WE'RE BEING **WATCHED.**

GET YOUR HANDS UP! GET YOUR GODDAMN HANDS UP!
Shit!

GAAH!

SHOOT HER! SHOOT HER!
BUDDA BUDDA BUDDA

BLAM

SAVIOR KILLER.
CROFT.

YOUR ATTENDANCE AT A RITUAL IS REQUESTED.
DROP YOUR WEAPON.
OR WE EAT THIS ONE'S BONES.

IF I GET KILLED HERE...
...I'M GOING TO COME AFTER LARA AND KICK HER ASS FROM MY **GRAVE.**
DON'T SAY THAT.

OKAY. BAD TASTE.
ALSO, BEING HERE MAKES IT SEEM NOT SO IMPOSSIBLE.
THIS GODDAMN ISLAND.

IT DREW US HERE. IT CALLED US BACK.
BULLSHIT.
BELIEVE WHAT YOU WANT, REYES.

THANK YOU, I WILL.
OKAY, WE HAVE NO PROVISIONS, NO WEAPONS, AND NO WAY BACK.
DO YOU HAVE A PLAN, JONAH?

YES.
FIND LARA AND HELP HER.
LIKE SHE WOULD HAVE DONE FOR **US.**

I am in the company of monsters.

I don't know what they are. I know what they LOOK like.
But that's impossible.
ENJOY YOUR LAST HOURS, SAVIOR KILLER.

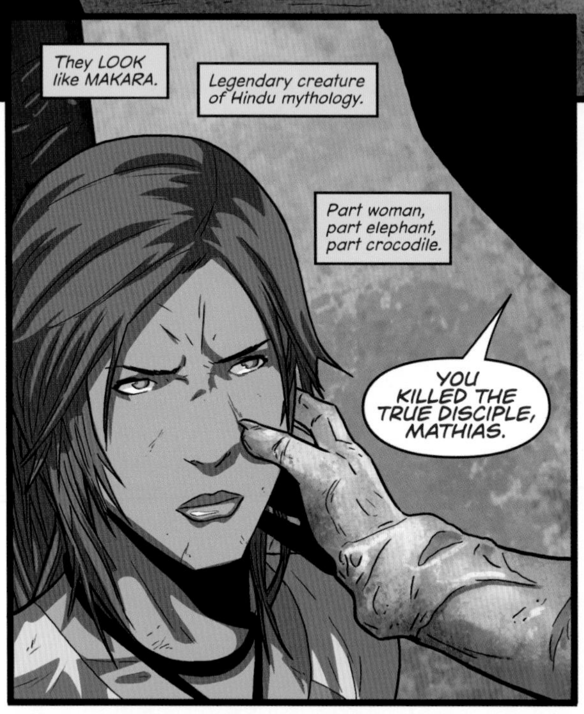
They LOOK like MAKARA.
Legendary creature of Hindu mythology.
Part woman, part elephant, part crocodile.
YOU KILLED THE TRUE DISCIPLE, MATHIAS.

AND YOU WILL BRING HIM BACK FROM THE GRAVE.
ONLY A GUARDIAN'S BLOOD SHALL DO.
Monsters.

HE WILL BE AVENGED.
...
HEY. HEY, LADIES.
But maybe they FORGOT something.

They forgot that they might not be the ONLY monsters in the room.
BE SEEING YOU.

DO YOU KNOW, PROFESSOR CAHALANE'S LAST WORD WAS YOUR NAME?
YES.
BEFORE I CRUSHED HIS SKULL TO RED PASTE IN MY HAND.
YES. WE WILL BE SEEING YOU.
REST WELL, LADY CROFT.
THEY'RE NOT MAKARA. THEY'RE MATSU'S OWN DAUGHTERS, IF YOU CAN BELIEVE THAT.
WHAT? HOW?
HYPNOSIS. MIND CONTROL. IT'S WHAT MATSU'S GROUP SPECIALIZE IN.
"IT'S ALL MAKEUP. PROSTHETICS AND FABRIC, YOU KNOW?
"BUT HE'S MESMERIZED THEM. THEY BELIEVE THEY ARE GODDESSES. I'VE SEEN THEM DO IMPOSSIBLE THINGS."
NOT EXACTLY FATHER OF THE YEAR, THAT GUY.
YOU'RE BLEEDING. ARE YOU OKAY?
ONE OF MATSU'S GOONS GOT ME WITH A KNIFE. I'M FINE.

I SMELL GAS.
THE ISLAND'S RIDDLED WITH POCKETS OF TRAPPED GAS...SOMETIMES A VEIN IS OPENED ACCIDENTALLY. IT'S COMBUSTIBLE. THEY GO WITHOUT HEAT OR FLAMES WHEN THAT HAPPENS, EVEN IN WINTER.
I THINK THAT'S WHY THEY SETTLED HERE. IT'S A EUPHORIC.

THAT MIGHT EXPLAIN THE DELUSIONS I SAW HERE.
IF THAT HELPS YOU SLEEP AT NIGHT, SURE.
I THINK YOU'D BETTER EXPLAIN WHAT YOU'RE DOING HERE, DANNY.
WHY DID YOU HELP US, BACK AT THE PUB?

BECAUSE THE SOLARII ARE EVIL, LARA.

AND MATSU'S PEOPLE WANT TO BRING THEM ***BACK.***

"AND IF MATHIAS AND HIS PEOPLE COME BACK...

"***THEY*** KNOW HOW TO BRING BACK THE ***SUN QUEEN.***"

AND THAT WILL BE THE END OF FREE WILL IN OUR WORLD.

THEY HAVE SAM.
I DON'T CARE WHAT THEIR MOTIVE IS.
I JUST WANT MY FRIEND BACK.
WE ARE NOT BARBARIANS, MISS CROFT.
YOU WISH TO SEE YOUR FRIEND, MISS NISHIMURA, I WILL TAKE YOU TO HER.
Grabby twit has my AXE!
WE ARE NOT GOING TO HURT HER. QUITE THE CONTRARY.
I AM THINKING OF MAKING HER INTO ONE OF MY MAKARA.
SHE SHOULD BE HONORED.
SAM? ONE OF THOSE... THINGS?
WE'LL SEE ABOUT THAT, ZEALOT.
IT ISN'T HER WE WANT, MISS CROFT. NOT NOW, ANYWAY.
IT IS YOU.
WHAT?
WHY?

I'VE READ THE SIGNS. I'VE STUDIED THE PROPHECY.
"HE WILL HAVE HIS HOUSE, WALL, FLOOR, ROOF, AND DOOR, AND EACH SHALL HAVE A GUARDIAN, AND EACH SHALL BEAR A CALAMITY."

THE ARTIFACTS YOU KNOW, WHEN YOUR GREED WAS REVEALED AND YOU STOLE THEM FROM THIS ISLAND.
THE CALAMITIES? THEY WERE THE BATTLES OF THE FOUR ELEMENTS.
I BELIEVE YOU HAVE FACED THEM THREE TIMES ALREADY?

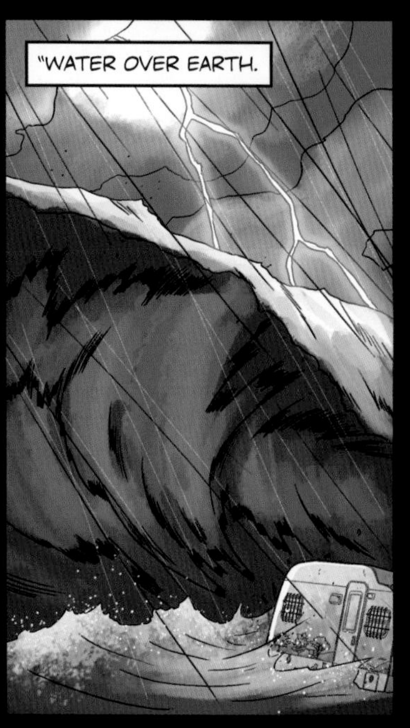
"WATER OVER EARTH.

"FIRE OVER WATER.

"EARTH OVER AIR."

LARA!
SAM!
OH, THANK GOD.

YOUR BLOOD WILL BRING MATHIAS BACK TO US.

He's mad. He's completely mad.

And worse...

...he has ALL the weapons in this scenario!

MATHIAS.
WE HAVE THE VESSEL.
WE HAVE THE PIECES OF YOUR HOUSE.

I WILL ASK THIS ONCE.
WHERE IN THAT SAD OLD DUMP HAVE YOU GOT LARA?

CUT HER.
THE TIME IS NIGH.
ONCE A GUARDIAN'S BLOOD TOUCHES THE ARTIFACTS ON THIS SIGIL, OUR SAVIOR WILL RETURN FROM THE ABYSS!

MATHIAS.
YOUR TRUE FOLLOWERS CALL TO YOU!

My God. What IS that?
WE ARE WITNESSING HIS BIRTH!
HE IS RISEN! HE WILL BE GIVEN FORM!

WE NEED MORE BLOOD.
GUARD. HER HEAD, PLEASE.
FOR OUR LORD AND SAVIOR.

It's LOATHSOME.
GAH.
Like a NIGHTMARE.

BLAMM
URK.

Oh.
My friends.
My beautiful FRIENDS.
LARA!

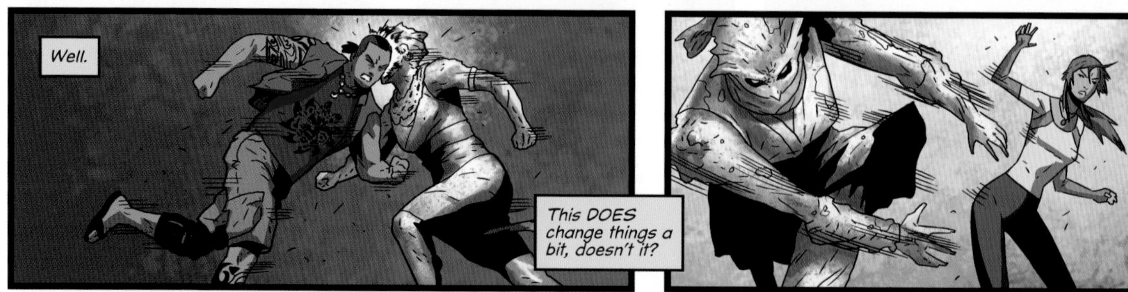
Well.
This DOES change things a bit, doesn't it?

I JUST WANT TO SAY.
I AM BEGINNING TO HATE ALL DEATH-WORSHIPING CULTISTS.

I CONFESS, I AM NOT FOND OF YOU EITHER, MISS CROFT.
ON YOUR KNEES, PLEASE.
WAIT. SAM. NO.

I'M NOT TIED UP NOW, YOU BASTARD!
Too LATE.

Only a GUARDIAN's blood shall do.
And MATSU...

...is a GUARDIAN.

RUN, SAM!

RUN!

HE RETURNS.

MATHIAS RETURNS AND I AM THE VESSEL!

FATHER!
FAAATHERRRR!
I AM NOT YOUR FATHER, MONSTERS.

Just this once...
AND MATHIAS NEEDS NO GUARDIANS.
I am hoping this IS just an illusion from the gas.

Good GOD.
His own DAUGHTERS. Good GOD.

IT'S COMING FOR US. WE HAVE TO DESTROY IT!
TAKE HER. TAKE SAM.
NO!
LARA...!
GO!

LARA.
YOU MURDERED ME, LARA.

LARA.
YOU OWE ME A LIFE.

The artifacts. The artifacts are his HOUSE. His PORTAL.
GO BACK TO HELL, YOU ROTTEN BASTARD.

So I will burn them DOWN.
With the guard's own GRENADES.
I'LL FIND YOU AGAIN, LARA.
I'LL FIND YOU.

JUMP! JUMP!
If that WAS really you, Mathias.
Go AHEAD. LOOK for me. Hunt me DOWN.

It'll give me a chance to kill you AGAIN, you evil SOD.

The front entrance was destroyed. It took an hour to find another DOORWAY.
The smell of the gas is much WORSE here. We can't even build a FIRE.
IT'S STEEP. BUT I THINK WE CAN DESCEND FROM HERE TO RENDEZVOUS WITH THE OTHERS.
LARA.

I'M SORRY, LARA. YOU ESCAPED THE MONASTERY.
BUT YOU TRAGICALLY FELL.
I TRIED TO SAVE YOU. I TRIED MY BEST.

WHAT ARE YOU SAYING?
I'M SAYING, LARA...
THAT I CAN'T LET YOU LEAVE THIS ISLAND.
NOT ALIVE.

SO YOU LIED? YOU'RE ONE OF THE SOLARII WORSHIPERS?
NO. I WAS.
BUT, LARA, THEY'LL TRY AGAIN TO BRING MATHIAS BACK. AND ALL HE WANTS IS THE SUN QUEEN.
I CAN'T SIT BY AND WATCH HUMANITY BE ENSLAVED BY HIMIKO.

EVERYTHING I TOLD YOU WAS TRUE, LARA. I DID WORK FOR YOUR FATHER.
THAT'S HOW I GOT MIXED UP IN THIS.

"HE ALWAYS WANTED TO KNOW THE UNKNOWABLE, LARA.
"AND WHEN WE FOUND A CULT THAT SPOKE OF A MAN, A MAN NAMED MATHIAS, WHO WAS GOING TO CHANGE THE WORLD...

"YOUR FATHER WANTED NO PART OF IT.
"I WAS NOT SO STRONG.
"I PLEDGED MY LOYALTY TO MATSU, WHO LED THE WORSHIPERS OF THE SOLARII."

YOU LEFT MY FATHER FOR WHAT, DANNY? FOR MONEY?
NO! I LOVED YOUR FATHER!
BUT MATSU HAD POWER, LARA.

"HYPNOSIS. MESMERISM. THEY ALL CAN DO IT. THEY MAKE PEOPLE DO WHAT THEY WANT.
"AND THEY TAUGHT ME HOW, AS WELL.
"IT WAS A TERRIBLE TEMPTATION. AND I FAILED THAT TEST."

YOU FOUR...YOU NEVER TOOK THE ARTIFACTS, LARA.
I MADE YOU THINK YOU DID.
ONLY, YOUR MIND FOUGHT BACK. YOUR MEMORIES WERE TOO STRONG. TOO VIVID.

BUT WHY? WHY GIVE US THE ARTIFACTS THAT COULD ALLOW MATHIAS TO BE REBORN?
"AND IT WORKED. THEY CAME FOR YOU!
"I SAVED THE WORLD, LARA!"
MATSU AND HIS MEN HAD GONE TO GROUND, LARA.
I NEEDED BAIT THEY COULD NOT RESIST.
THEN WHY DID YOU ATTACK THE JERUNG?
HOW DID YOU KNOW?
BECAUSE YOU AREN'T AS CLEVER AS YOU THINK, DANNY.
"THE BLOODSTAIN, RIGHT WHERE I SHOVED A SPEAR THROUGH A MASKED MAN IN A WETSUIT.
"IT WAS YOU."
YES. ALL RIGHT.
I CAN'T RISK YOU BEING ALIVE, LARA.
ONLY A GUARDIAN'S BLOOD CAN BRING BACK MATHIAS. AND YOU'RE THE LAST ONE.
ONCE MATSU WAS FOUND...YOU NEEDED TO DIE.
BE HAPPY, LARA. YOU'LL BE A MARTYR.
AND I'LL BE A HERO.
WELL, YOU KNOW, I BEG TO DISAGREE WITH THAT.

BECAUSE I THINK YOU'RE A TOSSER.
Everyone. My entire life.
Underestimated me. My family. My professors. MYSELF.
BLAM
He's no different.
AUCK.
CHUK
But if I get a vote in this thing...
...I vote not to DIE today.
GUHLK!
"A martyr," my ARSE.
GKKK.
STOP.
What?
Can't...can't MOVE.

THE CLIFF, LARA.
JUMP. NOW.

I can't stop my LEGS.
I'M SORRY IT HAD TO BE THIS WAY, LARA.

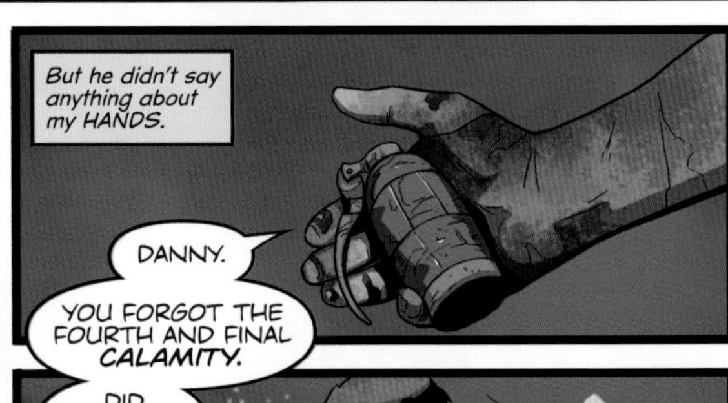
But he didn't say anything about my HANDS.
DANNY.
YOU FORGOT THE FOURTH AND FINAL CALAMITY.

DID YOU LOSE A GRENADE, DANNY?
NO. WAIT.
COMBUSTIBLE GAS. IN THE AIR.
NO!

NOOOOOOOOOOO!

Air over FIRE.
CALAMITY.

Well, what do you know, Danny?
Turns out YOU were the martyr, after all.

With only one good arm, it took a while to get down.
But I'm DONE underestimating myself.
I've lost a lot. My family, my innocence.

But I'm done living in the past...that's what destroyed everyone and everything ON this island.

Whatever spell Himiko had on this place is gone. I know it.

Time to appreciate what I have.

It was a lousy night.

But it's going to be a beautiful DAY.

TEN YEARS AGO, SNOWDONIA, WALES.

IN ONE OF THOSE EXCURSIONS (MAY THEY NE'ER FADE FROM REMEMBRANCE!) THROUGH THE NORTHERN TRACTS OF CAMBRIA RANGING WITH A YOUTHFUL FRIEND.

DID YOU JUST MAKE THAT UP, UNCLE ROTH?

NOT ME. WORDSWORTH. HE CLIMBED SNOWDON TOO.

HE WROTE ABOUT DAFFODILS, RIGHT? WE'RE STUDYING HIM IN ENGLISH.

GOOD FLOWERS, DAFFODILS. HARDY.

UGH, I SHOULDN'T THINK ABOUT SCHOOL. IT'S THE FIRST TIME THEY'VE LET ME OUT SINCE...AUNTIE'S FUNERAL.
YOU'RE RIGHT. LET'S LEAVE WORDS-WORTH AND FUNERALS BEHIND.
CAN WE SING THE *RHUBARB TART* SONG?

I WANT ANOTHER SLICE OF RHUBARB TART. I WANT ANOTHER LOVELY SLICE!

PYTHON SONG. ROTH AND I USED TO SING IT. THIS HIKE IS IN MEMORY OF HIM. WE NEED TO DO THIS RIGHT.
THE NEXT LINE IS "*I'M NOT DISPARAGING THE BLUEBERRY PIE.*"
RHUBARB TART...LOVELY SLICE. IS THIS A ***BRITISH*** THING? LIKE TOAD IN THE HOLE AND COMPLAINING ABOUT THE WEATHER?
YUP, IT'S A BRITISH THING.

LATER...
I GUESS I SHOULD BE GLAD YOU TWO DIDN'T CLIMB EVEREST TOGETHER.
OR THAT WE'RE NOT COMMEMORATING WHAT **YOU** GUYS DID TOGETHER.
GOOD TIMES.
HOW'S ALISHA NOW? CAN'T HAVE BEEN EASY FINDING OUT ABOUT HER REAL FATHER.
SHE SAYS SHE SUSPECTED FOR YEARS. HER WORDS WERE, "MOM, YOU'RE A LOUSY LIAR."
YOU'VE GOT A GOOD KID THERE.
I KNOW.
AGGGH!
CAREFUL!
THE ROCKS AROUND HERE ARE MUCH LOOSER THAN THEY LOOK.
DRINK THIS.
THANKS. DON'T WORRY. I DIDN'T SURVIVE YAMATAI TWICE ONLY TO DIE ON A WELSH MOUNTAIN!

A RHUBARB WHAT?
A **RHU**-BARB TART!
A RHUBARB TART!
A WHAT-BARB TART?
NEARLY AT THE SUMMIT.

WOW. OKAY, I'M IMPRESSED.

IT'S SO BEAUTIFUL.
THAT IT IS.
I'M GOING TO SEE IT, UNCLE ROTH. THE WORLD. ALL OF IT.
IT'S YOURS FOR THE TAKING.

WHAT ARE YOU DOING?
JUST SOME GARDENING. THEY'RE DAFFODIL BULBS.

HERE, TAKE THIS.
LARA.
UHN!
LARA.
LET... LET GO. LET GO OF ME!
LARA?
LARA. WHAT IS HAPPENING?
LARA, THERE'S NO ONE THERE!
HELP HER, LARA.

ALEX?
ALEX!
THEY ARE ON THEIR WAY TO KILL HER, LARA.
THEY ARE GOING TO KILL HER.

LARA.
I HAVE TO GO.
ALEX... YOU DIED. ON YAMATAI.
TO SAVE ME. TO SAVE ALL OF US.
YOU...YOU SHOULDN'T BE HERE.
...
OH.
GUESS NOT.
WANT TO HEAR SOMETHING FUNNY?
WHEN WE GOT TO PORT?
I WAS GOING TO ASK YOU ON A DATE.
LARA.
ALEX ISN'T HERE. HE'S DEAD.
LARA!

SHE'S RIGHT.
GRIEF, AND SURVIVOR'S GUILT, MOST LIKELY.
SAVE HER, LARA. BRING HER THE WATCH. THEN SHE'LL KNOW.
ROTH SAYS THANK YOU.
FOR THE DAFFODILS.
OH, AND ONE MORE THING.
LARA!
"WATCH YOUR STEP."
LARA!

UNGGG.
THUNK
OH, SHIT.
SHIT.
Just a casual, friendly hike, I said.
LARA!

YOU KNOW, THE ROCKS AROUND HERE ARE ***MUCH*** LOOSER THAN THEY LOOK!
YEAH... MAYBE WE SHOULD TAKE THE RAILWAY BACK DOWN.
THERE'S A ***RAILWAY?!***
I HATE YOU, YOU KNOW THAT?

There was a time when I believed that.
WELL. FORGIVE ME IF I LOVE YOU A LITTLE BIT RIGHT AT THE MOMENT.
I don't know if what I saw was a delusion or not.
It PROBABLY was.

But Alex died to save us. I have to find out for SURE.

And this woman would go with me, if I asked her.

So I will not ask her, not ever.

FORGET IT. I FIGURE I OWED YOU.

THANK YOU FOR SAVING MY LIFE.

Because I can't lose any more people I care about.

WHAT HAVE YOU GOT THERE?

NOTHING. JUST A WATCH I FOUND, SOMEWHERE.

To the greatest father ever. Love always, Alex and Kaz

REYKJAVIK, ICELAND.

‹WELCOME TO MY BAR, MY FRIEND! WE'RE NOT **QUITE** OPEN YET, BUT NEVER MIND! WHAT CAN I GET YOU?›
I DON'T SPEAK THAT DRIVEL.
AH. WELL. WOULD YOU LIKE A WHEATGRASS TEA, OR --
IN A MOMENT.

I'M LOOKING FOR **THIS** WOMAN.
I KNOW SHE COMES HERE.
I...I DON'T KNOW. I SEE A LOT OF PEOPLE.
PLACE LIKE THIS, WITH WHEATGRASS TEA AS THE SPECIAL?
I'M SURE YOU'RE SWAMPED.

SO, I'LL ASK AGAIN. HAVE YOU SEEN THIS WOMAN?

LOOK, I DON'T KNOW WHO YOU ARE.
BUT HASN'T SHE HAD **ENOUGH** TROUBLE?
SHE'S A GOOD GIRL.
CAN'T YOU JUST LEAVE HER **BE?**

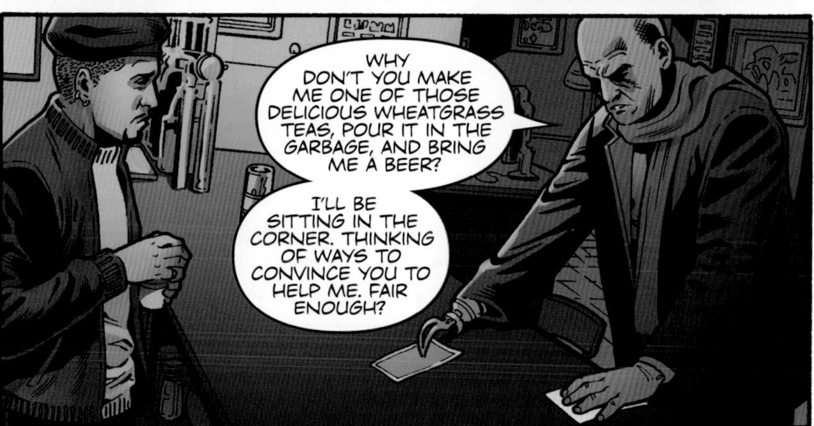
WHY DON'T YOU MAKE ME ONE OF THOSE DELICIOUS WHEATGRASS TEAS, POUR IT IN THE GARBAGE, AND BRING ME A BEER?
I'LL BE SITTING IN THE CORNER. THINKING OF WAYS TO CONVINCE YOU TO HELP ME. FAIR ENOUGH?

I WOULDN'T LEAVE ME TO THINK ALONE FOR TOO LONG.
WHEATGRASS GODDAMN TEA, FOR CHRIST'S SAKE.

AMERICAN, RIGHT?
I KNEW IT.
EXCUSE ME?

I'M A YANK, MYSELF, IF YOU CAN BELIEVE IT!
SHOCKING.
LET ME BUY YOU A DRINK, STRANGER.
NO, NO, THANK YOU.
OH, I INSIST.

DAMN.
I AM SO SORRY.
YOU CLUMSY IDIOT.

I AM SO EMBARRASSED. YOU'RE RIGHT.
LET ME HELP YOU WITH THAT.
MY WIFE USED TO CALL ME THE SAME EXACT THING!

BEFORE I STRANGLED HER WITH HER OWN FRENCH STOCKINGS. LIKE THE UNCLEAN FORNICATOR SHE WAS.
TRINITY ASKS YOU TO STOP YOUR QUESTIONS, MR. FEMON.

PLEASE. LEAVE HER ALONE. SHE'S BEEN THROUGH *ENOUGH*.
SHLK
SHLK
SHLK
SHLK
I'LL DECIDE WHEN SHE'S BEEN THROUGH ENOUGH, MR. FEMON.
REST WELL.
DRAFT BEER
Warsteiner
NOW. I'M GOING TO ASK THE SAME QUESTION MY FRIEND ASKED, KIND SIR.
BUT I WON'T BE *NEARLY* AS PATIENT.

I UNDERSTAND, MRS. WEISS. THANK YOU. I WILL TRY.

Of all the things I've had to do since returning to the world, calling the families of those who perished on Yamatai has been the hardest.
I WANT YOU TO UNDERSTAND ABOUT ALEX, MA'AM.
HE SAVED US ALL.
HE DIED A HERO.
YES.

And I will remember the words of this grieving mother until my dying day.
"You will understand if that is cold comfort, Ms. Croft."
WELL?

"WELL," WHAT?
WELL, WHERE ARE WE GOING?
THAT WAS ALEX'S MOTHER, RIGHT?
DIDN'T SHE SAY WHERE HIS SISTER IS NOW?

SHE **THINKS** KAZ IS IN THE UKRAINE. SHE LOST CONTACT A WEEK AGO.
BUT SHE SAYS SHE FEELS SHE'S IN TROUBLE.

SAM. I'M GOING ALONE.
NO, YOU'RE NOT.
SAM.
WE ALWAYS GO TOGETHER. ALWAYS.
It's true. We used to be inseparable.
But I owe Alex a debt, and someone's chasing his sister.

If my oxygen-deprived mind is to be trusted, of course.
NOT THIS TIME, SAM.

Sam would go. For me. And part of me wants to ask her to go.
But I won't. I will not.
PLEASE, SAM. TRY TO UNDERSTAND.
THIS IS NO PLACE FOR YOU.

"Cold comfort," indeed.
But she'll be ALIVE.

And I can live with that.
I'm coming, Kaz.
Your BROTHER sent me.

A UKRAINIAN DAWN.
Guess it was too much to hope that finding Kaz would be easy.
Or a comfy ride.
‹SHIPMENT FOR THE WORK NEXT WEEK.›
‹GOT NOTHING DOWN FOR TONIGHT. CAN'T LET YOU IN.›
‹SERIOUSLY?›
‹NOT WORTH MY JOB TO, FRIEND. COME BACK WHEN YOU'RE ON THE LIST.›
‹SCREW YOU AND YOUR LIST, FRIEND.›
Shit. My Russian is a little rusty, but I think that means we're not getting in.
At least not that way.

Guards, checkpoint, usual lines of communication out.

Let's go subtle.

No one's maintaining this perimeter fence.
Few people EVER want to see what's on the other side of it.

Shh, Lara.
CLICK
Damn it.
GAH!
SSSNAAAAP!
Wonder what they're trying to catch with these?
RUSTLE

Probably THAT.
GO ON, GET OUT OF HERE. I TOOK THIS ONE FOR YOU.

I guess the deer species owes me a little payback after Yamatai.
But a girl's got to eat.

GGRRRRR
And so have you.
GRRRRR
AND YOU.
GRRRR
OH, AND YOU TOO.
SO WHO'S GOING TO MAKE THE FIRST MOVE?

GRRRAAA!
BLAAM!
WHO'S NEXT?

SMART MOVE.
<SHOT CAME FROM OVER HERE!>
Bollocks! They heard it.

<WOLF'S BEEN SHOT.>
<POACHER?>
<POACHERS USE RIFLES, NOT PISTOLS.>
<TRAP HAS GOT BLOOD ON IT. IT'S HUMAN.>
<SEARCH THE AREA!>
Oh shit.

Can't risk another shot.
And they look like they'd REALLY like to use their guns.

‹EXTREME TOURISTS. WHAT DO THEY THINK WE HAVE A GODDAMN CHECKPOINT FOR?›

‹I'LL GIVE THEM SOMETHING EXTREME.›

THUNK!
OOOOFF...

YOU'LL LIVE TO FEEL THAT HEADACHE YOU'RE GOING TO HAVE.
SO I'D BETTER TAKE THIS.
I DON'T KNOW WHAT'S AHEAD OF ME.
ONLY THAT IT'S A PLACE FEW PEOPLE EVER WANT TO GO.

Pripyat. The ghost-city neighbor of CHERNOBYL.
WHAT THE HELL ARE YOU DOING **HERE,** KAZ?
OKAY, GROUP. GATHER, PLEASE.
THIS FAIRGROUND WAS BUILT TO CELEBRATE MAY DAY. IT WAS ONLY OPEN FOR ONE DAY BEFORE PRIPYAT WAS EVACUATED AFTER THE MELTDOWN.
LOOK AROUND, BUT DON'T **TOUCH** ANYTHING.
WOW. INCREDIBLE. JUST IMAGINE THAT, *HUH? ONE DAY?*
LONGER THAN YOU WILL LAST, LARA CROFT.
<SHE SAID THEY'D SEND SOMEONE.>
<THEY MUST BE STOPPED, BY ANY MEANS NECESSARY.>
<FOR LUCYA.>
<WE WILL AVENGE HER.>

There were many times.
But this was the first.
The first time I saved Alex's life.
ESC

I'VE GOT YOU. I'VE GOT YOU.
LARA? LARA!
JUST CALM DOWN.
DID YOU FALL IN TOO?
SURE... WHY NOT.
YEAH. SILLY ME, EH?
QUICK!
WAAAAAA HOOOOOO!
TAKE THIS!
ER, THANKS...
SUNSET SWIM? NO?
WATCH OUT BELOW!!

BOOOOOOM!!

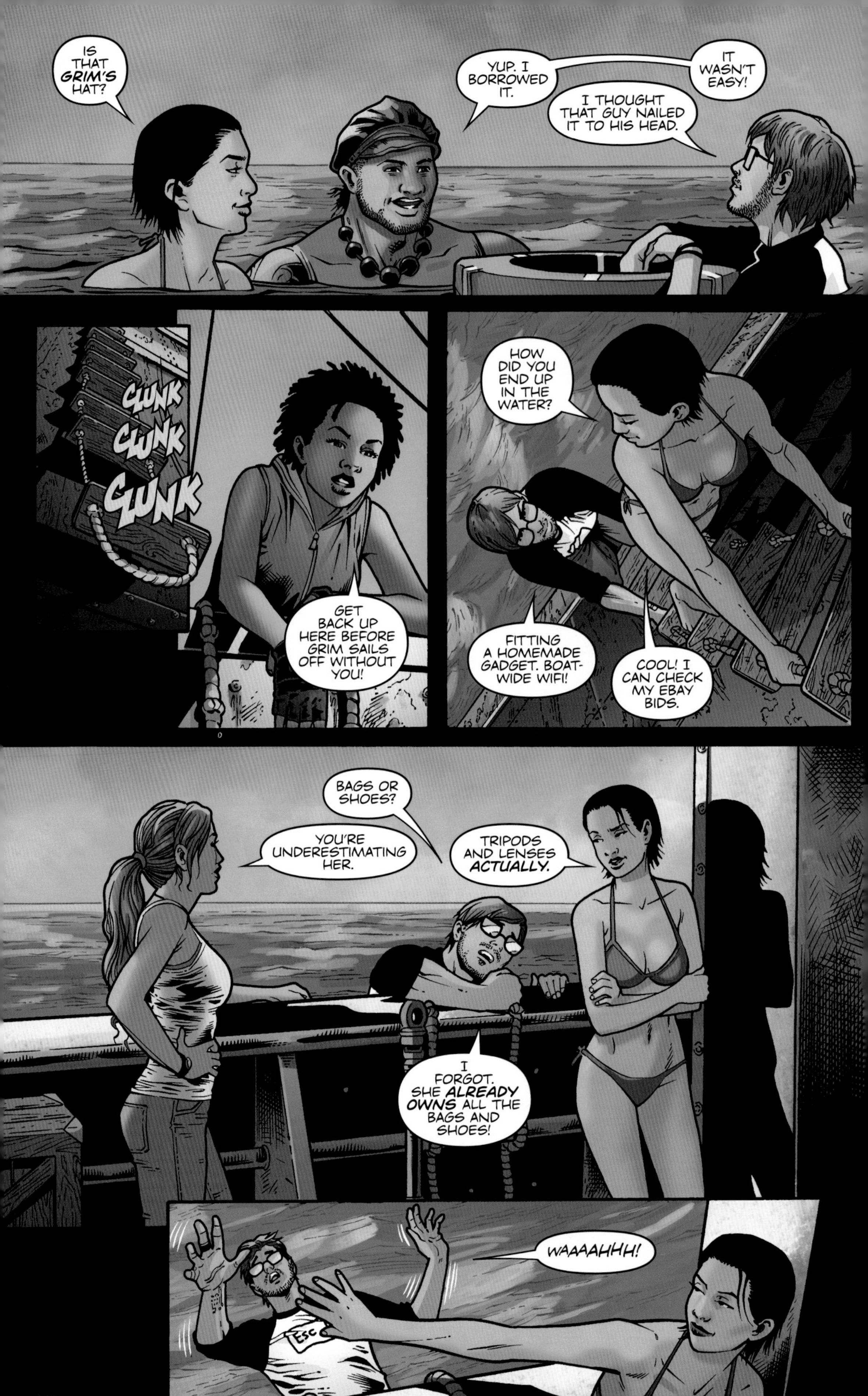

IS THAT **GRIM'S** HAT?
YUP. I BORROWED IT.
I THOUGHT THAT GUY NAILED IT TO HIS HEAD.
IT WASN'T EASY!

CLUNK CLUNK CLUNK
GET BACK UP HERE BEFORE GRIM SAILS OFF WITHOUT YOU!

HOW DID YOU END UP IN THE WATER?
FITTING A HOMEMADE GADGET. BOAT-WIDE WIFI!
COOL! I CAN CHECK MY EBAY BIDS.

BAGS OR SHOES?
YOU'RE UNDERESTIMATING HER.
TRIPODS AND LENSES ***ACTUALLY.***
I FORGOT. SHE ***ALREADY OWNS*** ALL THE BAGS AND SHOES!

WAAAAHHH!

YOU DON'T HAVE TO HELP HIM, YOU KNOW.
IF I DON'T, THEN WHO ELSE WILL?
AND WHAT DOES THAT TELL YOU?
AT LEAST MAKE HIM SWEAT A BIT.
HE'S JUST, YOU KNOW, AWKWARD. AND HE OVERCOMPENSATES. I USED TO BE AWKWARD ONCE.
YES, BUT, YOU WERE ADORABLY AWKWARD. HE'S JUST AN IDIOT.
LAAAAAARRRRRA!
I THINK HE MIGHT BE DROWNING... AGAIN.
OH, GO ON THEN! BUT BE CAREFUL!
THEY BROKE THE MOLD WHEN THEY MADE YOU, LARA.
And that was the second time...

But in the end, he saved me.
Saved all of us.
ESC
Kaz and Lucya's wedding. Alex was the best man.
Now I have to save HER. Kaz. Alex's sister.
After Alex...after he saved me. After he sacrificed himself so the rest of us could live.
I would walk through hell to pay that debt.
It's just...

I just didn't expect it to be quite that LITERAL.

PRIPYAT
3 KM FROM CHERNOBYL NUCLEAR PLANT

They call this a ghost city.

To me, it's more like a skeleton, like the BONES of a person after the FLESH decided to get up and LEAVE.

They proudly called this a "Nuclear City."

The city was just a teenager when it was evacuated. Sixteen years from founding to oblivion.

Fifty thousand souls were told to abandon their possessions and go, immediately. Another two hundred thousand from the surrounding area.

And the Earth has reclaimed it, poison and all.

Radiation levels are safe. For now.

The children were told to leave their toys. Many left their pets.
Everywhere I look tells a little tragedy.
Kaz, why in God's name would you come HERE?
SNAP
Someone's FOLLOWING me.
In the TREES.
Well, come on then, sneak.
SHOW yourself.
You again.
Science failed us. Let loose an environmental Kraken.
And the Earth took it down and laughed at humanity.
HANG ON, BEAUTY. I'M SURE I'VE GOT SOMETHING.

The area became the world's oddest wildlife sanctuary.
The animals came back. They're not only surviving, they're thriving, even with rad levels far higher than they should be.
And they look normal, which NO ONE expected.
THIS ISN'T EXACTLY HEALTH FOOD, DARLING.
Life finds a way to make us all feel foolish, somehow.
GOOD GIRL. GOOD GIRL.
She's not afraid.
Someone's been FEEDING her.
OKAY. LARA HAS A CHORE TO DO.
NICE MEETING YOU.
The official name for this area is CHERNOBYL EXCLUSION ZONE.
But there was a lonelier name, as well.
The ZONE OF ALIENATION.

<SHE MUST BE GOOD IF THEY SENT HER.>
<SHE'S DEFINITELY NOT WITH THE TOURIST GROUP.>
<NO. THEY NORMALLY KEEP THEM OUT OF OUR WAY. THAT'S THE UNDERSTANDING.>

<AT LEAST IF THEY WANT OUR HELP ON THE REACTOR.>
<MAYBE THEY WANT TO DO IT THEMSELVES NOW?>
<I DOUBT THAT. THEY KNOW A GOOD DEAL. WE'RE THE ONLY ONES WHO'D WILLINGLY BE HERE.>

COUGH COUGH COOOOUUUGH
<EASY, EASY. DID YOU TAKE YOUR MEDICATION TODAY?>
<YES.>

HUURK-- SPPAARR
<HAVE MINE AS WELL. I'VE NOT TAKEN IT YET.>
<WHAT ABOUT YOU?>

<I'LL LIVE. ALL OF US ARE GOING TO NEED OUR STRENGTH IF WE'RE GOING TO DEFEND HER.>
<AND KILL THAT GIRL.>
<LUCYA WOULD WANT THAT.>

OKAY. GO HOME NOW.
NO MORE RUBBISH FOOD, OKAY?
I'm beginning to think this deer's a BRIT.
ALL RIGHT. ENOUGH.
WE'RE NOT PARTNERS, IS THAT CLEAR?
DON'T YOU HAVE A DEER BOYFRIEND TO GET BACK TO? OR A DEER GIRLFRIEND, MAYBE?
SIGH
WELL, COME ON, THEN.
The battery's been taken.
Who'd want to loot in this place?
OH.
WE'RE HERE.

PRIPYAT AMUSEMENT PARK.
Welcome to Dismal Land, Lara Croft.
Welcome to the Unhappiest Place on Earth.
Not even VANDALS come here.
But Alex's sister went to ground right HERE, for God knows what reason.

SO **NOW** YOU GO!
But wolves wouldn't come this far into the city, would they?

OH SHIT.

I **LIKE** DOGS. DON'T MAKE ME SHOOT YOU.

GROWL

GROWL

GROWL

СТОП!
SHIT.
GET YOUR HANDS UP. GET YOUR GODDAMN HANDS UP!
THEY'RE UP.
Please don't tell me that this is...
...KAZ?
KAZ, I'M A FRIEND OF YOUR BROTHER'S. I'M A FRIEND OF ALEX!
I KNOW WHO YOU ARE, LARA CROFT.
THEN YOU WON'T MIND IF I TAKE THAT. THROW THE OTHER ONE DOWN.
I JUST DON'T KNOW WHY YOU'RE HERE.
YOUR DOGS, I PRESUME?
So what do I tell her? The ghost of her brother told me to come? Perhaps not.
THEY'RE THEIR OWN DOGS. BUT WE HAVE AN ARRANGEMENT.
CALL THEM OFF AND I'LL TELL YOU WHY I'M HERE.
PLEASE. YOU HAVE ALL THE GUNS.

CERBERUS, HEIMDALL, ALBERICH, STAND DOWN.

GOOD BOYS.

GUARDIANS. YOU NAMED THEM AFTER GUARDIANS.
YOU'RE SMART. I CAN SEE WHY ALEX LIKED YOU.
AND THEN YOU GOT HIM KILLED.

IT WASN'T LIKE THAT.
NONE OF YOU WOULD HAVE BEEN ON THAT ISLAND IF IT HADN'T BEEN FOR YOU.
ALEX MAILED ME. TOLD ME YOU WERE THE ONE THAT DECIDED WHERE THEY WERE GOING NEXT. INSISTED ON IT.

WE'RE COMING BACK TO THE FAIRGROUND AREA NOW. YOU'LL HAVE FIFTEEN MINUTES TO LOOK AROUND ON YOUR OWN.
IT'S A TOUR GROUP!
MOVE!
BOYS, YOU KNOW WHAT TO DO.

OKAY. IT'S JUST WILD DOGS. MOVE BACK, PEOPLE, MOVE BACK.

OH MY GOD! THEY LOOK DANGEROUS!

LET'S JUST MOVE AWAY. NICE AND SLOWLY.

One thing I've found in my travels.

There is no suffering so great that someone won't want to GAWK at it.

ARE THEY GOING TO ATTACK?

NOT UNLESS I ASK THEM TO.

YOU KEPT QUIET. THAT WAS COOL OF YOU.

I'M NOT HERE TO CAUSE TROUBLE. I'M HERE TO HELP.

AND I HAVE SOMETHING FOR YOU.

THIS WAS... MY FATHER'S WATCH. THEN, AFTER HE DIED, IT WAS ALEX'S.

HE WANTED YOU TO HAVE IT. I MEAN, THAT'S WHAT HE WOULD'VE WANTED. HE DIED SAVING US. YOU SHOULD KNOW THAT.

In a strange sense... it WOULD be ironic.
To come to this radioactive place, and die of LEAD poisoning.
STEP AWAY FROM HER.
OR WE WILL SHOOT YOU IN THE HEAD.
DO IT, NOW!
WHO?
WE KNOW WHO YOU ARE, ASSASSIN.
WE KNOW WHO YOU WORK FOR.
KAFF
ALL RIGHT, THEN.
WHO DO I WORK FOR?
I can hear it, the catch in his voice.
He means it.
VIKTOR, NO.
SHE'S NOT... SHE'S...
SHUT UP, KAZ! SHE'S BEEN HUNTING YOU, DO YOU NOT KNOW THAT?
SHE'S WITH TRINITY.
SHE'S COME FOR ALL OF US, JUST AS THEY DID FOR MY LUCYA!
NO. NO, VIKTOR.
PLEASE, PUT THE GUN DOWN.
YOUR FRIEND FEMON WENT LOOKING FOR YOU IN ICELAND, KAZ, AND NOW HE'S MISSING.
FOR ALL WE KNOW, SHE KILLED HIM, AS WELL.
He could kill me, right now. No police here, no law at all.
More than that, he WANTS to.

KAFFF
PAVEL, I TOLD YOU TO KEEP QUIET, YOU IMBECILE.
SORRY, VIKTOR.
While I, on the other hand...
...appreciate the distraction very MUCH, Pavel.
WHAT?

"WHAT," INDEED.

I MUST SAY.

RUSSIAN HOSPITALITY IS NOT ALL I'D HEARD.

TELL THEM, VIKTOR. TELL THEM TO LOWER THEIR GUNS.
OR YOU'LL FIND OUT FIRST HAND HOW I "HUNT."
LARA! STOP.
EVERYONE STOP.
LARA, THIS IS VIKTOR. HE'S...HE WAS MY BROTHER-IN-LAW.
I STILL AM, KAZ.
LUCYA WOULD WANT ME TO PROTECT YOU.
I KNOW, DEAR ONE. I KNOW. AND YOU MEAN WELL. BUT YOU'RE NOT A KILLER.
WHAT'S THIS ABOUT FEMON, VIKTOR?
HE'S MISSING. HE ENTERED A BAR IN REYKJAVIK.
NEVER CAME OUT...
LIKE A GHOST IN THE WIND.
WHO'S THIS FEMON, KAZ?
HE'S AN ANGEL. WHEN I WAS STRUNG OUT AND ON THE STREETS...

"HE FOUND ME IN A STUTTGART ALLEY. TOLD ME I WAS WORTH A BETTER LIFE.
"HE TAUGHT ME CERTAIN...WELL, VERY ILLEGAL COMPUTING SKILLS."

AND IT TURNED OUT I WAS GOOD AT IT.
HE CAN'T BE DEAD.

DON'T MOVE YOUR EYES AWAY FROM YOUR TARGET AT CLOSE QUARTERS, VIKTOR.
IT'S SLIGHTLY INSULTING, TO BE HONEST.
ALL RIGHT. WHO IS IT YOU'RE SO AFRAID OF?
WHO IS TRINITY?

LARA. TRINITY IS WHY I AM HIDING IN THE WORST PLACE ON EARTH, AND IT'S NOT FAR AWAY ENOUGH.
IF I TELL YOU...
...THEY WILL KILL YOU.

AND ALEX WOULD COME BACK FROM THE GRAVE TO HAUNT ME IF I ALLOWED THAT.
KAZ, I --
WHAT THE HELL?

IT'S A PACKAGE OF SOME KIND.
DON'T TOUCH IT. IT COULD BE A GRENADE!
WHO GIFT-WRAPS A GRENADE, VIKTOR?

OH, NO.
OH, GOD.

IT'S HIS PROSTHETIC.
IT'S FEMON'S PROSTHETIC.
Whatever terrible thing TRINITY is...

...it's now here BESIDE us.
VIKTOR. GIVE ME THE GUN.
...NO. NO, IT IS MY DUTY TO PROTECT HER, AND --
VIKTOR.
GIVE ME THE GUN.

GKKK.
PAVEL. I TOLD YOU TO KEEP QUIET. STOP THAT COUGHING.
Too late.

They're HERE.

OH, HE'S NOT COUGHING, MY FRIENDS.

GKK.

HE'S *DYING.*

JUST AS WELL. POOR BOY HAD RADIATION SICKNESS.

DID HIM A *FAVOR,* I'D SAY.

GOD'S *WORK,* REALLY.

Under different circumstances, this could have been a romp.
Abandoned spooky theme park, closed after being open just one day.
A goth's DREAM hangout.
Unfortunately, we're in the middle of the Chernobyl Exclusion Zone, and the mossy areas here emit dangerously high levels of radiation.
VERY PLEASED TO MEET YOU, FINALLY.
MY NAME IS MR. CRUZ.
I NEED TO KNOW, MISS WEISS.
WHOM DID YOU TELL?
WHOM DID YOU TELL OF TRINITY?
Oh, and a murderous ZEALOT is planning to kill us all.
Me, Alex's sister Kaz, and her odd Russian brothers-in-law.
Should have gone to the BIG park in PARIS, perhaps.

YOU DO KNOW I'M HOLDING A MUCH **BIGGER** GUN, YES?
TWO OF YOU WOULD BE DEAD BEFORE YOU COULD RAISE IT, MISS CROFT.
PERHAPS THREE.
I BELIEVE THE FLOOR IS **MINE?**

YOU'RE JUST GOING TO KILL US ANYWAY. WHY SHOULD I TELL YOU?
YOU KILLED MY **LUCYA.**
I DID.
HOW SHE **SQUEALED,** MISS WEISS.
I PUT BOTH HER STOCKINGS IN HER MOUTH AND **STILL** SHE WAS A SIREN!
MOST INCONVENIENT.

NOW, I KNOW THESE FINE GENTLEMEN MEAN SOMETHING TO YOU.
HOW WOULD THIS BE...?
YOU **PICK** ONE. THE MOST **EXPENDABLE,** I'D SAY.
NOW.

Kaz is right. He likes what he does.
He's going to kill us all like...
Like...

OR PERHAPS... THE **GIRL** YOUR BROTHER CARRIED SUCH A **TORCH** FOR?
DROP YOUR WEAPON, MISS CROFT.
OR YOU **WILL** GO FIRST.

KAZ... IT'S NO USE.
HE HAS US. HE'S GOING TO KILL US ALL.
LIKE **DOGS**.
WHAT?
WE HAVE NO **GUARDIANS**. HE'S **GOT** US.

WHAT ARE YOU **ON** ABOUT, MISS CROFT?
NOTHING.
I JUST WANT THIS DONE WITH.
WELL. THAT **IS** REFRESHING, I MUST SAY.

HERE YOU ARE.
I HOPE THE SHELL IN THE CHAMBER EXPLODES AND TAKES YOUR **EYE**.
YOUNG LADIES TODAY, ABSOLUTELY NO **CHARM** AT **ALL**.
Please, Kaz. I know you're too angry to think.
But one of us is going to DIE.

While SURPRISINGLY, one seems on the verge of RESURRECTION.
WHAT...?
KAAF
RUN, KAZ. **RUN!**
I DON'T **THINK** SO, PAVEL.
CERBERUS! HEIMDALL! ALBERICH!

KILL!
RIP HIM APART! TEAR HIS FILTHY THROAT OUT!
Kaz named her dogs after guardians.
How very APT.

GET OFF ME, YOU HELL BEAST!

OH, NO, YOU BASTARD.
I STILL HAVE SOME CHARM TO SHARE WITH YOU.
LARA. NO. YOU CAN'T FOLLOW HIM.

WE'VE BEEN WHERE THE CONCRETE IS...LOW-LEVEL RADS.
THOSE TREES ARE ANOTHER STORY.
IF THAT MAN GETS OUT OF HERE, NONE OF US WILL EVER STOP LOOKING BACK.

UNTIL WE TURN ONE NIGHT, AND SEE HIM, IN OUR LAST MOMENT.
I'M GOING.

WE GO WITH YOU, TERRIFYING FRIEND OF OUR SISTER-IN-LAW.
ABSOLUTELY NOT.
I MEAN, YOU HAVE TO GET PAVEL TO A MEDIC.

TAKE A SUIT, LARA. PLEASE.
THERE'S NO TIME, KAZ.
GET SOMEWHERE SAFE.

SHE IS VERY STUBBORN, THIS WOMAN, I THINK.
KAZ...?
WHAT ARE YOU THINKING?
I AM THINKING I AM GLAD MY BROTHER LOVED SOMEONE WORTHY OF HIM.
He was GUSHING blood.
And he has no GUN, unless it was concealed.
It's funny, on Yamatai, I was usually the one being hunted.
FUNNY how things CHANGE, isn't it?
SNAAPP
TSK.
IT'S ONLY YOU AGAIN, IS IT?
GO ON, SCOOT. IT'S DANGEROUS IN HERE.

SHIT.
CHUKKK
Should take my own ADVICE.
Fair-weather FRIEND.
GODDAMN IT, this creepy little tourist is fast.
SLLLSHSH
GIT.
THOSE ARE NASTY WOUNDS, MISS.
I THINK YOU'RE BLEEDING TO DEATH. WHAT DO YOU THINK?
I THINK YOUR DAYS OF COQUETTISH TEMPTATION ARE DONE.

I'M A CROFT. DYING OF BLOOD LOSS SIMPLY ISN'T DONE.
YOU, ON THE OTHER HAND...
...ARE NOT.

Bloodline or no, he's right.
BLASPHEMER.

I'm fading, and he's still got petrol in the tank.

But come hell or high water...
He's NOT leaving here to kill Alex's only SISTER.

YOU, Mr. Cruz, or WHOMEVER you are --
-- are FORTUNATE I don't have my AXE handy.
GUHH.
I...
I THINK WE BOTH MIGHT BE DYING, MISS CROFT.
I DID NOT PLAN FOR THAT.
UNFORTUNATE.

BUT I PROMISE YOU.
I WILL LIVE LONG ENOUGH TO KILL THAT CHATTY LITTLE BITCH.
I KNOW MY DUTY.

NOW, BE A GOOD GIRL AND LET ME WET MY BLADE IN YOU ONE LAST TIME, YES?
He's got the only weapon. And I am already losing peripheral vision.

I REGRET THAT I SHALL BE UNABLE TO OBLIGE.
MISS CROFT?
I need that bleeding GUN.

This is going to HURT.

Well.
Right AGAIN, Lara.

REMARKABLE.

DEVIL'S DAUGHTER!
Well. My AIM could be better.
But I admit I enjoy hearing him SQUEAL.

And then things go all BLACK for a bit.

MFF.

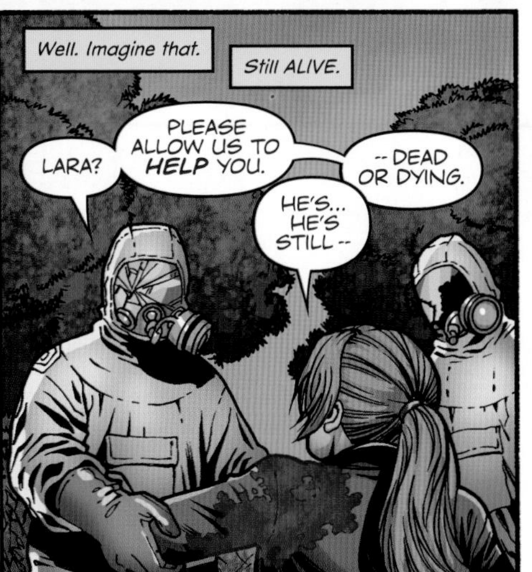
Well. Imagine that.
Still ALIVE.
LARA?
PLEASE ALLOW US TO HELP YOU.
HE'S... HE'S STILL --
-- DEAD OR DYING.

HE RAN. BUT HE RAN DEEPER INTO THE WOODS.
THE RADIATION LEVELS THERE... HE WILL NOT SURVIVE.
YOU CAME FOR ME?
WE COULD NOT LEAVE YOU BEHIND.
KAZ HAS TAKEN PAVEL TO HOSPITAL. YOU WILL NOT FIND HER, I THINK.

Despite their gear, they aren't really soldiers.
And yet, they stepped into the bear pit.
For me.
I...
THANK YOU.
YOU HAVE MADE A TERRIBLE ENEMY TODAY.
BUT YOU HAVE ALSO GAINED A FAMILY, I AM AFRAID.

FAMILY. I've never had much of a family before.
Mainly I was raised by books. Piles and piles of them. Anything I could get my hands on.
I loved adventure stories the best. Exciting tales from exotic lands.
I wanted that.
Someday. Somehow.

THERE YOU GO, REGINALD. THERE'S YOUR HEAD BACK.

And the staff of Croft Manor. They were good to me.

HARWOOD
Indulging the whims of the "Little Lady Lara."

As for Dad, he was away a lot.
Just like in my books. He was always off somewhere new.
Examining this, excavating that.
He always came back though.
With presents. Bribes.
To show what a good father he was.
And they pretty much worked.
For a smart kid, I could be easily BOUGHT, sometimes.

The best times were when he took me with him.
They weren't too often.
But they inspired my LOVE of archaeology. Of uncovering the mysteries of the world.
I became OBSESSED.
DAD! DAD!
But my father was a...little distracted.
THIS IS RIDICULOUS! I TOLD YOU WE HAVE ALL THE REQUIRED PERMITS AND PAPERS.
DAD, LOOK WHAT I FOUND!
IN A MINUTE, LARA, DARLING, IN A MINUTE.

ROTH, ROTH, LOOK WHAT I'VE FOUND.
ANOTHER PIECE OF BROKEN POTTERY?
NOW THAT IS QUITE SOMETHING. JADE. AND IN GOOD CONDITION TOO.
IT'S MY FIRST REAL FIND.
DID YOU SHOW YOUR FATHER?
HE'S BUSY.
OF COURSE.
HERE. TRY THIS.
I'LL NEVER TAKE IT OFF.

<IS SHE OKAY? WHY IS SHE HOLDING THAT PENDANT?>
<SHE PASSED OUT HOLDING IT.>

<IDIOTS! JUST STANDING THERE LIKE THE LEMONS! CAN'T YOU SEE SHE'S AWAKE?!>

<VIKTOR KIRILL! FILTHY HABIT!>

SORRY. THEY'RE OAFS, BUT MEAN WELL.
I HAVE TO **GO**. I HAVE TO FIND HIM.

NOT LIKE THAT. COME, I STITCH YOU.
THANK YOU...?
VARVARA.
VARVARA. WHERE AM I EXACTLY?
OUR HOME. THIS IS PAVEL'S ROOM. HE WON'T MIND YOU USING IT. KAZ IS GETTING HIM SEEN TO.

ARE ALL THESE HIS?
NONE. I COULD NOT AFFORD TOYS FOR THE BOYS WHEN THEY WERE LITTLE. AFTER THE DISASTER...WHEN THE OTHERS DIDN'T RETURN, HE SAVED THE CHILDREN'S THINGS.
PAINTED THEM. MENDED THEM.
JUST IN CASE THEY EVER COME BACK.

HE WAS ALWAYS SOFT LIKE THAT.

NOW WE MEND YOU. AHH, PRIPYAT TRIES TO BREAK US ALL.
YOU SHOULD'VE SEEN THE OTHER GUY.

YOU CAN TAKE THE PAIN. THAT'S GOOD.
I'VE HAD WORSE. A LOT WORSE.
DON'T MIND HIM.
HUURRRRGH
WHY DO YOU STILL LIVE HERE? WASN'T EVERYONE EVACUATED?

PRIPYAT, APRIL 27, 1986. ONE DAY AFTER THE CHERNOBYL DISASTER.
"MOST WERE.
"THEY WERE TOLD IT WAS JUST FOR A FEW DAYS.
"BUT THEY WERE NEVER ALLOWED TO RETURN.
"BUT MY HUSBAND WAS KILLED IN THE DISASTER.
"AND WE WERE, WHAT, JUST GOING TO LEAVE OUR **HOME?** ALL WE HAD **LEFT?**
"I DIDN'T BELIEVE THEM WHEN THEY SAID THEY WOULD BRING US BACK.
"I SAID NO.
"AND WE STAYED.
"THEY DIDN'T WANT TROUBLE. THEY HAD BIG PLATES FULL ALREADY.
"SO THEY LEFT US."
‹WE CAN'T **MAKE** THEM LEAVE.›
‹WE DID OUR JOBS. SENTIMENTAL FOOLS! THEY'RE NOT OUR PROBLEM NOW.›

"NOW GOVERNMENT **PAY** MY BOYS TO WORK ON THE REACTOR.

"PATCH UP THE CRACKS. KEEP IT SAFE. SAFE ***ENOUGH.***"

THEY EVEN GIVE US MEDS.
WE SCRATCH THEIR BACKS AND THEY LEAVE OURS ALONE.

WHAT ABOUT ***LUCYA?***
LEFT WHEN SHE WAS SEVENTEEN. I DON'T BLAME. THIS PLACE WASN'T FOR HER. SHE MARRIED KAZ TWO YEARS AGO.
SUCH A LOVELY GIRL.
THERE, ALL DONE.

THANK YOU, BUT I HAVE TO GO. CRUZ IS OUT THERE SOMEWHERE.
WHILST HE'S ALIVE KAZ WON'T BE SAFE.
NONE OF US WILL BE SAFE.

WHY DO YOU DO THIS? COME SO FAR FOR US?
A FAVOR TO A FRIEND. ALEX, KAZ'S BROTHER.
MUST HAVE BEEN QUITE A FRIEND.
HE WAS.

THWOCK THWOCK THWOCK
WHAT IS IT?
HELICOPTER. WE NEVER GET THOSE HERE. IT'S HEADING THIS WAY.

THWOCK THWOCK THWOCK

CRUZ MUST'VE CALLED IN ***REINFORCE-MENTS.***

THEY'RE AFTER ME. I HAVE TO GO. LEAD THEM AWAY.

NO!

WE ***FIGHT.***

ALL OF US. BASTARD KILLED ***OUR LUCYA.*** THIS IS ***PERSONAL.*** THIS IS ***FAMILY.***

HELLO AGAIN, MISS CROFT.

FIRE ON MY COMMAND.

PRIPYAT, 3 K.M. OUTSIDE CHERNOBYL.
In 1986 Chernobyl turned a thriving city into a ghost town.
WHOOOOOSSSH
WHOOOOOOSSSH
But some wouldn't go.
They would rather die in their homes than leave them.
And against the odds, they survived.
OH.
SHIT.
KABOOM
Once, Chernobyl brought death to Pripyat.
Now I have.

A secret group of zealots called TRINITY are hunting for Alex's sister Kaz.
I seem to have gotten in their WAY.

A good brain will serve you well.

But when a girl's in a tight spot?

One of THESE will do nicely.
BUDDA BUDDA BUDDA

GET IN THERE!
CHUK
CHUK
CHUK

CHUK
CHUK
TUNK
TUNK
TUNK
CHUK

OH GOD, VIKTOR.
HE'S DEAD.
And it's my fault. I came here hoping to help. Now people are dying.

A MOTHER KNOWS THESE THINGS.
GOT ANOTHER GUN?
URRRGGGG...

TAKE MINE.
TIME TO IMPROVISE A DISTRACTION.
Sorry, bear.
FUT
FUT
FUT
Needs must.

AND rifle club.

That's one thing the British public school system teaches you.

How to SURVIVE.
BUDDA BUDDA BUDDA
BUDDA BUDDA BUDDA
URRRRRG!
THERE'S TWO LEFT, AND THAT HELICOPTER.
KAZ WILL BE BACK FROM HOSPITAL SOON.
CAN YOU GET HIM OUT OF HERE? I CAN COVER YOU.
I AM NOT GOING NOWHERE.
YOU ARE. THAT'S FINAL.
HOW?
THEY'RE EVERYWHERE... EVERYWHERE. YOU DON'T KNOW WHAT... THEY'RE CAPABLE OF.
I'M STARTING TO.
Another friend, gone. But there's no time to mourn.

THEY WILL PAY FOR THIS. THEY WILL PAY, MY SON. I SWEAR IT.

PULL BACK!

SMITE HER A SECOND TIME! READY...

HE'S GOING TO FIRE AGAIN.
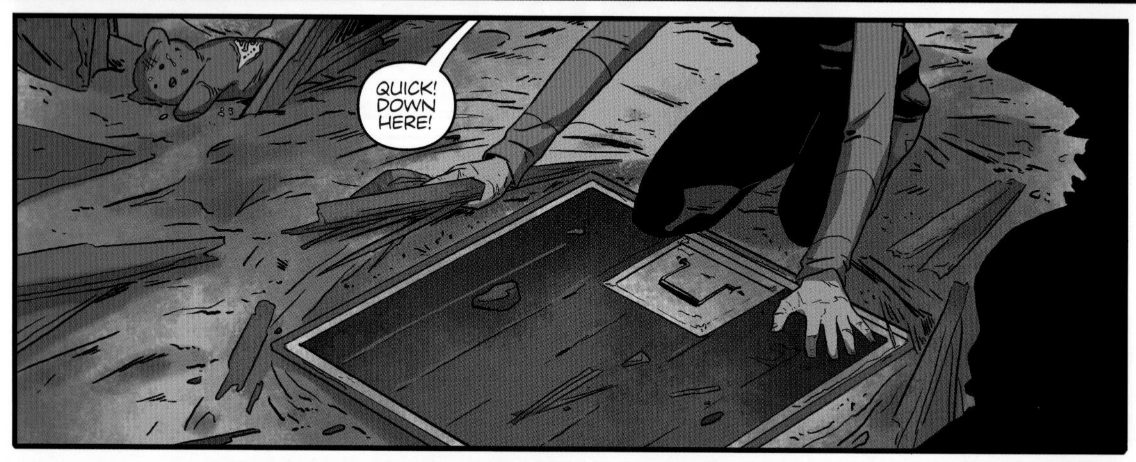
QUICK! DOWN HERE!

YOU FIRST.

You idiot, Lara.
WHOOSH
WHOOSH

No time.
WHOOOOOSH
WHOOOOOOOSH

BWOOOOOMM
BWOOOOOMM

QUICK THINKING.
This woman just lost her sons, but she's holding it together.
For NOW, anyway.

WHERE DID SHE GO?

NOT WITHOUT THIS.

SHE WON'T GET FAR.

LET'S SEARCH THE PLACE.

THEY'VE MOVED AWAY.

THEY'LL BE BACK. THERE'S SOME OF MY HOME **STILL STANDING.**

THERE'S DEBRIS HOLDING IT DOWN. IF I PUSH IT TOO HARD THEY'LL HEAR.
I ***MIGHT*** BE ABLE TO REACH A GUN IN TIME...
DO YOU HAVE GUNS DOWN HERE?
NO, THERE'S A BETTER WAY.
NOT GUNS...

BUT ***WEAPONS.***
YOU LIKE TO IMPROVISE, YES?

VARVARA, YOUR SONS.
THEY WERE GOOD MEN.
...

I'M...I'M SOR--
THEY WERE FOOLISH AND MAGNIFICENT, BOTH.
HELP ME OPEN THESE BOTTLES, CHILD.

NOT *THAT* ONE.

EXCUSE ME?

THAT ONE'S FOR US.
FOR **STRENGTH.**
WELL.
WHAT THE HELL, RIGHT?

IT WAS IN THE KITCHEN.

BUT THAT TIME IS PAST, I'M AFRAID.

There you go, trespassers.

That's from VARVARA.

AAAH, MERCIFUL GOD!

GET IT OFF ME!

We'll never get out of here with fire.

I need this one's GUN.

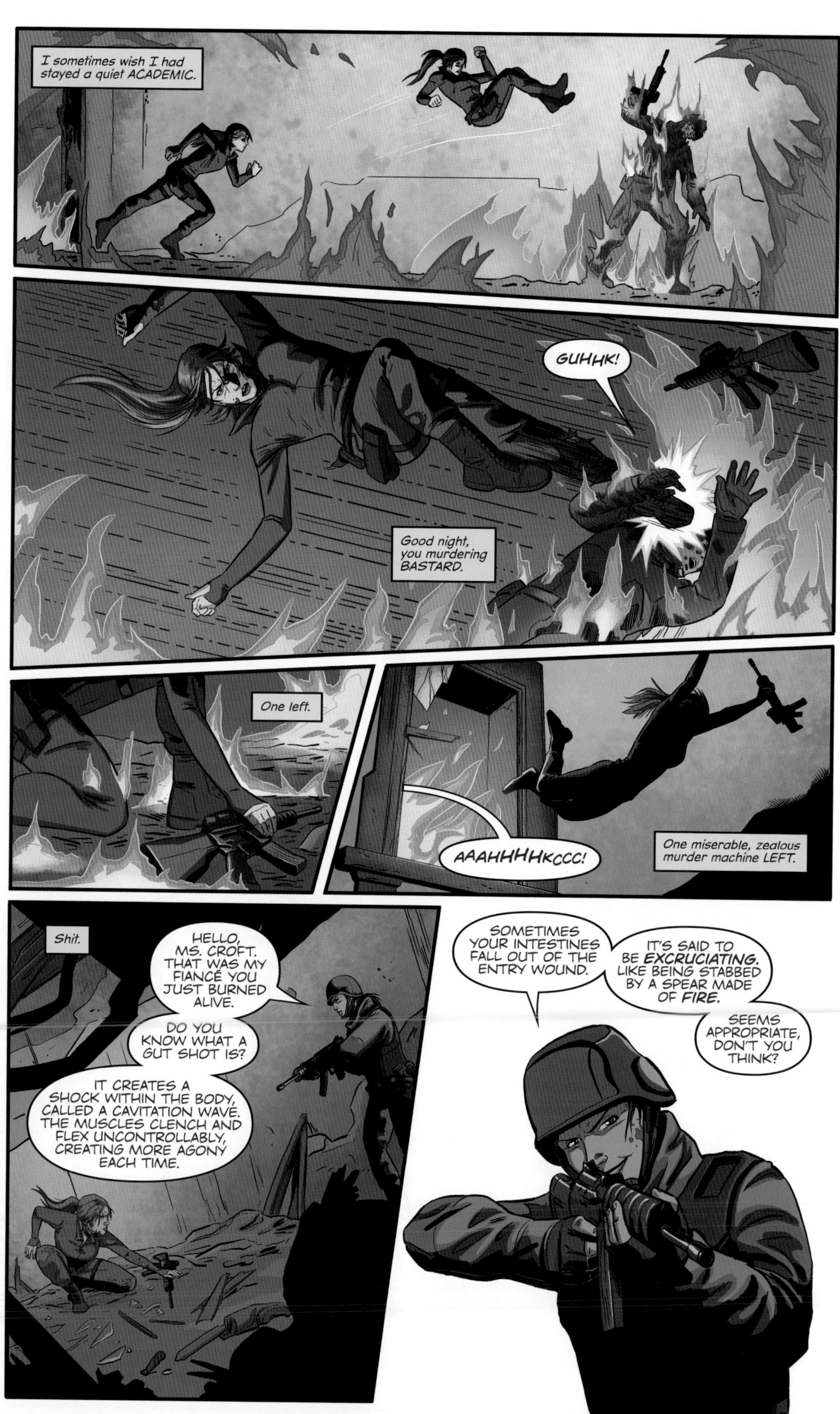
I sometimes wish I had stayed a quiet ACADEMIC.
GUHHK!
Good night, you murdering BASTARD.
One left.
AAAHHHHKCCC!
One miserable, zealous murder machine LEFT.
Shit.
HELLO, MS. CROFT. THAT WAS MY FIANCÉ YOU JUST BURNED ALIVE.
DO YOU KNOW WHAT A GUT SHOT IS?
IT CREATES A SHOCK WITHIN THE BODY, CALLED A CAVITATION WAVE. THE MUSCLES CLENCH AND FLEX UNCONTROLLABLY, CREATING MORE AGONY EACH TIME.
SOMETIMES YOUR INTESTINES FALL OUT OF THE ENTRY WOUND.
IT'S SAID TO BE EXCRUCIATING. LIKE BEING STABBED BY A SPEAR MADE OF FIRE.
SEEMS APPROPRIATE, DON'T YOU THINK?

BLAMM
OH.

KAZ!

THAT WAS CLOSE. IT'S GOOD TO SEE YOU.
YOU TOO. PAVEL WILL PULL THROUGH, BUT IT'S GOING TO TAKE TIME.
KAZ.
KIRILL AND VIKTOR, THEY--
I KNOW.
I KNOW.

THEY TOOK MY LUCYA. THEY TOOK THE BOYS. THEY TOOK MY HOME.
PERHAPS THEY SHOULD SEE HOW RUSSIANS **VIEW** SUCH MATTERS.

IT'S NOT ENOUGH. NOWHERE **NEAR.**
THEY HAVE AN **ASSAULT** HELICOPTER.
OH, VARVARA.
I AM...
I AM SO SORRY.

IF I... IF I HAD STAYED WITH TRINITY.
IF I HADN'T MARRIED YOUR **DAUGHTER.**
THEY'D STILL...THEY'D STILL BE...
CHILD.

HUSH.
NEVER SAY SUCH THINGS AGAIN TO MAMA.
DAMN YOU TO HELLFIRE, I NEED A **STATUS** REPORT!
OR SO **HELP** ME, I'LL FIRE ANOTHER **SIDEWINDER** WITH YOU STILL IN THE **GOD-CURSED HOUSE,** DO YOU **HEAR ME?**
And I have an idea.
It is ridiculous and completely suicidal.

I'm doing it ANYWAY.

YOU HAVE A **THREE COUNT**, SOLDIERS.

MAY THE TRINITY **BLESS** YOU, YOU COWARDLY, HELL-BOUND **INCOMPETENTS**.

"YOU SEE, I DON'T APPROVE AT ALL OF WOMEN THESE DAYS, PILOT. THEY ARE SLATTERNLY IN MANNER AND SPEECH.

"THEY ARE TOO PRESUMPTUOUS BY HALF. THEY ACT ALMOST AS IF FIT TO BE CALLED MEN, YOU SEE?"

BUT I MUST BE PROGRESSIVE AND GIVE CREDIT WHERE IT'S DUE. THEY **DO** MAKE FINE SOLDIERS.

THEY TAKE ORDERS EXTRAORDINARILY WELL, DON'T YOU FIND?

TELL THEM TO KILL, AND THEY SIMPLY **DO** IT.

Walk steady, Lara.

Walk STEADY.

SOMETHING.
SOMETHING NIGGLING.

I don't care if I die.
But let me get close ENOUGH, please.

IT'S HER. CAN YOU NOT SEE?
IT'S THAT CROFT GIRL!

ARE YOU MAD? THAT'S OUR AGENT!
SHOOT HER, YOU IMBECILE! HER SHOES, DO YOU NOT SEE HER SHOES?
Don't worry, Mr. Cruz, you stinking piece of human WASTE.

I'm not AIMING at YOU.

I'LL KILL YOU, YOU GOD-CURSED BITCH!
Somehow, Mr. Cruz...

I don't bloody well THINK so.

FWWOOOOMPH
You spoke of hell for others a great DEAL, Mr. Cruz.
I hope they all offer you the warm welcome you DESERVE.
I've shed a great deal of blood lately.
My own, and that of many others.
I hope to God it's all WORTH it.
LARA. YOU DID IT.
YOU HAVE TO GO. THERE ARE STILL SECURITY FORCES... THEY'LL SEE THE SMOKE. GO.
I...
I HAVE NOWHERE TO GO, MAMA. I HAVE NO ONE.
YES, WELL. ABOUT THAT.
HOW WOULD YOU FEEL ABOUT SHARING A MESSY FLAT IN LONDON WITH A FILMMAKER AND A FORMERLY QUIET ACADEMIC?

"ALTHOUGH I MAY HAVE SOME EXPLAINING TO DO TO SAM...

"BUT BEFORE WE GO...

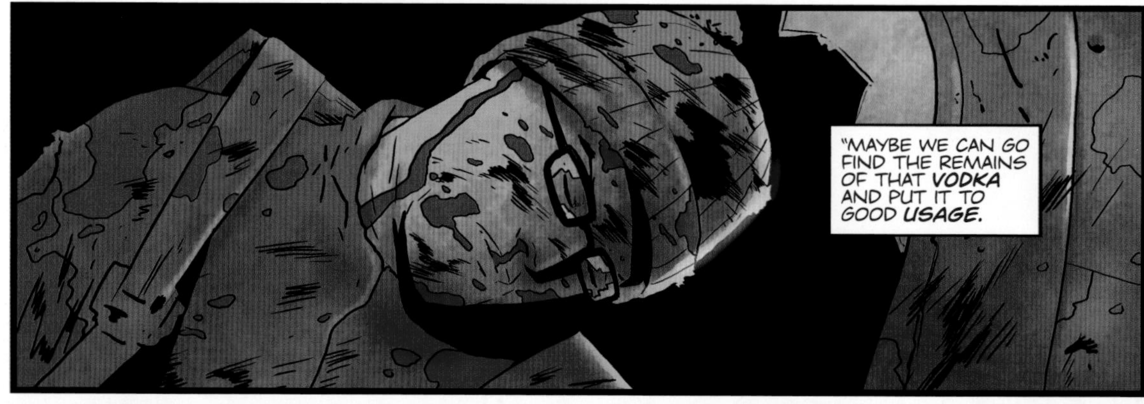
"MAYBE WE CAN GO FIND THE REMAINS OF THAT VODKA AND PUT IT TO GOOD USAGE.

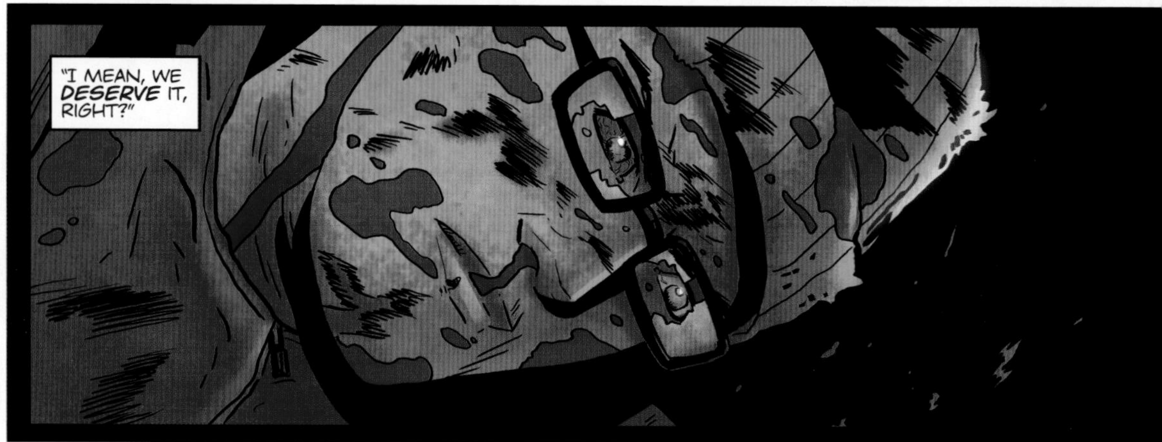
"I MEAN, WE DESERVE IT, RIGHT?"

ST. PETERSBURG HEALTH AND MEDICENTRE.
‹THE DECONTAMINATION WARD.›
‹IT'S... IT'S DOWN THIS HALL, SIR. YOU'LL NEED CLEARANCE.›
‹ARE YOU ALL RIGHT, JAN? WHAT'S WRONG?›
‹DID YOU SEE THAT MAN? HIS EYES!›
‹"THEY LOOKED LIKE WALKING DEATH."›
I'M HERE, MR. CRUZ.
TRINITY SENDS ITS REGARDS.
AUGER RAMILE.
WELL, THIS IS AN HONOR.

THE DOCTORS HERE ARE SURPRISED I AM ALIVE.
THEY DON'T KNOW OF OUR FAITH, OF COURSE.
DO YOU KNOW THEY PUT A CHEMICAL IN YOUR BODY THAT BINDS WITH THE RADIOACTIVE PARTICLES.
IT COMES OUT IN THE FECES, IS THAT NOT WONDERFUL?
YOU LITERALLY DEFECATE OUT THE POISON.
ARE YOU HERE TO KILL ME FOR MY FAILURE, MR. RAMILE?
I REQUEST THAT YOU BE QUICK.
PROFESSIONAL COURTESY, ONE KILLER TO ANOTHER.
TRINITY HAS SENT ME HERE TO FINISH YOUR TASK, MR. CRUZ. YOUR LOYAL SERVITUDE HAS NOT GONE UNNOTICED.
I'M NOT HERE FOR YOU. I'M HERE TO CLEAN UP.
AH. YES. LOOSE ENDS.
YES. THE ORIGINAL TARGET MUST BE ERASED. WE STILL DON'T KNOW HOW MUCH INFORMATION SHE GAINED ACCESS TO, OR HAS TOLD.
BUT THE OTHER ONE. SHE'S A KILLER AS WELL, LIKE US, IN HER WAY.
THE CROFT GIRL.
AS A PROFESSIONAL COURTESY, AND AS APT REWARD FOR MY "SERVITUDE"...?
I HAVE A REQUEST.
YES?

MAKE HER SUFFER.

Kill me now.
This is TORTURE.
DON'T KEEP COUGHING SO, KITTY, FOR HEAVEN'S SAKE!
HAVE A LITTLE COMPASSION ON MY NERVES. YOU TEAR THEM TO PIECES!
KITTY HAS NO DISCRETION IN HER COUGHS. SHE TIMES THEM ILL.

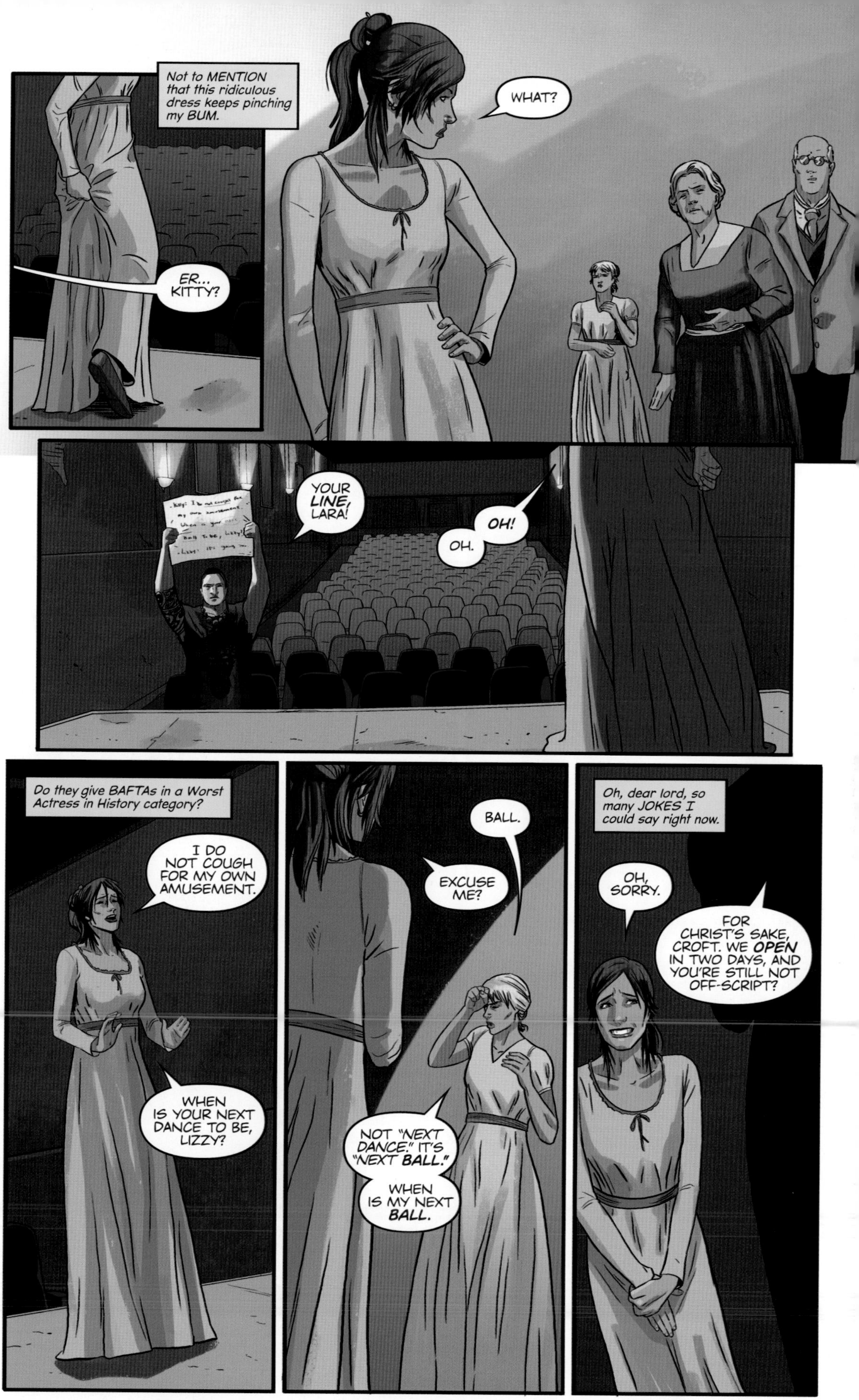

Not to MENTION that this ridiculous dress keeps pinching my BUM.
ER... KITTY?
WHAT?

YOUR LINE, LARA!
OH.
OH!

Do they give BAFTAs in a Worst Actress in History category?
I DO NOT COUGH FOR MY OWN AMUSEMENT.
WHEN IS YOUR NEXT DANCE TO BE, LIZZY?

BALL.
EXCUSE ME?
NOT "NEXT DANCE." IT'S "NEXT BALL."
WHEN IS MY NEXT BALL.

Oh, dear lord, so many JOKES I could say right now.
OH, SORRY.
FOR CHRIST'S SAKE, CROFT. WE OPEN IN TWO DAYS, AND YOU'RE STILL NOT OFF-SCRIPT?

THAT'S IT, I'M DONE.
I AGREED TO STAR IN THIS SHITTY PRODUCTION AS A LAUGH, BUT THIS IS TOO MUCH, JONAH.
DAMN.
THAT'S DINNER BREAK, EVERYONE. BACK IN AN HOUR, START AT THE TOP, ALL RIGHT?
FUNNY, THE RIDICULOUS THINGS YOU'LL DO FOR PEOPLE YOU LOVE.
JONAH, SHE'S RIGHT. I'M ABYSMAL.
CAN'T YOU JUST FIRE ME?
YOU'LL BE FINE, LARA. JUST...
JUST FOCUS, ALL RIGHT?
AND MAYBE DON'T SCRATCH YOUR BEHIND DURING THE PERFORMANCE?
Jonah, the guy with Maori tattoos and a Mohawk--
--turns out to be an amateur THEATRE buff.
And not enough girls auditioned for the sizable clan of BENNET sisters.
The least I could do was TRY.
But I am terrible at this, and the lead actress hates my INNARDS.
Dressing room
LARA, ANDREA'S ABOUT TO QUIT. FOR REAL, THIS TIME.
CAN YOU MAYBE GO HAVE SUPPER WITH HER?
TELL HER YOU'LL TRY HARDER?
THE GOLDEN LION THEATRE
PRESENTS: PRIDE AND PREJUDICE
"ALL RIGHT, JONAH. BUT IF YOU EVER DO ANOTHER PLAY...
"...I'M GOING BACK TO YAMATAI."
ANDREA! HEY!
WAIT UP!

WHAT DO YOU WANT? ACTING TIPS? YOU COULD USE THEM.
YOU'RE RIGHT, I'M A LITTLE OUT OF MY DEPTH.
A LITTLE.
OKAY, A LOT. THEATRE ISN'T REALLY MY FIELD OF EXPERTISE.
WHAT IS?
ARCHAEOLOGY.
Although I've EXPANDED my skill set a little.
REALLY? I ALWAYS WANTED TO BE AN EGYPTOLOGIST WHEN I WAS A KID, AFTER WATCHING ELIZABETH TAYLOR IN CLEOPATRA.
NO KIDDING?
IT WAS THAT OR AN ACTRESS.
YOU PROBABLY MADE THE RIGHT CHOICE.
WHAT A PIECE OF WORK IS THIS?
DEMON OR ANGEL?
OR BOTH?

I'M MEETING SOME FRIENDS HERE. WANT TO GET A DRINK?

UM... OKAY, SURE.

The Jolly Nag's Head

SHE'S THE ONE THAT GAVE ME THIS BROLLY. SHE THINKS IT'S ***HILARIOUS!***

LARA! ***LARA!***

THERE THEY ARE.

THIS IS ANDREA. SHE'S IN THE PLAY WITH ME.

SHE'S BEING KIND. THIS IS SAM AND KAZ.

HOW'S HER KITTY, ANDREA?

ER...IT COULD USE A BIT OF WORK.

WOW, YOUR ***HAIR!***

I KNOW... I'M STILL GETTING USED TO IT.

DON'T YOU JUST ***LOVE*** IT?

IT'S VERY DIFFERENT.

SHE LOOKS LESS LIKE A LARA ***UNDERSTUDY*** NOW.

A FRIENDLY ROUND LATER...
...I KNOW, THE IDEA OF JONAH AND THEATRE TOTALLY DON'T MIX, BUT HE'S REALLY A BUFF.
OH, I KNOW. HE TOOK ME TO SEE SKYLIGHT ABOUT A HUNDRED TIMES.
AND HE'S AN AMAZING COOK.
BE STILL MY HEART.
HE'S CUTE, BUT I HAVE A BOYFRIEND. AND SPEAKING OF, I'D BETTER GET BACK TO HIM.
I'LL WALK YOU TO THE TUBE.
GREAT TO MEET YOU. SEE YOU ON OPENING NIGHT!
OH, GOD, DON'T REMIND ME!
YOU'LL BE AWESOME, SWEETIE.
YOU'LL BOTH BE.
MWAH!
THANKS FOR THAT.
NO PROBLEM.
The Jolly Nag's

SEEMS I AM NOT THE ONLY PREDATOR IN TOWN TONIGHT.

OKAY... SO MAYBE I COULD GIVE YOU SOME ACTING TIPS.
THAT WOULD BE GREAT!

LET'S GO ANOTHER WAY.

BAGS, LADIES!
NO WAY!

LARA, JUST GIVE IT TO THEM, PLEASE.
THEY MIGHT HURT US.
NOPE!
I'D LIKE TO SEE THEM TRY.

SMACK
AHHH!
OOOOFFF!

SO... WE GOT A **LIVE** ONE.
NNNGGGG!

TWACK
ARRGGGGGG!
CRACK

GOT YA!
DO YOU?

ARRRRGGGH!

CRACCCK-

WHAT KIND OF ARCHAEOLOGIST ARE YOU?
THE KIND THAT DOESN'T TAKE SHIT FROM GUYS LIKE THEM.

LOOK, I, UM, APPRECIATE WHAT YOU DID. BUT FRANKLY YOU JUST SCARED ME MORE THAN THEY DID.
YOU ACTUALLY LOOKED LIKE YOU WERE ENJOYING IT.
I...

TELL JONAH I'M OUT OF THE PLAY.
SORRY.
YOU WALK A LONELY PATH, LARA CROFT. YOU ALWAYS WILL. I SEE THAT NOW.
IMPRESSIVE.

I always thought that brolly was ridiculous, anyway.

Jonah's going to KILL me.

BZZZT BZZZT BZZZT
YES?
DO BE QUICK, I'M QUITE BUSY.
MR. RAMILE? IT'S DR. PATEL, AT THE CLINIC.

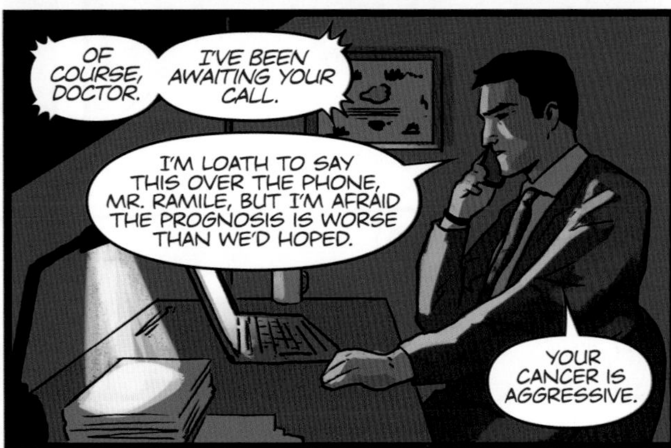
OF COURSE, DOCTOR.
I'VE BEEN AWAITING YOUR CALL.
I'M LOATH TO SAY THIS OVER THE PHONE, MR. RAMILE, BUT I'M AFRAID THE PROGNOSIS IS WORSE THAN WE'D HOPED.
YOUR CANCER IS AGGRESSIVE.

I SEE.
THANK YOU, DOCTOR. GOOD NIGHT.
WAIT. PERHAPS YOU SHOULD COME AND SEE ME AND WE CAN DISCUSS YOUR OPTIONS.
UNTIL THEN, DO YOU HAVE SOMEONE YOU CAN BE WITH?

"I SHOULDN'T HAVE THOUGHT SO, JUST A DAY AGO, DOCTOR.
"BUT YES. YES, I BELIEVE I DO.
"GOOD EVENING. WE WON'T SPEAK AGAIN."

IS IT DONE?
I ASK YOU, IS IT DONE?
<MR. CRUZ, I REALLY CAN'T ALLOW YOU TO SUBJECT YOURSELF TO ANY STRESS.>

NO. THERE'S BEEN A...
...DEVELOPMENT.
WHAT? ARE YOU INSANE?

YOU KNOW OUR EMPLOYERS. YOU KNOW HOW THEY TREAT INSUBORDINATION.
RAMILE. YOU KNOW!
<I AM GOING TO HAVE TO PUT THE PHONE AWAY, MR. CRUZ. YOUR RECOVERY-->

<YOU DROP THIS PHONE, YOU IGNORANT MEWLING COW, AND I'LL CUT YOUR EYES OUT AND LET YOU LIVE, DO YOU UNDERSTAND ME?>

IF YOU LET ME DOWN, MR. RAMILE...
...I WILL SHOW YOU HELL.
I WILL MAKE YOU CRAVE IT.

YOU CAN'T THREATEN A MAN FALLING OUT OF A PLANE WITH MORE GRAVITY, MR. CRUZ.
ALSO, MAY I SAY...
...I ALWAYS THOUGHT YOU WERE A BIT OF A PRAT.
GOODBYE.

DAMN POSH BITCH WITH HER TRICK BROLLY, FIGHTIN' DIRTY.
TOOK US BY SURPRISE, MATE, THAT'S ALL.
I SEEN HER AROUND. WE'LL GET OURS OFF HER.
TOO RIGHT.

WE GET THE LADS.
WE FIND HER.
YEAH. YEAH, WE FIND HER.
MESS UP HER FACE, MAYBE...NOT SO POSH THEN.

THE GOLDEN LION THEATRE
PRESENTS: PRIDE AND PREJUDICE
COURAGE, CROFT.

UM.
JONAH?
JUST A SECOND, LITTLE BIRD. THE THIRD ACT IS A **MESS.**
I HAD A CHAT WITH ANDREA.

YOU DID?
EXCELLENT, THAT'S ONE THING SORTED. THANK YOU.
ACTUALLY--
I WAS WORRIED I WOULDN'T BE ABLE TO PULL THIS OFF, BUT THINGS ARE FINALLY STARTING TO TURN OUR WAY, YOU KNOW?

JONAH.
LARA, WHY ARE YOU STILL HERE? YOU AND ANDREA GET READY, WE'RE DOING SECOND RUN-THROUGH IN **TEN.**
JONAH!

SHE'S GONE, JONAH.
SHE'S NOT COMING BACK.
I'M SO, SO SORRY.

One of the tiny handful of true friends I have.
I'd rather be SHOT AT than hurt him.

YOU'LL TAKE THE LEAD, THEN, LARA.
YOU'LL BE ELIZABETH.

WHAT? NO. WHAT?
ABSOLUTELY NOT.
I CAN'T!
YOU'RE HER UNDERSTUDY, LARA. YOU KNOW THE LINES, AND THERE'S NO TIME FOR ANYONE ELSE.

NO. I -- WAIT. WAIT.
I CAN'T ACT. EVERYONE HERE KNOWS I CAN'T ACT!
LARA, I KNOW YOU. YOU CAN DO ANYTHING YOU PUT YOUR MIND TO. AND THAT MEANS YOU CAN DO THIS.

AND YOU OWE ME.

I...
DAMMIT.
I absolutely DO!

WHO YOU CALLIN'?
SNIPE'S BRUVVER TERRY. HE WAS IN THE WAR, WEREN'T HE?
HE KNOWS HOW TO HURT A BODY. HE LIKES IT, I HEAR.
PARDON ME, BOYS.

BUT I'M AFRAID I CAN'T LET YOU DO THAT.
MISS CROFT IS UNDER MY PROTECTION, YOU SEE.

Oh, God...
KNOCK KNOCK

COME IN.
Please be Andrea, please be Andrea, please be Andrea.

FIFTY-MINUTE CALL, LARA. JONAH WANTS TO DO THE NETHERFIELD BALL SCENE FIRST.

SIGH I KNOW.
And I'm pretty sure that Jane Austen didn't write a gun and a climbing axe into that scene.
Pity. I'd feel much more comfortable.

IT'S SO BEAUTIFUL, ISN'T IT? LET ME HELP YOU GET READY.

WHAT DOES THIS WEIRDO WANT?
A GOOD KICKIN', I'D SAY.

WE'LL DO HIM AN' THEN WE'LL DO THE GIRL.
MAYBE JUST **BREAK** HIS LEGS SO HE CAN **WATCH.**

YOU SHOULD BE AWARE, GENTLEMEN, THAT THIS WILL NOT BE A FAIR FIGHT.

SHOULDN'T HAVE TANGLED WITH **TWO** OF US THEN!

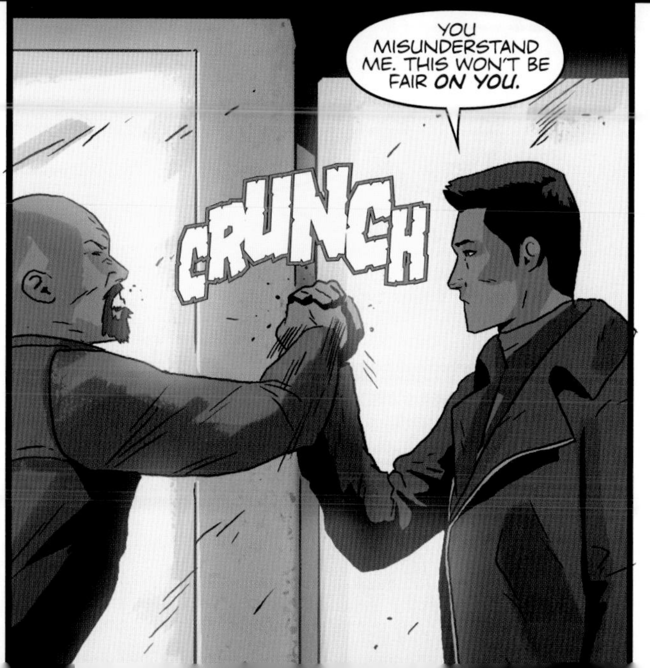
YOU MISUNDERSTAND ME. THIS WON'T BE FAIR **ON YOU.**
CRUNCH

CAN YOU BREATHE OKAY?
YES, THANKS.
Wish I couldn't though.
URRRRRRRG!
ARRRRRRG!
URRRG!
NEARLY THERE.
SLLLEEETTTHH
NOW THE GLOVES...

STOP, **STOP**. PLEASE.
I HAVE HEARD THAT MANY TIMES BEFORE. IT HAS NEVER WORKED.
AND IT NEVER WILL.

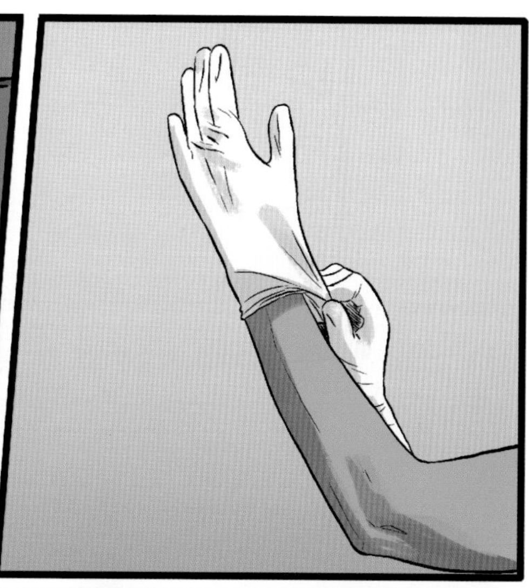

SCHHHUCK
URRRGGGGLLE...

DON'T TELL ANYONE I SAID THIS, BUT YOU LOOK BETTER THAN ANDREA.
YOU'RE AN OLD SOUL, LARA. USE IT.
It's just acting. I can do this. I CAN DO THIS.

MY ANGEL IS SAFE.
YOU SHALL NOT SPEAK OF HER AGAIN.
SHE IS THE ONE.
SHE WILL CONTINUE WHEN I CANNOT.

YOU CAN'T LEAVE, MR. CRUZ. YOU'RE NOT WELL ENOUGH.
I AM AS WELL AS I NEED TO BE.

SHE **WILL** SUFFER. THEY **ALL WILL SUFFER.**

STOP!
TOUCH ME AGAIN AND IT WON'T BE JUST **YOUR EYES** YOU LOSE.

LET HIM GO. HE'S NOT WORTH THE TROUBLE.
IT'S NOT **HIM** I'M WORRIED ABOUT.
IT'S WHO HE'S ***AFTER.***

"I HATE THIS FILTHY, DEGENERATE CITY.
"I HAD THE MISFORTUNE TO WORK HERE IN MY YOUTH. IN THE BOWELS OF THIS CITY THEY QUAINTLY CALL 'THE TUBE.'"

EVERYWHERE YOU LOOK IS TRIBUTE, NOT TO GOD, BUT TO MEN. WEAK, INBRED MEN.
EVERY BRICK LAID IS TESTAMENT TO EITHER *HUBRIS* OR *CARNALITY.*

THE AVERAGE CITIZEN THINKS MORE OF CURRY AND ADULTERY THAN OF HIS CREATOR.
WHEN I RUN TRINITY, THINGS WILL CHANGE.
THINGS WILL *CHANGE.*

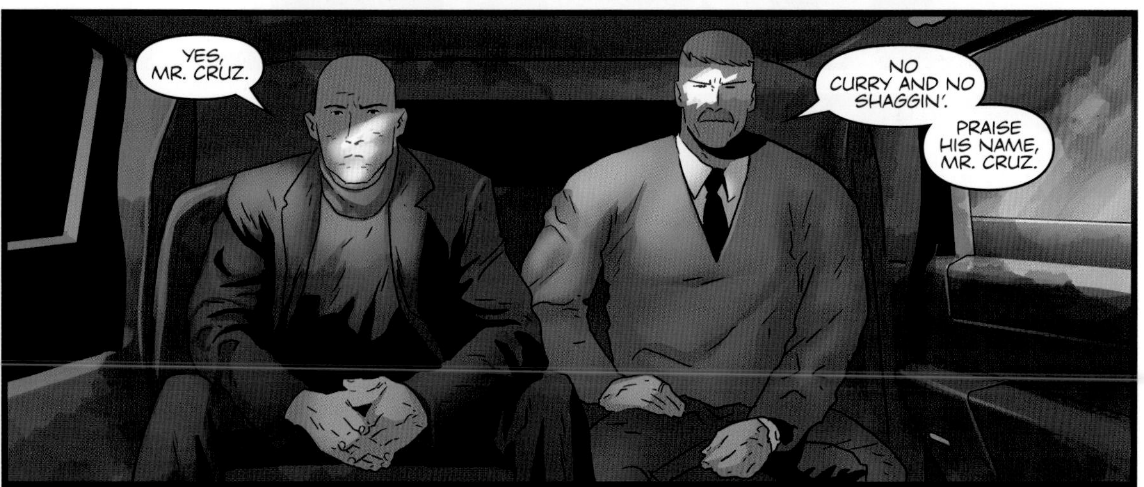
YES, MR. CRUZ.
NO CURRY AND NO SHAGGIN'.
PRAISE HIS NAME, MR. CRUZ.

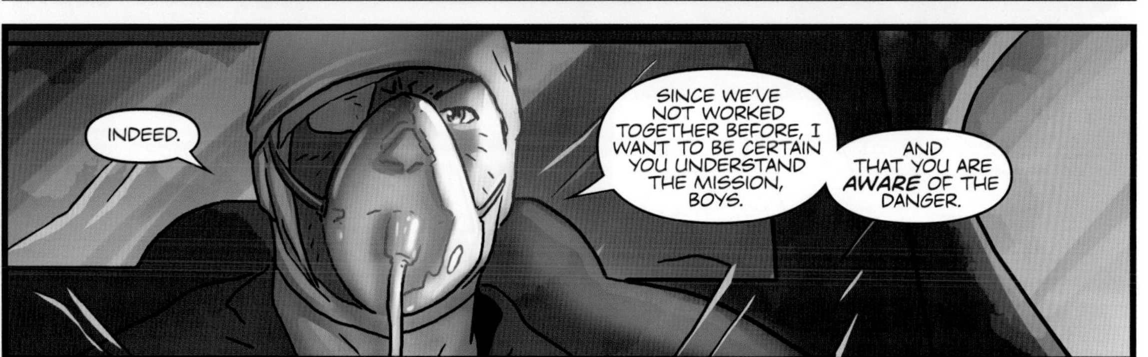
INDEED.
SINCE WE'VE NOT WORKED TOGETHER BEFORE, I WANT TO BE CERTAIN YOU UNDERSTAND THE MISSION, BOYS.
AND THAT YOU ARE *AWARE* OF THE DANGER.

OKAY. SOME BIRD NAMED KAZ HACKED INTO TRINITY, THEN FLED, MAYBE WITH SOME INFORMATION WE DON'T EXACTLY WANT **OUT**.
YOU SENT SOME FANCY BLOKE NAMED AUGER RAMILE TO TAKE HER OUT, ONLY HE'S BESOTTED WITH SOME TART WHO...
WELL. THAT IS, SOME GIRL WHO --
SAY WHAT YOU'RE THINKING, REGINALD.

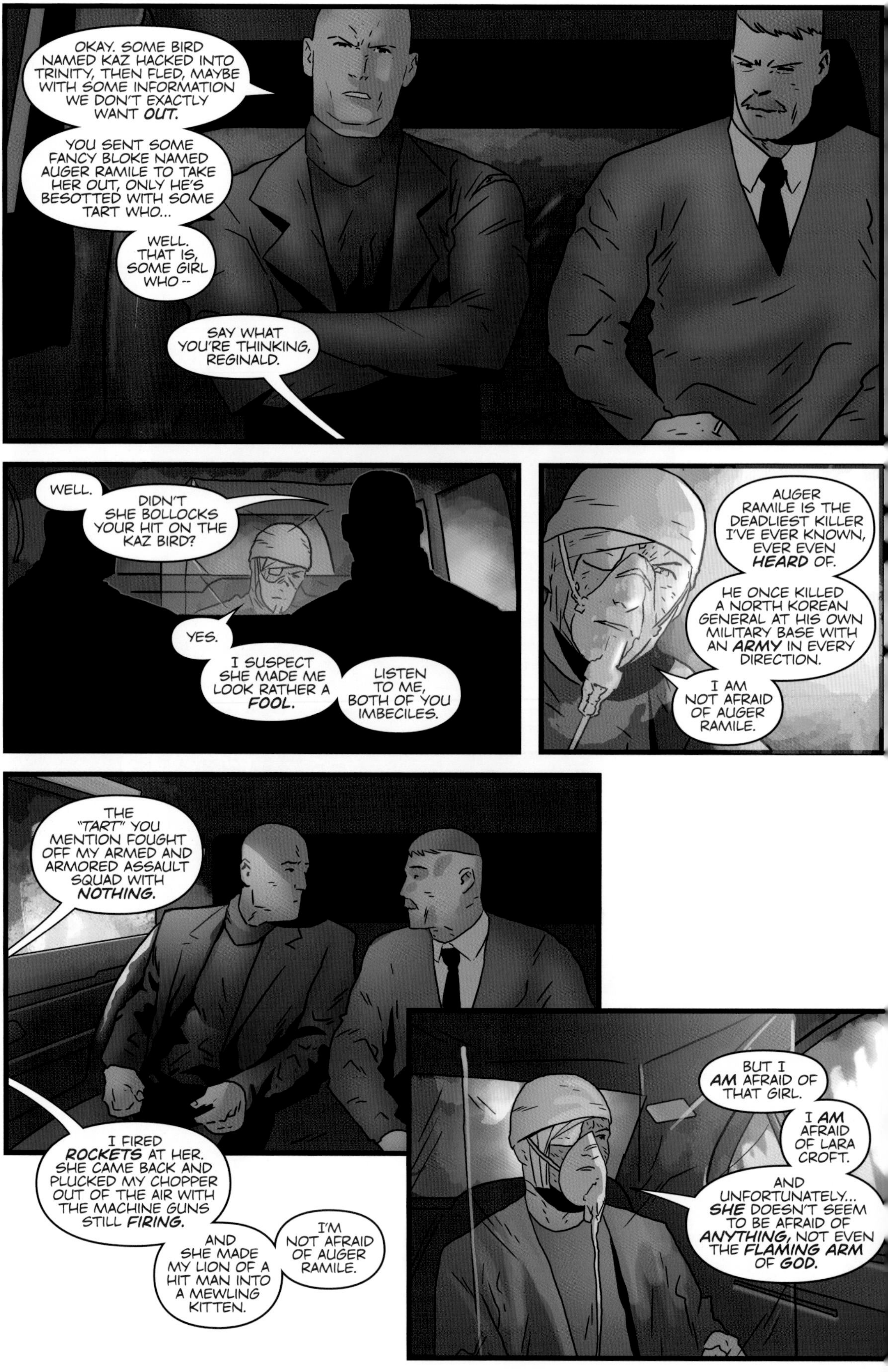

WELL.
DIDN'T SHE BOLLOCKS YOUR HIT ON THE KAZ BIRD?
YES.
I SUSPECT SHE MADE ME LOOK RATHER A **FOOL**.
LISTEN TO ME, BOTH OF YOU IMBECILES.

AUGER RAMILE IS THE DEADLIEST KILLER I'VE EVER KNOWN, EVER EVEN **HEARD** OF.
HE ONCE KILLED A NORTH KOREAN GENERAL AT HIS OWN MILITARY BASE WITH AN **ARMY** IN EVERY DIRECTION.
I AM NOT AFRAID OF AUGER RAMILE.

THE "TART" YOU MENTION FOUGHT OFF MY ARMED AND ARMORED ASSAULT SQUAD WITH **NOTHING**.

I FIRED **ROCKETS** AT HER. SHE CAME BACK AND PLUCKED MY CHOPPER OUT OF THE AIR WITH THE MACHINE GUNS STILL **FIRING**.

AND SHE MADE MY LION OF A HIT MAN INTO A MEWLING KITTEN.

I'M NOT AFRAID OF AUGER RAMILE.

BUT I **AM** AFRAID OF THAT GIRL.

I **AM** AFRAID OF LARA CROFT.

AND UNFORTUNATELY... **SHE** DOESN'T SEEM TO BE AFRAID OF **ANYTHING**, NOT EVEN THE **FLAMING ARM** OF **GOD**.

"AND A FEARLESS DEMON IS THE MOST DANGEROUS OF ALL."
RRAAALFFFFF!
Oh, God.
Please make it stop.
YOU ABOUT FINISHED THERE, KIDDO?
BECAUSE IT'S ONLY FINAL DRESS REHEARSAL.
KILL ME...
I CAN'T DO IT. I CAN'T.
SAM, YOU HAVE TO TELL JONAH I CAN'T PLAY ELIZABETH.
YOU CAN AND YOU WILL.
YOU HAVE TO HAVE SOMETHING IN YOUR STOMACH. HANG ON.
This is all my fault. I agreed to be the lead understudy for Jonah's tiny production of Pride and Prejudice.
THEN I scared away the star.

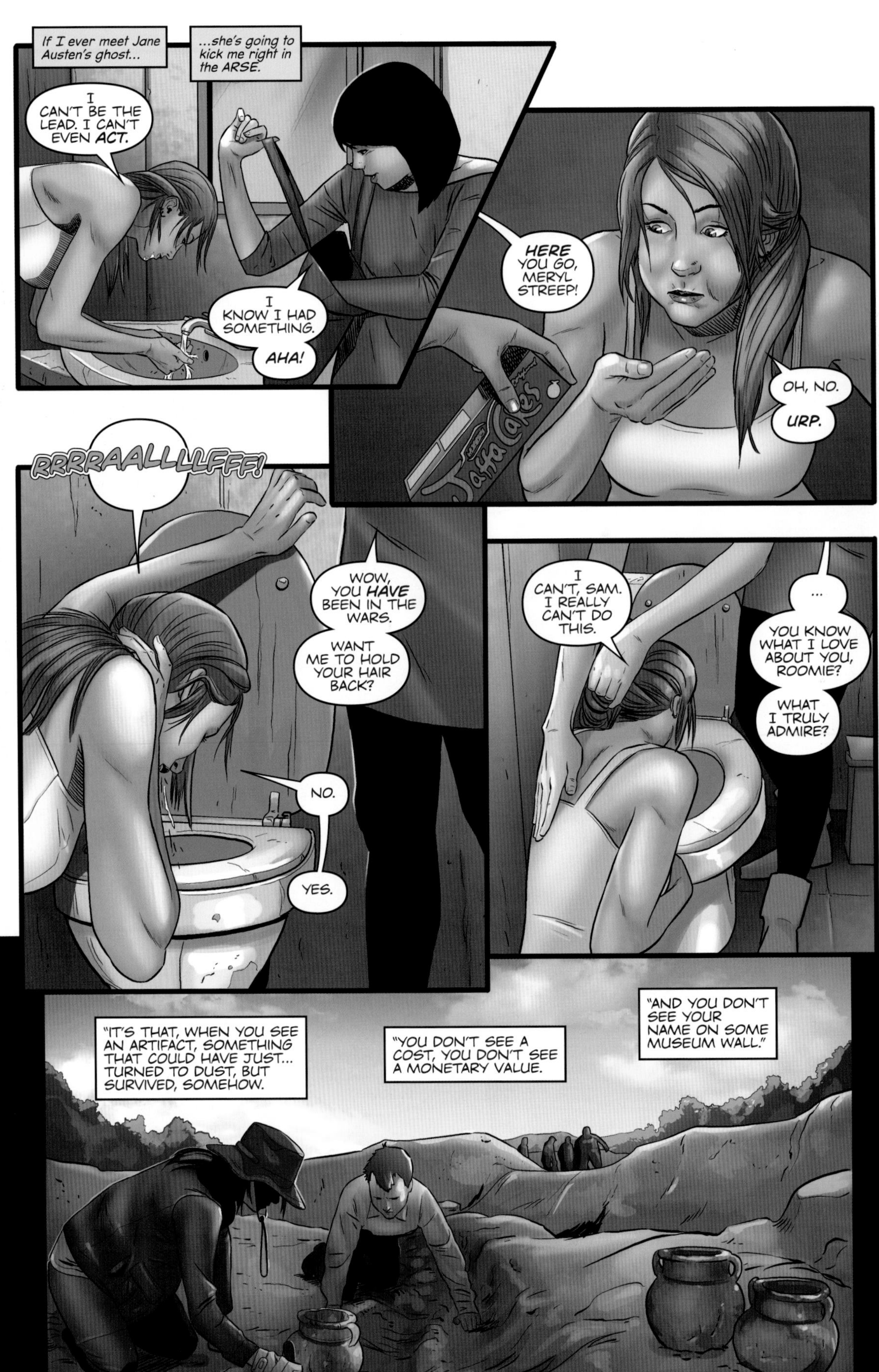
If I ever meet Jane Austen's ghost...
...she's going to kick me right in the ARSE.
I CAN'T BE THE LEAD. I CAN'T EVEN **ACT.**
I KNOW I HAD SOMETHING.
AHA!
HERE YOU GO, MERYL STREEP!
Jaffa Cakes
OH, NO.
URP.
RRRRAALLLLLFFF!
WOW, YOU **HAVE** BEEN IN THE WARS.
WANT ME TO HOLD YOUR HAIR BACK?
NO.
YES.
I CAN'T, SAM. I REALLY CAN'T DO THIS.
...
YOU KNOW WHAT I LOVE ABOUT YOU, ROOMIE?
WHAT I TRULY ADMIRE?
"IT'S THAT, WHEN YOU SEE AN ARTIFACT, SOMETHING THAT COULD HAVE JUST... TURNED TO DUST, BUT SURVIVED, SOMEHOW.
"YOU DON'T SEE A COST, YOU DON'T SEE A MONETARY VALUE.
"AND YOU DON'T SEE YOUR NAME ON SOME MUSEUM WALL."

YOU KNOW YOU DON'T.
WIPE YOUR MOUTH, BRANDO. AND SHUT UP. I'M SAYING BRILLIANT STUFF.
I DON'T?
"YOU SEE THE PERSON WHO MADE THE THING.
"YOU SEE THEIR HANDS MASTERING THEIR ART, AND THE FAMILY THEY DO IT FOR, AND THE COMMUNITY WHERE THEY LIVE."
IS THAT A BIG DEAL?
YOU KNOW IT IS.
AND THIS PLAY, LADY CROFT, THIS STORY.
IT'S MY FAVORITE. HAVE I EVER TOLD YOU THAT?
THE BOOK'S TWO HUNDRED YEARS OLD.
PEOPLE TODAY, WHO KNOW NOTHING ABOUT THE PERIOD, THEY DON'T JUST READ IT OUT OF OBLIGATION, LARA.
THEY LOVE IT. THERE'S NO OTHER WORD TO DESCRIBE IT.
IT LETS US, IT LETS EVERYONE, SEE THAT TIME THE WAY YOU WOULD.
IT'S ABOUT CLASS, AND LOVE, AND OBLIGATION. ABOUT KNOWING YOURSELF, BEING WHO YOU ARE.

AND THOSE THINGS SHOULD NEVER TURN TO DUST.
...
SO...
SO, GO BE LIZZIE AND LET PEOPLE SEE YOUR GIFT, ROOMIE.
MAKE-UP AND COSTUMING NEED YOU RIGHT NOW, MS. CROFT. DRESS IS IN FIFTEEN.
OH, GOD. OKAY.
OKAY.
I WON'T BACK OUT. GO AND TELL JONAH I'M GETTING READY.
AND SAM...
"...THANKS."
SOON...
THIS DRESS HATES ME.
WELL, IT WASN'T MADE FOR YOU. SO PERHAPS, TRY NOT TO BREATHE TOO MUCH.
THESE ARRIVED FOR YOU JUST NOW, MS. CROFT.
BREAK A LEG!
Oh, how I wish I would. BOTH, maybe.
NICE, NO ONE'S SENT ME FLOWERS IN YEARS.
FROM YOUR BEAU, MAYBE?
I DOUBT THAT.
Dear God.
We have Kaz, Miss Croft.
Walk the Piccadilly tube track going SW until you see us.
Don't be stopped or followed.
Come alone. And come right now.
Your friend,
Cruz

I HAVE TO GO.
THIS IS MORE IMPORTANT.
BUT IT'S THE LAST REHEARSAL IN A FEW MINUTES!
Oh God. He's still ALIVE.

CAN'T WAIT TO GET ONSTAGE, HUH? THAT'S MY GIRL.
COVER FOR ME, ***PLEASE!***

SO MUCH FOR MY INSPIRATIONAL SPEECH THEN!
IT'S NOT THAT.
THEN WHAT?
IT'S BEST IF I DON'T TELL YOU.
I'm not going to drag you into this, Sam. Not this time.

YOU'VE GOT THAT LOOK IN YOUR EYE. I'VE SEEN IT BEFORE. YOU'RE GOING TO DO SOMETHING DAFT, AREN'T YOU?
VERY PROBABLY.
AND I CAN'T STOP YOU, CAN I?
NO.
THEN ***PLEASE*** BE CAREFUL.
I WILL.

SHE'S GOING LIKE ***THAT?***
JONAH IS GOING TO HAVE A FIT.

THEATRE
PREJUDICE
Okay, which is the fastest way to Piccadilly?
PRESENTS PRIDE AND PREJUDICE
IT'S HER.
LOOK!
AH YES, SEE THE HISTORICAL STREETS OF LONDON COME TO LIFE BEFORE YOUR EYES!
SIRS, MADAMS, PLEASE EXCUSE ME.
SHE'S PROBABLY OFF TO FIND HER MR. DARCY.
AND HERE, ER, HE IS!
NO PHOTOGRAPHS!
Mr. Darcy I could handle.
It's Cruz I'm not so sure about.
UNDERGROUND
PICCADILLY

What the hell are you doing, Lara? Why would he take her here?

Damn. Unfortunately Lizzy Bennet does not carry an Oyster card.

METRO MAP
Got to be quick.

It's this or jumping the barriers, and I don't think this dress will allow for that.

HEY, YOU! YOU **IN THE HAT!**
I'LL CALL SECURITY, GIRL!
Uh-oh.
YOU **WILL** LEAVE HER ALONE. YOU WILL **NOT** GO AFTER HER. UNDERSTAND ME?
YYYES.
GOOD. SO MUCH BETTER WHEN PEOPLE UNDERSTAND.
Wish I was a little less conspicuous.

Need to get to the tracks somehow.

DANGER
AUTHORISED PERSONNEL ONLY

DANGER
AUTHORISED PERSONNEL ONLY
CLUNK
DAMN, IT'S LOCKED!

CLICK
GOT IT!

WAY OUT

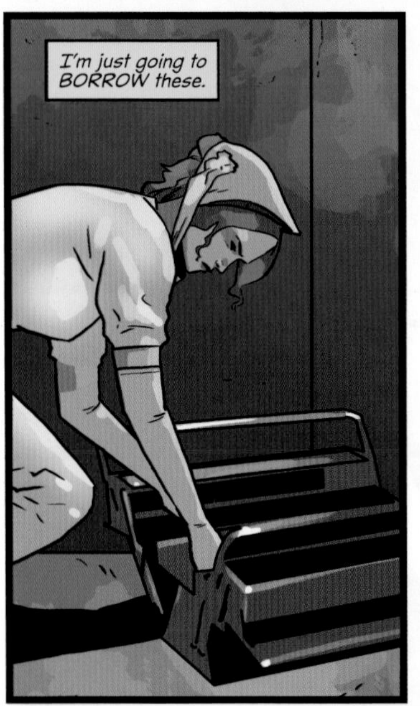
I'm just going to BORROW these.

I'd better take this too. I don't think Cruz will respond well to a bonnet and nice manners.

Okay, these must be the tracks. Just have to head southwest.

Have to avoid the rails. They're live, and I'd like to keep that way too.

Is it wrong to wish one of the maintenance men had left a climbing axe?
And maybe a Kalashnikov?

UH-OH.

SHIT.

SHIT SHIT *SHIT!*

GOD.

HELLO, MISS CROFT.
IS THIS THE NEW FASHION FOR YOUNG LADIES?
I APPROVE.
I WONDER IF YOU WOULD STEP THIS WAY, PLEASE.

WHY DON'T YOU STEP OVER BY ME AND WE'LL SETTLE THIS FOR GOOD, YOU CREEPY BASTARD?
AND MAY I SAY, YOU AREN'T **LOOKING** VERY WELL.
NO. NO, I AM NOT.
BECAUSE OF **YOU,** MISS CROFT.

BECAUSE OF **YOU,** I HAVE BEEN SHOT, STABBED, BEATEN, IRRADIATED, AND SET ON FIRE.
YOU'LL **FORGIVE** ME IF I HOLD A BIT OF A **GRUDGE.**

I'M GOING TO ASK AGAIN. COME HERE. EMPTY HANDED.
OR THINGS GET **TRAGIC** VERY **QUICKLY.**
LARA. YOU HAVE TO...
YOU HAVE TO RUN. **GO.**
KAZ. I...

I CAN'T.
I'M SORRY.
ALL RIGHT.
LET'S GET THIS OVER WITH.

IT'S FINAL **DRESS.** WHERE THE HELL IS **LARA?**
SHE'S GONE, JONAH. SHE JUST...
SHE JUST **LEFT!**

LARRAAAA!

MISS CROFT.
I SHOULD BE THANKING YOU, YOU KNOW.
WITHOUT YOU, I WOULD NOT HAVE KNOWN THE TRUTH ABOUT MYSELF.
WHAT'S THAT, PRAY TELL?
THAT I AM **IMMORTAL,** CHILD.
KNEEL IN FRONT OF YOUR BETTER, THE CHOSEN OF **GOD.**

IF SHE MOVES, SHOOT HER.
WE'RE GOING TO INTERROGATE THE TWO OF YOU, MISS CROFT.
FIND OUT WHAT YOU KNOW ABOUT TRINITY.
IT WILL BE... **EXTENSIVE.**

No, Mr. Cruz. You're not taking us to torture us to death.
THE CROWBAR, MISS CROFT. DROP IT.
NOW. YOU HAVE **NO CHOICE,** UNDERSTAND? I **WILL** SHOOT YOU!

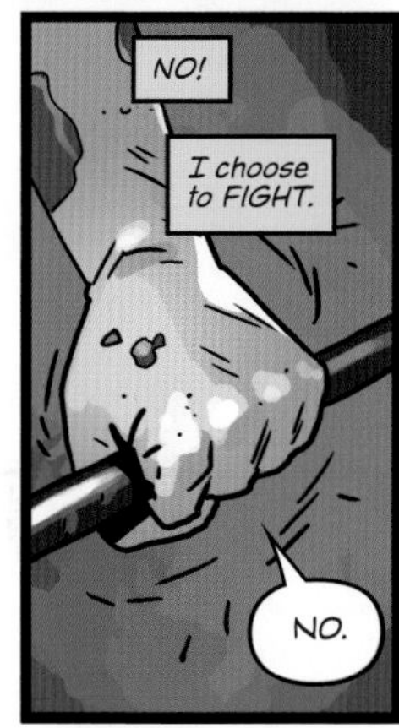
NO!
I choose to FIGHT.
NO.

DON'T LET THIS OUTFIT FOOL YOU, MR. CRUZ.
THE LAST GROUP OF ZEALOTS I CROSSED PATHS WITH?
EVERY LAST ONE OF THEM, **DEAD.**

AND I CAN SEE IT IN YOUR EYES.
EVEN WITH ALL THE GUNS AND ALL THE CARDS.
YOU'RE **AFRAID.**

SHOOT HER, YOU IDIOTS! **SHOOT** HER!

...I'm rather glad he's HERE.

GLLGHKK!

YOU KILLED MR. CRUZ!
Uh-oh.

Why do I always get the DEDICATED ones?
I'LL CHOKE THE LIFE OUT OF YOU!

Oh, good God.
NUH...
KLL YUH...
NO.
Doesn't this guy EVER stay down?

KILL UH...
UNCLEAN...

NO!
GGH!

ZTTTZZZTTTZZZTT
GGHHHHHNNNN!
GOOD RIDDANCE.

MAYBE IF I KILL YOU, TRINITY WILL GIVE ME CRUZ'S JOB.
If I'm going to die in this dress, then it's going to be onstage.
OOOOF.
I'm NOT letting Jonah down.
Not now. Not EVER!
NNNGGGG!
ZIIIINNG
FUTTT
I'D HOPED YOU WOULD BE THE ONE TO DO THIS. BUT THEN AGAIN, THERE ARE ALREADY PLENTY OF BODIES IN YOUR WAKE, LARA CROFT.
HOW DO YOU KNOW MY NAME?

LOOK, DON'T THINK I'M NOT GRATEFUL FOR YOUR HELP, BUT WHO THE **HELL** ARE YOU?

I AM THE ENDING TO YOUR BEGINNING.

I CAN MAKE YOU **EVERYTHING** YOU HAVE THE POTENTIAL TO BE.

UNLESS THAT INCLUDES A WITTY HEROINE FROM NINETEENTH-CENTURY LITERATURE, I'M REALLY **NOT** INTERESTED RIGHT NOW.

HE'S WITH TRINITY.

NOT FOR MUCH LONGER. LARA WILL TAKE MY POSITION. I SEE IT IN HER.

I CAN TEACH YOU. YOU WILL BE MY PROTÉGÉ. MY ANGEL OF DEATH.

I DON'T KNOW WHAT YOU **THINK** YOU'RE SEEING IN ME. BUT IT'S NOT TRINITY AND IT'S **NOT** YOUR PROTÉGÉ.

Oh God, I preferred it when people were just trying to kill me, not recruit me!

COME WITH ME. THERE ISN'T MUCH TIME.
I'M LEAVING HERE, BUT NOT WITH YOU.

YOU KNOW WHAT YOU ARE, LARA CROFT.
WHAT?
A KILLER. STONE COLD. I SEE IT IN YOUR EYES. I FEEL IT. YOU THINK YOU KILL TO SURVIVE, BUT YOU KILL BECAUSE IT IS IN YOUR NATURE.
I KNOW ABOUT YAMATAI, LARA.

YOU DON'T KNOW ME.
How the hell does he know about THAT?

HONK HOOOOOONK
PERHAPS I WAS WRONG.

HONK HONK HOOONK
THERE COULD ALWAYS BE A FIRST TIME.

CRRRUNNNCCH

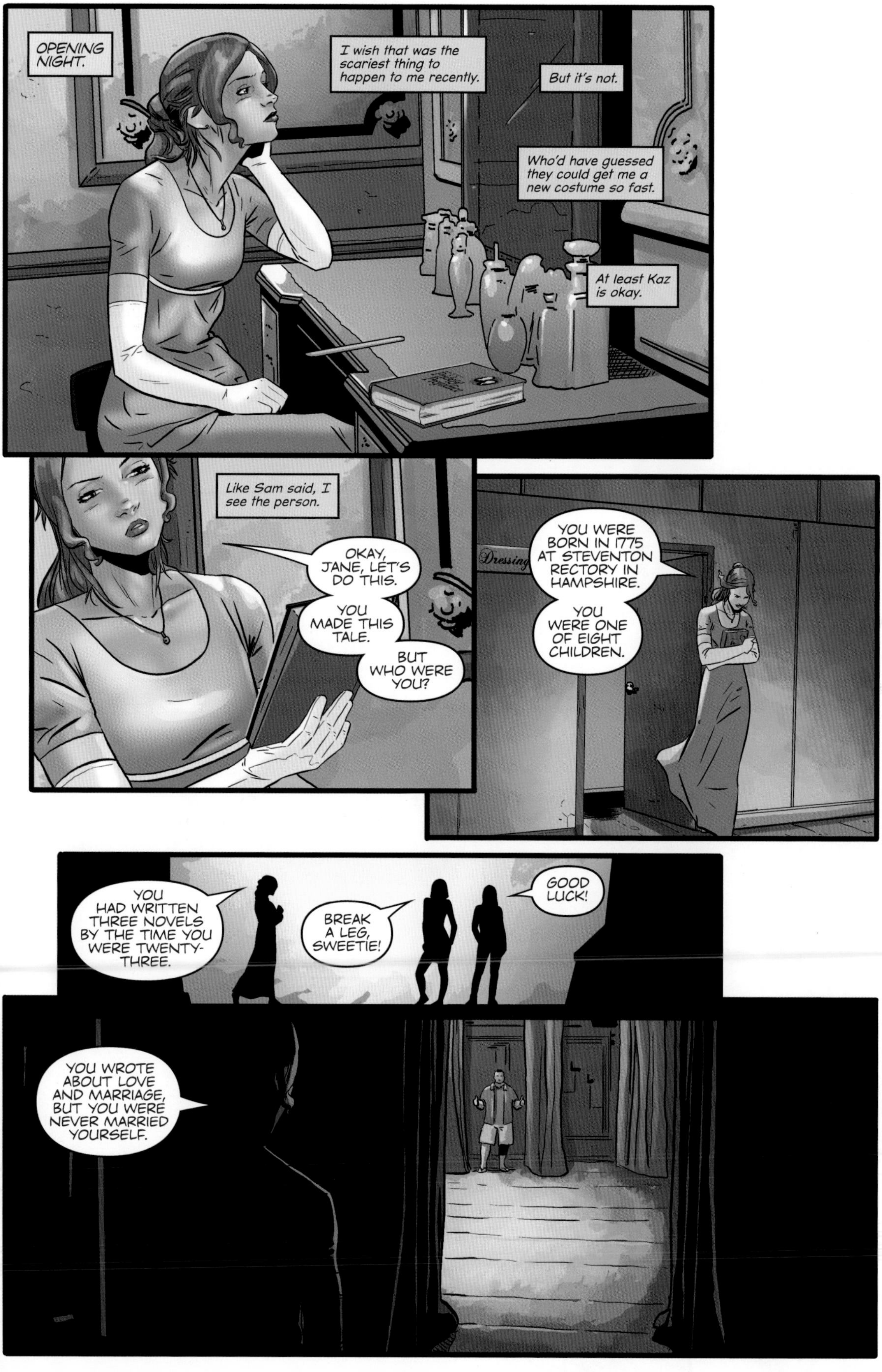

OPENING NIGHT.

I wish that was the scariest thing to happen to me recently.

But it's not.

Who'd have guessed they could get me a new costume so fast.

At least Kaz is okay.

Like Sam said, I see the person.

OKAY, JANE, LET'S DO THIS.

YOU MADE THIS TALE.

BUT WHO WERE YOU?

YOU WERE BORN IN 1775 AT STEVENTON RECTORY IN HAMPSHIRE.

YOU WERE ONE OF EIGHT CHILDREN.

YOU HAD WRITTEN THREE NOVELS BY THE TIME YOU WERE TWENTY-THREE.
BREAK A LEG, SWEETIE!
GOOD LUCK!
YOU WROTE ABOUT LOVE AND MARRIAGE, BUT YOU WERE NEVER MARRIED YOURSELF.

YOU DIED AT AGE FORTY-ONE.
JANE AUSTEN'S
Pride & Prejudice
SWWWOOSHH
The show must go on.
And so must I.

THE BRITISH MUSEUM, LONDON. AFTER CLOSING.
SECLUDED.
ALMOST.
Okay, so maybe this isn't...
...STRICTLY by the book. At least not when you work in a museum.
and let thy feet. millenniums hence set in midst of knowledge
But they'd never let me do this when it's open.
So I have to make do when it's closed.
Then it's mine.
Well, aside from a few kindly security guards, willing to look the other way.

Ancient Egypt. My favorite gallery.
HI, AMENHOTEP.
EVENING, AMENOPHIS.

It might not be Yamatai, or Chernobyl, but it's safer. A LOT safer.
Don't get me wrong. I kinda love it.
Only I'm not sure I'm too good at safe.
Not anymore.
Not after everything I've been through.
It makes me restless.
Is that bad?
LADIES.
SSCCCCUUF
HELLO?
Hmmm, must have imagined it. Security isn't due in this gallery for another hour.

ELSEWHERE IN LONDON.

HEY, NEW GUY!
JONAH.
WHATEVER. HURRY UP WITH THAT SAUCE.
YES, CHEF!

MUCK! WHAT THE HELL ARE YOU DOING?
IT'S NOT FINISHED YET.

WHAT DID YOU SAY?
IT'S NOT FINISHED YET, CHEF.
WHAT DID YOU SAY?
I MEAN... I'LL START AGAIN... CHEF.

SHIT!

THINKS
I DON'T KNOW
HOW TO MAKE
A SAUCE...

I KNOW
HOW TO MAKE
A SAUCE.

I KNOW
HOW TO MAKE
A HUNDRED
SAUCES.

I AM
MISTER
SAUCE.

SOMEWHERE ELSE IN LONDON.
CALL ME WHEN YOU'RE BACK, OKAY? WE NEED TO EDIT IN TIME FOR TRIBECA.
LOVE YOU! LOVE YOU!

OOH!
132 A

OH YES!
THAT'LL BE WHAT LARA NEEDS, I BET.

133
MAJOR BROWNIE POINTS FOR ME.
STILL NOT SURE WHAT ***THE HELL*** THOSE ARE.

SOMEONE'S FOLLOWING ME.

YUP. SUBTLE, BUDDY, SUBTLE.

HEY, THIS IS LARA. LEAVE ME A MESSAGE.

SHIT! PHONE ME. I'M BEING FOLLOWED.

THIS ISN'T HAPPENING. **NOT** AGAIN.

THIS CITY DRIVES ME NUTS SOMETIMES.
‹ME TOO!›

YAAAH!

WHAT THE --?
TO THE FRIENDS OF LARA CROFT
TO THE FRIENDS OF LARA CROFT

SSSSQQQUISSSH
AGGGG!

OOOOOOF!

WHY ARE YOU FOLLOWING ME?

GAAAH!
AHH!
YEAH, YOU'D **BETTER** RUN. I HAVE MORE CUPCAKES, YOU KNOW!

STAFF AREA NO PUBLIC ACCESS
CLONK
WHO'S IN THERE?
AAAAHHHHH!
STOP!
HEY! WATCH IT!
STOP HIM, SAM!

BE CAREFUL!
GET DOWN!
AGGGG!
ER, WHAT DID YOU JUST SAVE ME FROM, LARA?

SECURITY SAID THEY SAW NO ONE APART FROM YOU. HE MUST HAVE COME IN WHEN THE MUSEUM WAS STILL OPEN AND HID SOMEWHERE.
THIS IS TURNING INTO A **REALLY** WEIRD EVENING.

I THINK IT JUST GOT **WEIRDER.**
PLAY ME
LARA CROFT

CLICK

THAT LOOKS LIKE...

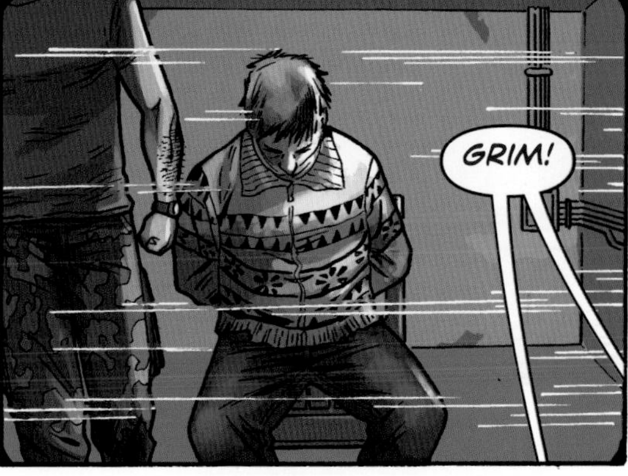
GRIM!

YOU'RE SEEING THIS TOO, RIGHT?
GRIM'S **ALIVE!**
I'M SEEING IT. I'M JUST NOT SURE I'M **BELIEVING IT.**

LARA CROFT. WE HAVE YOUR FRIEND, ANGUS GRIMALDI.
ER, HOW DOES SHE KNOW **YOUR NAME?**

IF YOU WISH TO SEE HIM ALIVE AGAIN, THEN WIRE FIVE MILLION U.S. DOLLARS TO THE FOLLOWING ACCOUNT.
OTHERWISE YOU WILL SEE HIM IN PIECES.
YOU HAVE TWO WEEKS. WE KNOW WHERE YOU LIVE AND WE KNOW WHO YOUR FRIENDS ARE.

"THIS CAN'T BE. I WAS **THERE.** HE WENT OVER THE EDGE."

DID YOU SEE HIS BODY?
WE HAVE TO GET THIS TO KAZ AND HAVE HER ANALYZE IT.
NO.
26892115
WE'D BETTER CALL JONAH TOO.

OVER AT KAZ AND JONAH'S PLACE.
OKAY, CAN'T GET MUCH INFORMATION ON THE ACCOUNT, OTHER THAN IT'S BASED IN MEXICO.
THIS IS INTERESTING.

I'VE SEEN THAT TATTOO BEFORE. THE GUY WHO WAS FOLLOWING ME HAD THE SAME ONE ON HIS ARM.
IT BELONGS TO A BANDIT GROUP KNOWN AS LAS SERPIENTES QUE CAMINAN.
THE SNAKES WHO WALK...

THEY'RE SAID TO OPERATE OUT OF THE LACANDON JUNGLE. THEIR LEADER'S A WOMAN KNOWN AS "THE SERPENT QUEEN."
I'M GUESSING THAT'S HER ON THE VIDEO.
THEY'VE KIDNAPPED PEOPLE BEFORE, TOURISTS AND THE LIKE. THEY'RE SERIOUS!

I CAN'T BELIEVE I LEFT HIM THERE, AND HE WAS STILL ALIVE. I SHOULD'VE CHECKED.
IT'S NOT YOUR FAULT, LARA. YOU DIDN'T KNOW.

KNOCK KNOCK
KAZ, YOU IN THERE?
COME IN, JONAH. SAM AND LARA ARE HERE.

WHAT'S THAT?

YOU NEED TO SEE IT FOR YOURSELF.

THAT'S GRIM'S, ISN'T IT?
OH GOD.
YES. AND THERE'S BLOOD ON IT.
I THINK THIS IS WHAT'S KNOWN AS SENDING A MESSAGE.

WHAT ARE WE GOING TO DO?
PAY THE RANSOM.
HOW? MY UNCLE WON'T HELP US AGAIN AFTER YAMATAI, AND YOU DON'T HAVE THAT MUCH.
NO. BUT I KNOW WHO DOES.

NEW HIGH QUALITY A/C OFFICES TO LET
YOU'VE NOT SEEN YOUR UNCLE IN YEARS.
THAT'S BECAUSE HE'S A SHIT. HE ALWAYS BLAMED DAD FOR WHAT HAPPENED TO MUM. BUT HE'S STILL THE EXECUTOR OF THE CROFT ESTATE.

THIS IS IT.
DO YOU THINK HE'LL JUST HAND IT OVER? I MEAN, HE DOESN'T HAVE A CHOICE, RIGHT?
HE HAS TO AUTHORIZE IT STILL, AND WE'VE NEVER BEEN CLOSE, SO...

STILL, YOU ARE **ROCKING** MY SUIT.
IT SAYS **CONFIDENCE.**
FEELS WEIRD.
I'M PRETTY SURE IT SAYS, *"I AM A WOMAN WHO SHOULD BE IN TROUSERS!"*

TRUST ME.
JUST IMAGINE HE HAS A WEAPON OR SOMETHING.
HE **DOES,** SAM.
It's just not one I can disarm.

I thought I would never have to touch the money, the estate.
I've supported myself for so long.
Thought I could leave it all behind. All the memories.

Here we go. Hating this, hating this.

I'M HERE TO SEE MR. DeMORNAY.
NAME?
LARA. LARA CROFT.

OH, *YOU'RE* THE ONE. GO ON THROUGH.

PLEASE SIT.

HOW HAVE YOU BEEN, UNCLE?
LET'S NOT PRETEND TO CARE NOW ABOUT SUCH THINGS, SHALL WE?
And that's why it's been five years since I last saw him.

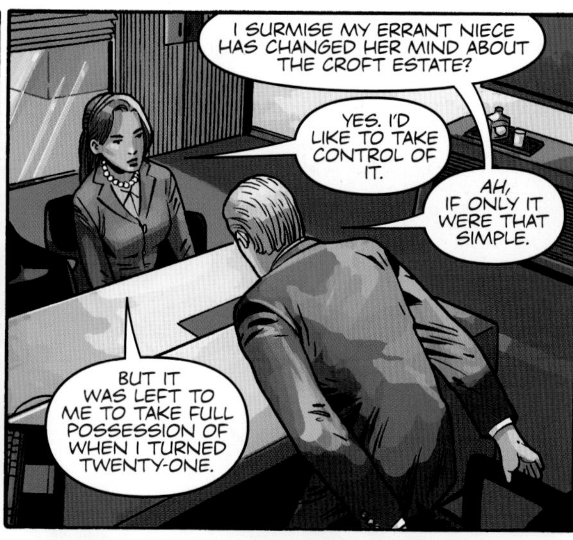
I SURMISE MY ERRANT NIECE HAS CHANGED HER MIND ABOUT THE CROFT ESTATE?
YES. I'D LIKE TO TAKE CONTROL OF IT.
AH, IF ONLY IT WERE THAT SIMPLE.
BUT IT WAS LEFT TO ME TO TAKE FULL POSSESSION OF WHEN I TURNED TWENTY-ONE.

WHICH YOU DID NOT BOTHER TO DO.
INSTEAD YOU WENT ON A JAUNT AROUND THE WORLD, GETTING YOURSELF SHIPWRECKED. ON A VOYAGE, MY SOURCES TELL ME, THAT LEFT SEVERAL CREW **DEAD.**
AND **THEN** YOU ENDED UP IN, WHERE WAS IT? AH YES, **CHERNOBYL!**

LARA!
Damn, even just thinking about that feels good.
PAY ATTENTION!
I AM, UNCLE. WHAT HAVE MY TRIPS GOT TO DO WITH THE CROFT ESTATE?

THEY HAVE EVERYTHING TO DO WITH IT. ONE OF THE CONDITIONS OF YOU TAKING OVER WAS THAT YOU WERE DEEMED FIT TO DO SO. BY ME.

AND YOU DON'T THINK I AM? YOU'RE NOT EVEN LIVING THERE. YOU'RE NOT EVEN A CROFT!

DO THOSE ADVENTURES SOUND LIKE THE ACTIONS OF A SANE PERSON? THEY DO NOT.
I'M FINE!
Really DO NOT feel fine right now. Keep calm, Lara. Keep calm.

IT'LL TAKE MORE THAN A SURLY ATTITUDE AND A NICE SUIT TO CONVINCE ME.
STOP THIS CRAZY BEHAVIOR. GET HELP. PROFESSIONAL HELP.
THEN I'LL CONSIDER WHETHER YOU ARE RESPONSIBLE ENOUGH TO TAKE OVER THE CROFT ESTATE.

Ah, if only it were that simple.
Damn. Maybe he has got a point.

SO I JUST GOT OUT OF THERE.
WHAT A BASTARD! HERE YOU GO.
THANKS.
MAYBE WE COULD GO TO THE AUTHORITIES?
AND TELL THEM *WHAT?*

THAT WE WERE SHIPWRECKED ON AN ISLAND FULL OF MAD CULTISTS WORSHIPING AN IMMORTAL SUN QUEEN?
AND OUR FRIEND DIED, ONLY HE'S NOT REALLY DEAD, BUT TAKEN BY BANDITS IN THE MEXICAN JUNGLE AND NOW THEY WANT FIVE MILLION DOLLARS FOR HIM?
Modern Day Monsters
SO, NOT THE AUTHORITIES THEN.

I'M **REALLY** WORRIED, SAM. THESE PEOPLE, THEY CAME AFTER **ALL** OF US.
OKAY, SO THEY WEREN'T TRYING TO HURT US. **YET.**
BUT WHAT HAPPENS IN TWO WEEKS?

I'VE BEEN WORKING ON AN IDEA. WELL, JONAH, KAZ, AND I HAVE. A PLAN B. HEAR ME OUT...
LET'S GO THERE!
TO MEXICO?
Modern Day
YES! ALL OF US.

NO WAY!
I'LL TRY MY UNCLE AGAIN.
YOU'RE NOT PUTTING YOURSELF THROUGH THAT A SECOND TIME.
Modern Day Monsters
SO YOU, WHAT, WANT TO GO TO MEXICO AND STORM THEIR STRONGHOLD?

NO. BUT ONE THING'S FOR CERTAIN -- WE'RE NOT SAFE HERE. AND GRIM'S NOT SAFE THERE.
AND I HAVE AN IDEA THAT COULD GET US CLOSE, WITHOUT CAUSING TOO MUCH SUSPICION.
HOW?

WITH THIS!
Modern Day

AND THIS!

YOU SEE, WE WON'T BE GOING INTO THE JUNGLE TO FIND THE BANDITS.
WE'LL BE GOING INTO THE JUNGLE TO FIND...
Modern Day

CHUPACABRA!

JUMP, LARA!
Here I am again.

I can feel the spray on my face. The smell of burning in the air. The sound of twisting, groaning metal.
I'LL CATCH YOU!

Like it was yesterday.

And he saves me.
But it's not him.

It's HER. HIMIKO.

And she's only interested in saving herself.
ARRRRRGGGGGH!
NO. NO!
Her grip is like iron. I can't get free.
KNOCK KNOCK
HANG ON!

I WAS TAKING A NAP, SAM!

OH...
HI! SORRY IF I WOKE YOU.
What the hell? Am I still dreaming?

SURPRISE! IT'S YOU.
WELL, THE STAND-IN YOU.
WE HIRED THEM TO PLAY US WHILE WE'RE GONE. REMEMBER?
OH, RIGHT. OF COURSE, SORRY.
I'M LILY. FROM SAM'S ACTING CLASS.
LARA.

UNCANNY, RIGHT? I MEAN, WE HAD TO DYE HER HAIR, AND SHE'LL NEED CONTACTS. MAYBE HEELS.
I DON'T WEAR HEELS.

I KNOW, SWEETIE. SO LET'S HOPE OUR SPYING FRIENDS OUT THERE DON'T NOTICE.
Envoys from Las Serpientes Que Caminan. "The Snakes Who Walk."
Watching to see that we deliver the ransom for Grim's return.
Only we have other plans.

MEET JULIA, THE EMERGENCY ME.
SHE'S **WELL PAID** TO BE.
SHE'S GOOD.
THIS IS GOING TO BE **SO** MUCH FUN.
OKAY, SO YOU KNOW YOUR PARTS. AND YOU'VE GOT NOTES ABOUT THE PLACES WE HANG OUT.
BE SEEN, BUT NOT TOO MUCH. KEEP THINGS LOCAL. AVOID ENGAGE-MENT.
I'VE GOT TIME OFF FROM THE MUSEUM, SO DON'T WORRY ABOUT GOING THERE.
THESE GUYS OUT THERE, ARE THEY DANGEROUS?
NO. THEY'RE JUST WATCHING. AS LONG AS THEY THINK YOU'RE US AND WE'RE STILL HERE, IT'LL BE FINE.
CALL REYES IF YOU'RE WORRIED. SHE CAN DEAL WITH THEM.

ARE YOU **SURE** ABOUT THIS, SAM?
I **CAN** GO ON MY **OWN.**
WE DON'T HAVE A LOT OF OPTIONS. IT'S JUST TWO WEEKS.
I REMEMBER WHAT HAPPENED **LAST** TIME YOU DID THAT. SO NO, WE'RE ALL GOING **TOGETHER.**

OKAY, LADIES. ARE YOU READY?
THEN WE'LL SEE YOU TONIGHT.
YES.
YUP.

THAT EVENING.
THEY'LL BE THERE, WON'T THEY?
YES, STOP WORRYING.
OUR FRIENDLY STALKERS STILL FOLLOWING?
YUP.
SAM, YOU THERE?
IT'S THEM.
WE'RE HERE.
WE'RE IN POSITION. WAITING FOR YOU.
OKAY, WE'RE CLOSE.
CAN YOU BUY US SOME SPACE?
SURE.
‹SHIT! WHAT ARE THEY DOING?›
‹KEEP UP!›

SCREEEEEEECH
DAMN IT.
TAKE A RIGHT, THEN A LEFT.

WHERE'D YOU LEARN TO DRIVE, LARA? NASCAR?
WE'RE COMING.
READY.

GO!

THEY TOOK THE BAIT.

A FEW HOURS LATER.
I CAN FEEL YOU HATING BEING IN ECONOMY.
HELL, IT'S ALL I CAN AFFORD AT THE MOMENT.
DO YOU THINK WE CAN REALLY PASS AS A DOCUMENTARY CREW?
SURE. I'VE GOT THE PAPERWORK, THE GEAR. I'VE TAUGHT YOU ENOUGH. THE REST YOU CAN JUST FAKE.
HE NORMALLY HATES FLYING.
HE STILL DOES, BUT I SLIPPED HIM A VALIUM. WE MAY HAVE TO CARRY HIM OFF.
I'VE CHARTERED A BOAT FROM CANCÚN TO TAKE US DOWN THE COAST AND INLAND.
AND THEN WHAT?
A GUIDE'LL TAKE US FURTHER INTO THE JUNGLE TO WHERE CHUPACABRA MYTHOLOGY OVERLAPS WITH LAS SERPIENTES QUE CAMINAN'S TERRITORY.
PLANES, I LIKE. BOATS I LOVE. BUT JUNGLES, I'M NOT SO SURE ABOUT.
YOU DIDN'T HAVE TO COME, KAZ. YOU NEVER EVEN MET GRIM.
ALEX WOULD WANT ME TO KEEP THE BIG MAN HERE SAFE.
BESIDES, I OWE YOU GUYS MORE THAN A THOUSAND CRAZY JUNGLE TREKS COULD EVER REPAY.

OKAY, THAT'S THE LAST ONE.

HERE YOU GO, MY SOUND GIRL.

MY CAMERA GUY. AND TAKE CARE OF MY FRIEND, HERE. WE'VE BEEN TOGETHER A LONG TIME.
YOU GOT IT.

AND YOU, LARA CROFT...
YOU KNOW I HATE GOING ON CAMERA, SAM.
TOUGH. YOU'RE GOING TO BE MY STAR.
PRETEND STAR.
SURE. BUT YOU STILL HAVE TO CARRY THINGS.

LET'S GET TO THE BOAT!
I SEE SHE'S NOT CARRYING MUCH.
I GUESS DIRECTORS DON'T HAVE TO!

THIS IS IT.
SHOULDN'T THERE BE A CREW OR SOMETHING?
I'M AFRAID I'M IT.
SO LET'S HOPE SOME OF YOU KNOW ABOUT BOATS, HUH?
I DROVE ONE OF THESE FOR TOURISTS A FEW SUMMERS BACK. SHE'S BEAUTIFUL ...ER?
ARTURO. ART. AND THANK YOU, SHE IS.
ALICE IS THE ONLY GIRL WHO'S STUCK BY ME.
OKAY, I HAVE ONE RULE. WHAT I SAY GOES, OKAY?
GUESS HE WENT TO THE CONRAD ROTH SCHOOL OF CAPTAINING.
IT'LL BE BETTER THIS TIME.
I'M NOT SO SURE ABOUT THAT.
WE'RE TOGETHER. THAT'S WHAT MATTERS.
Alice

THAT EVENING.
JUST CATCHING DINNER.
SO I SEE.
STORM'S COMING.
SHIT.
I remember the last one only too well.
AND IT'S JUST A STORM. LOOKS LIKE A SMALL ONE TOO. LET'S GO INSIDE. WE'LL COOK THESE. WE'LL DRINK A LOT.
DRINK UNTIL WE STOP REMEMBERING.
I'LL WAKE UP SAM.

SAM?

ARE YOU OKAY?

SAM?
WHAT'S THE MATTER?
LEAVE ME ALONE.

LEAVE ME ALONE, LARA CROFT!
OKAY, OKAY, I'M SORRY. I'LL LEAVE YOU TO SLEEP.

EVERYTHING OKAY?
YEAH. FINE. SAM IS JUST... RESTING, THAT'S ALL.
JONAH'S JUST TAKING A SHOWER. HE'LL BE OUT SOON.
ANY IDEA HOW LONG THIS STORM'S GOING TO LAST?
SHOULDN'T BE MORE THAN AN HOUR OR SO. I'M TRYING TO STEER US AROUND THE OUTSIDE OF IT.
BUT IT'S MOVING FAST.
WHAT'S SAM DOING OUT THERE?
WHAT THE --? I JUST LEFT HER DOWNSTAIRS.
HEY, LADY! GOING FOR A WALK?
SAM?
WHAT IS WRONG WITH YOU?

AHHHH!
PLEASE GET DOWN!
STOP THIS! WHATEVER'S WRONG, WE CAN SORT IT OUT, OKAY?
NOOOOOOO!

KAZ, TAKE THE WHEEL. KEEP HER CLOSE.
What the hell? What happened to the storm?
OH GOD.
GET OUT OF THE WATER, ART!
SAM, WAKE UP!
Bull shark. Not friendly.

If you want her, you'll have to go through me.

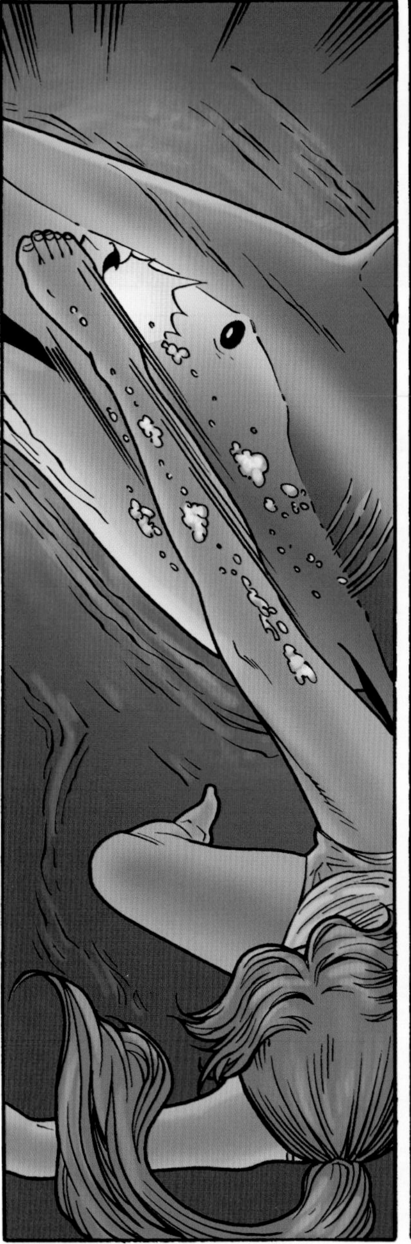

HOW DID I GET IN THE WATER?
NO TIME TO EXPLAIN, WE JUST NEED TO GET OUT!

ART, WATCH OUT!

GAAAAAHH!

AGGGHH!
AGGGGGH!

WE HAVE TO GET HIM BACK TO THE SHIP.
IF IT COMES CLOSE AGAIN, KICK OUT, PUNCH. SCARE IT OFF.
OKAY.
Alice

LARA!
IT'S COMING!
JUST KEEP SWIMMING.
TAKE ART FIRST.
LARA, COME ON!
SAM!
GAAAAAH!
GOTCHA!

REMIND ME NOT TO MAKE YOU ANGRY, SAM.

USE THIS FOR THE BLOOD.

WE HAVE TO GET HIM TO A MAINLAND HOSPITAL.
HOW LONG WILL IT TAKE US TO GET ANOTHER BOAT?

IT'S NOT JUST THE TIME--IT'S THE MONEY. I CAN'T AFFORD ANOTHER BOAT.

DAMN, HE'S PASSED OUT. WE ***HAVE*** TO GET HIM MEDICAL ATTENTION.

THERE'LL BE AN AMBULANCE WAITING FOR US. WE PASS HIM OVER AND GO.

YOU SURE?

I JUST DON'T WANT TOO MANY QUESTIONS ABOUT THIS. WE DON'T HAVE TIME, AND I'M NOT SURE I EVEN UNDERSTAND.

WHAT HAPPENED?

I DON'T KNOW. SAM WAS ACTING SO STRANGELY IN THE CABIN.

I THOUGHT SHE WAS JUST CRABBY BECAUSE I'D WOKEN HER.

HOW DID SHE GET KNOCKED INTO THE WATER?
SHE DIDN'T. SHE *LET* HERSELF FALL.
GOD.

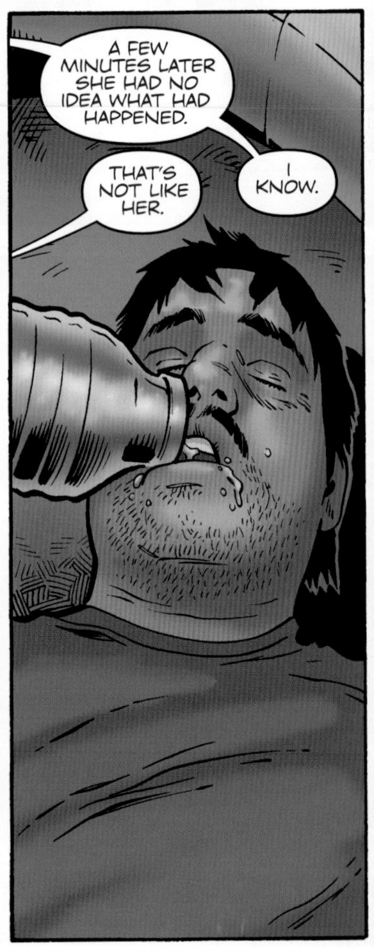

A FEW MINUTES LATER SHE HAD NO IDEA WHAT HAD HAPPENED.
THAT'S NOT LIKE HER.
I KNOW.

WHAT NOW? MAYBE I COULD RAID MY SAVINGS. GET ANOTHER BOAT.
NO! NO WAY.
I'M NOT GOING TO LET YOU DO THAT.
TAKE HER.
TAKE ALICE.
ARE YOU SERIOUS?
YOU SAVED MY LIFE. IT'S THE LEAST I CAN DO.
JUST BRING HER BACK IN ONE PIECE.
THANK YOU, ART. WE WILL.

SOME TIME LATER.
A new adventure's starting. Exhilarating and terrifying.
Down the rabbit hole we go.
Down the rabbit hole with Alice.

"I WOKE TO THE SOUND OF THE GOATS SCREAMING."
MMMMMMAAAAAAAARRRRWW
BBBBBAAAAAAAAAAAA

"I CREPT OUT TOWARDS THE SHED."
WAAAAA! BBBBWWAAAA!
WAAAAAAAA! WAAAAA!

"MY PRIZE GOAT WAS DEAD. ITS BLOOD WAS DRAINED. THE OTHERS WERE TERRIFIED AND SO WAS I."
"THEN I HEARD *IT*. *HIM! CHUPACABRA!*"
GRRRRRRRRWWW

"IT LEAPT AT ME! MUST HAVE BEEN ABOUT A METER TALL. SPINES! SCALES! HORRIBLE!

"THEN IT RAN OFF ACROSS THE FIELD."

"*THAT* WASN'T CHUPACABRA!

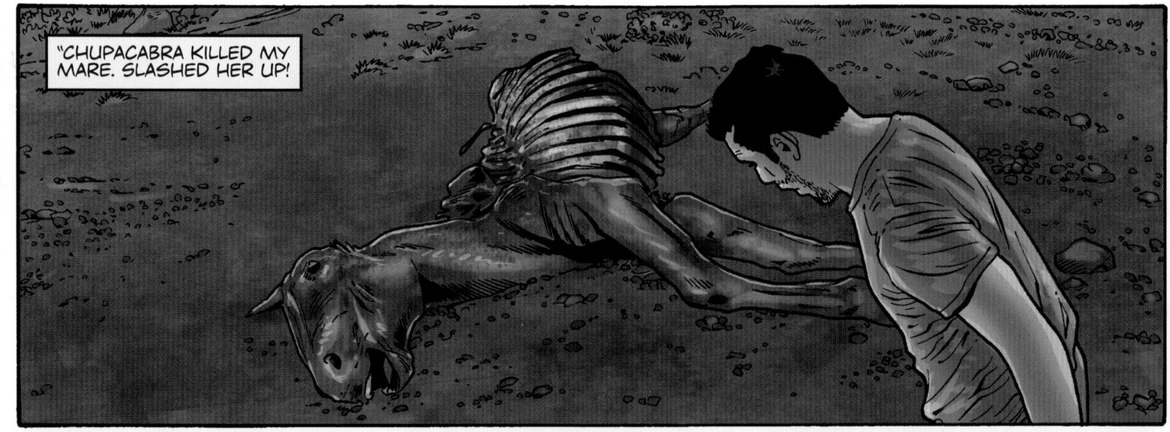
"CHUPACABRA KILLED MY MARE. SLASHED HER UP!

"THEN HE CAME FOR ME!
"AND HE WAS BIG. TWO METERS, MAYBE. AND COVERED IN HAIR!

"SO I RAN. HE WAS FASTER...

"BUT I WAS SMARTER.

"I STAYED THERE ALL NIGHT. IN THE MORNING, CHUPACABRA WAS GONE."

YOU WERE CHASED BY A **WOLF**, THAT'S ALL.
NO! IT WAS ***HIM!***
HE **SUCKS** BLOOD. HE DOESN'T SLASH THINGS.

I'M TELLING YOU, IT WAS ***CHUPACABRA!***
THE MIC'S IN SHOT.

SORRY!
I'LL JUST BE A MO, SAM.
Looks like she wants to say something, but isn't comfortable with the camera.

HI. DID YOU WANT TO TALK TO US?

I...I... NO. IT WOULDN'T HELP ANYWAY.

ARE YOU SURE?

DID SOMETHING HAPPEN TO YOU?

NOT TO ME -- TO MY LITTLE DAUGHTER, MARI.

Oh God.

I DON'T WANT TO BE FILMED. NO CAMERAS.
NO CAMERAS. IT'S JUST US.
MY DAUGHTER, MARI, AND I WERE IN THE JUNGLE COLLECTING RARE ORCHIDS A FEW DAYS AGO.

I TURNED MY BACK FOR A MINUTE AND SHE WAS GONE.
JUST VANISHED.
I'M SO SORRY.

WE'VE NOT HEARD ANY REPORTS OF CHUPACABRA ATTACKING CHILDREN.
IF IT CAN KILL A HORSE, THEN A LITTLE GIRL WOULD BE NO TROUBLE.
DID THE AUTHORITIES DO ANYTHING?
THEY AREN'T INTERESTED IN US.

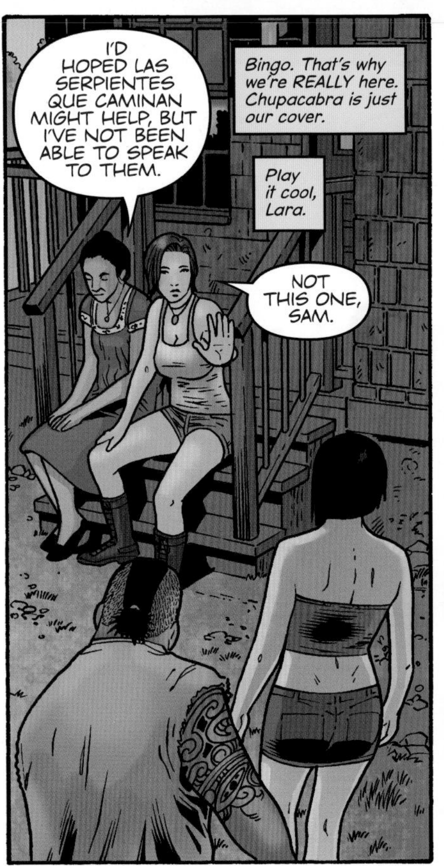
I'D HOPED LAS SERPIENTES QUE CAMINAN MIGHT HELP, BUT I'VE NOT BEEN ABLE TO SPEAK TO THEM.
Bingo. That's why we're REALLY here. Chupacabra is just our cover.
Play it cool, Lara.
NOT THIS ONE, SAM.

WHO ARE LAS SERPIENTES QUE CAMINAN?
A...LOCAL GROUP, BUT RECLUSIVE. THEY'RE RUMORED TO OPERATE NEAR WHERE MARI WENT MISSING.
WHERE WAS THAT?
A COUPLE OF KILOMETERS BEYOND THE OLD CRYSTAL FALLS. NEAR WHERE THE MONKEY FACE ORCHIDS GROW.

WE'LL KEEP A LOOK-OUT FOR HER, I PROMISE.
THANK YOU. I HAVE PRAYED TO THE SPIRITS FOR HER SAFE RETURN.

CHUPACABRA "CHILD KILLER"? WOW.
WE REALLY SHOULD HAVE GOT THAT ON TAPE.
SHE WOULDN'T HAVE TOLD ME ANYTHING IF YOU'D POINTED THAT CAMERA AT HER.
AND THIS WAY WE'VE GOT A LEAD TO LAS SERPIENTES QUE CAMINAN.
The snakes who tried to shake me down for Grim's ransom.
HEY, JONAH. LET'S GET A SHOT OF THIS...RITUAL THING.
IT'S A FRUIT OFFERING. AN ISOGUÍ EBÓ. TO THE SPIRITS OF SANTERIA. PROBABLY FOR THE GIRL.
WHO ARE YOU?
HI, I'M SAM. WE'RE JUST DOING SOME FILMING.
WE'RE DISTURBING HER. LET'S GO.
I SEE YOU! NOW TELL ME WHO YOU ARE!
I... URRRG...
HEY, TAKE IT EASY. DON'T SHOUT AT HER. WE'RE LEAVING, OKAY?
SAM? SAM?
GOD, SHE'S FAINTED.
LET'S GET HER BACK TO THE BOAT.

LATER...
I REMEMBER YOU TALKING TO THAT WOMAN ABOUT HER DAUGHTER, AND THAT'S IT.
SO YOU DON'T REMEMBER THE LADY DOING THE RITUAL?
NO.
BUT I CAN SMELL SOMETHING ON MY CLOTHES.
COULD BE THE HERBS SHE WAS BURNING. YOU PROBABLY JUST HAD A BAD REACTION TO THEM.

I GUESS SO.
SO WHEN DO WE HEAD FOR THE WATERFALL?
YOU'RE NOT GOING ANYWHERE. I'M WORRIED ABOUT YOU. ESPECIALLY AFTER WHAT HAPPENED ON THE BOAT.

RIGHT. NO ONE GETS TO BE THE HERO BUT YOU, DO THEY, LARA?
THAT'S NOT IT, SAM.
IT'S EXACTLY IT. DO YOU KNOW WHAT IT'S LIKE, HAVING YOU RESCUE ME, OVER AND OVER AGAIN? DO YOU KNOW WHAT THAT FEELS LIKE?
I USED TO THINK WE WERE EQUALS.
WE ARE, SAM.
NOT ANYMORE.

ARE YOU SAYING I SHOULDN'T HAVE SAVED YOUR LIFE?
I'M SAYING YOU CAN'T HELP IT! YOU HAVE TO CONTROL EVERYTHING. YOU CAN'T LET ME IN ANYMORE!
JUST RELAX, SAM.
STAY OUT OF IT, KAZ.

STAY AWAY FROM ME. ALL OF YOU.

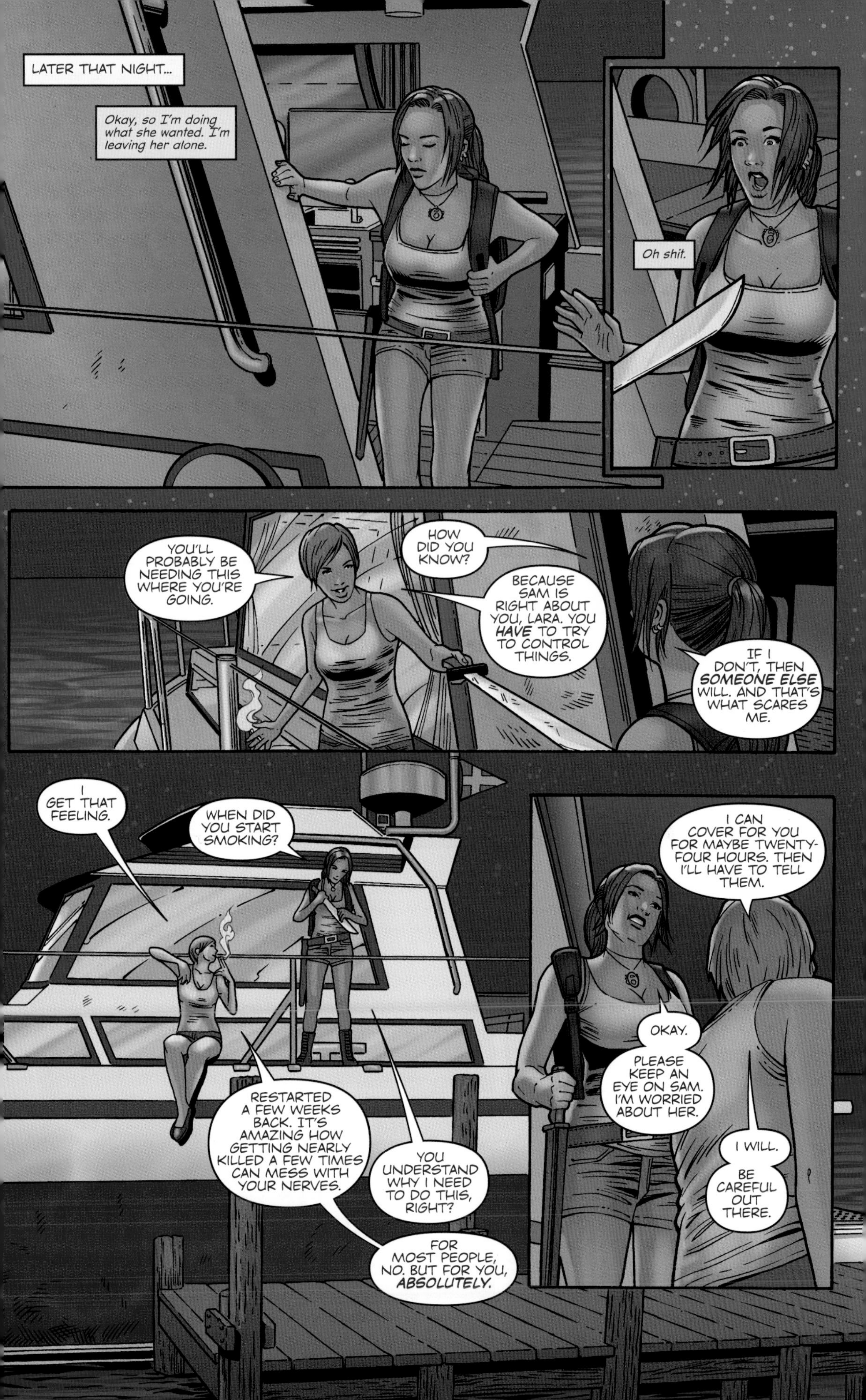
LATER THAT NIGHT...
Okay, so I'm doing what she wanted. I'm leaving her alone.
Oh shit.
YOU'LL PROBABLY BE NEEDING THIS WHERE YOU'RE GOING.
HOW DID YOU KNOW?
BECAUSE SAM IS RIGHT ABOUT YOU, LARA. YOU HAVE TO TRY TO CONTROL THINGS.
IF I DON'T, THEN SOMEONE ELSE WILL. AND THAT'S WHAT SCARES ME.
I GET THAT FEELING.
WHEN DID YOU START SMOKING?
RESTARTED A FEW WEEKS BACK. IT'S AMAZING HOW GETTING NEARLY KILLED A FEW TIMES CAN MESS WITH YOUR NERVES.
YOU UNDERSTAND WHY I NEED TO DO THIS, RIGHT?
FOR MOST PEOPLE, NO. BUT FOR YOU, ABSOLUTELY.
I CAN COVER FOR YOU FOR MAYBE TWENTY-FOUR HOURS. THEN I'LL HAVE TO TELL THEM.
OKAY.
PLEASE KEEP AN EYE ON SAM. I'M WORRIED ABOUT HER.
I WILL.
BE CAREFUL OUT THERE.

Better not use my torch yet--
don't want to attract attention.
The moon should give me enough light.
Have to make sure I don't get lost in there. The jungle's so dense that it'd take weeks for anyone to find me.
If I follow this stream then maybe it'll lead to the waterfall.
I'll just check it out and report back.
That's all. Not too controlling.
Yeah, right. Keep telling yourself that, Lara.
A FEW HOURS LATER.
OKAY. WHICH WAY NOW?
IF I'M LOOKING FOR A WATERFALL, THEN THE WATER WILL HAVE TO RUN DOWN TO SOMETHING TO FALL OFF.
SO LEFT IT IS.
SHOULD'VE GONE RIGHT.
I'm thinking this probably isn't the Old Crystal Falls.
BUT THAT COULD BE.

It's MAGNIFICENT! To think that something like this could be hidden in the heart of the jungle.
I have to admit that it's nice to have some time on my own.
Especially after what Sam said. She's been acting really strangely lately.
Still, I hope she's not hating me too much right now.
Orchids! That's what Mari's mother said they were collecting.
MONKEY FACE ORCHIDS!
Pretty cute for a flower. I should save it for Sam.
What are those stones?
OH MY GOD!
THEY'RE NOT STONES. THEY'RE BRICKS!

Bricks mean a MANMADE structure. And this deep into the jungle they'd have to be...
MAYAN!
This is amazing. These are genuine Mayan ruins!
Untouched for centuries.
Late to Terminal Classic period, I'd say.
NO ONE'S BEEN HERE FOR...
mffff mffffff mffffff
...CENTURIES.
OR MAYBE NOT.

HELLO? IS SOMEONE THERE?

mmmmaaa mmmmmmmma

It's coming from over there.

Something has fallen through here.

HELLO? IS THERE SOMEONE DOWN THERE?

MAMA?

MARI? IS YOUR NAME MARI?
YES. DO YOU KNOW WHERE MY MAMA IS?
HANG ON! I'M COMING DOWN TO GET YOU.

THANK GOD I BROUGHT THIS. HOPE IT'S LONG ENOUGH.

Can't tie it off further away or I won't have enough rope to get down there.
THIS'LL HAVE TO DO.
OKAY, I'M COMING DOWN.

IT'S OKAY, I'M COMING. IT'S OKAY.
CRACK
AHHHHH!
SHIT!
MARI, GET BACK!
AAAAGHHGGG!

OOOFFF!

ARE YOU OKAY?
YES. YOU SAID A BAD WORD.
I DID. I'M SORRY.
And I fear it probably won't be the last.
LOOKS LIKE WE WON'T BE GETTING OUT THAT WAY.

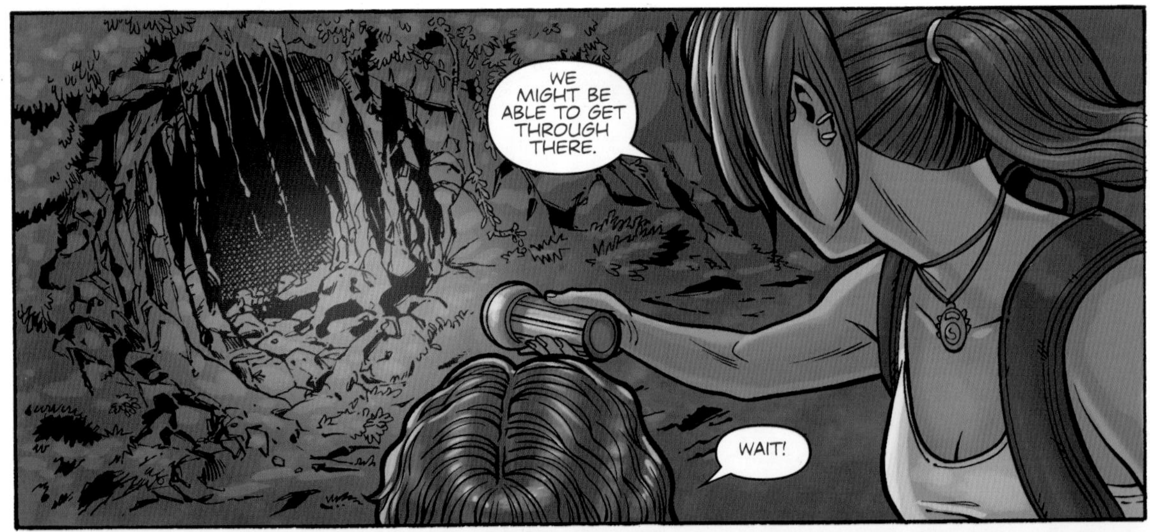
WE MIGHT BE ABLE TO GET THROUGH THERE.
WAIT!

WHO *ARE* YOU?
God, Lara. Now is NOT the time for controlling. Now is the time for gentleness.

I'M SORRY. I'M LARA. YOUR ENGLISH IS VERY GOOD.
I KNOW. I'VE HAD LESSONS. DID MAMA SEND YOU?
SORT OF, YES. SHE'S VERY WORRIED ABOUT YOU.

I'M MARI, BUT YOU KNOW THAT.
HOW DID YOU SURVIVE DOWN HERE?
I ATE SOME MOSS AND FOUND WATER IN THE NEXT CAVE.
CAN YOU SHOW ME?

SURE.
THIS WAY.

THE WATER'S FRESH.
HOW?
IT ALSO MIGHT BE OUR WAY OUT.
IT CAME IN, SO IT MUST GO OUT SOME-WHERE.

LARA...
I'M SCARED.

ME TOO. BUT I THINK WE CAN DO THIS.
WE'LL TAKE IT SLOW, OKAY?

DO YOU THINK WE CAN REALLY FIND A WAY OUT?
I DO.
What I mean is, "I hope."
THINK OF IT LIKE AN ADVENTURE.

I TRIED TO ADVENTURE WHEN I FIRST FELL DOWN HERE. BUT I HEARD NOISES AND I COULDN'T SEE. SO I STAYED IN THE LIGHT.
ADVENTURES ARE BETTER WHEN THERE ARE TWO OF YOU.
I actually managed to say that like I believed it.

CAN YOU SWIM?
YES.
ARE YOU OKAY?
IT'S SO C-C-COLD.
CLIMB ON MY BACK.
TAKE THE TORCH. KEEP IT SHINING AHEAD.
GO SLOW, REMEMBER.

HSSSSSSSSSS
THE NOISES! THAT'S WHAT I HEARD!

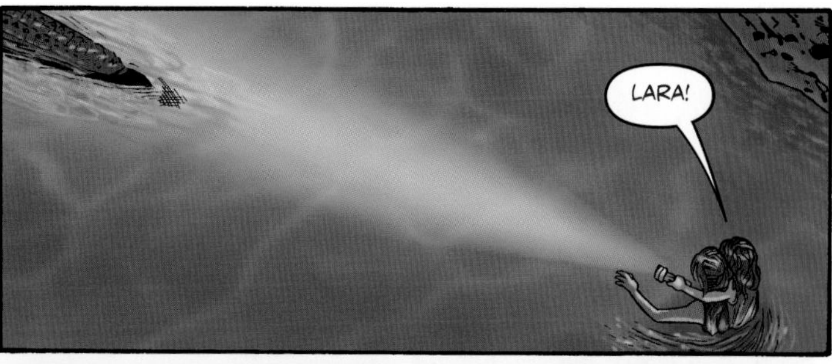
LARA!

QUICKLY, OUT OF THE WATER.
Oh god, it couldn't be, could it?

Alligator!

NO! GO AWAY!
THUNK
Brave kid!

IS IT GOING? DID I SCARE IT?
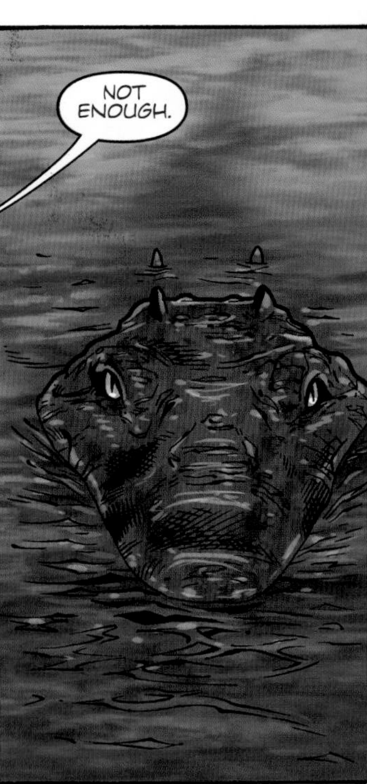
NOT ENOUGH.

GET READY WITH THE TORCH. IF IT GETS CLOSE, SHINE IT RIGHT IN ITS EYES!

HSSSSSSSSSSS

COME ON, BEFORE ANY MORE OF THEM TURN UP.
YOU JUST... KILLED IT.
SOMETIMES YOU JUST HAVE TO DO THAT.
BESIDES, IT WOULD HAVE KILLED US.
LOOK, THERE'S LIGHT UP AHEAD.
I KNOW THIS PLACE!

WHAT IS IT?

WHEN PEOPLE LOSE A CHILD THEY COME HERE TO ASK THE SPIRITS TO BLESS THEM IN THE AFTERLIFE.

PINKY!

MY MOTHER MUST HAVE PUT IT THERE. SHE MUST THINK I'M DEAD.

I THINK SHE WAS ASKING THE SPIRITS FOR HELP FINDING YOU.
ARE YOU A SPIRIT THEN?
I HOPE NOT.

BZZZZZ

HELLO, LARA CROFT.

LOCH NESS, SCOTLAND.
I GOT BREWS. I'LL CATCH YE. EVEN IF I HAVE TO WAIT **ALL** NIGHT. **EVERY NIGHT.**
WHERE ON EARTH AM I?
THAT'S GRIM!
HEY, GRIM!

THAT *DOESN'T* LOOK GOOD.

GRIM! SOMETHING'S COMING!
OH GOD.
WHAT THE HELL?
HUUURRRNNGH

WATCH OUT!
NESSIE!
HOW ABOUT A FACE FULL O' DANDRUFF, PAL!
CRRRRUNCCCH
GLASGOW KISS! YAAAAY!

DON'T YE GO TOUCHING THE BREW, GIRL. IT'LL WASTE YER LIFE.
BUT I'D SAY IT'S ABOUT TIME YOU GOT **YER** KISSING FACE ON.
HUH?
LOOKS LIKE HIS MAMMY'S IN TOWN.
SHE DON'T POSE FOR PHOTOGRAPHS.

SHE JUST EATS YE!
LARA!

DEEP IN THE MEXICAN JUNGLE...

LARA! WAKE UP!

STOP! IT'S ME, MARI!

YOU WERE HAVING A **BAD DREAM!**

I'M SORRY.

Good God! You nearly attacked a kid who's already survived being trapped in ruins, underground rivers, and an alligator!

Pull yourself together, Lara!

WHO'S GRIM?
OH...WAS I TALKING IN MY SLEEP?
YES.
HE'S AN OLD FRIEND.

THIS IS HIM.
I'VE SEEN THIS MAN!

"WHERE?"
"WHEN I GOT LOST I SAW THESE HUTS DEEP IN THE JUNGLE.
"THERE WERE MEN WITH GUNS THERE. I THINK...I **THINK** THEY WERE LAS SERPIENTES QUE CAMINAN."
"THE SNAKES WHO WALK."
"YES! I WAS HOPING I MIGHT SEE THE ONE THEY CALL THE QUEEN OF SERPENTS.
"BUT...I WAS TOO SCARED TO ASK THEM FOR HELP."

<SHE SAYS WE GOTTA MOVE HIM.>
<PUT HIM IN WITH HER **FRIENDS?**>
<NOT YET, BUT SOON.>
"I SAW THEM WITH A MAN.
"THEY HAD HIM TIED UP.
"HE LOOKED JUST LIKE YOUR FRIEND."

DO YOU REMEMBER WHERE THE BASE WAS?
NOT THAT FAR FROM WHERE YOU FOUND ME.

COULD YOU DRAW ME A MAP?
COULD YOU GET ME BACK TO MY VILLAGE?

SURE, LET'S GO.
If I ever have kids then they HAVE to be like this one!

LATER...
CAN YOU GO THE REST OF THE WAY?

YOU'RE NOT COMING? AREN'T YOUR FRIENDS HERE?
THEY ARE. BUT I'M NOT READY TO SEE THEM YET.
I'm not sure they're ready for me, either.

COULD YOU GIVE THIS TO THEM, PLEASE? THEY'RE MOORED AT THE DOCKS NEAR YOUR VILLAGE. IT'S A BOAT CALLED THE *ALICE*.
OKAY.

HERE. YOU KNOW THE OLD CRYSTAL FALLS, RIGHT?
YES. THANK YOU.

I LIKE YOU. DON'T DO ANYTHING SILLY.
YOU SOUND LIKE MY FRIENDS.
GOOD.
OKAY. I'LL...**TRY** NOT TO.
TRY **REALLY** HARD.

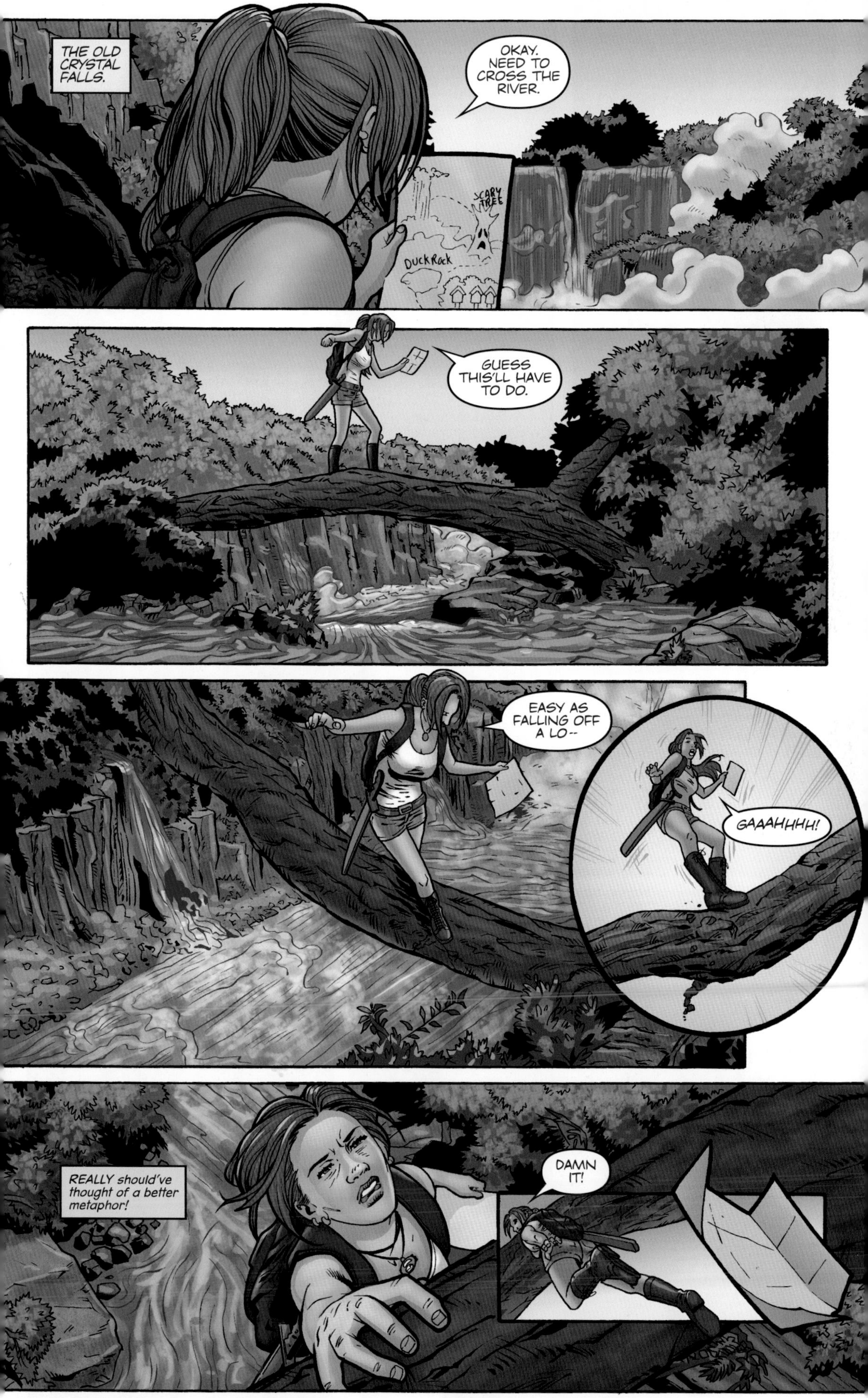

THE OLD CRYSTAL FALLS.

OKAY. NEED TO CROSS THE RIVER.

SCARY TREE

DUCK Rock

GUESS THIS'LL HAVE TO DO.

Okay, what was it she wrote? Some kind of scary tree...

If there's one thing I'm not short of here...it's TREES. But none of them look particularly scary.

Okay -- I'm Mari, I'm lost...I'm looking at all the trees...

Let's get some perspective on this.

Oh! There we go! SCARY tree!

Got the tree. Now, it was some kind of bird--no, a rock. A DUCK rock, that was it.
NONE OF THESE LOOK DUCK SHAPED.
Hmmm, she didn't mention this.
Someone small went this way.
I have to DUCK to get through.
I get it, Mari.
Total kid joke.
That must be it!

Quite the operation they've got going here.
This is probably the "something silly."
Sorry, Mari.
Where is everyone?
There's one.
Guess this place doesn't get many visitors.
Explains why there aren't many guards.
HHHSSSSS

HHHSSS
SSSSCHHHS
SSSCHH
OH GOD.
No, THAT explains why there aren't many guards.
Unless this IS the guard.
EASY, EASY...
SSCHHSSCHHSSS
WHUD
SMART ONE, AREN'T YOU.
HHHSSS

Shit!

HANDS!

Strangely, this is a relief.

WHERE WERE YOU LOT HIDING?
WE DON'T HIDE, LARA CROFT. WE JUST KNOW THIS JUNGLE BETTER THAN YOU DO.
SO YOU'VE BEEN EXPECTING ME?
OF COURSE.
<BAG THIS ONE. WE NEED TO TAKE HER UP. **SHE** WANTS TO SPEAK TO HER.>

Keep calm, Lara, keep calm. Now you might finally get some answers.

I AM NOT TALKING TO HER THROUGH A SACK. SHOW ME HER FACE!

YOU SEEM VERY RELAXED FOR SOMEONE IN SUCH A PREDICAMENT.
IT'S NOT MY FIRST PREDICAMENT.
LEAVE US.
ARE YOU SURE, MA'AM?

I SAID, LEAVE US!

I'M GUESSING YOU'RE "THE QUEEN OF SERPENTS"?
YOU GUESSED RIGHT.
THE TAPE OF GRIM? THE PEOPLE WHO FOLLOWED US IN LONDON? THAT WAS YOU?
CORRECT. ALTHOUGH YOU DEFINITELY GAVE THEM A RUN FOR THEIR MONEY.
AND THE DECOYS WERE A NICE TOUCH. THE IDIOTS DIDN'T NOTICE FOR OVER A WEEK.
AND THAT CHUPACABRA COVER? SMART. ALWAYS GUARANTEED TO GET THE LOCALS TALKING.

IS GRIM STILL ALIVE? IF YOU'VE HURT HIM, I'LL KILL YOU, I SWEAR.
HE'S STILL ALIVE. MOSTLY. HOW LONG HE STAYS THAT WAY IS RATHER UP TO YOU.
I'm sure I can loosen these bindings. Just have to keep her talking.

YOU HAVE YOUR FATHER'S EYES, LARA.

WHAT DO *YOU* KNOW ABOUT MY FATHER?

A GREAT DEAL. ONCE UPON A TIME...

"WE MET WHEN HE WAS MORE OF A DREAMER AND I STILL HAD SOME OPTIMISM LEFT.

"I WAS PROTESTING THE PROPOSED DRAINING OF SOME JUNGLE SWAMPLANDS.

"THREE DAYS CAMPED OUT IN FRONT OF THE MACHINES.

"I'D SAY THEY WERE ABOUT READY TO SHOOT US.

"THEN *HE* CAME ALONG.

"AND MADE IT *ALL* GO AWAY."

RICHARD CROFT.
LETICIA CORTEZ.
"IT WAS HARD NOT TO BE IMPRESSED.
"HE SAID HE HAD COME LOOKING FOR RUINS IN THE SWAMPLANDS AND NEEDED A LOCAL GUIDE.

"AND SO I OFFERED TO TAKE HIM.

"AT FIRST I THOUGHT HE WAS JUST SOME RICH TOURIST WHO'D READ TOO MUCH JULES VERNE.

"AND HAD COME LOOKING FOR HIS GREAT ADVENTURE.

"BUT IT TURNED OUT HE WAS PRETTY CAPABLE. FOR A BRIT.

"AND WHEN HE SAW THE RUINS...THE LOOK ON HIS FACE WAS LIKE NOTHING I'D SEEN BEFORE.

"TO MANY THEY WOULD HAVE JUST BEEN OLD ROCKS FROM A PAST THAT NO LONGER MATTERED.

"BUT TO HIM THEY WERE ***WONDROUS.***

"I GREW RATHER FOND OF HIM. IT WAS HARD NOT TO.

"HE TOLD SUCH AMAZING STORIES. BUT THEY WEREN'T JUST TALL TALES TO HIM.
"HE REALLY **BELIEVED** THERE WAS SOMETHING MORE OUT THERE.
"THAT THERE WERE STILL GREAT SECRETS TO BE DISCOVERED. AND HE WAS GOING TO BE THE ONE TO DO IT.
"HE TALKED ABOUT HIS DAUGHTER. YOU WERE JUST A KID BACK THEN.
"HE SAID HE HOPED ONE DAY TO SHOW YOU THE MYSTERIES OF THE WORLD.
"I COULD TELL FROM THE WAY HE SPOKE THAT HE WAS PROUD OF YOU.
"IT WAS THE SECOND TIME I SAW WONDER ON HIS FACE.
"BUT WHEN HE LEFT, I KNEW I'D NEVER SEE HIM AGAIN."

I ALWAYS WONDERED WHAT HAPPENED TO THAT LITTLE GIRL AND HER NECKLACE.
WELL, NOW YOU KNOW.
CARE TO LET MY FRIEND AND ME GO NOW?
NO. LIKE I SAID, I WAS AN OPTIMIST BACK THEN. NOW I'M A REALIST.

A KIDNAPPER, YOU MEAN?
A BUSINESS-WOMAN.
SOME BUSINESS!
I HELP PEOPLE REALIZE WHAT IS IMPORTANT TO THEM. I'D SAY THAT HAS VALUE.
WELL, I DON'T HAVE YOUR RANSOM MONEY. I NEVER DID!

AH, YES. FLAWED ORIGINAL INTEL, I'M AFRAID. IT WAS SIMPLY UNIMAGINABLE TO US THAT YOU HAD REJECTED YOUR FAMILY'S MONEY FOR SO LONG.
I ADMIRE YOUR PRINCIPLES. BUT THEY ARE OF LITTLE USE TO ME.
The bindings are getting looser. Should be able to get free soon.

WHERE ARE YOUR FRIENDS? YOU DIDN'T COME TO MEXICO ALONE.
THEY'VE GONE BACK.

I DOUBT THAT SOMEHOW.

I WOULD SERIOUSLY RECONSIDER WHAT YOU'RE DOING, LARA.
SLIP YOUR BINDINGS AND I WILL SHOOT.

HOW MUCH DO YOU THINK THEY WOULD PAY FOR *YOU?*
YOUR FRIEND SAMANTHA NISHIMURA, FOR INSTANCE. QUITE THE WEALTHY FAMILY, I BELIEVE.
LEAVE SAM OUT OF THIS!
LOOK, IF SHE COULD'VE PAID A RANSOM SHE WOULD'VE DONE SO.
STILL, I HAVE A FEELING SHE MIGHT GO THE EXTRA MILE FOR *YOU*, LARA.
PERHAPS EVEN VENTURE OUT HERE ON A LITTLE TREK OF HER OWN.
I SUSPECT HER FAMILY MIGHT PAY A GREAT DEAL FOR *HER* SAFE RELEASE.
IF YOU HURT HER...
YOU'LL KILL ME...YES, YES. IS THAT YOUR ANSWER TO EVERYTHING?
SAYS THE WOMAN WITH THE GUN IN MY FACE.
HECTOR! FELIX!

YES, MA'AM?
PUT HER WITH THE OLD MAN. THEY CAN REMINISCE WHILE WE SEARCH FOR HER FRIENDS.
OF COURSE, TELL US WHERE THEY ARE, AND IT WILL GO EASIER FOR THEM.
OF COURSE, SET ME FREE, AND IT'LL GO EASIER FOR YOU.
GOOD TO SEE THAT THE NEXT GENERATION OF CROFTS IS AS IDIOTIC AND STUBBORN AS THE LAST.
They must be taking me to Grim.
He really IS alive.
‹WHAT'S SHE SMILING ABOUT?›
‹DOESN'T KNOW WHAT'S IN STORE FOR HER, I GUESS!›
‹I CAN SPEAK SPANISH, YOU KNOW.›
Between us we'll break out of here, no problem.

AHHHHH!
GRIM?
SORRY, MISS. I'M NOT HIM.

We started out as seven.
We came back as four.
Three lives lost. Three friends gone.
ESc
Angus Grimaldi... Grim, as we called him, was the first to go. He sacrificed himself so that I might have a chance to help the others.
I thought he was dead. We all did.
GRIM!
PLAY ME LARA
Until I received THAT. He was alive. Kidnapped and in Mexico, but definitely not dead.
And so we came looking for him. Under the pretext of filming a documentary about the chupacabra.
And our world got turned upside down.
Again.
I thought I'd found him.
WHAT?
I'M **NOT** GRIM.
AND BELIEVE ME, RIGHT NOW I **REALLY** WISH I WAS.
That makes two of us.

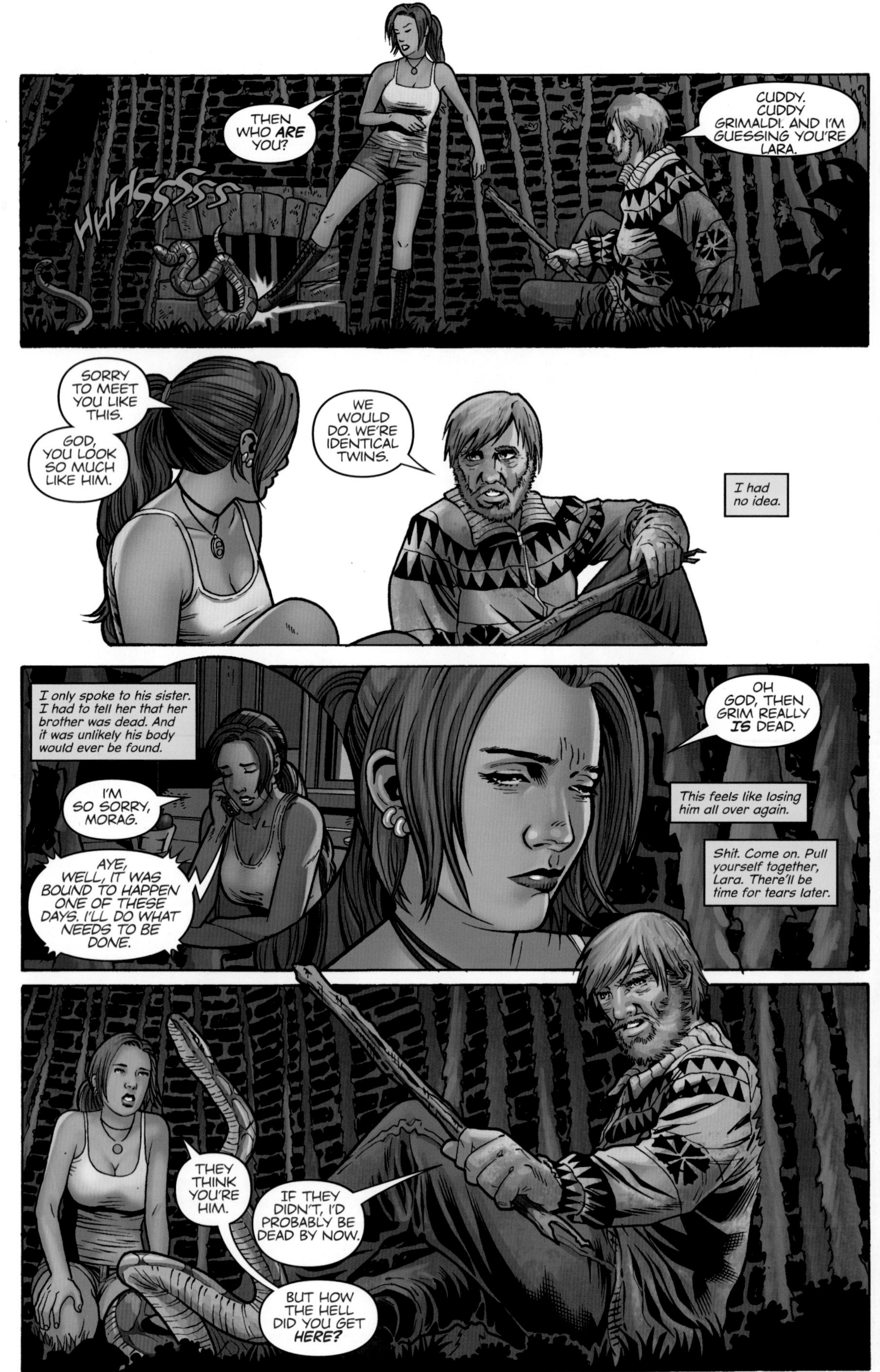
THEN WHO ARE YOU?
CUDDY. CUDDY GRIMALDI. AND I'M GUESSING YOU'RE LARA.
HHHSSSSSS
SORRY TO MEET YOU LIKE THIS.
GOD, YOU LOOK SO MUCH LIKE HIM.
WE WOULD DO. WE'RE IDENTICAL TWINS.
I had no idea.
I only spoke to his sister. I had to tell her that her brother was dead. And it was unlikely his body would ever be found.
I'M SO SORRY, MORAG.
AYE, WELL, IT WAS BOUND TO HAPPEN ONE OF THESE DAYS. I'LL DO WHAT NEEDS TO BE DONE.
OH GOD, THEN GRIM REALLY IS DEAD.
This feels like losing him all over again.
Shit. Come on. Pull yourself together, Lara. There'll be time for tears later.
THEY THINK YOU'RE HIM.
IF THEY DIDN'T, I'D PROBABLY BE DEAD BY NOW.
BUT HOW THE HELL DID YOU GET HERE?

"ANGUS WAS ALWAYS THE RISK TAKER. I WAS ALWAYS THE SENSIBLE ONE. EVEN WHEN WE WERE NIPPERS.
"STILL, WE USED TO BE CLOSE BACK THEN.
"WE FELL OUT WHEN MA GOT SICK. ANGUS COULDN'T HANDLE IT. WENT OFF ON MORE OF HIS ADVENTURES.
"LEFT ME AND MORAG TO DEAL WITH HER."
JUST COME BACK!
"DIDN'T EVEN COME BACK FOR THE FUNERAL.
betty
"WE DIDN'T SPEAK AFTER THAT.
"WHEN MORAG TOLD ME HE'D DIED I WENT TO TAKE CARE OF HIS BOAT.
"AND HIS BOYS -- TATTIE AND NEEPS.
the Bonny Betty
"THEY WERE MORE AT HOME ON THE WATER THAN LAND. JUST LIKE HIM.
"SOMETHING ABOUT BEING IN THAT BOAT MADE ME REALIZE WHAT I'D BEEN MISSING.
"ON A DAFT WHIM I DECIDED TO HEAD OFF ON MY OWN ADVENTURE.
"BANDITS PICKED ME UP OFF THE COAST. ANGUS'S PAPERWORK WAS STILL ON BOARD, SO THEY THOUGHT I WAS HIM."

THEY TRIED TO BLACK-MAIL US INTO PAYING YOUR RANSOM. WELL, GRIM'S RANSOM.
I'M SORRY. I DON'T KNOW WHAT I WAS THINKING. I'M AN **ACCOUNTANT,** FOR GOD'S SAKE! I'M NOT EVEN BRAVE!
WE DECIDED TO FIND OUT WHAT THE HELL WAS GOING ON.
I'M SUCH A NUMPTY.

I'M GOING TO TRY CLIMBING UP.
WHAT ABOUT **THE SNAKES?**
THEY CAN WATCH ME.

BE CAREFUL, SNAKE ABOVE YOU.
THAT ONE'S NOT POISONOUS. IT JUST LOOKS IT.

I DON'T THINK I CAN DO THAT.
YOU WON'T HAVE TO.
THERE ARE GUARDS OUTSIDE THE DOOR. YOU'LL NEVER GET OUT THAT WAY.

I'M NOT TRYING TO GET US UP AND OUT.

I'M GOING TO TRY AND GET US **THROUGH** AND **OUT.**
THESE BARS ARE TOUGH THOUGH.

WE NEED TO WEAKEN THEM FIRST.
HE CAN HELP US.

WHAT ARE YOU DOING?
TRYING TO MAKE IT THINK THAT IT'S WRAPPED AROUND FOOD.

THAT'S IT. GOOD BOY!
CREEEEEK

WE SHOULD BE ABLE TO GET THROUGH THAT.

HOW DO YOU KNOW THAT IT LEADS SOMEWHERE?
BECAUSE SHE MIGHT ENJOY KEEPING **US** SOMEWHERE LIKE THIS, BUT SHE TREATS HER SNAKES BETTER.
THEY MUST BE COMING FROM SOMEWHERE OUTSIDE.
THIS'LL HELP CLEAR THE WAY.

I DON'T THINK I CAN DO THAT.
IF GRIM COULD, THEN YOU CAN.
Way to be sensitive, Lara.
SORRY, I MEAN, IT'LL BE OKAY. I'LL CLEAR THE SNAKES.

WE WATCHED TOO MANY HUMPHREY BOGART MOVIES AS KIDS. ANGUS WAS CUT OUT FOR THIS KIND OF THING. I'M NOT.
I USED TO THINK I COULDN'T DO STUFF LIKE THIS EITHER.
BUT YOU CAN SURPRISE YOURSELF.

‹I'M TELLING YOU, HE WON'T LAST IN THERE.›
‹WHAT ABOUT **HER?**›
‹SHE'LL HOLD OUT. LETICIA'S BETTING ON THAT.›

‹HAVE THEY MOVED HIS BOAT YET?›
‹YEAH, IT'S DOWN BY THE RIVER.›
‹PRETTY NICE CRAFT.›

‹WE SHOULD JUST SELL IT, DUMP THEM, AND CUT OUR LOSSES.›
‹COME ON. I THINK THE QUEEN WANTS US TO JOIN THE OTHERS AT THE VILLAGE.›

CREEEEEK

QUICK, BEFORE THEY COME BACK.

IF THOSE BASTARDS SELL THE *BONNY BETTY* ANGUS'LL BE BACK TO HAUNT ME!
I'M MORE WORRIED ABOUT MY FRIENDS. I THINK SHE'S GOING TO GO AFTER THEM.
CAN YOU WARN THEM?
IT'LL TAKE US AGES TO GET BACK THERE.
DOUBT THE DARK'S GOING TO HELP US.
TRUTH BE TOLD, I'M NOT THAT STEADY ON MY FEET IN THE LIGHT!
THE RIVER'S CLOSE. LET'S HEAD FOR THAT AND SEE IF WE CAN FIND YOUR BOAT.
FOLLOW ME.
I...
YOU CAN DO THIS. WE'LL GO SLOW, OKAY?

I SEE A GUARD.
LETICIA'S OBVIOUSLY KEEN TO PROTECT HER **INVESTMENT.**
WE NEED TO GET CLOSER.

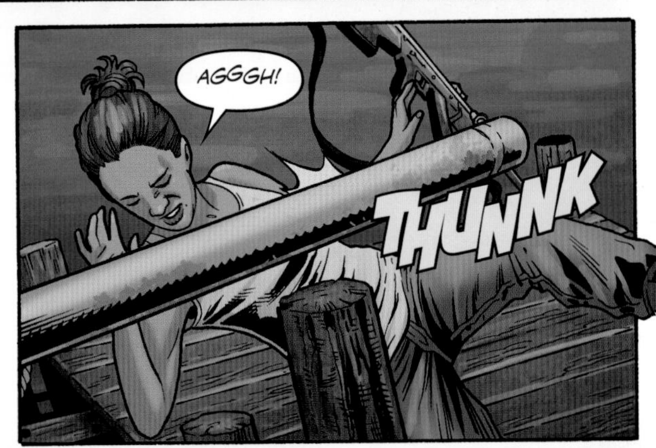
AGGGH!
THUNNK

SPLUSSH

IS SHE...?
NO.
BUT WE'D BETTER MOVE BEFORE SHE COMES ROUND.
I REALLY HOPE SHE DIDN'T HAVE THE KEYS.
I KNOW WHERE ANGUS KEPT A SPARE.

THEY'RE STILL HERE.
CLICK
<HOW THE HELL DID YOU GET OUT?>

<WHERE'S ROSA? **WHERE IS SHE?**>
<JUST TAKE IT EASY, OKAY? THE BOAT WAS EMPTY.>
TOILET

<I'M SURE THE QUEEN IS GOING TO BE GLAD TO SEE YOU BACK.>
<OR MAYBE SHE'D BE HAPPIER TO JUST SEE **YOUR BODIES.**>
<I WOULDN'T KILL US IF I WERE YOU. WE'RE HER PAYDAY.>
SCRRITCCH SCRITTCCH

<SO YOU GOT ANOTHER FRIEND HIDING HERE, HUH?>
<TRYING TO STEAL **HER** PROPERTY.>
IT'S **NOT HERS,** YOU DAMN SCUNNER!
There's the GRIMALDI SPIRIT!

YAWWWAAAAA
ROOOOOOWWWLL
TATTIE!
NEEPS!

CRRUNCH
OOOOOOFFF
AGGGGG!
WHO TAUGHT YOU *THAT?*
YOUR BROTHER.

FFFUTT
FUUTTTT
FUTTT
DAMN, YOU MISSED!
I MEANT TO.
I'M NOT SHOOTING A FLEEING UNARMED MAN.
SHE'LL KNOW WE ESCAPED.
SHE PROBABLY ALREADY DOES. SO WE'D BETTER GET GOING.

THESE ARE A COUPLE OF TOUGH KITTIES.
WELL, THEY **ARE** GLASWEGIAN.
THEY GO IN AND OUT OF THE *BONNY BETTY* AS THEY PLEASE. THEY'VE GOT NOOKS AND CRANNIES EVERYWHERE.
STOP HERE, BEFORE THE BEND.
WE'RE THERE?
NOT YET.

I'VE GOT A BAD FEELING. I JUST WANT TO CHECK OUT THINGS ON FOOT FIRST.
DO YOU WANT TO STAY HERE?
I THINK I'M PROBABLY SAFER WITH YOU.

THANK YOU.
FOR WHAT?
FOR NOT LEAVING ME THERE WHEN YOU FOUND OUT I WASN'T GRIM.
Does he really think I'd do that?

ADVENTURES ARE SELDOM WHAT YOU THINK THEY'RE GOING TO BE.
BESIDES, GRIM WAS LIKE FAMILY.
WELL, YOU'VE GOT SOMEONE TO DO YOUR TAXES FOR YOU FOR THE REST OF YOUR LIFE.
SO worth it.

OH GOD.

WHERE IS SHE?
WE'VE NOT SEEN HER.
SHE **ESCAPED** WITH THE OLD MAN. THIS WOULD'VE BEEN THE FIRST PLACE SHE'D GO.
LOOK, SHE ***ISN'T HERE!***

WHAT ABOUT YOU? WHY SO QUIET, BITCH? WHAT DO YOU KNOW?

GET THAT THING ***OUT*** OF MY FACE!
WE **WAIT.** SHE'S BOUND TO TURN UP SOONER OR LATER.

THE GUN'S BACK AT THE BOAT.
NO MORE BULLETS LEFT.
THEN WHAT?
WE NEED SOME KIND OF DISTRACTION.

I'VE GOT AN IDEA. HAVE YOU EVER SEEN THE *AFRICAN QUEEN?*
IT'S ONE OF MY FAVORITES.

A SHORT TIME LATER.

HERE WE GO. I KNEW THE OLD BASTARD HADN'T GIVEN UP SMOKING WHEN HE GAVE UP THE DRINK.

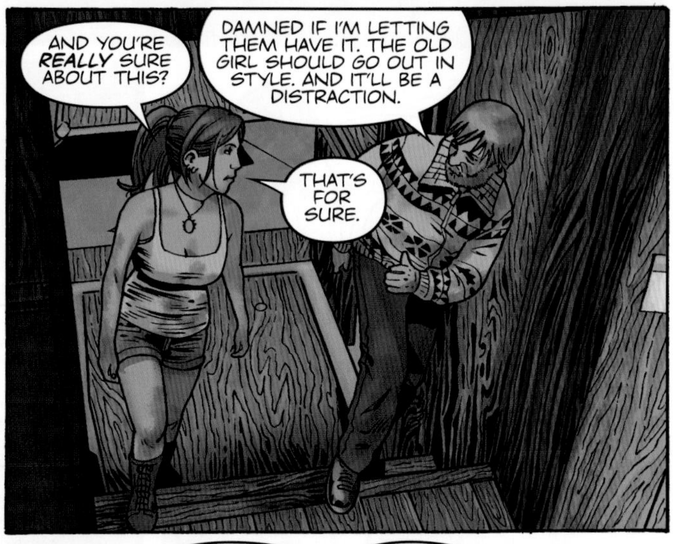
AND YOU'RE ***REALLY*** SURE ABOUT THIS?
DAMNED IF I'M LETTING THEM HAVE IT. THE OLD GIRL SHOULD GO OUT IN STYLE. AND IT'LL BE A DISTRACTION.
THAT'S FOR SURE.

WON'T GRIM HAUNT YOU IF YOU DESTROY HIS BOAT?

AH WELL, WE'VE PROBABLY GOT A LOT TO CATCH UP ON.

ARE YOU SURE YOU DON'T WANT **ME** TO DRIVE?

NO. YOU GO FOR THE OTHERS. I NEED TO DO THIS. IT'S A FAMILY THING.

ONCE YOU'VE LOCKED THE WHEEL, GET OUT OF THERE AS SOON AS YOU CAN.

THROW THE LIGHTER AS YOU JUMP. THEN GET TO COVER.

GOT IT.

GOOD LUCK.

YOU TOO.

AND TO THINK A FEW HOURS AGO HE THOUGHT HE WASN'T BRAVE.

OKAY, FELLAS, YOU STAY SAFE.
MMMMOWW
BRRRRRRR

A SHORT TIME LATER...

Here we go.
<LOOK!>
<SHIT!>

KAAABOOOOM

<WHAT THE HELL HAPPENED?>
<IS SHE IN THE WATER? IS SHE SHOOTING?>
SAM. ARE YOU OKAY? **SAM?**

SAM! NO!
SSSSHLTH
GULURRRRRRGGG
HE'S... DEAD. YOU KILLED HIM... YOU KILLED HIM!

I...WHAT? WHAT DID I DO?

LARA, THEY'RE COMING. WE'VE GOT TO GO.

TATTIE! NEEPS! COME ON!

START THE BOAT, CUDDY!

BLAM
BLAAM

‹SHE'S GONE. AND THE OLD GUY. WE LOST THE BOAT, AND CARLOS.›
‹SHE'S A DIFFERENT CREATURE FROM HER FATHER. THAT'S FOR SURE.›

‹YOU SOUND IMPRESSED.›
‹HE ALWAYS SPOKE OF HER SO FONDLY. I ALWAYS WONDERED HOW SHE MIGHT TURN OUT.›
‹AND NOW I KNOW.›

‹I'M NOT SURE IF HE'D BE PROUD OR HORRIFIED. EITHER WAY SHE'S GOT A BUMPY ROAD AHEAD OF HER.›

WELL, SHE'S PRETTY MUCH OUT OF IT. I COULDN'T EVEN GET HER IN THE SHOWER TO WASH THE BLOOD OFF. SHE'S JUST SITTING THERE.
ME TOO.
I'M **REALLY** WORRIED ABOUT HER.

LET HER REST. SEE HOW SHE IS IN THE MORNING.

It's only been a few weeks, but it feels like a lifetime.

I THINK **THIS** IS THE NEAREST I WANT TO GET TO ADVENTURE. I'VE DEFINITELY HAD MY FILL.

I APPRECIATE THE JOB RECOMMENDATION.

SORRY YOU LOST YOURS.

IT WAS TEMPORARY. BESIDES, I WAS GONE QUITE A WHILE. CAN'T SAY I BLAME THEM.

I PROBABLY WOULD HAVE FIRED ME.

I KNOW I WASN'T EXACTLY WHO YOU WERE HOPING TO BRING BACK. BUT THANK YOU. AGAIN.
YOU WERE... UNEXPECTED, ADMITTEDLY. BUT I THINK I NEEDED A DOSE OF THAT.

SEE YOU AT THE WEEKEND. JONAH DOES A MEAN SUNDAY ROAST.
GREAT! I'LL BRING THE PUDDING. BACK TO NORMAL LIFE AT LAST!

Normal life...

I used to know what that was.

Even thought I'd managed to get it back again, despite everything that's happened.

I was wrong. VERY wrong.

I used to like peace and quiet. Now I prefer the noise. The constant hum of the city.
TELEPHONE

Helps drown out the memories.

But somehow they always seem to break through.
SOMETIMES YOU'VE GOT TO MAKE SACRIFICES, LARA. YOU CAN'T SAVE EVERY-ONE.
I KNOW ABOUT SACRIFICES.

NO. YOU KNOW ABOUT LOSS. A SACRIFICE IS A CHOICE YOU MAKE. A LOSS IS A CHOICE MADE FOR YOU.

Those gut punches. That pain inside that you always carry with you.
It never leaves. You just learn to bury it deeper, so you can go on living.

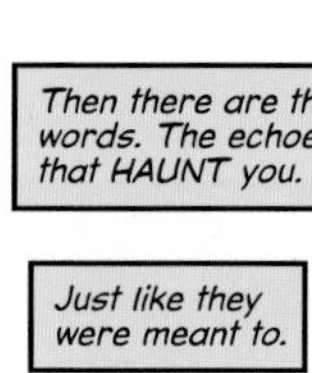
Then there are the words. The echoes that HAUNT you.
Just like they were meant to.

YOU KNOW WHAT YOU ARE, LARA CROFT.
A KILLER. STONE COLD. I SEE IT IN YOUR EYES. I **FEEL** IT.

But words from strangers only cut so deep. They don't know you. Not really. At least that's what I tell myself.
But the words from those that know you. Those are the ones that CHILL you to the bone.

DO YOU KNOW WHAT IT'S LIKE, HAVING YOU RESCUE ME, OVER AND OVER AGAIN? DO YOU KNOW WHAT THAT **FEELS** LIKE?
I USED TO THINK WE WERE EQUALS. NOT ANYMORE.

I'M SAYING YOU **CAN'T HELP IT!** YOU HAVE TO CONTROL **EVERYTHING.** YOU CAN'T LET ME IN ANYMORE!

COOKIES
NO ONE GETS TO BE THE HERO BUT YOU, DO THEY, LARA?

I KNOW my mind plays tricks on me.
Mace
SEBASTIAN & ALEX

Makes me jittery.

Shit.
But I'm honestly not quite sure what's real anymore. Not completely.
And I can't take any chances.

OVER THERE!

Damn it. What's wrong, Lara?
COME ON, THERE'S THE CAR.
THERE'S GOT TO BE A BETTER PUB AROUND HERE SOMEWHERE!
SQQIIISH

WHAT THE HELL IS
WRONG WITH YOU?

But you pick yourself up and you carry on.

Because what else is there to do?

HEY, SAM!
HI.

ANOTHER RUN, HUH?
YES.
YOU'VE BEEN TAKING A LOT OF THOSE.

WHY DON'T YOU STAY? WE'VE NOT HUNG OUT FOR A WHILE. I BOUGHT YOU A CUPCAKE.

IT'S A *LITTLE* SQUASHED.

MAYBE LATER.
WE NEED TO TALK ABOUT WHAT HAPPENED IN MEXICO.
NO, WE DON'T.
IT'S GOING TO HAVE AN EFFECT ON YOU. MORE THAN YOU CAN IMAGINE.
AND YOU'RE GOING TO HAVE TO DEAL WITH THAT.
AND HOW DID YOU DEAL WITH THAT...OH YES...YOU TRIED TO GET AS FAR AWAY FROM ME AS POSSIBLE!
IT WASN'T ABOUT YOU, SAM.
LOOK, I AM DEALING WITH IT. IN MY OWN WAY.
AND AS SOON AS I FEEL THE NEED TO DASH OFF TO THE ASS END OF NOWHERE, I'LL LET YOU KNOW.
I'M SURE YOU'LL BE ALL OVER THAT.

LATER...
KNOCK KNOCK
COME IN!

LARA?

THANKS FOR COMING.
NO WORRIES. SORRY WE DIDN'T GET HERE BEFORE YOU WENT INTO HIBERNATION!

DON'T MOCK THE BLANKET CAVE. DON'T EVER MOCK THE BLANKET CAVE.

YOU'RE RIGHT...IT DOES HAVE A CERTAIN SOMETHING.
CHOCOLATE!

GOING TO SEND SOMEONE AFTER YOU, SHE WOULD'VE DONE IT BY NOW.
I'M NOT SO SURE.
CLEARLY. I THOUGHT YOU BRITS DIDN'T DO GUNS HERE IN THE MOTHERLAND. ISN'T IT ALL HEAVY SARCASM AND RAISED EYEBROWS?
ONCE UPON A TIME THAT WAS ENOUGH.
BUT JONAH'S RIGHT. SHE'S NOT GOING TO MESS WITH YOU AGAIN.
ARE YOU SURE YOU'RE NOT LOOKING FOR AN EXCUSE TO GET OUT OF TOWN AGAIN?
NOW YOU'RE SOUNDING LIKE SAM.
HEY, DID SOMETHING HAPPEN WITH YOU TWO?
WE HAD A BIT OF A FIGHT.
WHERE IS SHE NOW?
SHE WENT OUT RUNNING. BUT THAT WAS AGES AGO.

MAYBE SHE'S RIGHT...
WELL, YOU DON'T SEEM TO LIKE BEING IN ONE PLACE FOR LONG. AND **BELIEVE ME,** I'VE BEEN **GRATEFUL** FOR THAT IN THE PAST.

DIDN'T THAT FAMILY FRIEND OF YOURS RECOMMEND SOMEONE YOU COULD TALK TO ABOUT ALL THIS?
SHE'S DAD'S OLD GIRLFRIEND, AND YES, ANA SAID SHE KNEW SOMEONE GOOD. AND TRUSTWORTHY. BUT I DON'T KNOW...

Would someone even believe what I've been through?
Not sure I even believe it myself.

OKAY, I AM CUTTING YOU OFF!
HEY!

IS THAT YOU AND YOUR DAD?
YES.
THAT BRAID IS **ADORABLE.**
WHAT'S GOT YOU TRIPPING DOWN MEMORY LANE?

"THE SERPENT QUEEN -- LETICIA CORTEZ -- SAID SHE KNEW HIM.

"I MEAN ***REALLY KNEW*** HIM.

"AND HE TALKED ABOUT ME TO HER.

"SAID ONE DAY HE HOPED TO SHOW ME THE SECRETS OF THE WORLD.

"I THINK DEEP DOWN SHE BLAMED ME FOR HIM LEAVING HER TO PURSUE THEM.

"OR MAYBE SHE WAS JUST CURIOUS.

"EITHER WAY SHE ENJOYED MAKING ME SQUIRM."

BUT YOU KNEW THERE WERE OTHER WOMEN, RIGHT?
AFTER MUM? YES, OF COURSE. BUT IT WASN'T THAT.
I NEVER THOUGHT HE WAS THAT INTERESTED IN ME.

DAD'S RESEARCH TAPES. I'VE BEEN LISTENING TO A FEW OF THEM.
IT'S SO STRANGE HEARING HIS VOICE AGAIN AFTER ALL THESE YEARS...
I DO NEED SOMETHING, JONAH. I'VE GOT NO JOB. SAM WOULD RATHER I WASN'T HERE. SO I MIGHT AS WELL NOT BE.
WHERE ON EARTH WOULD YOU GO?
I DON'T KNOW. BACK TO YAMATAI MAYBE?
HONESTLY, LARA, FOR SOMEONE WHO IS SO SMART YOU CAN BE A REAL IDIOT SOMETIMES.
I'VE NEVER BEEN TO THAT PLACE AND I HATE IT! LET IT GO!

YOU DON'T UNDERSTAND WHAT HAPPENED THERE, KAZ.
MAYBE NOT. BUT I KNOW IT WAS HELL FOR YOU. ***ALL*** OF YOU. I LOST MY BROTHER THERE, REMEMBER.

I REMEMBER...
I SAW THINGS THERE THAT...I CAN'T EVEN BEGIN TO UNDERSTAND.

I GET THAT. BUT RUNNING RIGHT BACK INTO THE MOUTH OF HELL BECAUSE YOU'RE TOO AFRAID OF MOVING FORWARD IS ***NOT*** THE WAY TO DEAL WITH THIS.
Brrrrrrrriinnnnng
brrrriiinnngggg

THEN I'LL GO SOMEWHERE ELSE.

HELLO?
IS THAT MISS LARA CROFT?
YES.
THIS IS THE WESTMINSTER POLICE DEPARTMENT. I'M AFRAID YOUR FRIEND SAMANTHA HAS BEEN ARRESTED FOR ASSAULT.

MISS CROFT? ARE YOU THERE?

H.M. PRISON HOLLOWAY.
THE NEXT DAY.
5
H.M.Prison Holloway

THIS IS CRAZY. WHY COULDN'T THEY KEEP HER AT THE STATION?
THEY SAID SHE WAS A DANGER TO HERSELF AND OTHERS, AND I COULDN'T AFFORD HER BAIL.
AND HE WAS JUST ASKING SAM FOR DIRECTIONS, THAT'S *ALL?*
Prison Holloway

YES. WE'VE BEEN THROUGH THIS.
EVEN SAM TOLD THEM THAT. SHE JUST CAN'T REMEMBER WHAT HAPPENED NEXT.
I KNOW. I JUST DON'T BELIEVE IT.
UNTIL THEY WERE PULLING HER OFF HIM.

5
THAT'S SOUNDING A BIT TOO FAMILIAR...
I KNOW. ALTHOUGH I WON'T BE TELLING THEM THAT.
DO YOU WANT US TO COME IN WITH YOU?

BEST NOT. SHE'S NOT EXACTLY BEEN THAT COMMUNICATIVE.
EVEN WITH ME.
Holloway
ning left

OF ALL OF US, I NEVER THOUGHT SAM WOULD BE THE ONE TO END UP SOMEWHERE LIKE THIS.

HOW'S SHE DOING?
QUIET TODAY. ROUGH NIGHT LAST NIGHT.

IF YOU NEED ME, YELL OR HIT THE ALARM. I'LL BE JUST OUT HERE.
Shit, is she serious?

She seems almost catatonic again. Like she was on the boat.
Those scratches...

WHAT HAPPENED TO YOUR ARMS? DID SOMEONE DO THAT TO YOU?
Or did you do it to yourself?
SAM?
HELLO? CAN YOU HEAR ME?

WE CAN HEAR YOU. WE'RE FINE.
WE'RE fine...oh God. No, it couldn't be. Not again.
Just keep calm.
SAM, IT'S LARA. COME BACK TO ME. **PLEASE** COME BACK TO ME!

IT'S GOING TO BE **OKAY.**
I'M GOING TO FIND A WAY TO RAISE YOUR BAIL. GET YOU OUT OF HERE. GET YOU HELP. **PROPER** HELP.
YOU KNOW I WILL, RIGHT?

I... KNOW.
Got her!

SO YOU'LL BE GOING AWAY THEN?
I... I...MAYBE. I DON'T KNOW.

GO!
Lost her...

SAM! COME BACK! **SAM!**

LATER...
So...that went well.

This is what she wants.

Well, fine.

What are you doing, Lara?

You're just using Sam as an excuse to get away.
RUN away.
Kaz was right.

We never talked about it. What happened on that island. At least not publicly.

Maybe we were wrong.
Maybe we were ALL just running away.
If the pen is mightier than the sword...
Then perhaps the keyboard is mightier than the pistol.

Dad never got to reveal the secrets of the world to me. But maybe I've stumbled on them myself.
I KNOW I saw something. I won't lie. I won't bury this.
The Journal might even publish me.

It won't be for nothing. You won't be forgotten, I promise.
One last thing.

Time to embrace the light.

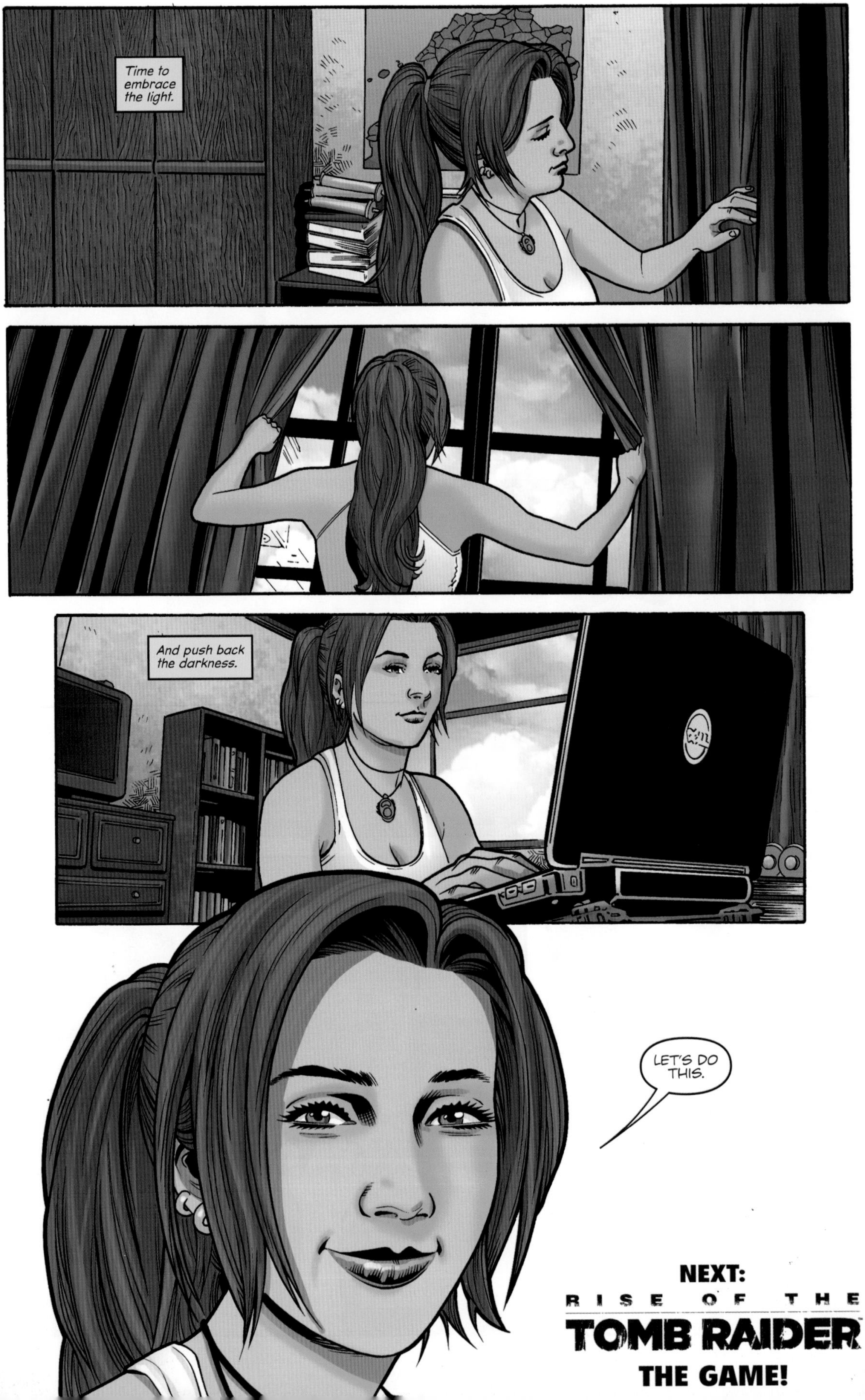

And push back the darkness.

LET'S DO THIS.

NEXT:
RISE OF THE TOMB RAIDER
THE GAME!

Artist **DAN DON SANTOS**

Artist **DAN SCOTT**

Artist **ARIEL OLIVETTI**

Artist **STEPHANIE HANS**

Artist **BRIAN HORTON**

Artist **DAN SCOTT**

Artist STEPHANIE HANS

Artist **STEPHANIE HANS**

Artist **ANDY PARK**

Artist **ANDY PARK**

Artist **DAN SCOTT**

Artist BRIAN HORTON

Artist **BRENOCH ADAMS**

Artist BRENOCH ADAMS

Artist **ANDY PARK**

Artist **ANDY PARK**

Artist **BRIAN HORTON**

Artist **BRIAN HORTON**

Artist **ANDY PARK**

Artist JENNY FRISSON

JUSTICE LEAGUE
VS. SUICIDE SQUAD

JUSTICE LEAGUE VS. SUICIDE SQUAD

JUSTICE LEAGUE VS. SUICIDE SQUAD

JOSHUA WILLIAMSON * TIM SEELEY
ROB WILLIAMS * SI SPURRIER
writers

JASON FABOK * TONY S. DANIEL * JESUS MERINO * FERNANDO PASARIN
ROBSON ROCHA * HOWARD PORTER * CHRISTIAN DUCE
RILEY ROSSMO * SCOT EATON * GIUSEPPE CAFARO
GIUSEPPE CAMUNCOLI * SANDU FLOREA * ANDY OWENS * MATT RYAN
WAYNE FAUCHER * JAY LEISTEN * DANIEL HENRIQUES
OCLAIR ALBERT * FRANCESCO MATTINA
artists

ALEX SINCLAIR * HI-FI * IVAN PLASCENCIA
MAT LOPES * GABE ELTAEB * JEREMIAH SKIPPER
colorists

ROB LEIGH * PAT BROSSEAU
RICHARD STARKINGS AND COMICRAFT * JOSH REED
letterers

JASON FABOK and ALEX SINCLAIR
collection cover artists

SUPERMAN created by **JERRY SIEGEL** and **JOE SHUSTER**
By special arrangement with the Jerry Siegel family
MAXWELL LORD created by **J.M. DEMATTEIS** and **KEITH GIFFEN**
AMANDA WALLER created by **JOHN OSTRANDER** and **JOHN BYRNE**

JUSTICE LEAGUE VS. SUICIDE SQUAD

DC Comics, 2900 West Alameda Ave., Burbank, CA 91505
Printed by LSC Communications, Salem, VA, USA. 5/19/17. First Printing.
ISBN: 978-1-4012-7226-5

Library of Congress Cataloging-in-Publication Data is available.

CURRENT TEMPERATURE... COLDER THAN YOU'D EXPECT.

IT'S... SNOWING? HERE?

THANK GOD. I WAS GONNA PASS OUT IN THIS STUPID SUIT. IT'S LOUISIANA, FOR GOD'S SAKE!

THAT STUPID SUIT MAY JUST KEEP YOU **ALIVE**, SOLDIER. SO STOW THE CHATTER AND WEAPONS READY.

YES, **COLONEL FLAG**.

NEW ARRIVAL, BOYS AND GIRLS.
LET'S SEE IF WE CAN BEAT LAST MONTH'S FATALITIES RECORD, SHALL WE?
ONE THING MY DADDY ALWAYS SAID ABOUT *PEOPLE*.
EVERYONE HAS A WARM HEART, BABY. SOME JUST KEEP IT BURIED DOWN DEEP, IS ALL.

OKAY. FIRST DAY IN PRISON. SO, WHAT DO YOU DO?
YOU DON'T ALLOW FEAR. YOU THINK ABOUT IT SURGICALLY AND WITH A SCIENTIST'S METHODOLOGY. YOU THINK ABOUT IT COLDLY.
YOU WILL ENCOUNTER NOTHING BUT PREDATORS. MONSTERS. SO, QUICKLY IDENTIFY THE DEADLIEST ALPHA...
AND LIVE UP TO YOUR DAMN NAME...
JAILERS OF BELLE REVE, MEET DR. CAITLIN SNOW.
A.K.A. KILLER FROST.
A HEAT VAMPIRE. HIGHLY DANGEROUS. SHE WILL SUCK THE LIFE RIGHT OUTTA YOU, STORE IT AND THEN TRANSMUTE IT INTO ICE PROJECTION. RAZOR-SHARP ICE PROJECTION. THE TYPE THAT SEVERS ARTERIES...
WOW, A GREETING LIKE THIS COULD GIVE A GIRL AN EGO, YOU KNOW.

JUSTICE LEAGUE VS. SUICIDE SQUAD

PRELUDE:

Warm Heart

ROB WILLIAMS: writer
GIUSEPPE CAMUNCOLI: layouts
FRANCESCO MATTINA: finished art
HI-FI: colorist
JOSH REED: letterer
BRIAN CUNNINGHAM: group editor
HARVEY RICHARDS: associate editor
ANDY KHOURI: editor

AH, NOW THAT'S NOT FAIR. THOSE SUITS YOU'RE WEARING ARE INSULATING YOUR HEAT REGISTERS. SO I CAN'T...ENJOY YOU.
ARE YOU TRYING TO STOP ME FROM GETTING HUNGRY?

BECAUSE I'M ALWAYS HUNGRY.
THAT'S IT, CAITLIN. KEEP UP THAT COCKY PATTER.

THE SUITS'LL COME OFF SOON, DR. FROST...
COOL LIKE A CRYOGENIC FONZ ON THE SURFACE.

...WHEN WE HAVE YOU UNDER CONTROL.
ALL THAT FEAR BUBBLING BENEATH.

DOWN DEEP WHERE NO ONE CAN FIND IT.
WELCOME TO YOUR NEW HOME.
YEAH, I READ YOUR FILE. YOU WERE A BIGSHOT SCIENTIST FOR S.T.A.R. LABS WORKING ON AN ADVANCED THERMODYNAMIC ENGINE IN THE ARCTIC.
WOW.
SOME FEAT OF ENGINEERING.
YOUR BASE WAS ATTACKED BY H.I.V.E. AGENTS. THEY TRIED TO KILL YOU WHILE YOU WERE STILL INSIDE THE ENGINE.
TO TRY AND SURVIVE, YOU--
HOTWIRED THE COOLANT SYSTEM.
I MERGED WITH IT. SAVED MY LIFE. CHANGED MY LIFE.
AND HOW DO YOU KNOW ALL THIS ABOUT ME, MR....?
COLONEL RICK FLAG. TASK FORCE X TEAM LEADER. AND THIS IS MY SECOND-IN-COMMAND--
KATANA.
SEVER.
HEAD.

DR. FROST, AS OF NOW YOU ARE RECRUITED INTO TASK FORCE X.
A COVERT METAHUMAN PARAMILITARY TEAM THAT UNDERGOES DISAVOWED MISSIONS ON BEHALF OF THE UNITED STATES GOVERNMENT.
INMATE
IS THAT DEADSHOT? HIS HEART IS...
...COLD.
THESE INDIVIDUALS WILL BE YOUR TEAMMATES IN THE FIELD.
THAT'S HARLEY QUINN. SHE'S OUR WILD CARD.
HEY, FLAG, WHY ARE ALL YOU GUYS ON THE CEILING?
KILLER CROC. MUSCLE.
HMMM...ONE MAN'S INTIMIDATION IS ANOTHER GIRL'S HOT MEAL, COLONEL FLAG. TELL ME...
WHEN ARE YOU GOING TO SHOW ME THE REAL MONSTERS?
I'M HUNGRY.
OH, THEY'RE COMING.
TRUST ME.

CASE IN POINT-- THIS IS JUNE MOONE. JUST AN ORDINARY, UNASSUMING GRAPHIC DESIGNER...
HER HEART'S BLACK...?
...WHO IS POSSESSED BY--AND SOMETIMES TRANSFORMS INTO... GENTLEMEN, HIT JUNE WITH A 40 PERCENT BRAIN JOLT, PLEASE...
WHO DARES SUMMON FORTH THE BIBLE-BLACK EPHEMERAL ENERGIES OF THE ENCHANTRESS?!
SHE ALLITERATES. YOU GET THE PICTURE.
OI! OI! CAN'T A BLOKE GET A BIT OF PRIVACY WHEN HE'S DUNNYING?
OHMYGOD.
BOOMERANG. AUSTRALIAN.
THAT'S CAPTAIN BOOMERANG TO YOU! SHOW SOME RESPECT!
AND THIS IS EL DIABLO. HE'S--
--BEAUTIFUL.

Y'KNOW, FLAG, I'LL LEVEL WITH YOU. ON THE CHOPPER IN, I WAS GENUINELY A LITTLE SCARED. BUT NOW THAT I'VE MET THEM ALL...
I SHOULDN'T HAVE BEEN.

FROST...
FFFTTTT
... I COULDN'T CARE LESS IF YOU'RE TERRIFIED OR FEEL RIGHT AT HOME...

...YOU WILL FOLLOW MY ORDERS IN THE FIELD.
YOUR DESTINATION...
THAT DOOR...THE ROOM BEHIND THAT DOOR... IT'S...

...IT'S THE COLDEST PLACE IN HERE.
DON'T ALLOW FEAR.

YOU WILL ENCOUNTER NOTHING BUT PREDATORS.
MONSTERS...

DR. SNOW. WELCOME.

MY NAME IS AMANDA WALLER AND TASK FORCE X IS UNDER MY CONTROL.
I'D LIKE TO OFFER YOU A DEAL. JOIN OUR OPERATION AND YEARS WILL BE TAKEN OFF YOUR SENTENCE. YOU COULD EVEN GET OUT OF HERE WITH A CLEAN SLATE.
IF YOU AGREE, I WILL INSERT A BOMB INTO YOUR BRAIN. THIS WILL ENSURE YOU CANNOT ESCAPE, AND THAT YOU WILL FOLLOW MY AND COLONEL FLAG'S ORDERS.
SO, CRIMINAL...
...DO YOU WANT TO JOIN THE SUICIDE SQUAD?
MY DADDY ALWAYS SAID EVERYONE HAS A WARM HEART, SOME JUST KEEP IT BURIED DEEP DOWN.
...
...MY DADDY WAS WRONG.

FABOK
·2016·

FABOK
·2016·

Death Valley, California.
"Power does not corrupt. Fear corrupts...perhaps the fear of a loss of power." --John Steinbeck
THUNK
GOOD MORNING, GENTLEMEN.
AUTHORIZED PERSONNEL ONLY, SIR.
SIR! YOU NEED TO STOP RIGHT THERE.
WE'RE UNDER STRICT ORDERS TO CALL IN ANY--
THAT WON'T BE NECESSARY.
YOU'D BOTH RATHER KILL EACH OTHER INSTEAD.

BANGBANGBANG
BANG BANG
THANK YOU.
THE CATACOMBS. THE MOST TOP SECRET PRISON IN THE WORLD...
...CONSTRUCTED TO HOLD ONLY A HANDFUL OF DANGEROUS CONVICTS.

W-WHAT ARE YOU DOING HERE?
RELEASE THE PRISONERS, DOCTOR.
YOU DON'T KNOW WHAT WE WENT THROUGH TO GET THEM CONTAINED!
DO YOU UNDERSTAND WHAT THEY ARE?
THEY DON'T BELONG IN THIS WORLD!
I KNOW.
NOW... LET THEM OUT.

WHY WOULD YOU DO THIS?
BEEP
OPEN
DOOR LOCK

BECAUSE I BELIEVE IN SECOND CHANCES.

FFSSSHHH
FFFSSSSHHH

DON'T LET THEM ESCAPE!
SOMETIMES I FEEL LIKE THE END OF THE WORLD HAS ALREADY COME AND GONE...

SLASHH
BUT I STILL HAVE *HOPE*...

...THAT I CAN INSPIRE US TO DO *BETTER.*
AAHHH!!!

ALL I NEED ARE *BRAVE SOULS* WILLING TO TAKE ON THE WEIGHT OF THE *WORLD*...

UK--

IT HURTS...

...WILLING TO PUT THEIR VERY *LIVES* ON THE LINE TO SAVE OTHERS.

SPLAT

OH GOD...

RIPPP

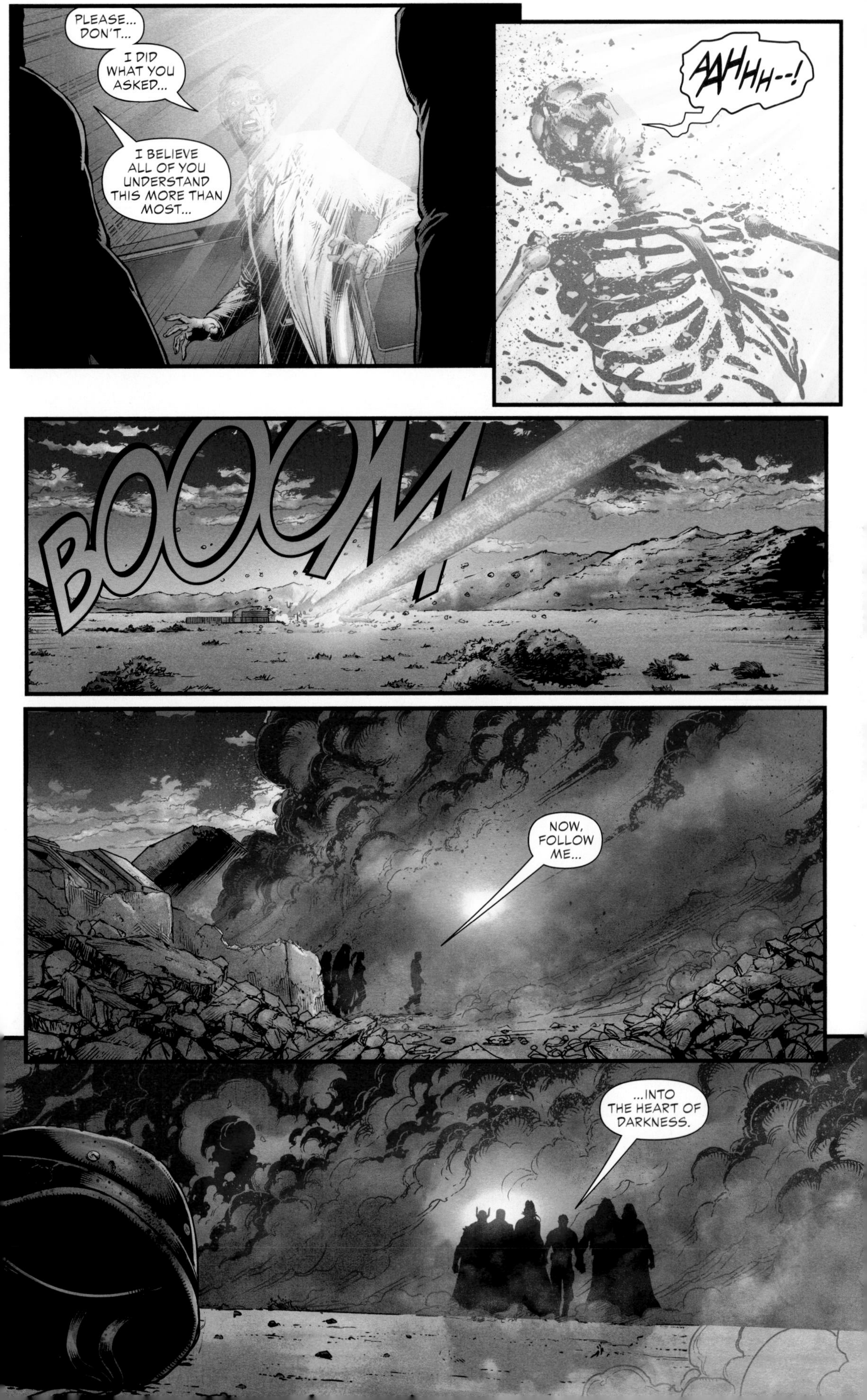

PLEASE... DON'T...

I DID WHAT YOU ASKED...

I BELIEVE ALL OF YOU UNDERSTAND THIS MORE THAN MOST...

AAHHH--!

NOW, FOLLOW ME...

...INTO THE HEART OF DARKNESS.

JOSHUA WILLIAMSON Writer JASON FABOK Artist
ALEX SINCLAIR Colorist ROB LEIGH Letterer

JASON FABOK AND ALEX SINCLAIR Cover
AMEDEO TURTURRO Assistant Editor
JESSICA CHEN AND HARVEY RICHARDS Associate Editors
ANDY KHOURI Consulting Editor BRIAN CUNNINGHAM Editor

Badhnisia.
WHAT A LOVELY DAY TO DIE!

"WHAT THE
HELL, WALLER?!
"YOU SENT THE SUICIDE
SQUAD ON A MISSION
WITHOUT ME?!"

Belle Reve Penitentiary, Louisiana.
WHAT HAPPENED TO NEEDING ME TO KEEP YOUR INMATES IN LINE?
SHORT NOTICE, FLAG. I MADE AN EXECUTIVE DECISION.
CAITLIN SNOW IS WITH THEM? SHE'S TOO INEXPERIENCED--

"KILLER FROST IS A SURVIVOR, FLAG.
"SHE MIGHT NEED TO FEED ON THE LIFE FORCE OF THE LIVING, BUT HER FREEZING POWERS FELT...SUITED TO THIS MISSION."

WHICH IS?

TWO HOURS AGO, A DEATH CULT CALLED THE BRIMSTONE BROTHERHOOD STOLE A QUAKE PULSAR FROM S.T.A.R. LABS.

"THE BROTHERHOOD PLANS TO USE THE PULSAR TO CAUSE AN EARTHQUAKE THAT WILL DESTROY THE SMALL ISLAND OF BADHNISIA."

THEY'RE LED BY A MAN NAMED APEX, WHO PLANS TO USE THE ISLAND'S DESTRUCTION AS A RITUAL SACRIFICE TO THEIR GOD.
THE SQUAD NEEDS TO RETRIEVE THE QUAKE PULSAR FROM APEX BEFORE HE ACTIVATES IT.
WHY DO WE CARE ABOUT A STUPID ISLAND IN THE MIDDLE OF NOWHERE ANYWAY, WALLER?
THE UNITED STATES HAS A SECRET OUTPOST THERE AND AN EARTHQUAKE COULD DRAW ATTENTION TO IT.
KILLER CROC. BRAWLER. BREATH LIKE BAD SUSHI.
THE EARTH WILL SHAKE AND TAKE THE SOULS OF MANY.
DEADSHOT. EXPERT MARKSMAN. HAS A DEATH WISH.
SQUAD! KEEP THE BROTHERHOOD DISTRACTED WHILE I GET A SHOT AT APEX HIMSELF!
ENCHANTRESS. WITCH. SCARY.
I'M HEADING OUT THERE! THEY'RE GONNA NEED A PICKUP WHETHER THEY SUCCEED OR FAIL...
DO ALL YOUR MISSIONS GO THIS BADLY?!
SHUNK
YOUR FIRST TIME IS ALWAYS A BIT OF A ROUGH RIDE, ICE PRINCESS...

...BUT YOU CAN TRUST OL' DIGGER TO SHOW YA A GOOD TIME, LUV.
CAPTAIN BOOMERANG. ASSASSIN. THEY'RE NOT TOYS.

I'M SURE.
GIVING ME THE COLD SHOULDER, eh? THAT'S A'RIGHT...
...I'VE NEVER MINDED A GIRL WHO WAS ICY TO THE TOUCH.
KILLER FROST'S TOUCH COULD KILL YOU.
Eh...ALWAYS FIGURED I'D DIE BY A WOMAN'S HAND.
EL DIABLO. PYROKINETIC. MARTYR COMPLEX.

YA SICK, DIGGER!
YOU SHOULD SEE SOMEONE!
HARLEY QUINN. YOU KNOW WHO SHE IS.
THAT YER PROFESSIONAL OPINION, DOC?!
I'LL LIE DOWN ON YER COUCH ANYTIME.

FROSTY, BABY... STICK WITH ME AN' YOU'LL MAKE IT OUT OF THIS IN ONE PIECE!
PROBABLY.
WHAT IF WE JUST TOLD WALLER WE QUIT?

THEN SHE'D MAKE YER NOGGIN GO KABLOOEY!
WAIT--WALLER WAS SERIOUS ABOUT THAT?!
HAVING A BOMB INJECTED INTO YER NECK HAS A WAY OF CHANGING YER P.O.V., DON'T IT?
NOW LET'S FIND THIS DAMN QUAKE PULSAR BEFORE APEX TURNS IT ON.
HOW WILL WE KNOW IF HE DOES?
...BECAUSE IT WILL BE YOUR LAST ACT ON THIS EARTH.
YOUR SOULS WILL BE A GIFT TO OUR GOD!
CALL IT WOMEN'S INTUITION.
THIS REMINDS ME OF THE TIME MISTAH J SPIKED THE ARKHAM GUARDS' DINNERS WITH JOKER VENOM AND THEY STARTED A MOSH PIT IN THE MESS HALL.
THAT WAS A FUN THANKSGIVING.
I HOPE YOU ENJOYED KILLING MY BROTHERS TODAY...
"RECENTLY, I'VE BEEN BUILDING A FILE ON A TOP SECRET GOVERNMENT SANCTIONED PROGRAM CALLED...TASK FORCE X."

INCARCERATED CRIMINALS ARE GIVEN A REDUCED SENTENCE IF THEY COMPLETE A SERIES OF DANGEROUS MISSIONS...HENCE THE NICKNAME...
THE SUICIDE SQUAD.
THIS PROGRAM IS MADE UP OF OUR ENEMIES.
BATMAN. DARK KNIGHT DETECTIVE.
I'VE NOTICED A FEW TEAM-UPS AMONG THEM BEFORE, BATMAN... BUT I BELIEVED IT WAS JUST HONOR AMONG THIEVES.
THAT'S WHAT THEY WANT US TO THINK, AQUAMAN.
IF THE SUICIDE SQUAD WERE CAUGHT, IT WOULD JUST BE CHALKED UP TO ANOTHER CRIMINAL ACT.
SUPERMAN. MAN OF STEEL.
AND NO ONE WOULD QUESTION IT?
GREEN LANTERN. SIMON BAZ.
THEY'D HAVE PLAUSIBLE DENIABILITY...
CORRECT.
AQUAMAN. KING OF ATLANTIS.
IF I DISCOVERED BLACK MANTA WAS A PART OF SOMETHING LIKE THIS...
RIGHT?
HOW CAN WE ENSURE ANY KIND OF JUSTICE IF CRIMINALS ARE BEING GIVEN A HALL PASS?
FLASH. FASTEST MAN ALIVE.
WHO'S BEHIND THIS?

AMANDA WALLER. A HIGH-RANKING GOVERNMENT BUREAUCRAT.
I RECENTLY WORKED WITH HER ON A MISSION TO SANTA PRISCA AND SAW FIRSTHAND HOW DESTRUCTIVE THIS GROUP CAN BE.*
WALLER USED THE OPPORTUNITY TO BREAK INTO THE BATCAVE WHILE I WAS GONE TO INVESTIGATE EXACTLY HOW MUCH I KNEW ABOUT HER AND TASK FORCE X.
WALLER USED ME. JUST LIKE SHE USES THE SQUAD.
*SEE BATMAN VOL. 2: I AM SUICIDE.
THESE CRIMINALS SHOULD HAVE A CHANCE TO BE REHABILITATED...THEY SHOULD...BUT THIS IS NOT THE RIGHT WAY.
HOW MANY TIMES HAVE WE STOPPED A VILLAIN NOT KNOWING THEY WERE SECRETLY WORKING FOR AMANDA WALLER?
GOOD QUESTION, FLASH.
WAIT...THESE ARE BAD GUYS, RIGHT? WHY WOULD THEY EVER SIGN UP TO WORK FOR THE GOVERNMENT? WHY DON'T THEY JUST ESCAPE?
GREEN LANTERN. JESSICA CRUZ.
CYBORG. HALF-MAN, HALF-MACHINE.
WONDER WOMAN. AMAZON PRINCESS.
PERHAPS WALLER IS CONTROLLING THEM?
SHE THINKS SHE CAN CONTROL THEM, BUT SHE'S GOING TO BE ON THE WRONG SIDE OF--
BATMAN?
I'VE BEEN MONITORING THE WATCHTOWER'S DATABASE OF KNOWN INCARCERATED CONVICTS AND CHECKED FOR ANY SIGHTINGS OF TWO OR MORE TOGETHER IN THE SAME LOCATION...
...AND YOU WON'T BELIEVE WHAT I JUST FOUND IN BADHNISIA...
"IT IS AN HONOR THAT YOU DIE IN OUR GOD'S NAME."

THIS DEVICE WILL ENSURE IT!
VVRRRMMMMM
ALLOW ME TO SHOW YOU A TRUE GOD TO WORSHIP.
RISE FROM THE DARK--
VVRRMMMMM
HEY, WALLER... WE MIGHT HAVE A BIT OF A PICKLE HERE!
FINISH IT, HARLEY. OR I FINISH YOU.
I HAVE NO QUALMS DYING AS PAR OF THIS SACRIFICE!
YOU WANT US TO BURN THIS PSYCHO, WALLER?
I'LL MAKE HIM BURN.
THAT'S THE SPIRIT, DIABLO.

RUMMBLE
RUMBLE

EVERY TIME APEX USES THE PULSAR, IT RAMPS UP THE SEISMIC ACTIVITY.
I DON'T THINK THIS ISLAND CAN TAKE MUCH MORE.
LEAST YOU DIE WITH OL' DIGGER BY YOUR SIDE, LUV.

THE OCEAN WILL BE OUR GRAVE--

BANG

DONE.
YOU SHOULD JUST SEND ME SOLO, WALLER.

HEY, I STEPPED IN APEX'S BRAINS...THAT MEANS I HELPED, RIGHT?
BLOODY HELL. DEADSHOT'S ALWAYS STEALING ME GLORY.

WE GOT LUCKY. THOSE EARTHQUAKES WERE NO JOKE.
Ehhhh, WHAT'S A FEW TREMORS?

KRRKT
TSHH
DIOS MIO...
IT'S COMING DOWN--THERE'S PEOPLE INSIDE...
KR-KRNK-AK
THIS ISN'T GOOD.
ENCHANTRESS! USE YOUR MAGIC!
SHE'S STILL OUT!
WAKE HER UP!
MAYBE WALLER WILL STILL SEE THIS AS A WIN-LOSS...?
I DON'T CARE ABOUT WALLER... HOW ARE WE GOING TO SETTLE THIS WITH OUR OWN SOULS?

$#&%!
CAN'T JUMP THAT...
BEEN ON BORROWED TIME FOR A WHILE ANYWAY.
NO MORE BULLETS LEFT TO FIRE, BABY GIRL...
SEE YOU IN HELL, AMANDA WALLER.

NOT TODAY, DEADSHOT.

BUILDING IS SECURE!
WE GOT THE PEOPLE ON THE GROUND!
IT'S GOING TO BE OKAY...
YOU'RE SAFE NOW.
WHAT THE HELL IS THE JUSTICE LEAGUE DOING HERE?
CLEANING UP OUR MESS, CROC.
YOU DROPPED THIS.
THANKS. NOW IF YOU'LL EXCUSE US--
TASK FORCE X IS **OVER,** DEADSHOT.

IT WOULD BE IN YOUR BEST INTERESTS...
...TO COME ALONG WILLINGLY.

HARD PASS, BATS.

THIS ISN'T A CONVERSATION, HARLEY.
BUT THIS IS A MISUNDERSTANDING, BATMAN.

IT'S REALLY NOT, LAWTON.
WE KNOW YOU'RE WORKING FOR AMANDA WALLER.
THAT SHE SENT YOU ON THIS DISASTER.
WHAT IF WE HADN'T BEEN HERE TO STOP THAT BUILDING FROM COLLAPSING?

SLOW YOUR ROLL, BATMAN.
THE EARTHQUAKE AIN'T ON US.

ARE WE REALLY ABOUT TO DO THIS?
AW, DON'T WORRY ABOUT THESE PARTY POOPERS.
WHATCHA GONNA DO...
LOCK US UP?

WALLER IS USING YOU.
WE CAN HELP YOU GET AWAY FROM HER. SOMEPLACE SAFE.

I GOT A SHOT.
YOU CRAZY?

ISN'T THIS A LITTLE ONE-SIDED?
THAT DUDE JUST HAS BOOMERANGS.

DON'T UNDERESTIMATE CAPTAIN BOOMERANG. HE'S A KILLER.
YEAH, BUT AREN'T BOOMERANGS A LITTLE LAME?

YOU DID NOT JUST BLOODY--

THE HEAT IS ON, WALLER.
WHAT DO YOU WANT US TO DO HERE?
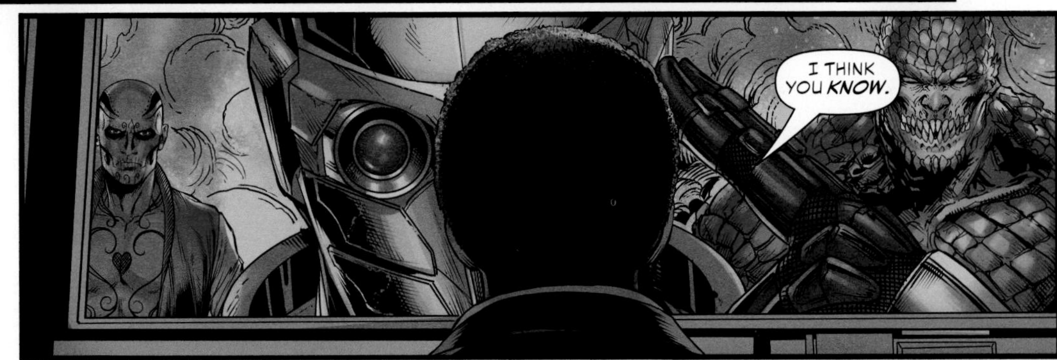
I THINK YOU KNOW.

I WANT TO HEAR YOU SAY IT.

DO NOT LET THE JUSTICE LEAGUE TAKE YOU ALIVE.
OR YOU'RE DEAD.
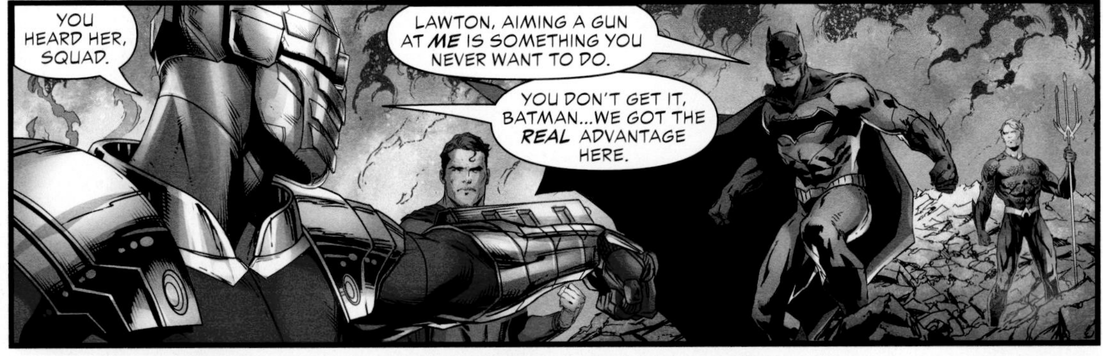
YOU HEARD HER, SQUAD.
LAWTON, AIMING A GUN AT ME IS SOMETHING YOU NEVER WANT TO DO.
YOU DON'T GET IT, BATMAN...WE GOT THE REAL ADVANTAGE HERE.
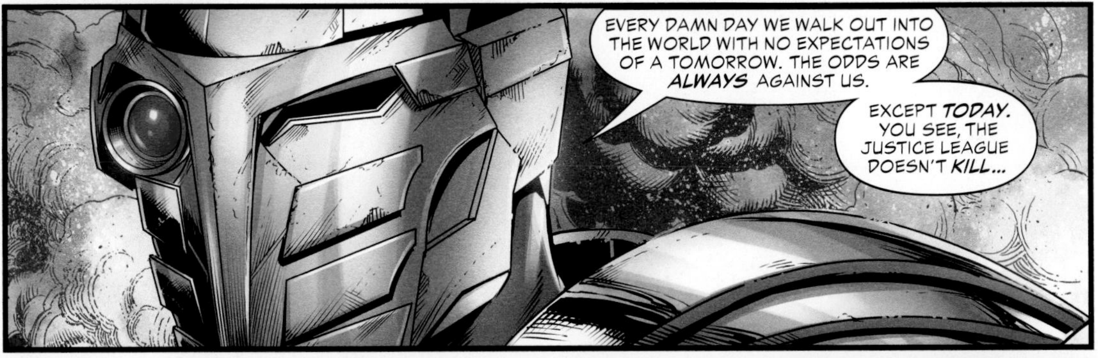
EVERY DAMN DAY WE WALK OUT INTO THE WORLD WITH NO EXPECTATIONS OF A TOMORROW. THE ODDS ARE ALWAYS AGAINST US.
EXCEPT TODAY. YOU SEE, THE JUSTICE LEAGUE DOESN'T KILL...

...BUT WE DO!

"IT TOOK ME A LONG
TIME TO FIND YOU."

The Swiss Alps.
"I LOVE THIS WORLD...
"...BUT SOMETHING HAS HAPPENED...
"...THERE HAS BEEN A CHANGE.
IT SEEMS LIKE I'M THE ONLY ONE WHO CAN SEE THAT HUMANITY IS BROKEN.
AND THE PEOPLE WITH THE POWERS TO FIX IT DON'T KNOW HOW.

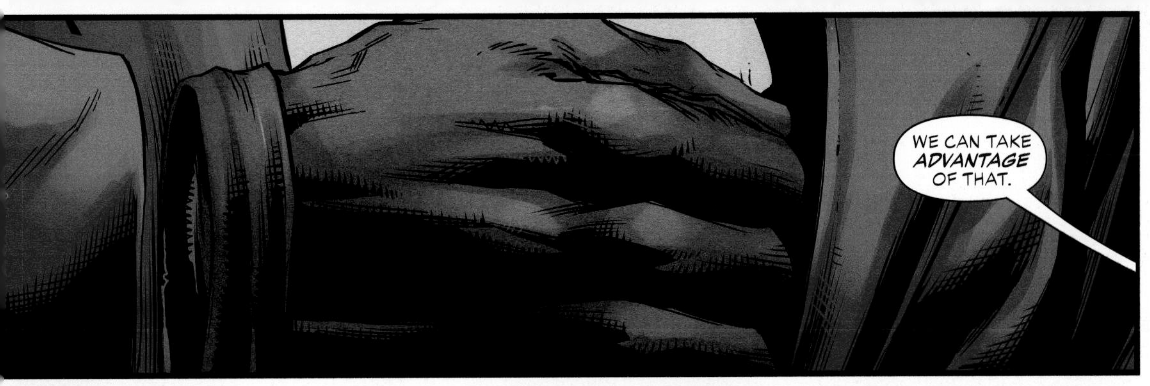
WE CAN TAKE ADVANTAGE OF THAT.
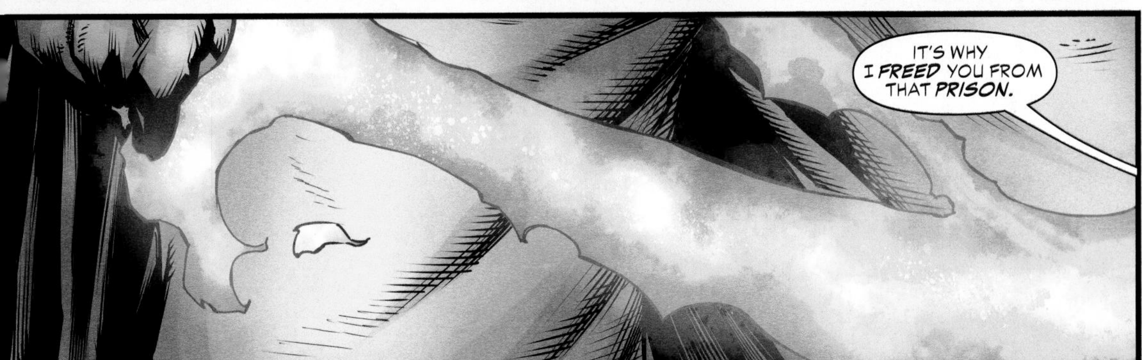
IT'S WHY I FREED YOU FROM THAT PRISON.
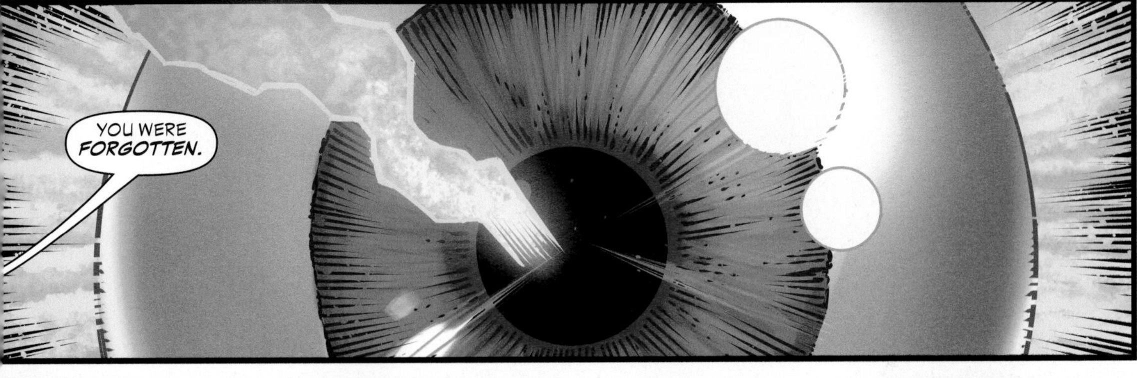
YOU WERE FORGOTTEN.
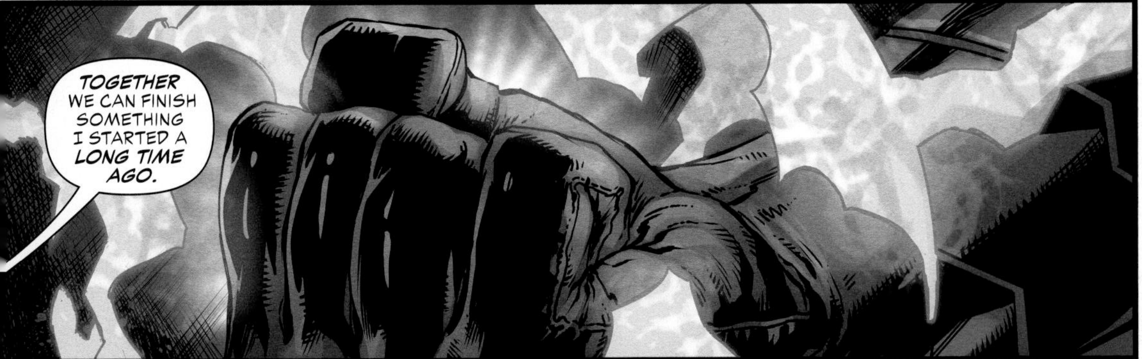
TOGETHER WE CAN FINISH SOMETHING I STARTED A LONG TIME AGO.
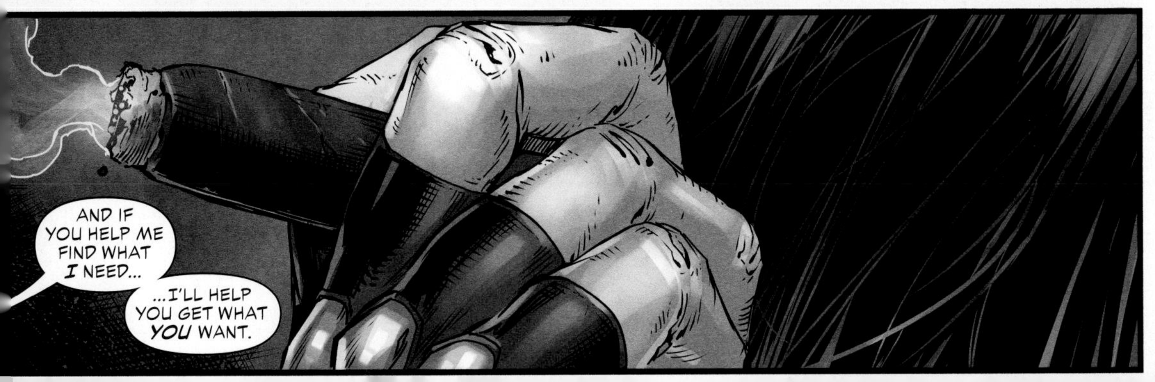
AND IF YOU HELP ME FIND WHAT I NEED...
...I'LL HELP YOU GET WHAT YOU WANT.

ALL OF YOU.
I'LL HELP YOU KILL AMANDA WALLER.
DOCTOR POLARIS
EMERALD EMPRESS
LOBO

JOHNNY SORROW
RUSTAM
SAY WE DO ALL THAT...

...WHAT'S IN IT FOR YOU?
ME?
I'M GOING TO SAVE THE WORLD.
MAXWELL LORD

TONY
AND
MORALES
-2016-

SUICIDE SQUAD!
YOU WILL DO AS I SAY!

Belle Reve Penitentiary.
OR I'LL BLOW THOSE BOMBS IN YOUR BRAINS!
HOW FAR OUT IS COLONEL FLAG?
TEN MINUTES FROM THE ISLAND, MA'AM.
TELL HIM HE HAS FIVE.

HEY, WALLER...

Badhnisia.

...I KNOW I'M ***NEW*** TO THE SUICIDE SQUAD, BUT...

...YOU'RE ***JOKING*** ABOUT TAKING DOWN THE LEAGUE, RIGHT?

YOU HAVE A ***Ph.D.,*** KILLER FROST. I THOUGHT THIS WOULD BE ***EASY*** FOR YOU TO FOLLOW.

FLAG IS ON HIS WAY TO EXTRACT YOU NOW.

BUT IF THE SUICIDE SQUAD IS CAPTURED BY THE JUSTICE LEAGUE BEFORE THEN...

WE GO ***BOOM.***

GOT IT.

BUT IT'S GOING TO BE HARD TO GET AWAY...

"...SINCE WE'RE STUCK ON A DAMN ISLAND!"
CAN'T MIND YOUR OWN DAMN BUSINESS, CAN YOU, BATMAN?
YOU'RE GOING TO A REAL JAIL, KILLER CROC. NO MORE SECRET MISSIONS!
I'D RATHER DIE FIGHTING!
BIFF
THE SQUAD HAS DONE A LOT OF GOOD THINGS THAT YOU HAVE NO CLUE ABOU--
UNH!!
IT WON'T BRING BACK ALL THE LIVES YOU'VE TAKEN! YOU'RE A KILLER, LAWTON.
AND YOU'LL NEVER BE MORE THAN THAT.
ALONE, YOU'RE DANGEROUS.
TOGETHER, THE SQUAD IS EVEN WORSE!
FFT
FFT
FFT

BAM BANG
BATMAN'S GIVEN ME AN IDEA!
SUICIDE SQUAD!
BANG
SCATTER!
YOU TELLING US TO RUN FROM A FIGHT, DEADSHOT?
NEVER, EL DIABLO! WE DON'T HAVE A CHANCE IN HELL FIGHTING THE JUSTICE LEAGUE WHEN THEY'RE TOGETHER...
...WE'RE NOT SPLITTING US UP...
...WE'RE SPLITTING THEM UP!
"I KNOW THERE ARE THINGS THAT YOU WANT..."

Swiss Alps.
...YOUR OWN PERSONAL GOALS.
AND YOU'RE FREE TO GO AND ACCOMPLISH THEM.
HOWEVER, I SUGGEST THAT TOGETHER, WE COULD HELP EACH OTHER.
SO THAT YOU MAY SAVE THIS WORLD, MAXWELL LORD?
WHY WOULD WE WANT TO DO THAT?
EVER SINCE THE KING OF TEARS GIFTED ME WITH A NEW LIFE, I'VE HAD A CONNECTION TO MULTIPLE DIMENSIONS... AND THIS ONE HAS BEEN MANIPULATED...
JOHNNY SORROW IS CORRECT... THE EMERALD EYE OF EKRON FEELS LIKE TIME IS MISSING.
I MUST FIND THE LEGIONNAIRE.
I PROMISE YOU, EMERALD EMPRESS, I CAN HELP WITH YOUR SEARCH.
I KNOW THINGS.
THEN ANSWER THIS, MAXIE...

...HOW DO WE KNOW YA AIN'T USING YER LITTLE MIND-CONTROL GARBAGE ON US?
I WOULDN'T DARE DO THAT TO YOU, LOBO.
YA DAMN SKIPPY.
YOU TRY THAT ON THE MAIN MAN AND YOU'RE A DEAD BASTICH.
JUST HEAR ME OUT. PLEASE.
IF YOU DON'T LIKE WHAT I HAVE TO SAY...
WE'VE BEEN DOWN A PATH LIKE THIS BEFORE, LORD...
...WHAT MAKES YOU ANY DIFFERENT?

WE ALL HAVE ONE THING IN COMMON, RUSTAM.
HATE.
IF YOU HELP ME GET WHAT I WANT, YOU GET THE ADDED BONUS OF REVENGE ON THE PERSON YOU HATE THE MOST...AMANDA WALLER.

MAX IS RIGHT.
SHE DESERVES TO PAY FOR WHAT SHE DID TO US.

I'M SO GLAD YOU SEE THIS MY WAY, DOCTOR POLARIS. YOUR CONTROL OVER METAL WILL BE ESPECIALLY USEFUL FOR WHAT WE HAVE TO DO...
LET'S SAY WE DID AGREE TO YOUR...TERMS. WHAT EXACTLY DO YOU HAVE IN STORE FOR US?
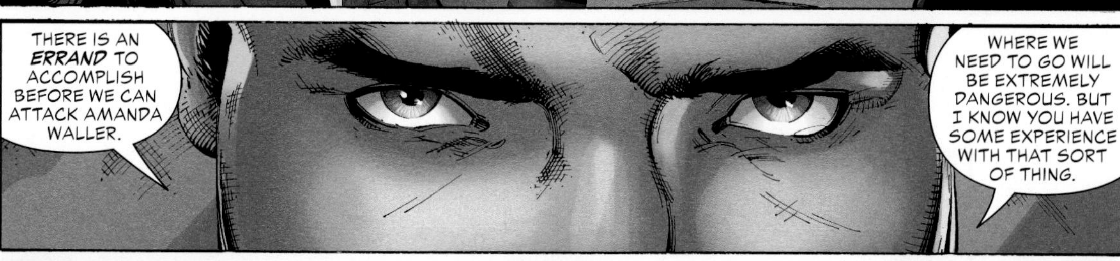
THERE IS AN ERRAND TO ACCOMPLISH BEFORE WE CAN ATTACK AMANDA WALLER.
WHERE WE NEED TO GO WILL BE EXTREMELY DANGEROUS. BUT I KNOW YOU HAVE SOME EXPERIENCE WITH THAT SORT OF THING.

WHAT ABOUT THE HEROES? THE JUSTICE LEAGUE?
THE JUSTICE LEAGUE AND I ARE OLD FRIENDS, AND I LOOK FORWARD TO THEIR EVENTUAL INVOLVEMENT...BUT RIGHT NOW, I BELIEVE THEY HAVE THEIR HANDS FULL.
"I KNOW WHO YOU ARE, ENCHANTRESS..."

...JUNE MOONE... A BRIGHT YOUNG DESIGNER POSSESSED BY AN EVIL WITCH. AND NOW YOU'RE A PAWN OF AMANDA WALLER'S.
YOU CAN FIGHT BACK, JUNE!
YOU...YOU'RE RIGHT. I CAN. THANK YOU, SUPERMAN.
WE CAN GET YOU HELP, JUNE...
CRETIN! YOU THINK I CARE ABOUT JUNE?
YOU WILL BURN AS JUNE MOONE'S SOUL DOES!
AHH!
SO THE MIGHTY HERO HAS A WEAKNESS...
MAGIC.
"I KNOW WHAT HAPPENED TO YOU WASN'T AN ACCIDENT, KILLER FROST."

YOUR ENGINEERING TEAM BETRAYED YOU AND TURNED ***CAITLIN SNOW*** INTO ***KILLER FROST.*** THEY'RE THE REASON YOU NEED TO FEED ON PEOPLE'S ***LIFE FORCE*** TO LIVE.
EVEN NOW, MY SCANNERS ETECT THAT YOU'VE USED UP ALL THE ENERGY YOU HAVE FIGHTING AGAINST US AND ARE GROWING WEAK.
H-HOW DO YOU KNOW SO MUCH ABOUT ME, CYBORG?
I JUST ACCESSED OUR ***A.R.G.U.S.**** FILES ONLINE. I EVEN READ YOUR COLLEGE ENTRY EXAM...
...A YOUNG WOMAN WHO WAS TOLD SHE'D NEVER E AN ENGINEER, WHO ANTED TO GIVE THE WORLD A BETTER FUTURE...
*ADVANCED RESEARCH GROUP UNITING SUPER-HUMANS
...YOU CAN STILL HAVE THAT.
WHAT IF I DON'T WANT THAT ANYMORE?!
RIGHT NOW YOUR ***MACHINE PARTS*** ARE WORKING IN OVERDRIVE TO SAVE YOUR VULNERABLE ***HUMAN*** SIDE...
AND THEY'RE LOSING!
S-STOP-P-P!
"MAN, THIS IS SOME B.S.!"

YOU TWO AIN'T GREEN LANTERNS!
I'M TRYING REAL HARD RIGHT NOW TO NOT BE *INSULTED*... BUT THEY SEND A PAIR OF NOBODIES AFTER US?
WHERE'S THE *RESPECT?*
WE MIGHT BE NEW TO THIS...BUT WE STILL KNOW HOW *FIRE* WORKS!
SUFFOCATE HIS FLAMES, JESSICA!
HOPE HE'S NOT CLAUSTROPHOBIC, SIMON. I'D BE FREAKING OUT RIGHT NOW IF I WERE HIM.
YOU MEAN THE GUY WHO CALLED US *NOBODIES?* HE'LL LIVE.
"YOU AND I GO WAY BACK, FLASHER."

I KNOW THERE'S NO POINT TRYING TO OUTRUN YOU AND YER RED PAJAMAS, MATE.
THE TRICK IS...

...TO MAKE YOU CHASE AFTER SOMETHING ELSE!

DAMMIT, BOOMERANG!

YOU JUST CAN'T HELP BUT SAVE LIVES, FLASH...
...EVEN WHEN IT PUTS YOU IN DANGER.

ARE THE ROGUES ANGRY THAT YOU'RE TWO-TIMING THEM WITH THE SUICIDE SQUAD?

OR DID THEY FINALLY REALIZE THAT YOU WERE THE WEAK LINK?

WE'VE GOT AN OPEN RELATIONSHIP, MATE.
NOW...C'MON, FLASH... I KNEW YOU'D CATCH MY DARLING THERE...TOSS 'ER BACK, WILL YA?

YOU'RE RIGHT... WE DO GO WAY BACK. AND I KNOW THE BEST WAY TO STOP YOU IS TO...
...TAKE AWAY YOUR TOYS.
SNAP

I SEE I WENT AND MADE YA UPSET...
...YA GOT ME. BUT SAVE ME THE INTERROGATION. I'LL TELL YOU WHATEVER YOU WANNA KNOW...
"YOU CAN'T OUTSWIM ME, CROC!"

AFTER WHAT YOU DID TO ME IN AMNESTY BAY, I STAY AS FAR AWAY FROM YOU AS I CAN, AQUAMAN!
AMNESTY BAY? HAVE WE MET BEFORE?
AND HERE I THOUGHT I HAD A FACE NO ONE COULD FORGET!
KRAK
MAYBE YOU'RE CONFUSING ME WITH ONE OF MY FRIENDS...
A GREAT WHITE?!
HEH. ALWAYS WONDERED HOW MY CLAWS WOULD MEASURE UP AGAINST "JAWS"!
RIPPP
NOOO!!
IT'S TOO THICK... TO SEE...

CHOMP
GAH!
RAGH!
YOUR SKIN--IT'S ROCK HARD!
SO'S MY FIST.
SPLOOSH
"YOU'RE A COWARD, DEADSHOT!"

IT'S NO SURPRISE YOU'VE NEVER STOOD UP TO WALLER.
YOU ALWAYS TAKE THE *EASY* WAY.
LIKE WHEN YOU KILLED A MAN IN FRONT OF YOUR OWN *DAUGHTER.*

TO *SAVE* HER!
IT'S A SHAME THAT SHE'LL ALWAYS KNOW YOU'RE NOTHING BUT A *HIRED GUN.*

YOU TALK PRETTY TOUGH FOR A GUY WHO PUSHES *CHILDREN* INTO BATTLE!

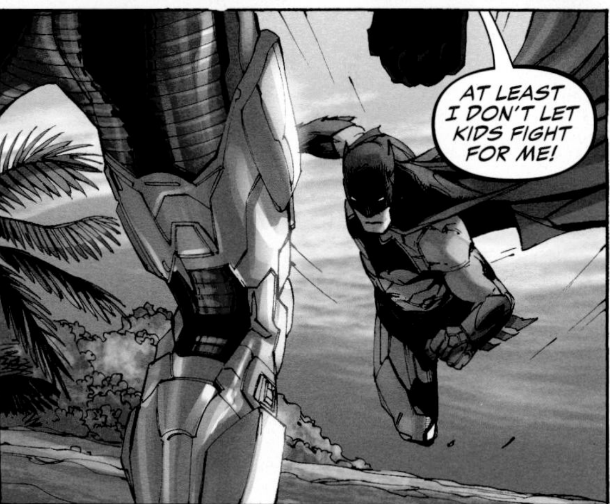
AT LEAST I DON'T LET KIDS FIGHT FOR ME!

WHAT DOES THAT SAY ABOUT *YOU?!*
BANG

≠HH≠
NO BULLETPROOF VEST IS THAT GOOD, BATMAN.
BANG
TRSH
TRSH
THE PAIN IS WORTH IT...
...TO MAKE SURE...
...THAT I STOP YOU FROM EVER ENDANGERING YOUR DAUGHTER AGAIN!
KRAK
"EXCUUUUSE ME!"

MOVE IT OR LOSE IT!
STOLEN MOTORCYCLE COMING THROUGH!

VVRROOOMM

CITIZENS OF BADHNISIA.

MAKE WAY.
WHOOOOSSHHH

WHAT GIVES, WONDER LADY?!

WHERE'S MY HUGS AND KISSES AT?!

LAST TIME WE SAW EACH OTHER I THOUGHT WE PINKIE-SWORE TO BE **B.F.F.s!**

I'M NOT FRIENDS WITH DERANGED CRIMINALS WHO **KILL PEOPLE!**

TNG

TNG

TNG

IS THIS BECAUSE BATMAN, SUPERMAN AND OL' HARLEY QUINN ARE THE NEW TRINITY?
OR IS THIS REALLY ABOUT HOW YOUR MAMA MADE YA FROM MUD?
TALK TO ME. TELL ME HOW YA FEEL.
THE GODS GAVE ME LIFE AND I'M THANKFUL EVERY DAY FOR IT. EVERY DAY SO I CAN--
THIS'LL PUT A SMILE ON YOUR MUG! DOCTOR'S ORDERS!
HARLEY, THE PEOPLE! THEY COULD BE--
EVERYONE GET BACK! RUN!
POOF
GODS... I WOULD RATHER FIGHT THE ERINYES OF HADES THAN TO MATCH WITS WITH...
...WHERE IS SHE?
HEY, WONDY WOMAN!

MADE YA LOOK!
KA-BOOM
Sigh...
BATMAN... I GOT HARLEY.
GOOD. THE SUICIDE SQUAD IS NEARLY IN OUR CUSTODY.

KILLER FROST AND KILLER CROC ARE STILL ON THE RUN!
HURRY!
GOING AS FAST AS I CAN! YOU TRY TAKING A PUNCH TO THE FACE BY--
FWASSH
KILLER FROST! THERE IS NO USE RUNNING!
BATMAN! CAPTAIN BOOMERANG TOLD ME THAT THEY'VE GOT WALLER TALKING IN THEIR EARS!
ALWAYS KNEW YOU'D BE THE FIRST TO BETRAY ME, DIGGER.
I WARNED YOU, SUICIDE SQUAD. I CAN'T HAVE YOU JEOPARDIZING EVERYTHING I'VE--
WAIT! WALLER, NO! DON'T!
THERE HAS TO BE SOMETHING I CAN--

BOOM
YOU WILL DIE BY MY HAND, MAN OF STEEL...
SUPERMAN...?
FROST! THIS IS YOUR LAST CHANCE!
SUPERMAN IS POWERED BY THE SUN.
ABSORB HIS LIFE FORCE!

BUT...
TAKE HIM!
TAKE HIM NOW!
I... I CAN FEEL IT!
HIS POWER...
...WOW.

I...DIDN'T KNOW...
...I COULD DO THAT.

UHHGASP!
WHERE...?
YOUR MIND MIGHT BE YOUR MOST DANGEROUS WEAPON, BATMAN, BUT IT'S NOTHING IF YOU DON'T HAVE ACCESS TO YOUR BODY.
SO I HAD THIS CELL MADE SPECIFICALLY FOR YOU.
JUST LIKE I DID FOR T REST OF YO FRIENDS.

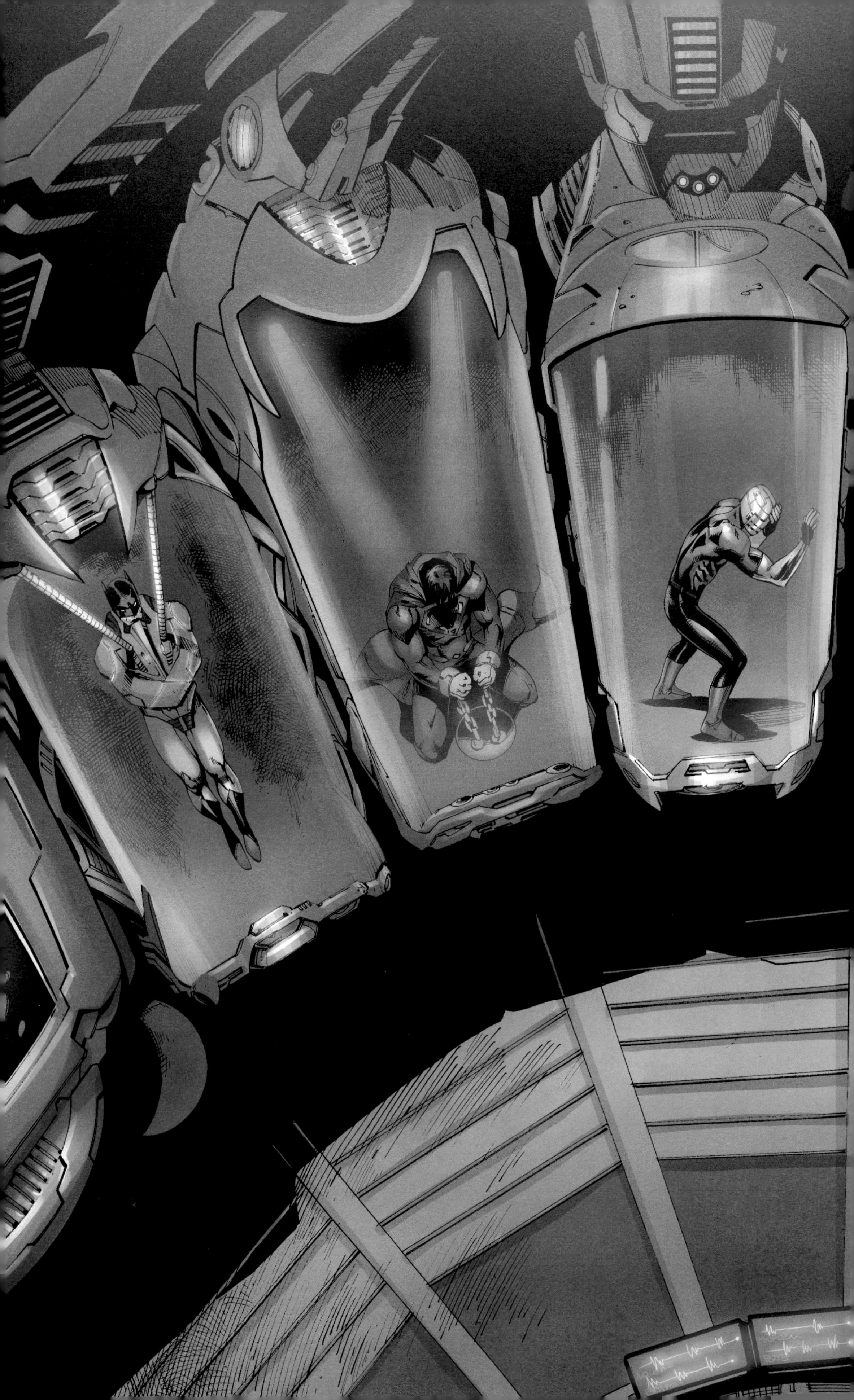

YOU'RE NOT THE *ONLY* ONE WHO PLANS FOR EVERY CONTINGENCY, BATMAN.
JUSTICE LEAGUE...

...WELCOME TO THE SUICIDE SQUAD.
JUSTICE LEAGUE VS. SUICIDE SQUAD
Chapter Two
JOSHUA WILLIAMSON Writer • TONY S. DANIEL Penciller • SANDU FLOREA Inker
ALEX SINCLAIR Colorist • ROB LEIGH Letterer • TONY S. DANIEL, MARK MORALES & ALEX SINCLAIR Cove
AMEDEO TURTURRO Asst. Editor • JESSICA CHEN & HARVEY RICHARDS Assoc. Editors
ANDY KHOURI Consulting Editor • BRIAN CUNNINGHAM Editor

TONY S. DANIEL 2016
S. FLOREA

2016
S. FLOREA

CICERO, ILLINOIS.
TASK FORCE X BLACK SITE.
PLEASE STATE YOUR NAME AND RANK FOR THE RECORD.
*THIS STORY IS SET BEFORE THE EVENTS OF JUSTICE LEAGUE VS. SUICIDE SQUAD.
MAXWELL LORD IV.
DIRECTOR AND BLACK KING OF THE U.N.'S PEACE-KEEPING OPERATION CHECKMATE.
MY HOBBIES INCLUDE GOLF AND COLLECTING CIGAR BANDS.
BUT YOU ALREADY KNEW THAT. IT'S YOUR JOB TO KNOW EVERYTHING...
...ISN'T IT, AMANDA?
YOU'LL REFER TO ME AS DIRECTOR WALLER. IT'S MY JOB TO PURSUE JUSTICE.
DO YOU KNOW WHY YOU'RE HERE, MR. LORD?
HM.
IT MUST BE ALL THOSE UNPAID PARKING TICKETS.

THREE DAYS AGO. SOUTHWEST KENTUCKY.
HAD I SEEN MY OL' PAL THE WALL, MAYBE WE COULD HAVE AVERTED BLOODSHED.
BUT YOU WERE HIDING BEHIND A BUNCH OF INTERNATIONALLY KNOWN AND WANTED SUPERCRIMINALS!
NEXT TIME YOU MIGHT WANT TO CONSIDER STANDING OUT IN FRONT, OR MAYBE HAVE YOUR CRONIES WEAR A SIMPLE PATCH ON THEIR SHOULDERS SAYING TASK FORCE DAMN X!

A MISTAKE? A MISTAKE?!
WHAT POSSIBLE REASON COULD CHECKMATE HAVE FOR ATTACKING ONE OF MY DAMN TRAINS?!
WE WERE ACTING ON VERY GOOD INTELLIGENCE THAT KOBRA CULTISTS WERE SEEKING TO COMMANDEER THIS PRISONER TRANSFER!
WAPOW
YOU WANT ME TO PUT ONE BEHIND HIS EAR OR--?
NO, DEADSHOT. SECURE HIM. I WANT MR. LORD TO LEARN THE CONSEQUENCES OF QUESTIONING MY CONTROL.

YOU GRAB MY ARM WHEN I'M A METER MAID, OR AFTER YOU BOTCH A PRISON TRANSFER, YOU GET THE SAME RESULT.
TOUCHY.
YOU HAVE AN IMPRESSIVE RÉSUMÉ. SINGLE REMAINING ROYALTY-RANKING MEMBER OF CHECKMATE. CO-HEAD OF THE CADMUS PROJECT, AND EXECUTIVE COMMISSIONER OF THE OMAC INITIATIVE.
BUT YOU'VE GOT SOME RED MARKS.
WHENEVER YOU WERE TASKED WITH WORKING WITH OTHER AGENCIES, CONFLICTS AROSE. YOU HAVE VERY POOR REVIEWS FROM THE HEADS OF BOTH S.H.A.D.E. AND SPYRAL.
YOU DON'T PLAY WELL WITH OTHERS. OR MAYBE IT'S THAT YOU HAVE AN ISSUE WITH AUTHORITY FIGURES AND FOLLOWING CHAIN OF COMMAND.
I THOUGHT THIS WAS AN INQUISITION, BUT THIS IS GETTING DANGEROUSLY CLOSE TO A PSYCH EVALUATION.
WOULD YOU LIKE ME TO TELL YOU ABOUT MY FATHER?

NO NEED. LIKE YOU SAID, I KNOW ALMOST EVERYTHING. BUT IN THE CASE OF YOUR FATHER, I DIDN'T HAVE TO DIG FAR.
ALBERT LORD.
ENTREPRENEUR AND SELF-MADE MAN. STARTED CHEMTECH PHARMACEUTICALS AND MADE MORE MONEY IN A WEEK THAN MY OL' MAN MADE IN A LIFETIME.
BUT THEN THERE WAS THAT BOMBSHELL REVELATION THAT ONE OF CHEMTECH'S WEIGHT-LOSS PILLS CAUSED CANCER.
CHEMTECH HEAD SUICIDE SHOCKS SHAREHOLDERS
CEO DEAD AFTER CANCER PROBE
I MEAN, I GUESS THAT IS ONE WAY TO LOSE WEIGHT.
POOR ALBERT. HE TOOK IT HARD.
THAT MUST HAVE EEN DIFFICULT FOR J AND YOUR FAMILY. ESPECIALLY YOUR MOTHER.
HM. THERE'S NOT MUCH ABOUT HER, THOUGH. SHE DROPPED OUT OF THE PUBLIC EYE.
IF THIS FEELS SO MUCH LIKE A PSYCH EVAL TO YOU, WE CAN ALWAYS GO ALL IN.
"PLEASE, MIZTER LORD. TELL ME ABOUT YOUR MOZZER."
NO.

MARBLEHEAD, MASSACHUSETTS. TWENTY-THREE YEARS AGO.
NO!
MRS. LORD! WERE YOU PERSONALLY AWARE OF THE INSUFFICIENT RESEARCH YOUR HUSBAND COMMISSIONED?
HOW WILL ALBERT'S DEATH AFFECT THE ONGOING LAWSUITS AGAINST CHEMTECH?
WHAT WILL YOU TELL MAXWELL?
VULTURES, ALL OF THEM.
MOM? DAD IS...DAD IS REALLY GONE.
WHAT'RE WE GOING TO DO NOW?
IT'S OKAY, MY SWEET BOY.
WHAT WE'RE GOING TO DO IS BURY YOUR FATHER. WE'RE GOING TO SHAKE HANDS AND SHED TEARS.
AND THEN THERE'LL BE NO MORE PAMPERING. NO MORE WEAKNESS. NO MORE HEADACHES AND BLOODY NOSES AND HEARING VOICES, MAX.
I NEED YOU TO FIND YOUR OWN *VOICE.*
BECAUSE YOU'RE GOING TO PROMISE ME TO NEVER BE ANYTHING LIKE YOUR COWARDLY, PATHETIC FATHER.

WHEN I MET YOUR FATHER I WAS ATTRACTED TO HIS DRIVE. HIS INTELLIGENCE. HIS COMPASSION.

HIS POWER.

BUT YOUR FATHER WASN'T WORTHY OF THAT POWER, MAX. HIS COMPASSION LET THE NEEDS OF THE FEW GET IN THE WAY OF THE NEEDS OF THE MANY. HE JUST COULDN'T DO WHAT HAD TO BE DONE.

I SHOULD HAVE RUN THE COMPANY. I COULD HAVE COVERED UP THE PILLS. I COULD HAVE SMUDGED THE REPORTS. BUT I COULDN'T TAKE AWAY WHAT ALBERT HAD.

I...I LOVED HIM.

PROMISE ME, MAX. YOU'LL NEVER LET COMPASSION OR AFFECTION GET IN THE WAY OF *NECESSITY.*
AND WHEN YOU FIND PEOPLE ***UNWORTHY OF POWER,*** YOU'LL ***PLUCK*** THEIR NFLUENCE AND CONTROL AWAY...

...UNTIL THERE'S ***NOTHING LEFT.***

WELL, THEN LET'S TALK ABOUT WORK. YOU ENTERED CHECKMATE OUT OF COLLEGE, TURNING DOWN LUCRATIVE OFFERS TO WORK IN THE PRIVATE SECTOR. ROSE FROM RANK OF PAWN TO KING'S KNIGHT IN A RECORD TEN YEARS.
YOU SERVED BLACK KING JASON CAMERON FOR THREE YEARS UNTIL--
AH, YES. POOR JASON.
HE DIED TO SAVE US ALL.
EIGHT YEARS AGO.
THE CASTLE. CHECKMATE OPERATIONS HEADQUARTERS.
WELL, ISN'T THIS LOVELY, MAX?
IT'S DOWN TO YOU AND ME NOW.
ON ONE SIDE WE'VE GOT AN ENCROACHING ARMY OF "BLOOD CULTISTS," WHOSE PREFERRED METHOD OF DEALING WITH CAPTURED ENEMY AGENTS IS TO SACRIFICE THEM PIECE BY PIECE TO A SIX-EYED FIEND NAMED TRIGON.
AND ON THE OTHER SIDE WE'VE GOT ALL OUR PRETTY LITTLE DIGITAL SECRETS, AND A TWO-HUNDRED-METER DROP THAT'LL PUT OUR HEADS QUITE LITERALLY UP OUR @%$.

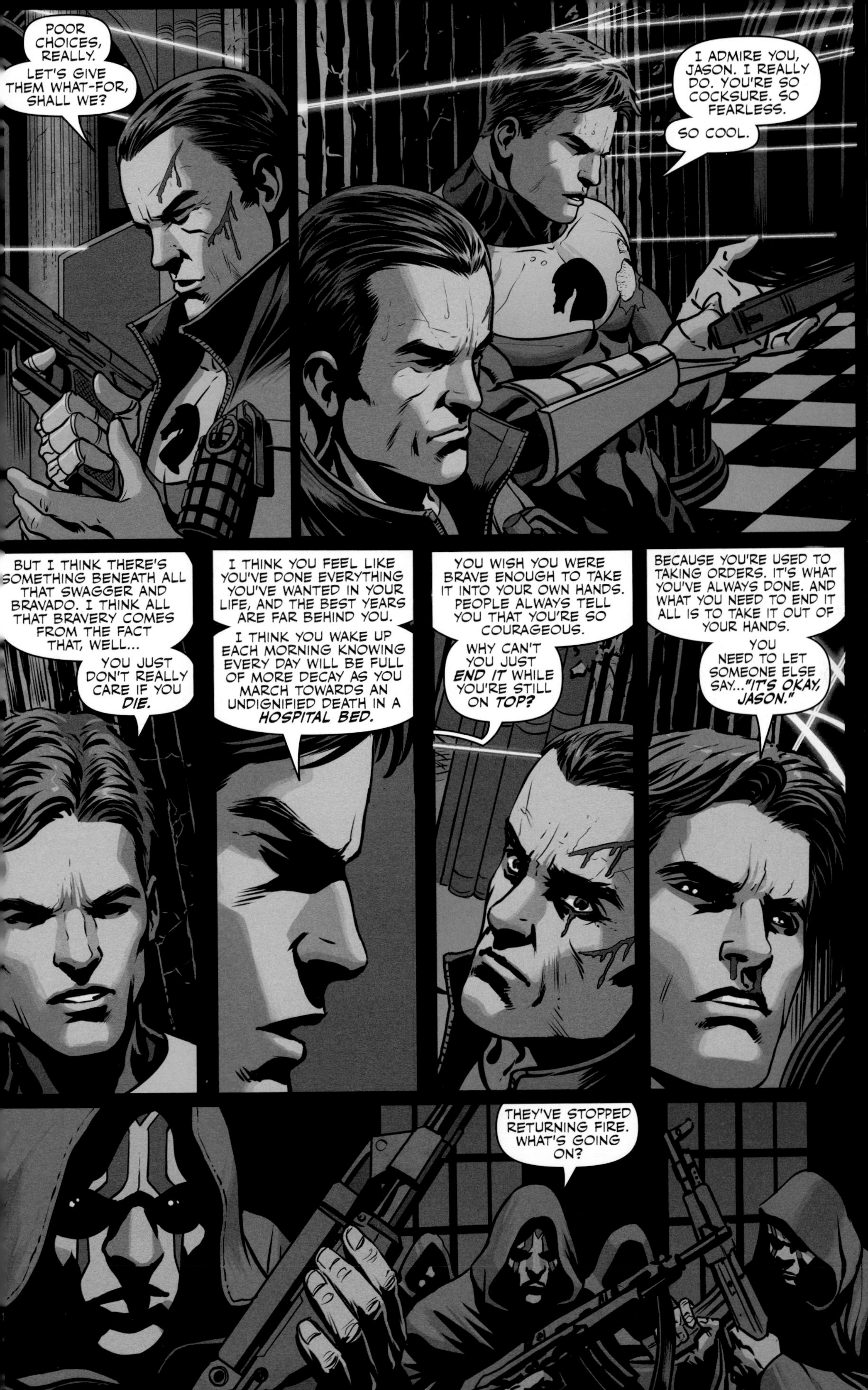
POOR CHOICES, REALLY.
LET'S GIVE THEM WHAT-FOR, SHALL WE?
I ADMIRE YOU, JASON. I REALLY DO. YOU'RE SO COCKSURE. SO FEARLESS.
SO COOL.
BUT I THINK THERE'S SOMETHING BENEATH ALL THAT SWAGGER AND BRAVADO. I THINK ALL THAT BRAVERY COMES FROM THE FACT THAT, WELL...
YOU JUST DON'T REALLY CARE IF YOU DIE.
I THINK YOU FEEL LIKE YOU'VE DONE EVERYTHING YOU'VE WANTED IN YOUR LIFE, AND THE BEST YEARS ARE FAR BEHIND YOU.
I THINK YOU WAKE UP EACH MORNING KNOWING EVERY DAY WILL BE FULL OF MORE DECAY AS YOU MARCH TOWARDS AN UNDIGNIFIED DEATH IN A HOSPITAL BED.
YOU WISH YOU WERE BRAVE ENOUGH TO TAKE IT INTO YOUR OWN HANDS. PEOPLE ALWAYS TELL YOU THAT YOU'RE SO COURAGEOUS.
WHY CAN'T YOU JUST END IT WHILE YOU'RE STILL ON TOP?
BECAUSE YOU'RE USED TO TAKING ORDERS. IT'S WHAT YOU'VE ALWAYS DONE. AND WHAT YOU NEED TO END IT ALL IS TO TAKE IT OUT OF YOUR HANDS.
YOU NEED TO LET SOMEONE ELSE SAY..."IT'S OKAY, JASON."
THEY'VE STOPPED RETURNING FIRE. WHAT'S GOING ON?

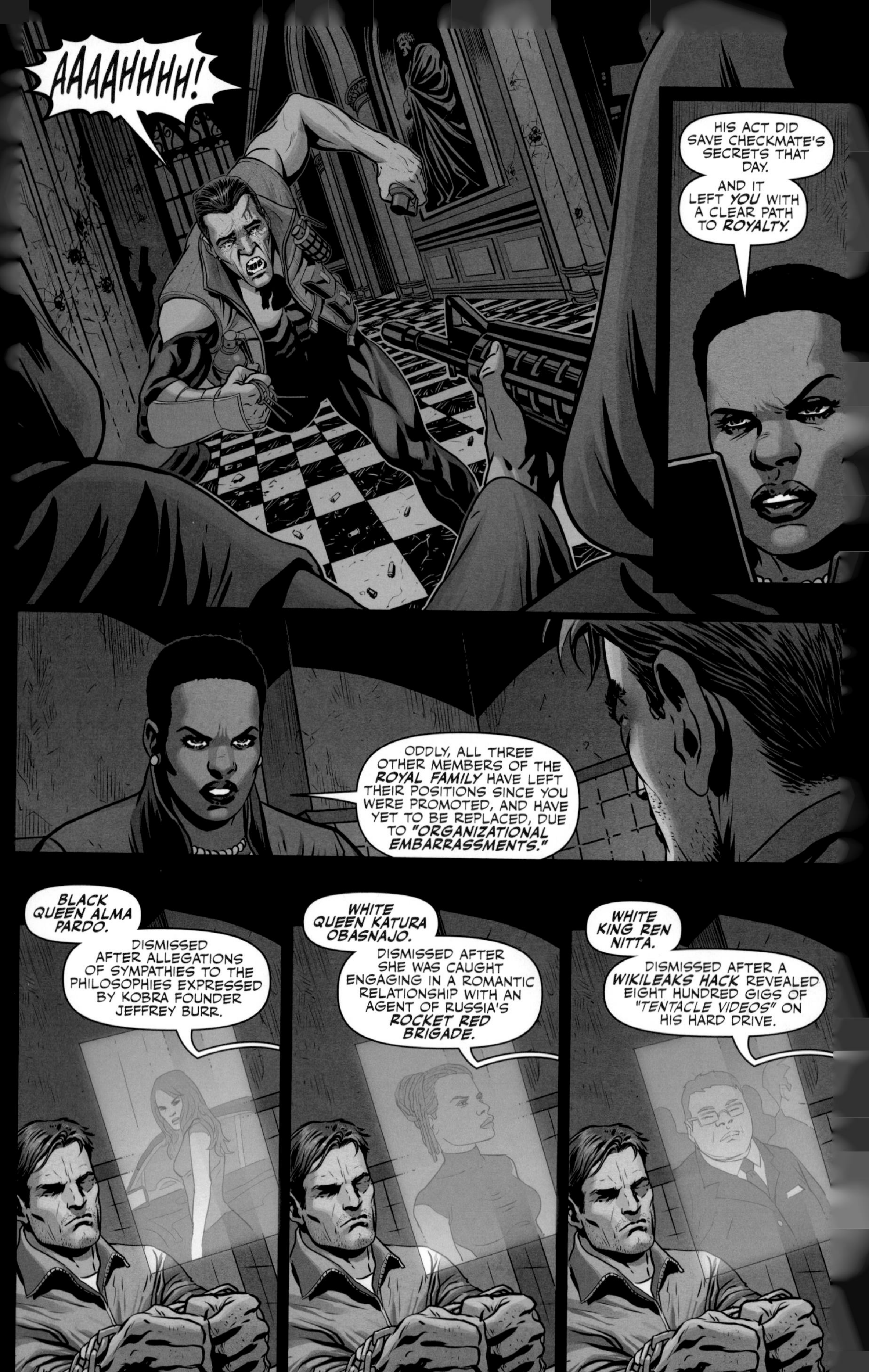
AAAAHHHH!
HIS ACT DID SAVE CHECKMATE'S SECRETS THAT DAY.
AND IT LEFT YOU WITH A CLEAR PATH TO ROYALTY.
ODDLY, ALL THREE OTHER MEMBERS OF THE ROYAL FAMILY HAVE LEFT THEIR POSITIONS SINCE YOU WERE PROMOTED, AND HAVE YET TO BE REPLACED, DUE TO "ORGANIZATIONAL EMBARRASSMENTS."
BLACK QUEEN ALMA PARDO.
DISMISSED AFTER ALLEGATIONS OF SYMPATHIES TO THE PHILOSOPHIES EXPRESSED BY KOBRA FOUNDER JEFFREY BURR.
WHITE QUEEN KATURA OBASNAJO.
DISMISSED AFTER SHE WAS CAUGHT ENGAGING IN A ROMANTIC RELATIONSHIP WITH AN AGENT OF RUSSIA'S ROCKET RED BRIGADE.
WHITE KING REN NITTA.
DISMISSED AFTER A WIKILEAKS HACK REVEALED EIGHT HUNDRED GIGS OF "TENTACLE VIDEOS" ON HIS HARD DRIVE.

REN DID ENJOY HIS MOLLUSKS.
IT'S A VERY HIGH-PRESSURE JOB, I'M SURE YOU UNDERSTAND. NOT EVERYONE IS CUT OUT FOR IT.

IT'S CLEAR YOU BELIEVED *YOU WERE.*
IN THE AFTERMATH OF THE INITIAL ATTACKS BY FORCES FROM THE PLANET APOKOLIPS, YOU LOBBIED FOR CHECKMATE'S CONTRACT AS A GLOBAL PEACEKEEPING UNIT WITH THE UNITED NATIONS TO BE EXPANDED...

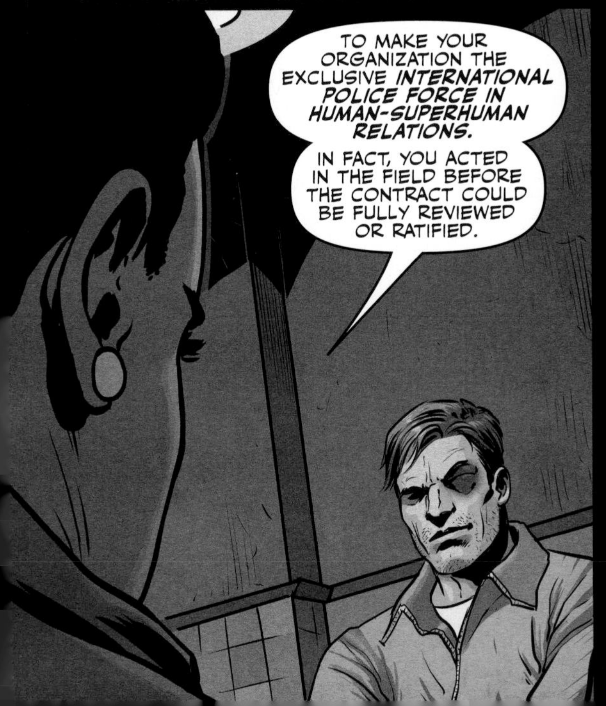
TO MAKE YOUR ORGANIZATION THE EXCLUSIVE *INTERNATIONAL POLICE FORCE IN HUMAN-SUPERHUMAN RELATIONS.*
IN FACT, YOU ACTED IN THE FIELD BEFORE THE CONTRACT COULD BE FULLY REVIEWED OR RATIFIED.

AW. MS. WALLER, ARE YOU FEELING WISTFUL FOR OUR FIRST MEETING?

METROPOLIS. YEARS AGO.
HUP HUP HUP HUP
THIS ISN'T LOOKING GOOD, TREVOR.
ALL WE HAVE TO DO IS HOLD OUT, WALLER. SHE'LL BE HERE. THEY'LL BE HERE!
SECURE THE PERIMETER!

AS OF THIS MOMENT, METROPOLIS BELONGS TO CHECKMATE.
ARE YOU THE COMMANDING OFFICERS IN CHARGE HERE?
CAPTAIN TREVOR. U.S. ARMY.
AMANDA WALLER. NONE OF YOUR DAMN BUSINESS.
WELL, AREN'T YOU A PEACH?
I'M TAKING OVER THIS OPERATION ON AUTHORITY OF THE UNITED NATIONS SECURITY COUNCIL, HONEY.
HONEY?!
AS COMMANDER OF THIS OPERATION, I WANT ALL FORCES TO ENGAGE ALL NON-HUMAN FORCES--DEMONS, SUPER-PEOPLES, WHATEVER.
I WANT THOSE SELF-APPOINTED GODS BROUGHT DOWN TO EARTH.
ARE YOU INSANE? THOSE SELF-APPOINTED GODS...

"...ARE THE ONLY ONES WHO CAN SAVE US."

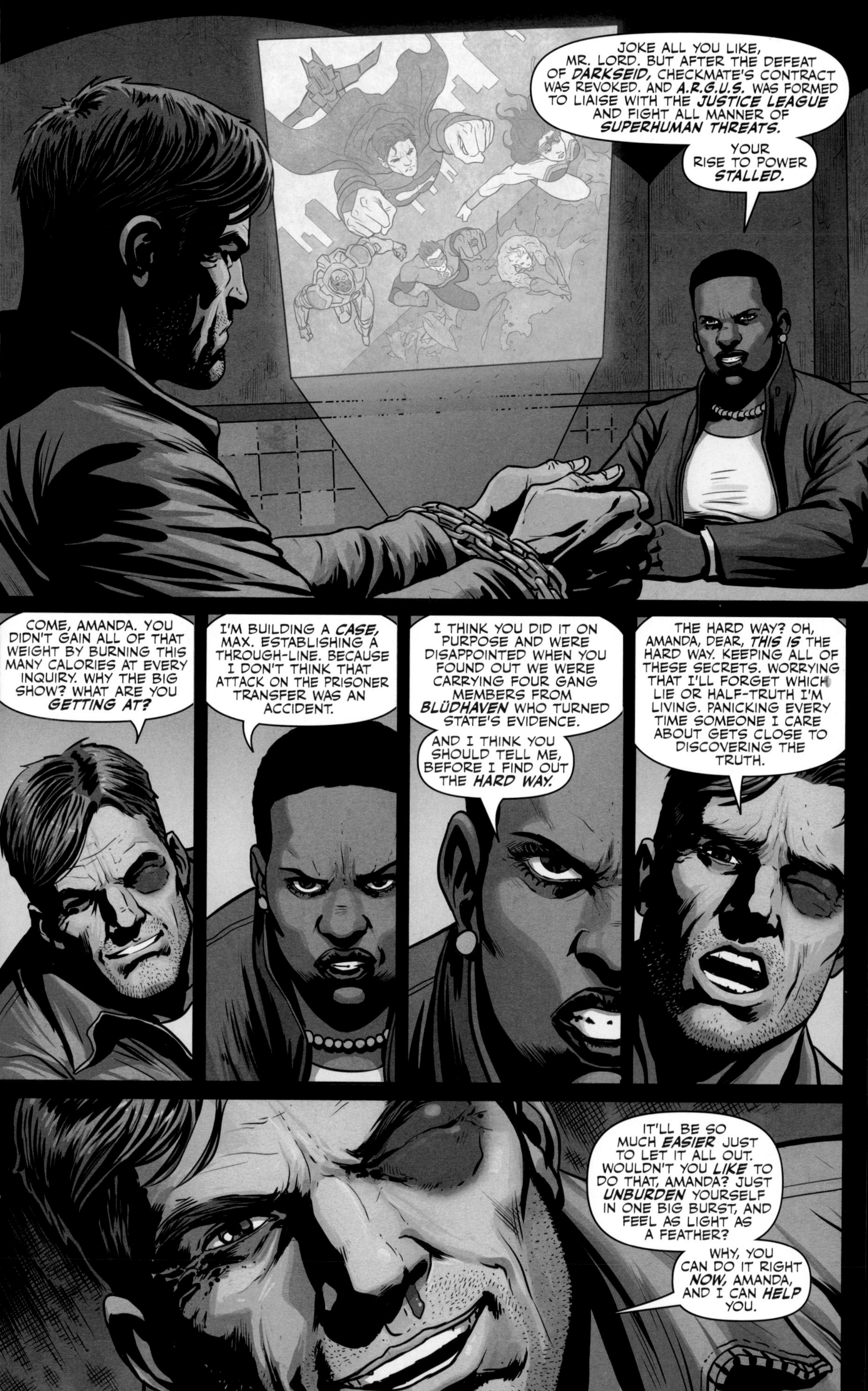
JOKE ALL YOU LIKE, MR. LORD. BUT AFTER THE DEFEAT OF DARKSEID, CHECKMATE'S CONTRACT WAS REVOKED. AND A.R.G.U.S. WAS FORMED TO LIAISE WITH THE JUSTICE LEAGUE AND FIGHT ALL MANNER OF SUPERHUMAN THREATS.
YOUR RISE TO POWER STALLED.
COME, AMANDA. YOU DIDN'T GAIN ALL OF THAT WEIGHT BY BURNING THIS MANY CALORIES AT EVERY INQUIRY. WHY THE BIG SHOW? WHAT ARE YOU GETTING AT?
I'M BUILDING A CASE, MAX. ESTABLISHING A THROUGH-LINE. BECAUSE I DON'T THINK THAT ATTACK ON THE PRISONER TRANSFER WAS AN ACCIDENT.
I THINK YOU DID IT ON PURPOSE AND WERE DISAPPOINTED WHEN YOU FOUND OUT WE WERE CARRYING FOUR GANG MEMBERS FROM BLÜDHAVEN WHO TURNED STATE'S EVIDENCE.
AND I THINK YOU SHOULD TELL ME, BEFORE I FIND OUT THE HARD WAY.
THE HARD WAY? OH, AMANDA, DEAR, THIS IS THE HARD WAY. KEEPING ALL OF THESE SECRETS. WORRYING THAT I'LL FORGET WHICH LIE OR HALF-TRUTH I'M LIVING. PANICKING EVERY TIME SOMEONE I CARE ABOUT GETS CLOSE TO DISCOVERING THE TRUTH.
IT'LL BE SO MUCH EASIER JUST TO LET IT ALL OUT. WOULDN'T YOU LIKE TO DO THAT, AMANDA? JUST UNBURDEN YOURSELF IN ONE BIG BURST, AND FEEL AS LIGHT AS A FEATHER?
WHY, YOU CAN DO IT RIGHT NOW, AMANDA, AND I CAN HELP YOU.

LET'S START WITH A EASY ONE...
WHERE ARE YOU KEEPING T SO-CALLED "LO PRISONERS"
CATACOMBS PRISON. DEATH VALLEY.
YOU SEE, I HAD TO GET YOU ALONE SO YOU COULD TELL ME THAT. WASN'T THAT A RELIEF? CONFESSING LIKE A CATHOLIC ON SUNDAY.
THERE'S ONE MORE THING, AMANDA, AND AFTER THAT, YOU'LL BE FREE TO FORGET THIS EVER HAPPENED.
TELL ME... IS THE ITEM STILL IN THE BOWELS OF BELLE REVE?
THE-- I-ITEM?
N--HNRGUK--

YOU SON OF A--I CAN FEEL YOU IN MY HEAD! YOU'RE SOME KIND OF TELEPATH!
HNH. SOME CALL IT THAT. SOME CALL "SUPERHUMANLY CHARMING."
GET HIM!
KRAK
HNGH. NOW BOYS, NO NEED TO WORK SO HARD. YOU HATE THIS JOB, DON'T YOU? IT'S SO BORING. YOU WANTED TO BE FIELD AGENTS. HEROES.
HNH. SHUT HIS MOUTH...
YOU JUST WANT TO GIVE ME YOUR GUNS, AND WALK OUT WITH ME.

MAKE A MOVE AND THEY DIE, AMANDA. ANYONE MAKES A MOVE UNTIL I'M WELL OUT OF HERE, AND THEY DIE.
I'M GOING TO *FIND* YOU, MAX. IT DOESN'T MATTER WHERE YOU RUN, I'M GOING TO FIND YOU, AND I'LL BE STANDING RIGHT OUT IN DAMN FRONT.
YOU BROKE AWAY FROM MY INFLUENCE, AMANDA. NO ONE HAS EVER DONE THAT BEFORE. NO ONE.
BUT FOR ONE GLORIOUS MOMENT, I GOT TO BE THE MAN WHO TOOK *CONTROL* FROM AMANDA WALLER.

OLD BURIAL HILL CEMETERY. MARBLEHEAD, MASSACHUSETTS. TWO DAYS LATER.

I'M SORRY IT'S BEEN SO LONG SINCE I VISITED.

I'VE BEEN...BUSY. I'VE BEEN USING ***MY VOICE*** TO MAKE SURE EVERY DOMINO IS FALLING INTO PLACE, DESPITE THE OPPOSITION IN FRONT OF ME.

THE LEADERSHIP OF CHECKMATE.

THOSE COMPASSIONATE AND WEAK-WILLED GODS, ***THE JUSTICE LEAGUE*** AND THEIR ILK.

THE SELFISH AND ARROGANT BUREAUCRATS LIKE AMANDA WALLER.

YOU SEE, MY VOICE ONLY MAKES PEOPLE DO WHAT THEY WANT TO DO ANYWAY. I CAN PUSH THEM, NOT TRULY CONTROL THEM. I'M *"PERMISSION,"* NOT *"MANDATE."*

BUT IT WON'T MATTER ONCE I HAVE THEM: ***THE LOST PRISONERS.***

THEY'LL GET ME WHERE MY VOICE CAN'T. THEY'LL BREAK DOWN THE DOORS, SO I CAN TAKE WHAT ONLY *I* SHOULD HAVE.

I PLUCKED THEM ALL FOR YOU, MOM.
AND SOON THE *ONE MAN* WHO'S TRULY WORTHY OF THE POWER...
WILL BE IN TOTAL AND ABSOLUTE *CONTROL.*
MAXINE LORD
Loving mother and Wife
ALBERT LORD
Loving father and Husband
MAX LORD: REBIRTH
TIM SEELEY WRITER / CHRISTIAN DUCE ARTIST
MAT LOPES COLORIST / RICHARD STARKINGS & COMICRAFT LETTERER
TONY S. DANIEL, SANDU FLOREA & TOMEU MOREY COVER / AMEDEO TURTURRO & DIEGO LOPEZ ASSISTANT EDITORS
ANDY KHOURI CONSULTING EDITOR / BRIAN CUNNINGHAM EDITOR

WHAT THE HELL WAS THIS PLACE?

IN ALL MY TIME IN THE MARINE CORPS AND WITH TASK FORCE X, I NEVER HEARD OF THE CATACOMBS.
HAVE YOU, KATANA?
NO...

CAN YOU SMELL THAT?
BLOOD. IN THE AIR...

THEN WHY'RE YOU PUTTING THE SOULTAKER AWAY?
WE DON'T KNOW WHAT'S--
CALM YOURSELF, RICK FLAG. MY BLADE WON'T BE NECESSARY...

...WE'RE THE ONLY SOULS HERE.

IT MUST HAVE BEEN A PRISON OF SOME KIND.
BUT ONE THAT ONLY HAS A HANDFUL OF CELLS.
WHY WOULD WE BUILD A PRISON FOR JUST A FEW PEOPLE?
THIS WAS ABOUT MORE THAN HOLDING THEM. THEY WERE HIDDEN...
WALLER TOLD US TO JUST RETRIEVE THE SECURITY BLACK BOX AND LEAVE...I'M NOT GOING TO PLAY DETECTIVE, KATANA.
SOLID STEEL... CUT WITH A VERY HOT BLADE...
WHEN DID YOU START FOLLOWING WALLER'S ORDERS WITHOUT QUESTION?
IN MY SHORT TIME WORKING WITH THE SUICIDE SQUAD, I'VE LEARNED WALLER EITHER GETS HER WAY...
...OR SHE LETS YOU GET YOURS.
ALL RIGHT... FOUND THE BLACK BOX.
LET'S GET THE HELL OUT OF HERE...
"...I'M SURE WALLER'S GOING TO NEED HELP WITH HER NEW GUESTS."
Belle Reve Penitentiary.

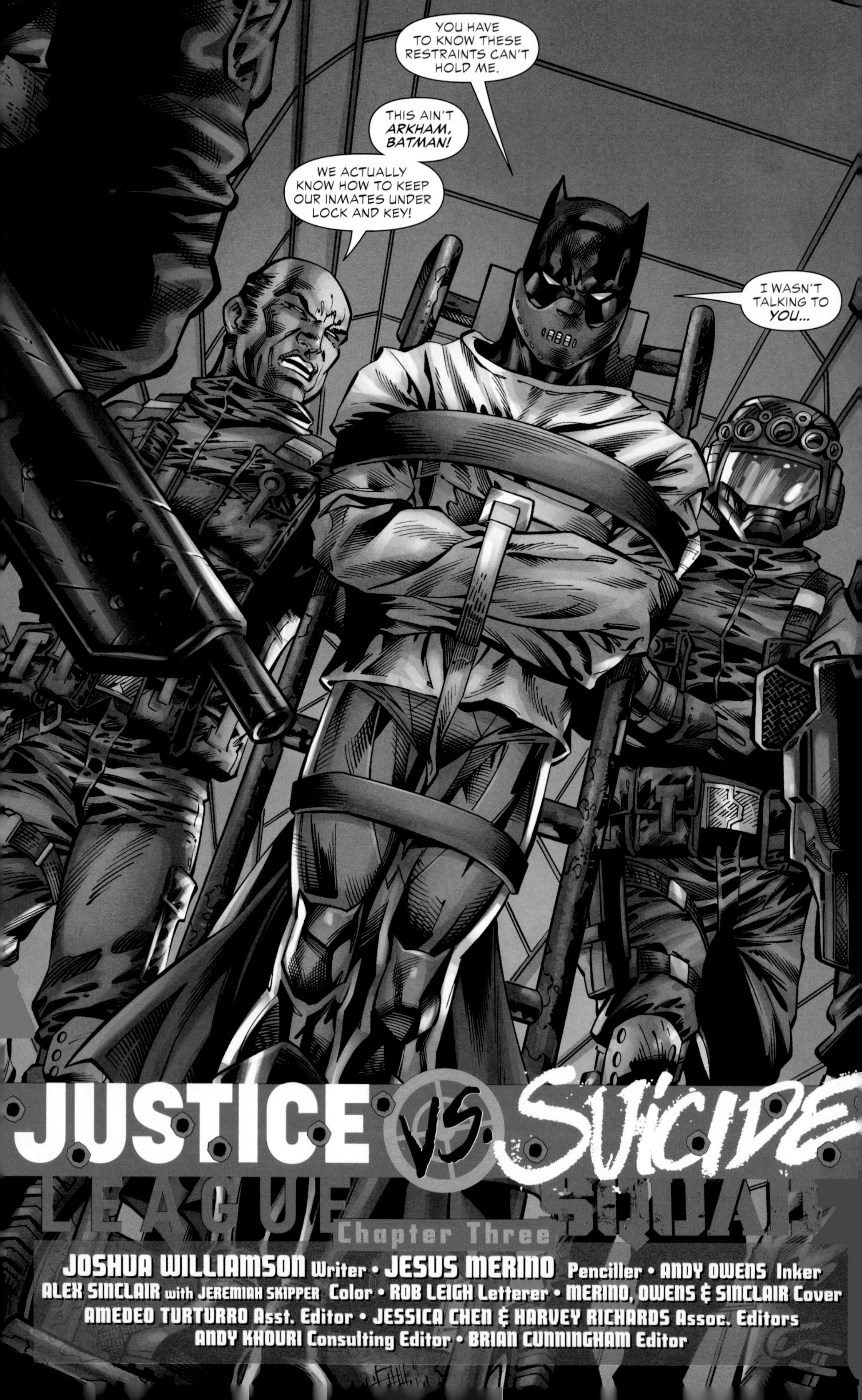
YOU HAVE TO KNOW THESE RESTRAINTS CAN'T HOLD ME.
THIS AIN'T ARKHAM, BATMAN!
WE ACTUALLY KNOW HOW TO KEEP OUR INMATES UNDER LOCK AND KEY!
I WASN'T TALKING TO YOU...
JUSTICE LEAGUE VS. SUICIDE SQUAD
Chapter Three
JOSHUA WILLIAMSON Writer • JESUS MERINO Penciller • ANDY OWENS Inker
ALEX SINCLAIR with JEREMIAH SKIPPER Color • ROB LEIGH Letterer • MERINO, OWENS & SINCLAIR Cover
AMEDEO TURTURRO Asst. Editor • JESSICA CHEN & HARVEY RICHARDS Assoc. Editors
ANDY KHOURI Consulting Editor • BRIAN CUNNINGHAM Editor

KLUNK
...I WAS TALKING TO YOUR BOSS!
TAKE HIM DOWN!
I KNOW YOUR MEN ARE JUST DOING THEIR JOBS...IF A BIT OVERZEALOUSLY.
I PROMISE TO NOT HURT THEM...
CAMERA-6
KRAKK
...MUCH.
STOP HIM--HE'S GONNA--
THUK
YOU ARE GOING TO ANSWER...
...TO ME...

...AMANDA WALLER!
TOOK YOU LONG ENOUGH, BATMAN.
I FIGURED YOU'D HAVE BROKEN FREE AT LEAST AN HOUR AGO.
RELEASE THE JUSTICE LEAGUE, WALLER!
CALM DOWN. YOUR TEAM IS SAFE.
WHY WERE YOUR MEN BRINGING ME TO THE INFIRMARY?
YOU SEE THIS? IT'S MY FAVORITE TOY.
IT INJECTS A SMALL EXPLOSIVE DEVICE INTO A PERSON'S BRAIN.
IT'S HOW I KEEP THE SQUAD IN LINE.
I COULD HAVE USED THIS ON YOU AND THE JUSTICE LEAGUE...
...BUT I DIDN'T.
ARE WE SUPPOSED TO BE GRATEFUL?
I HAD HOPED YOU'D VIEW THIS AS A SIGN OF TRUST... AN OLIVE BRANCH BETWEEN OUR TWO TEAMS.
LOCKING UP THE JUSTICE LEAGUE IS A HUGE RISK. YOU WOULDN'T MAKE A MOVE LIKE THAT UNLESS YOU WERE IN TROUBLE.
TELL ME THE TRUTH, WALLER...

..WHY ARE WE
EALLY HERE?"
ANYBODY
NOW HOW WE
GOT BACK TO
BELLE REVE?
LAST I REMEMBER, WE WERE GETTING OUR BUMS HANDED TO US BY THE JUSTICE LEAGUE, AND THEN BAM! I WOKE UP IN MY CELL FEELING A BIT SHORT IN ME KNICKERS...
I DID IT.
"I FROZE THE SUICIDE SQUAD AND THE JUSTICE LEAGUE TO STOP WALLER FROM BLOWING US UP."
SO... THE SUICIDE SQUAD BEAT THE JUSTICE LEAGUE?
NICE.
IF THAT'S SO, THEN...
...WHERE... ARE... THEY?
POP

Harley
4(0)-ever

I'LL BE DAMNED.
THE JUSTICE LEAGUE IN BELLE REVE.
CYBORG
FLASH

AWWW, IS THE BIG BAD BELLE REVE TOO MUCH FOR YOU?!

WELCOME TO OUR WONDERFUL WORLD OF INCARCERATION!

HEY, ROBO-HERO, I HEARD YOU HAVE THE POWER TO CLEAR MY FATHER'S RECORD. THAT TRUE?

TAP TAP

L-L-LET ME OUT, EL DIABLO... AND I'LL...SHOW YOU...

EVEN THOUGH YOU TRIED TO DO ME WRONG...

...I PROMISE I'LL WRITE YOU EVERY DAY, WONDER WOMAN.

WELL WELL WELL...

...IF ONLY THE OTHER ROGUES COULD SEE YOU NOW, *FLASHER.*
THIS IMAGE OF YOU LOCKED UP IS BEING FILED AWAY IN ME HEAD...

Y'KNOW, BOOMERANG...EVEN IN HERE...I CAN SMELL YOUR *BAD BREATH...*
YOU BLOODY...
I DON'T CARE IF YOU'RE BEHIND BARS-- I'M GONNA--

AHGAGAGAG!!

YOU...KNEW THAT WAS GOING TO HAPPEN... DIDN'T YOU?
I COULD FEEL THE ELECTROMAGNETIC PULSE IN THE GLASS. NOT ENOUGH TO KILL US, BUT WOULD GIVE US A SHOCK...SO... *YES, I DID.*

YOU LAUGHING AT US?
CALM DOWN...I DON'T THINK YOU WANT A ROUND TWO.
YA GOTTA ADMIT, CROC... IT *WAS* KINDA FUNNY SEEING DIGGER YELLIN' IN PAIN...
AHGAGAGAG!!
HA HA HA HA HA HAHAHA HA HA
KILLER... FROST...

WHY...DID YOU HESITATE...?
WHAT?
WHEN I WAS WEAK FROM MY FIGHT WITH ENCHANTRESS...
WHAT'RE YOU TALKING ABOUT? I DIDN'T...
BEFORE YOU TOUCHED ME TO DRAIN MY LIFE FORCE...
"...YOU PAUSED."
I COULD HEAR WALLER YELLING AT YOU IN YOUR HEAD... TELLING YOU THAT IF YOU DIDN'T ATTACK ME... SHE WOULD KILL YOU.
AND YET... YOU STILL HESITATED...
IT...WAS BECAUSE I REMEMBERED THE FIRST TIME I EVER SAW YOU...BEFORE I BECAME KILLER FROST.
I WAS IN METROPOLIS.
YOU WEREN'T FIGHTING ANYONE.

"YOU JUST FLEW OVER ME.
"IT WAS A REAL METROPOLIS MOMENT.

I WAS THERE FOR A SYMPOSIUM WITH A RESEARCH GROUP...
...A PROFESSOR ON THE TRIP WITH US HAD JUST TOLD ME HE DIDN'T THINK I HAD WHAT IT TOOK TO GAIN MY Ph.D.... THAT I'D NEVER MAKE IT.
I WAS ABOUT TO CALL IT QUITS AND GO HOME...BUT THEN I SAW YOU...AND I THOUGHT...

...IF A MAN COULD FLY... I COULD STAY IN COLLEGE.

I DIDN'T KNOW DRAINING YOUR LIFE FORCE WOULD AFFECT MY POWERS THE WAY IT DID...
BUT I'M... GLAD YOU SURVIVED.
SO IF THE NEXT TIME WE FIGHT YOU COME GUNNING FOR ME...I'LL UNDERSTAND.

KILLER...
CAITLIN... WAIT.

WHEN I FIRST REVEALED MYSELF TO THE WORLD, THERE WERE SOME WHO THOUGHT I WAS A DANGER...
...AND THERE WERE SOME WHO WANTED TO USE MY POWERS FOR THEMSELVES.
JUST AS WALLER USES THE SUICIDE SQUAD.
BUT AFTER I PROVED MYSELF, THE WORLD ACCEPTED ME, AND I BELIEVE YOU WANT TO BE MORE THAN WALLER'S PAWNS.
YOU'RE ALL CAPABLE OF BEING BETTER THAN--
CUT THE INSPIRATIONAL SPEECH, SUPERMAN.
THE WORLD DOESN'T CARE ABOUT US.
HELL, WALLER NEEDS US AND SHE DOESN'T GIVE A DAMN ABOUT US.
WE COULD DIE TOMORROW AND WALLER WOULD JUST PICK A WHOLE NEW GROUP OF PRISONERS. I'VE SEEN IT HAPPEN.
THE SQUAD ISN'T A TEAM.
WE'RE JUST THE ONES WHO KEEP ON SURVIVING...
IT'S JUST A MATTER OF TIME BEFORE SOMEONE BIGGER AND BADDER COMES ALONG AND PUNCHES OUR TICKET.
"THERE IS AN ISLAND IN THE SOUTH PACIFIC..."

"...AND ON IT RESIDES WHAT I NEED TO SAVE THE WORLD.
"BUT TOURISM IS HIGHLY DISCOURAGED.
"IT'S PROTECTED BY AN ARMY OF DEADLY SHAMANS WHO DON'T TAKE KINDLY TO VISITORS.
"THEY WILL PROTECT THE ISLAND'S SECRETS TO THE DEATH..."

MAX SAID THESE SHAMANS WERE GOING TO BE A *CHALLENGE*...
EMERALD EMPRESS
JOHNNY SORROW
IT WAS WORTH IT TO WARM UP MY SCIMITAR.
LOBO
RUSTAM
FFT
THE MAIN MAN DON'T FRAG NOBODY WITHOUT A GOOD REASON. OR A *CONTRACT.* SO MAX BETTER HURRY THE HELL UP WITH THAT HIGH PRIEST.
"HE CAN*NOT* BE UNLEASHED AGAIN...

...THE WORLD IS ALREADY CORRUPT ENOUGH...

EXACTLY.
THIS WORLD... IT'S REALLY GOING ALL TO HELL, ISN'T IT? IT'S MADNESS.
SOMEONE HAS TO PUT A STOP TO IT.
Unnh...

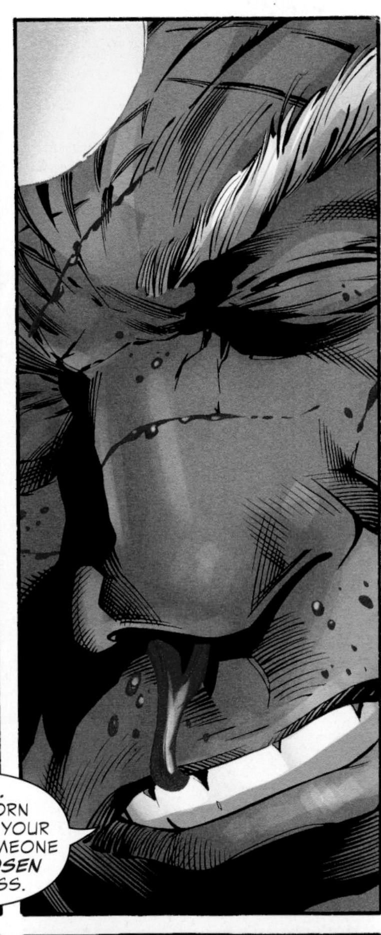
NOT YOU... YOU WERE BORN A MAN. BUT IN YOUR EYES I SEE SOMEONE WHO HAS CHOSEN THE DARKNESS.

YOU AND I BOTH KNOW HE'LL GET FREE AGAIN.
WOULDN'T IT BE BETTER IF THERE WERE SOMEONE WHO COULD CONTROL HIM?

YOUR POWERS ARE USELESS.
YOU MIGHT BE ABLE TO MANIPULATE A PACK OF WILD DOGS... BUT YOU ARE NOT POWERFUL ENOUGH TO CONTAIN HIM.

FINE... JUST GIVE ME WHAT I WANT... AND THEN FINALLY I'LL BE ABLE TO DO WHAT'S BEST FOR EVERYONE.
I PROMISE YOU, IF YOU HELP ME...

DOCTOR POLARIS

...I CAN MAKE THE *PAIN* GO AWAY.

I WILL *NEVER* HELP YOU, MAXWELL LORD.

IS THAT SO?
MAYBE YOU JUST NEED ANOTHER... *PUSH*.

AAAAAAAHHHHHHHHHH--*
CAN WE GO NOW?
IT TOOK SOME PERSUASION, BUT I WAS ABLE TO CONVINCE THE SHAMANS' HIGH PRIEST TO GIVE ME WHAT I WANTED.
WHAT ABOUT WHAT I WANT?
WHEN'RE WE GOING AFTER WALLER?!
I APPRECIATE YOUR...PATIENCE, LOBO.
BUT NO MORE WAITING. IT'S TIME...

"...FOR REVENGE."
THE JUSTICE LEAGUE DOESN'T BELONG HERE, DEADSHOT.
NOT WITH US.
THE JUSTICE LEAGUE SHOULDN'T BE ANOTHER OF WALLER'S TOOLS...THEY SHOULD BE IN THE WORLD SAVING LIVES AND BEING ON HAPPY MEALS.
BUT THE SUICIDE SQUAD... WE...
HAD YOUR SHOT.
EVERYONE IS CAPABLE OF GOOD AND EVIL.
AND THE SQUAD IS FAR PAST THE POINT OF REDEMPTION.
THE JUSTICE LEAGUE IS FREE TO GO.
FTTRRSSSSHHHH
BUT THERE IS SOMETHING YOU SHOULD ALL SEE.

THIS IS A BLOODY *JOKE.*

IF *I* WERE IN *YER* SHOES, I'D ALREADY BE IN SYDNEY WITH SOME HOT YOUNG BIRD IN *ONE* HAND AND A DRINK IN THE *OTHER.*

WE'RE NOT *YOU,* DIGGER.
IT CAN'T BE THIS *EASY,* BATMAN. WALLER JUST LETS US GO...?
BECAUSE WHILE THE JUSTICE LEAGUE WAS WASTING TIME HUNTING DOWN *MY* TEAM...

...THERE WAS A PRISON BREAK AT A TOP-SECRET LOCATION CALLED *THE CATACOMBS* AND A *REAL* DANGER WAS FREED INTO THE WORLD.
RICK FLAG AND KATANA HERE WERE ABLE TO RECOVER THE SECURITY FOOTAGE...

STOP THEM!
"EMERALD EMPRESS. WIELDS THE EMERALD EYE OF EKRON--A WEAPON CAPABLE OF IMMENSE MYSTIC ENERGY.
FFWWOOSH
"RAZA KATTUAH, A.K.A. RUSTAM, AFTER THE LEGENDARY PERSIAN HERO ROSTAM. FANCIES HIMSELF A RIGHTEOUS ASSASSIN, AND WITH HIS FLAMING SCIMITAR THAT CAN CUT THROUGH ANYTHING...
Raza Kattu
a.k.a.
RUSTAM
"DOCTOR POLARIS, A.K.A. DOCTOR NEAL EMERSON. FORMER A.R.G.U.S. SCIENTIST. HIS EXPERIMENTS ON HIMSELF DROVE HIM MAD BUT GAVE HIM THE ABILITY TO CONTROL ELECTROMAGNETIC WAVES."
Dr. Neal Emerson
a.k.a.
DOCTOR
POLARIS

"CLAIMS SHE'S FROM THE FUTURE. OUR STUDIES HAVE SHOWN THAT THE EYE HAS ELEMENTS OF GREEN LANTERN TECHNOLOGY.
EMERALD EMPRESS
...HE'S ONE OF THE GREATEST SWORDSMEN IN THE WORLD.
RRTTSSSHH
KRRUNCH
BLARG.

"JOHNNY SORROW, FORMER ACTOR TURNED PSYCHO. WAS TRAPPED IN ANOTHER DIMENSION BUT EXCHANGED HIS PHYSICAL BODY TO BECOME AN EMISSARY OF A GOD CALLED THE KING OF TEARS.

WHY?
BECAUSE ONE LOOK AT SORROW'S REAL FACE, AND EVERYONE IN THIS ROOM WOULD BE DEAD.

NO ONE LOCKS UP THE MAIN MAN!

ZZTT--

WE HAD TO EDIT THIS PIECE OF HIS FOOTAGE...

"SORROW HAS ACCESS TO EXTRA-DIMENSIONAL POWERS THAT WE STILL DON'T UNDERSTAND.

JOHNNY SORROW

AND THEN THAT BRINGS US TO THE MAIN EVENT...

"...*LOBO.* A BOUNTY HUNTER FROM THE PLANET CZARNIA. CLAIMS TO HAVE KILLED HIS WORLD'S ENTIRE *POPULATION.* HE'S STRONG AND FAST...BUT IT'S HIS ABILITY TO HEAL FROM *ANY* INJURY THAT MAKES HIM A REAL CHALLENGE.

THEY ARE *EFFICIENT KILLING MACHINES.*
AS INDIVIDUALS, THEY ARE SOME OF THE WORST VILLAINS TO EVER STEP FOOT ON THIS OR *ANY* PLANET...

...TOGETHER THEY ARE ***UNSTOPPABLE SADISTS.***

THEY COULD HAVE JUST ***ESCAPED*** THE CATACOMBS.

INSTEAD, THEY TOOK THEIR ***TIME.*** THEY MADE SURE TO ***MURDER*** EACH AND EVERY SINGLE PERSON THERE AS HORRIFICALLY AS POSSIBLE BEFORE MAKING THEIR EXIT.

AND THE MAN WHO ***RELEASED*** THEM...

...AND ***MANIPULATED*** THEM...

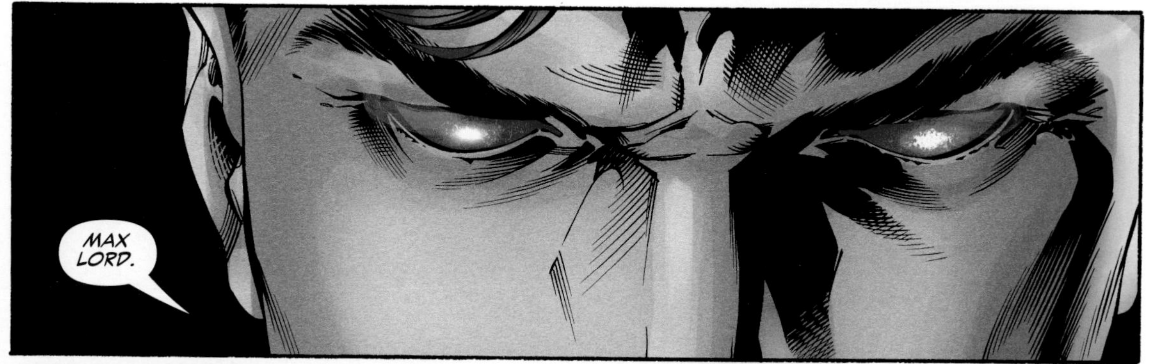
MAX LORD.

OF ALL OF THEM... MAX IS THE ONE WE NEED TO WORRY ABOUT.
THAT GUY?!

TRUST.
ME.
I'LL, ah... TAKE YA WORD FOR IT.
YA CAN TURN YOUR EYES OFF, MATE.

MAXWELL LORD'S PAST IS A BIT OF A MYSTERY...EVEN TO ME. WHILE DIRECTOR OF CHECKMATE, HE DID WHATEVER BEST SUITED HIS NEEDS, BUT EVENTUALLY WENT ROGUE.
HE HAS THE ABILITY TO...SUGGEST THINGS...MANIPULATE PEOPLE INTO DOING WHAT HE WANTS.

YOU TWO SHOULD BE BEST BUDS THEN!
SO WHAT'S HE AFTER?

ME.
THEY WANT TO KILL ME.
AND I WANT *YOU* TO PROTECT ME.
HAHAHAHAHAHAHAHAHAHAHAHAHAHAHAHAHAH
SETTLE DOWN.
GO ON, WALLER. YOUR HEAD ISN'T *ALL* THEY'RE AFTER.

BASED ON HIS MOVEMENTS SINCE THE ESCAPE, WE BELIEVE MAX LORD IS SEARCHING FOR A WEAPON THAT COULD HELP HIM GET SOMETHING HE'S ALWAYS WANTED.
ABSOLUTE CONTROL OF THE WORLD.

SO YOU WANT US TO TARGET THEM AND TAKE THEM OUT BEFORE THEY FIND IT.
THE JUSTICE LEAGUE CAN DEAL WITH THIS...BUT WHAT MAKES YOU THINK WE'D WORK WITH THE SUICIDE SQUAD?

YOU HAVE NO CHOICE. THE WEAPON THEY'RE SEARCHING FOR IS HOUSED IN BELLE REVE. THEY'RE COMING HERE.
NOW.

WHAT?! HERE?!
WHO'D BE DUMB ENOUGH TO BREAK INTO BELLE REVE?

EVEN WITHOUT MAX, THEY'RE FULLY CAPABLE OF INVADING BELLE REVE AND RETRIEVING THE WEAPON.
THEY WORK AS A TEAM.

AND HOW DO YOU KNOW THAT?

BECAUSE I MADE THEM A TEAM...

"...THEY WERE THE FIRST
SUICIDE SQUAD."

PROTECT THE **PEOPLE.**
EVERYTHING ELSE IS DETAILS.
OKAY, SCUM. SHUT UP AND LISTEN.

Kabul
Xi'an
Shanghai
Tokyo
JAPAN
North Pacific Ocean
Midway Islands (U.S.)
Taiwan
JANGSUN
Northern Mariana Islands (U.S.)
Saipan
Wake Island (U.S.)
Johnston Atoll (U.S.)
MARSHALL ISLANDS
Kolonia
Majuro
Kingman Reef (U.S.)
JANGSUN. ISLAND NATION IN THE NORTH PACIFIC.
BEEN UNDER THE RULE OF A TOTALITARIAN NUT-JOB DICTATOR NAMED ***YOUNG*** FOR THE PAST 23 YEARS.

YOUNG HATES... EVERY COUNTRY THAT ISN'T JANGSUN, PRETTY MUCH. THREATENING WAR EVERY COUPLE OF WEEKS. THE WORLD WILL COWER BEFORE US, YADDA YADDA...
NO BIGGIE. HE'S NEVER HAD THE WEAPONRY. UNTIL NOW...

RECORDING
JANGSUN HAS RELEASED THIS FOOTAGE. IT'S A WEAPONS TEST. THEY HAVE SOMEHOW DEVELOPED A TEAM OF METAHUMANS. HE CALLS THEM ***JANGSUN GODS.***
YOUNG CLAIMS THIS ONE--CODE NAME: ***MISSILE***--CAN REACH THE PACIFIC COAST AND HAS ENOUGH POWER TO TAKE OUT CALIFORNIA ON IMPACT.

HE BOASTED OF A WEAPONS TEST. WE PICKED UP THIS IMPACT JUST 200 MILES OFF THE COAST OF CATALINA YESTERDAY. IF HE CAN GET THAT CLOSE...
THIS IS ***EXACTLY*** THE TYPE OF THREAT I PUT THIS TEAM TOGETHER TO COMBAT. SO, BUCKLE UP...

BELLE REVE PENITENTIARY, LOUISIANA.

SEVERAL YEARS AGO...

IT'S TIME TO SEE WHAT *THE SUICIDE SQUAD* CAN DO...

RUSTAM, *Task Force X field commander.*

THE FIRST AND LAST MISSION OF SUICIDE ZERO

ROB WILLIAMS & SI SPURRIER WRITERS RILEY ROSSMO ARTIST
IVAN PLASCENCIA COLORS PAT BROSSEAU LETTERER RILEY ROSSMO COVER
BRIAN CUNNINGHAM GROUP EDITOR AMEDEO TURTURRO ASSISTANT EDITOR
HARVEY RICHARDS ASSOCIATE EDITOR ANDY KHOURI EDITOR

EMERALD EMPRESS, owner: one giant creepy eye from space.
DOCTOR POLARIS, Magnetism manipulator. Insane.
LOBO, alien killer-for-hire.
JOHNNY SORROW, madder than a bag of undead snakes.
WALLER, YOU KNOW THE MAIN MAN'S MANTRA, BABY DOLL. AND I'M SURE I SPEAK FOR THESE BUNCHA INGRATES, TOO, WHEN I SAY...
WE'LL KILL ALL THE FOREIGN PEOPLE, LONG AS THE PRICE IS RIGHT.

THE TARGET WILL DO. THEN YOU'LL GET WHAT YOU WANT, LOBO.
THIS IS MADNESS, WALLER. I'VE BEEN A GOOD SOLDIER FOR YOU, BUT THESE...THINGS...

"THEY'RE CRIMINALS... OR WORSE.
"THEY CANNOT BE CONTROLLED."

CONTROL'S WHAT I DO, RUSTAM.
YOU CAN TRUST ME.

JUST LIKE WE PLANNED, SQUAD, YOU WILL FOLLOW RUSTAM'S ORDERS IN THE FIELD.
GET IN. WIPE OUT JANGSUN'S GODS AND THE TECH THAT MADE THEM SO THEY CAN'T REPEAT THE PROCESS. END THE THREAT. IF CAPTURED...
...THAT WILL NOT HAPPEN...
...YOU ARE JUST ANOTHER TEAM OF GREEDY-ASS SUPER-VILLAINS. YOU ARE NOT ACTING UNDER THE AUSPICES OF THE UNITED STATES GOVERNMENT. WE WILL NOT START A WORLD WAR HERE.

AND IF YOU SUCCEED I WILL GIVE YOU YOUR HEART'S DESIRE.
WHETHER IT BE HARD CASH, THE LOCATION OF YOUR ENEMIES, A COMMUTED SENTENCE...

AND ME, WALLER?
I GET MY FREEDOM, RIGHT? YOU...
YOU PROMISED.

WHO'S THE TOOTHPICK?
LOOK, HE RECOILS IN FEAR OF US. HE IS ***NOT*** OUR EQUAL.
CYCLOTRON,
[Redacted.]

WHY'S ***HE*** HERE? I WASN'T BRIEFED.
THERE WASN'T TIME. ***SUICIDE SQUAD!*** MEET YOUR NEWEST MEMBER. YOU CAN GET FAMILIAR EN ROUTE.

AMANDA WALLER'S MISSION *REPORT--REF: SSQ/001. [EYES ONLY.]*
SQUAD INSERTION WAS, OF COURSE, TEXTBOOK.
IT'S FRANKLY THE ONLY PART OF THE EXPEDITION I COULD PERSONALLY CONTROL. HENCE THE ONLY PART THAT WENT PERFECTLY TO PLAN.

AT 1148 HOURS THE SQUAD CONFRONTED THE ENEMY'S METAHUMAN ASSETS. INTEL ON THE JANGSUN "GODS" WAS--PREDICTABLY--PATCHY:

"STATUE": Carbonized shell, beam-weapon tech; probably cybernetic.

"ISLAND": He's...well, he's an island. Look. See? An island.

"WIND": As in, "runs like the". Speedster. Laziest code name ever.

YOU JUST...JUST STAY OUT OF THE WAY, OKAY?

IN THE EARLY PHASES, THE RISK TO NEARBY CIVILIANS WAS ADMITTEDLY **HIGH...**

"GROWTH": Reflects the great and prosperous people's dream by getting all enormo and smashing things.
"MISSILE": You already met.
ATTACK PATTERN T-DELTA! PICK TARGETS!
REMEMBER YOUR TRAINING--ALTERNATE ON THE HALF-MINUTE!
AND... CYCLOTRON--?
...27...28... 29... 30! ALL CHANGE ROUND!
BUT ONE MUST TAKE A PRAGMATIC VIEW ON SUCH THINGS. THE SQUAD WAS UNDENIABLY EFFECTIVE.
AW! THESE LOSERS AIN'T ANY KINDA MATCH FOR THE BASTICH BRIGADE!

GIVEN WHAT WAS AT STAKE, I RELUCTANTLY JUDGED THE SECONDARY LOSSES TO BE...ACCEPTABLE.

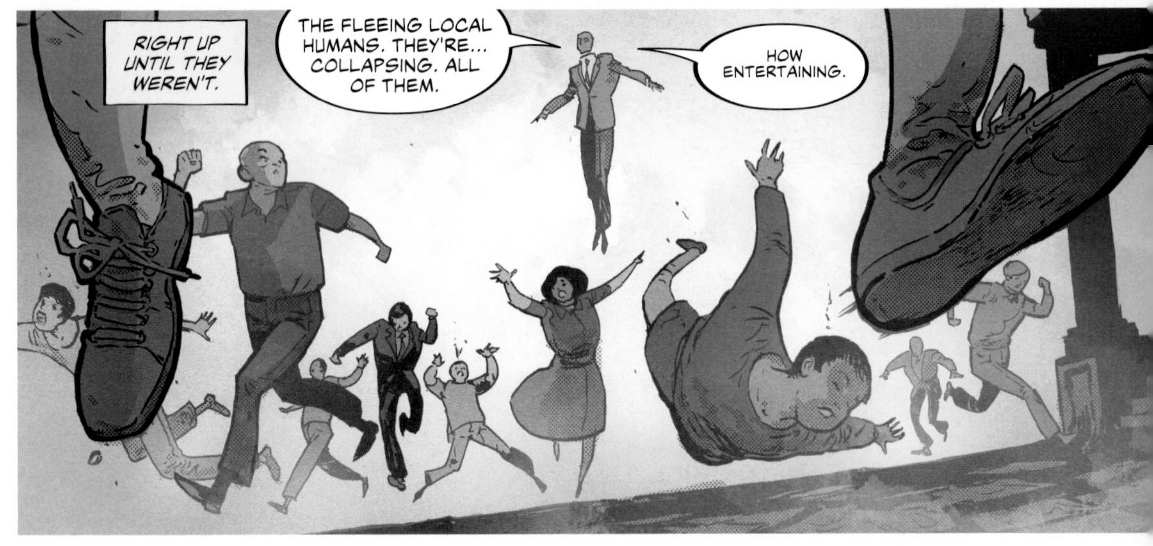

RIGHT UP UNTIL THEY WEREN'T.
THE FLEEING LOCAL HUMANS. THEY'RE... COLLAPSING. ALL OF THEM.
HOW ENTERTAINING.

WHAT'S GOING ON? WHAT JUST HAPPENED?
UH...WE HAVE...WE HAVE DOZENS OF CIVILIANS DOWN. HUNDREDS, COULD BE. A-ARE THEY--
DEAD--YES. THE KING OF TEARS CAN TASTE THEIR LOSS. THESE WARRIORS ARE LINKED SOMEHOW TO THE POPULACE.
TO KILL THE GODS IS TO KILL THE PEOPLE. I FELT IT THE MOMENT WE ARRIVED...
B-BUT YOU DIDN'T SAY ANYTHING?! ABORT MISSION! ABORT MISSION!
WE NEED TO FIND SOME OTHER WAY T--
WAIDDAMINUTE, BOSS LADY--YOU PROMISED US A REWARD FOR MURDERISIN' THESE ASSHATS.
QUITE. AND YOU CHOSE US FOR A REASON:
WE'RE NOT THE SORT TO DO HALF A JOB.
SO MURDER TIME IT IS!

FOR EVERY ONE OF THE JANGSUN GODS WHO FELL, A THOUSAND OF THE LOCALS DIED WITH THEM.
OH GOD.

O-OH SAAY CAN YOU SEEEEE--
BY THE DAWN'S EARLY LIIIIIGHT--

IMPERIALIST SCUM! STAY BACK!

THE *GOD-ENGINE* WILL NOT BE DEFILED BY CAPITALIST TOUCH!

"GOD-ENGINE"? WHAT'S--

GREAT PEOPLE'S REVOLUTIONARY DEVICE! NO GODS BUT THOSE WE CREATE! PUNISH IMPERIALIST DOGS THROUGH MANDATED STATE METAPHYSICS!

QUIET, FOOL! DON'T *TELL* THEM!

S'NO WAY TO TALK TO A *LADY,* BUB.
THIS TECHNOLOGY IS... *EXTRAORDINARY.* IT APPEARS TO TRANSMUTE *PSIONIC ENERGY* INTO *ASTRAL DRONES.*
MEANING?

MEANING IT USES HUMAN LIFE AS FUEL TO CREATE PUPPET GODS...
DESTROY IT! DESTROY IT! DESTROY IT!
OR.

SORRY, SORRY, I'M JUST SAYING, WE COULD, SORT OF...
...USE IT?
...WHO'S THIS GUY AGAIN?
LET HIM SPEAK...
LOOK--THIS WALLER LADY. I GOT NO IDEA WHY SHE SENT ME OUT HERE WITH THE BIG GUNS BUT, C'MON...
IT'S CALLED FREAKIN' SUICIDE SQUAD. WE'RE ALL DISPOSABLE. AND WHAT'S SHE OFFERING IN RETURN, HUH?
"SERIOUSLY, THESE JANGSUN DUMMIES HAD PRETTY LOW AMBITIONS, TOO-- LOOK WHERE IT GOT THEM.
"ALL THAT JUNK WALLER'S OFFERING US...? IT'S NOTHING COMPARED TO WHAT WE COULD TAKE FOR OURSELVES.
"ALL WE'D HAVE TO DO IS REACH OUT WITH THIS TECH...AND FEED IT THE BRAIN WAVES OF A BILLION PEOPLE...
"HEY PRESTO: DIVINE WRATHFUL PUPPETS OF YOUR VERY OWN."

FAT WAD.
INTEL ON SATURN GIRL.
ONE MILLION HYMNS TO THE KING OF TEARS.
SHE'LL TELL ME WHERE MY FATHER IS...SO I CAN HURT HIM...
THE WAY I UNDERSTAND THIS TECHNOLOGY, IT FEEDS ON PEOPLE'S BRAINWAVES.
...WELL THERE'S A THOUGHT.
AT 12:02 HOURS THE SITUATION BECAME... PROBLEMATIC.

IT'S POSSIBLE-- JUST POSSIBLE-- THAT I MAY HAVE OVERESTIMATED THE EFFICACY OF A REWARD-BASED INCENTIVE.
RUSTAM. FOR THE GOOD OF YOUR ADOPTED COUNTRY--
--DESTROY. THAT. MACHINE.
STEP AWAY, SOLDIERS. THIS IS OFF-MISSION.
YOU CAN COUNT OUT TH' MAIN MAN, TOO. BEIN' A GOD SOUNDS LIKE A LOTTA DAMN EFFORT. ALL I WANT'S MY MONEY.
I'M SORRY, RUSTAM. WE DON'T FOLLOW YOUR ORDERS ANYMORE.
AAAH!
THEN AGAIN, WE ARE ON THE CUSP OF GODHOOD.
SO BY ALL MEANS START PRAYING.
...
...
LOBO.

HIP FLASK...
HIP FLASK...
HIP FL--
LOBO, LISTEN TO ME, DAMMIT...

I NEED YOU TO KILL CYCLOTRON.
NOW. LET'S SSSEEEE...

WHAT? WHY?
BECAUSE I'LL DOUBLE YOUR MONEY.

AAAGGHHH
AAAGGHHHH

FAIR ENOUGH.
WHAT'RE Y--
WAIT--

ALL THE SAME. A DEAL'S A DEAL.

WHERE'D WE BE IN THIS WORLD WITHOUT HONOR, EH?

HEY, WHAT'S WITH THE PRETTY LIGHTS?
WHAT DID YOU DO?
WHAT DID YOU DO?!

GOD TOLD ME TO DO IT.

CYCLOTRON... HE'S A BOMB... THAT'S ALL HE EVER WAS. A FAILSAFE TO TAKE YOU ALL OUT IF YOU CROSSED THE LINE.
WHAT? WHY DIDN'T YOU SAY?
BECAUSE WALLER ORDERED HIM NOT TO.

GET BACK! VILLAINS!
I'M NOT ONE OF YOU! YOU HEAR ME? I'M...
RUSTAM. FOR WHAT IT'S WORTH...

...I'M SORRY.
I SERVED YOU, WALLER! I WAS YOUR SOLDIER!
DAMN YOU! DAMN YOU TO...

HELL.

...
I WILL ADMIT THAT THIS OUTCOME...
...TROUBLED ME.

BUT A COMMANDER ACCEPTS THE POSSIBILITIES OF LOSSES ON ANY MISSION.

WE, THE PROTECTORS, LONG AGO LEFT BEHIND THE LUXURY OF RESTFUL SLEEP.

THAT PRIVILEGE BELONGS TO THE AMERICAN PEOPLE.

THE SQUAD SURVIVED THE BLAST, WHICH... SURPRISED ME.
LOBO IS VIRTUALLY UNKILLABLE, BUT THE OTHERS... I CAN ONLY ASSUME DOCTOR POLARIS MANAGED TO DEFLECT THE BULK OF THE ELECTROMAGNETIC ENERGY. THEY WERE, HOWEVER, COMATOSE.
EASILY COLLECTED.
AND FILED.
AS FAR AS THE WORLD WAS CONCERNED, JANGSUN'S METAHUMAN PROJECT HAD SIMPLY EXPLODED IN ITS FACE.
CYCLOTRON'S BLAST TOOK OUT ALL COMMUNICATIONS, CAMERAS, COMPUTERS, EVERYTHING. ALL EVIDENCE OF TASK FORCE X WIPED AWAY.
THERE WAS NO U.S. INVOLVEMENT.
CRIMINALS COULD BE USED IN THIS MANNER. PERHAPS JUST LESS...ERRATIC SUBJECTS. THESE CREATURES WERE JUST TOO DANGEROUS TO RELEASE INTO THE WORLD.
WHILE RUSTAM KNEW TOO MUCH.
CONTROL. THAT WOULD BE KEY GOING FORWARD. PERHAPS INTER-CRANIAL 'BRAIN' BOMBS COULD BE INSERTED...
THE THREAT HAD BEEN NEUTRALIZED. THE SUICIDE SQUAD WAS--WITH CERTAIN CAVEATS--A SUCCESS.
THE REST WAS JUST DETAILS.

Belle Reve Penitentiary.
BOOM
KRRTSSSHH
FOR TOO LONG, AMANDA WALLER HAS MANIPULATED THE POWERFUL INTO MAINTAINING THE *STATUS QUO* FOR HER.
TODAY THAT WILL FINALLY *END*.

WELL, WELL, WELL...
...THE SELF-APPOINTED SAVIORS OF JUSTICE.
STANDING SIDE BY SIDE WITH THE SUICIDE SQUAD.
SHOULD WE BE FLATTERED BY THIS TEAM-UP?
JUSTICE LEAGUE VS. SUICIDE SQUAD
Chapter Four

JOSHUA WILLIAMSON Writer • FERNANDO PASARIN Penciller • MATT RYAN Inker
LEX SINCLAIR with JEREMIAH SKIPPER Color • ROB LEIGH Letterer • PASARIN, RYAN & SINCLAIR Cover
MEDEO TURTURRO Asst. Editor • JESSICA CHEN & HARVEY RICHARDS Assoc. Editors
NDY KHOURI Consulting Editor • BRIAN CUNNINGHAM Editor

WALLER TOLD US EVERYTHING, MAX.
I HAVE TO HAND IT TO YOU...YOU ALWAYS WANTED TO INSPIRE PEOPLE TO COME TOGETHER... AND BY UNLEASHING THESE MONSTERS, YOU HAVE.
LOBO... I'M SURPRISED YOU'D ALLOW YOURSELF TO BE USED BY MAX LORD.
NOBODY'S CONTROLLING THE MAIN MAN, BLUE!
WALLER KEPT THEM LOCKED UP AND SHE NEEDS TO PAY, SUPERMAN.
YEAH! WALLER KEPT US LOCKED UP AND SHE NEEDS TO PAY!
SUPERMAN, IT WOULD REALLY BE IN YOUR BEST INTEREST TO JUST FLOAT ASIDE AND LET US DO OUR WORK.
I KNOW TOO WELL HOW FAR YOU'RE WILLING TO GO FOR WHAT YOU THINK IS BEST, MAX. YOU DON'T JUST PUSH PEOPLE TO DO WHAT YOU WANT...
...YOU PUSH THEM TO THEIR BREAKING POINT.
ENOUGH TALK!
I WILL END THIS... MY MIND CANNOT BE MANIPULATED BY THE LIKES OF YOU, HUMAN.
YOU'RE RIGHT. YOUR MIND IS A LOCKED BOX, ENCHANTRESS...

...BUT JUNE MOONE'S MIND ISN'T.
JUNE...? I KNOW YOU'RE IN THERE. AREN'T YOU ANGRY THAT WALLER HAS KEPT YOU TRAPPED WITH THE ENCHANTRESS...?
WOULDN'T YOU LIKE TO DO SOMETHING ABOUT THAT?
I JUST WANTED HELP...BUT SHE...
JUNE... WHAT...? YOU DON'T HAVE ACCESS TO MY MAGIC...
BUT I DO.
EEEEWIII!!!
WHAT ARE YOU DOING TO HER?!
ALERT. UNKNOWN LANTERN TECHNOLOGY DETECTED. DANGEROUS SITUATION IMMINENT--
LANTERN TECH...?
DANGER DANGER DANGER
THE RING IS REALLY NOT A FAN OF THAT GIANT GREEN EYEBALL--
SIMON, BE CAREFUL--

STAY BACK, GREEN LANTERN!
KRASH
KRSH
KRSH
SIMON!
Uh-oh.
POP

THIS IS OUR MOMENT.
REMEMBER WHAT YOU CAME FOR!
FRET NOT, MAX...
...I BELIEVE I CAN THINK OF A FEW WAYS TO ENTERTAIN OUR HOSTS.
AW NAH YA DON'T.
WE KNOW WHAT HAPPENS WHEN YOU SHOW OFF THAT UGLY MUG, MATE!
IF YOU ARE A CRITIC OF MY PERFORMANCE...
...I PRESENT MY SUPPORTING CAST.
WHEN I WAS KEPT IN WALLER'S CELL, I WASN'T ALONE. THE SCREAMS IN THE DARK KEPT ME COMPANY.
IT WAS THE KING OF TEARS' ARMY DEMANDING TO BE...

...FREE!
SECURE THE PERIMETER! WE CANNOT LET ANYONE GET TO THE CONTROL ROOM AND RELEASE THE PRISONERS!
FWWOSSH

FWOOSH
FORGIVE ME, MY FRIENDS. I'M FAMILIAR WITH THE LOYALTY WALLER DEMANDS.
BUT IF WE ARE TO TRULY DEFEAT THE DEVIL...IT CALLS FOR MORE THAN CUTTING OFF HER HEAD...
...WE MUST OPEN THE GATES OF HELL THEMSELVES!

CLANG

YOU ARE UNKNOWN TO ME, GIRL. BUT I RECOGNIZE THE ***SOULTAKER*** BLADE. OF COURSE WALLER WOULD HAVE SOMETHING SO ***EVIL*** IN HER EMPLOY.

MY NAME IS ***KATANA.*** YOU WILL ***LEARN*** IT.

CLANG

CLANG

CLANG

I WAS AN ***INNOCENT*** PLACED BEHIND WALLER'S BARS...

...WHO KNOWS HOW MANY LOCKED WITHIN THESE WALLS CAN SAY THE ***SAME?***

I HAVE LIVED AMONG THE PRISONERS OF BELLE REVE...

...AND THEY ARE SOME OF THE ***WORST*** SOULS THE WORLD HAS TO OFFER.

...THE VAULT IS MINE.
YOU DO LIKE TO BURY THINGS YOU DON'T WANT TO DEAL WITH, DON'T YOU, AMANDA?
"REVENGE WAS NEVER MY FIRST PRIORITY, UNLIKE THE REST OF MY ALLIES...
...BUT I KNEW THERE WAS NO WAY I'D EVER GET DOWN HERE WITHOUT THEIR HELP.
"IF AMANDA WALLER DIES...
...THAT'S... A WELCOME...
...BONUS...?
NOT ONE FOR SUBTLETY, ARE YOU...

...KILLER FROST?
NEVER BEEN THE PASSIVE-AGGRESSIVE TYPE, MAX.
FREEZING YOU SHOULD SLOW DOWN YOUR MOTOR SKILLS... MAKE IT TOUGH FOR YOU TO "MAGIC TALK" YOUR WAY OUT OF THIS.
YOU WON'T BE ABLE TO MAKE ME--
I DON'T MAKE ANYONE DO ANYTHING.
I MERELY SHOW PEOPLE THE DIRECTION THEY ALREADY WANT TO GO.
DON'T YOU WANT TO SEE ME TAKE OUT AMANDA WALLER?
WALLER... unh...USES PEOPLE, BUT SHE--
THEN D-DON'T YOU WANT TO MAKE S-SURE THAT WALLER NEVER F-FORCES HER WILL ON ANYONE AGAIN?
WALLER... SHOULD NEVER FORCE HER WILL ON ANYONE AGAIN...
...YOU'RE RIGHT.
I KNEW YOU'D SEE IT MY WAY.
AND YOU'RE GOING TO HELP ME...

"...SAVE THE WORLD FROM ITSELF."
WHAT'S YER KILL COUNT, FLASHER?!
I'M NOT KILLING THEM, DIGGER!
YOU TELLING ME YOU WON'T EVEN KILL MONSTERS?!
SLISSHH
WE DON'T KNOW WHAT THEY ARE. BETTER TO INCAPACITATE THEM AND SEND THEM BACK TO WHEREVER THEY CAME FROM.
YER A REAL PIECE OF WORK, FLASH.
NO WONDER THE REST OF THE SQUAD ALWAYS SAID I HAVE THE EASY HERO.
YOU CAN'T HIDE FROM THIS CZARNIAN, WALLER!
BANG BANG BANG BANG
JUST KEEP UP, DEADSHOT.
WE CAN'T SHAKE THIS GUY, WALLER!
BANG BANG BANG BANG
MAX IS MANIPULATING YOU, LOBO!
MAX FREED ME!

NO!
TKK
NO ONE MAKES ME MISS A FRAGGIN' SHOT!
EVEN WITHOUT ONE OF MY BRAIN BOMBS IN YOUR HEAD, YOU STILL END UP WORKING FOR ME, BATMAN.
JUMP!
KRAKOOM
WHERE IS SUPERMAN WHEN YOU NEED HIM?

IF YOU ONLY KNEW WHAT THE FUTURE HOLDS, SUPERMAN...YOU'D LET MAX GET WHAT HE WANTS!
THE FUTURE?
YOU'RE BETTER OFF DEAD THAN EVER KNOWING THE TRUTH!
NO!
ANOTHER GREEN LANTERN? DO YOU BELIEVE YOU HAVE A BETTER CHANCE AGAINST THE EMERALD EYE OF EKRON?
YOU SUCKER-PUNCHED SIMON! YOU'RE NOT PULLING THE SAME MOVE TWICE!
THE EYE... IT WON'T FIRE ON YOU. WHY?
MAYBE GAME RESPECTS GAME.
ALERT! TEMPORAL ENERGY DETECTED. ALERT!
WHAT...?

GET AWAY FROM THE EYE, JESSICA!
KRIKK
KRAKK
NO!
IF THE EYE BREAKS I'LL BE TRAPPED HERE...
BUT... I HAVE TO FIND HER...
I HAVE TO FIND SATURN GIRLLLLLL...
WHO IS SATURN GIRL?
WE'LL DEAL WITH THAT LATER*-- WE NEED TO PUT A STOP TO THIS...
*OH, YOU WILL, SUPERMAN! IN THE PAGES OF SUPERGIRL!

"...BEFORE SOMEONE GETS HURT."
ME BOOMERANGS GOT LODGED--!
THIS DEATH SUCKS--!
EEEEEE!!!
YOU CAN STOP SCREAMING, DIGGER. JEEZ.
YA...YA SAVED ME?!
I PROMISE NOT TO TELL THE ROGUES IF YOU DON'T.
DEAL.
BANGBANGBANGBANGBANGBANG
WHERE THE HELL IS KATANA?

UF!

RUSTAM, STOP! I KNOW YOU DON'T WANT THIS! I'VE BEEN IN YOUR SHOES, MAN.

YOU LED WALLER'S FIRST SUICIDE SQUAD INTO THE FIELD...THAT'S MY ASSIGNMENT NOW!

THEN KILLING *YOU* WOULD BE A *MERCY!*

NOTHING CAN STOP MY BLADE!

I'M *COUNTING* ON IT.
TSSCHHH
AAAHHH!!

"YOU ARE NOT MY *TRU* ENEMY..."

...BUT THE SHOW MUST GO ON, WONDER WOMAN.
IF WE'RE NOT YOUR ENEMY, WHY ARE YOU HELPING MAX LORD?
BECAUSE I LIKE TO WATCH PEOPLE SUFFER.
STAY AWAY FROM MY BESTIE!
HARLEY, DON'T LOOK--
...
CUTE FACE.
NO CLOWN WILL UPSTAGE ME! WITNESS THE TRUE FACE OF MADNESS.
WONDER WOMAN, NO!
SORROW REMINDS ME OF MEDUSA...

...I WONDER WHAT HAPPENS WHEN HE LOOKS AT HIS OWN FACE?

NO ENCORE FOR YOU, BUDDY!

EXIT STAGE LEFT!

IT APPEARS THE KING OF TEARS' MONSTERS CAN'T EXIST ON THIS PLANE WITHOUT JOHNNY SORROW.

HARLEY...HOW DID YOU SURVIVE LOOKING AT SORROW'S FACE?
OH, PLEASE... ONCE YOU'VE LOOKED INTO ONE ABYSS YOU'VE SEEN 'EM ALL.
YOU SAVED MY LIFE TODAY.
IT'S NO BIG.

AW, WHO AM I KIDDING?!
WE'RE A TEAM AGAIN, SISTER! WE SHOULD BE THE NEW WONDER TWINS!
WE SHOULD ASSIST THE OTHERS, HARLEY.

SCREAM FOR ME!
DO YOU FEEL THAT? IT'S THE IRON IN YOUR BLOOD TWISTING AND BURNING INSIDE OF YOU!
THAT'S ENOUGH, DOCTOR POLARIS!
THEY SENT A MAN MADE OF METAL TO STOP ME?

I'VE HAD THIS BODY FOR A BIT NOW.
YOU REALLY THINK I DIDN'T PLAN FOR MAGNETS?
BY CHANNELING ELECTRICITY THROUGH MY METAL BODY I CAN CREATE MY OWN ELECTROMETRIC FIELD...
...THAT CANCELS YOURS OUT!
YOU'RE LUCKY I DON'T BOOM-TUBE YOUR BUTT INTO DEEP SPACE!
WWWRRRRRTTTTTT
THANKS, CYBORG.
DID YOU JUST GOOGLE THAT MAGNET STUFF...?
NAH, MAN... LEARNED THAT IN KINDERGARTEN.
WHO'S LEFT OF MAX'S TEAM?

LOBO TAKES EVERYTHING WE THROW AT HIM! HE JUST KEEPS HEALING!
ARMORY
I NEED BOTH OF YOU TO STAY HERE AND SLOW HIM DOWN.
WHERE THE HELL ARE YOU GOING?
JUST KEEP LOBO BUSY!
NUTHIN'S GONNA STOP ME, WALLER!
POOM
POOM
POOM
POOMPOOMPOOM

HA.
THAT THE BEST YA GOT?!
TAKES A LOT...
...TO KILL...
THE MAIN MAN.
AH!
MAX...⇝KAFF⇜... MAX IS...⇝KK⇜... CONTROLLING... YOU...
NO WAY MAXIE'D PULL THAT ON ME.
YOU BURIED ME ALIVE, WALLER. YOU EARNED THIS.

YOU'RE BEING CONTROLLED BY MAX LORD WHETHER YOU WANT TO BELIEVE IT OR NOT, LOBO!
YOU'VE LEFT ME...

...NO CHOICE!
TSH

DUNNO WHAT YOU JUST INJECTED ME WITH AND I DON'T CARE. YER DEAD, WALLER!

IT'S A BRAIN BOMB.

THAT SUPPOSED TO SCARE ME?
WALLER PUTS THEM INSIDE HER SUICIDE SQUAD'S HEADS...

...AND IT'S THE ONLY WAY TO STOP YOU.

DEECT

BOOM

DAMN, BATMAN.
HERE WE ARE, KILLER FROST. ALL THAT STANDS BETWEEN US AND THE POWER TO CHANGE THE WORLD IS ONE LAST DOOR.
NOW DESTROY THE VAULT.
Nn... NO.
DO IT!
NOW!
WHAT IS MAX REALLY AFTER, WALLER?
YOU SAID IT WAS A WEAPON... BUT THIS IS BIGGER THAN THAT. WHAT ARE YOU HIDING?
IT'S A DIAMOND... CONTAINING AN INCREDIBLY MALEVOLENT POWER.

"ANYONE WHO TOUCHES IT BECOMES CORRUPTED BY IT..."
KRAKKRAKKRAKOOM
WE NEED TO STOP MAX!
I KNOW WHERE THE VAULT IS. LET'S GO...
"IT DOESN'T MATTER HOW PURE OF SOUL...OR STRENGTH OF WILL...THE DARKNESS WITHIN INFECTS YOU AT YOUR CORE...
"IN SOME PARTS OF THE WORLD IT'S BEEN CALLED 'NALUSA CHITO' ...OR THE 'ECLIPSO DIAMOND,' BUT IT'S MOST COMMONLY CALLED THE HEART OF DARKNESS..."
FINALLY.
CONTROL... WILL...BE...
...MINE.

F MAX CAN USE HIS ABILITIES TO CONTROL HE HEART OF DARKNESS, HE WON'T JUST BE ABLE TO SUGGEST PEOPLE OBEY HIM...
"...MAX WILL BE ABLE TO FORCE EVERYONE TO BECOME THE WORST VERSIONS OF THEMSELVES.
"AND WE'LL HAVE ALREADY LOST."
STOP.
ARGH!
NNGH!
NNH-.
IS MAX TRY'N TO CONTROL THEM?
WHY NOT US?
BECAUSE WHY WOULD I WANT TO CONTROL A GROUP OF LOSERS...
...WHEN I CAN USE THE GREATEST POWERS IN THE UNIVERSE?

AND NOW WITH THE ECLIPSO DIAMOND, THE JUSTICE LEAGUE WILL HELP MAKE THE WORLD SAFE...
...MY WAY.

ROBSON

ROBSON
DANIEL
SINC

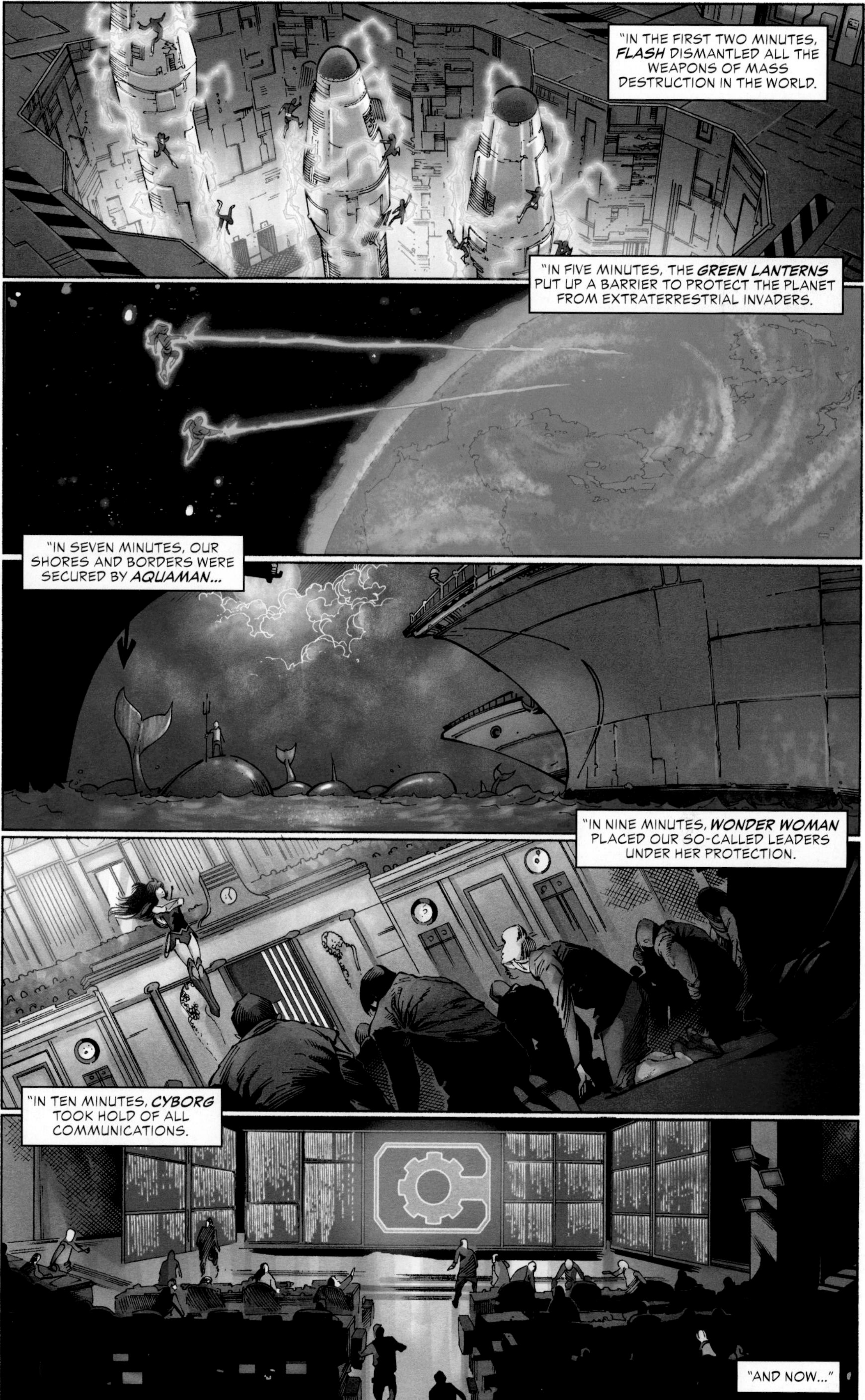
"IN THE FIRST TWO MINUTES, FLASH DISMANTLED ALL THE WEAPONS OF MASS DESTRUCTION IN THE WORLD.
"IN FIVE MINUTES, THE GREEN LANTERNS PUT UP A BARRIER TO PROTECT THE PLANET FROM EXTRATERRESTRIAL INVADERS.
"IN SEVEN MINUTES, OUR SHORES AND BORDERS WERE SECURED BY AQUAMAN...
"IN NINE MINUTES, WONDER WOMAN PLACED OUR SO-CALLED LEADERS UNDER HER PROTECTION.
"IN TEN MINUTES, CYBORG TOOK HOLD OF ALL COMMUNICATIONS.
"AND NOW..."

"...THE WHITE HOUSE."
KRA-KOOM
THOOOM
BRAK-A-BRAK-A-BRAK-A-BRAK-BRAKK

WHOOSH
WITHIN THIRTEEN MINUTES...

...THE UNITED STATES IS SAFE.
JUSTICE LEAGUE VS. SUICIDE SQUAD
Chapter Five
JOSHUA WILLIAMSON Writer • ROBSON ROCHA Pencill
JAY LEISTEN, DANIEL HENRIQUES, SANDU FLOREA & OCLAIR ALBERT Inke
ALEX SINCLAIR with JEREMIAH SKIPPER Colorists • ROB LEIGH Letterer • ROCHA, HENRIQUES & SINCLAIR Cov
AMEDEO TURTURRO Asst. Editor • JESSICA CHEN & HARVEY RICHARDS Assoc. Edito
ANDY KHOURI Consulting Editor • BRIAN CUNNINGHAM Edit

YOU'RE A *BORE,* SUPERMAN.
IT'S NO FUN SAVING THE WORLD IF THERE'S NO ONE TO *ENJOY* IT WITH.

I NEED SOMEONE WHO WILL *APPRECIATE* WHAT I'VE ACCOMPLISHED.

"WHERE IS AMANDA WALLER?"

KRTRCHH

ARE WE DEAD?

Belle Reve Penitentiary.
NEW TECH I'VE BEEN DEVELOPING. WIRE MESH SHIELDING DEPLOYED DURING EARTHQUAKES.
THAT DIDN'T FEEL LIKE ANY EARTHQUAKE, BATS...
...BUT WE'RE STILL TRAPPED WITH YOUR LOVELY HEADLESS HANDIWORK.
NOT THE FIRST TIME I'VE BEEN BURIED UNDERGROUND WITH A DEAD BODY...
DAMMIT. BELLE REVE COMMUNICATIONS ARE DOWN. I HAVE NO IDEA IF THE HEART OF DARKNESS IS STILL SECURE...
MORE THAN BELLE REVE IS JAMMED, WALLER. I CAN'T CONNECT TO MY OWN SYSTEMS.
WHY EVEN KEEP THAT THING HERE TO BEGIN WITH?

"I BURIED THE HEART OF DARKNESS DIAMOND UNDER BELLE REVE TO STOP IT FROM EVER BEING USED AS A WEAPON.
IF MAX GOT HIS HANDS ON IT...
THE JUSTICE LEAGUE MIGHT HAVE STOPPED MAX AND YOUR ORIGINAL SUICIDE SQUAD, WALLER.
WE JUST NEED TO FIND A WAY OUT OF HERE.
IF THE JUSTICE LEAGUE WON...WHERE THE HELL ARE THEY?
SHUT IT, DEADSHOT...
WHAT'RE YOU GONNA DO? BLOW ME UP LIKE YOU DID LOBO?
CRAP!
RELAX... I KNOW THAT SOUND.
THANK YOU, SUPERMAN. HOW DID YOU FIND...

...US.
I COULD HEAR YOUR ANNOYING VOICE FROM MILES AWAY, BATMAN... BUT I DIDN'T COME FOR YOU.
MAX LORD REQUESTS YOUR PRESENCE, AMANDA WALLER.
STAY BACK, WALLER.
I'VE HAD TO STOP SUPERMAN BEFORE.
YOUR KRYPTONITE RING? YOU ARE DESPERATE.
BUT PAIN IS NO LONGER A CONCERN FOR ME, BATMAN.

IT'S OVER.
YOU'VE SPENT YOUR ENTIRE LIFE TRYING TO PROTECT ONE CITY...
...AND FAILED.
MAX SAVED THE WORLD WITHIN A MATTER OF MINUTES.
YOU OF ALL PEOPLE KNOW THE POWER OF THE LEAGUE, MY FRIEND. DON'T COME FOR US.
WHOOSH
KRRSSSHH
WAS THAT LITTLE GREEN ROCK YOUR BEST SHOT AT TAKING YOUR BOY DOWN?
WE'RE SO SCREWED.

BASTICH!

BATMAN! YOU BLEW ME UP?!
YOU HEALED FROM EVERYTHING WE THREW AT YOU, LOBO. BUT IF ANYTHING COULD BREAK MAX'S CONTROL OVER YOU, IT'D BE ONE OF WALLER'S BRAIN BOMBS.
I LIKE YOUR STYLE, YA BAT-FREAK.
BUT WHERE THE HELL IS MAX LORD?
I TOLD THAT LITTLE SNOT THAT IF HE PULLED HIS VOODOO MUMBO JUMBO ON ME, I'D FRAG HIM.
IT'S MORE COMPLICATED THAN THAT NOW, LOBO--
NOT REALLY, BATS!
KRAK!
DAMN.
GOOD TO SEE YOU, TOO, DEADSHOT.
PARTS OF BELLE REVE HAVE BEEN WRECKED, BUT THE PRISONERS ARE CONTAINED.
LOBO IS WITH US, FLAG...FOR NOW. WHERE'S THE REST OF MAX'S TEAM?
ENCHANTRESS AND EL DIABLO ARE LAID UP IN THE INFIRMARY. POLARIS AND RUSTAM ESCAPED. THE SQUAD IS DEALING WITH ONE OF MAX'S NEW SLAVES...
KEEP HIM DOWN!

CYBORG'S POSSESSED!
DON'T LET GO, CROC!
STOP... ZZT
FOOL ME ONCE, YA BUCKET'A BOLTS!
THWACK

GET AWAY FROM CYBORG!

OI!
THE LEAGUE TOSSED THE JOINT AND THEN TORE OUTTA HERE!
BUT CYBORG STAYED BEHIND TO FINISH US OFF!

THEN WHY ISN'T HE FIGHTING BACK, HARLEY?!

PLEASE... ZZT... STOP.

VIC...?
MAX ZZT HAS TAKEN HOLD OF ME...

MY HUMAN SIDE ⋮ZZT⋮ IS *LOST.*

LUCKILY I CREATED ⋮ZZT⋮ SECURITY PROTOCOLS IN CASE MY SYSTEMS WERE EVER ⋮ZZT⋮ COMPROMISED.

IT'S KEEPING SOME OF MY ***MACHINE SIDE*** FREE ⋮ZZT⋮ FROM MAX'S CONTROL.

MAX ORDERED THE JUSTICE LEAGUE ⋮ZZT⋮ TO TAKE OVER THE UNITED STATES, I HAD NO CHOICE...I SEIZED ALL COMMUNICATIONS...

EVEN NOW I'M WORKING ACROSS THE GLOBE TO ACCESS DATABASES FOR MAX... MAX'S WORDS STILL COMMAND ME...

"IT'S AN EVIL BEYOND ANYTHING WE'VE EVER KNOWN.
"UNBRIDLED RAGE... AND HATE...
...IT'S UNLOCKING MY WORST FEARS... NOT FEARS...NO... MY OWN DARK THOUGHTS.
EVERY DARK IMPULSE I'VE EVER HAD...IT WANTS ME TO ACT ON THEM...
...AND THE VOICE KEEPS GETTING LOUDER...
...I CAN'T TELL IF IT'S MINE ANYMORE.
HEY, SO LISTEN...I'M NOT ONE TO LOOK A GIFT HORSE IN THE MOUTH BUT...
...WHY DON'T ANY OF US LOOK LIKE, uh, THAT?
YEAH! WHAT BOOMERANG SAID!
AFTER MAX AND THE JUSTICE LEAGUE GOT ALL BLUE IN THE FACE AND CREEPY... THEY WHOOSHED RIGHT PAST US LIKE--
WE'RE NOTHING?
MAX BELIEVES THAT WE DON'T HAVE THE POWER TO STAND A CHANCE AGAINST HIM...
...AND HE'S RIGHT.
"WE'RE A RARE BREED, AMANDA..."

...WE UNDERSTAND THAT SACRIFICES HAVE TO BE MADE FOR THE GREATER GOOD.
I NEEDED THE JUSTICE LEAGUE TO HELP ME MAKE THE UTOPIAN WORLD THAT SOCIETY HAS DREAMED OF...EVEN IF I HAD TO FORCE THEM.
MAX, THAT DIAMOND... IT WILL INFECT YOU...
AMANDA... PLEASE.
YOU REALLY THINK I DIDN'T TAKE PRECAUTIONS?
I FORCED THE HIGH PRIEST OF DIABLO ISLAND TO BRAND ME WITH THEIR SACRED SIGIL SO I'D HAVE AN EDGE OVER THE DIAMOND.
FOR YEARS, I STRUGGLED TO CONTROL PEOPLE WITH MY POWERS...
...BUT NOW, WITH THE HEART OF DARKNESS...I CAN MAKE PEOPLE DO WHATEVER. I. WANT.
MAX...THROUGHOUT HISTORY THERE HAVE BEEN RECORDINGS OF A BLACK DIAMOND AT SOME OF MANKIND'S WORST MOMENTS... THE BLACK PLAGUE, SALEM, THE INQUISITION...
OUR RESEARCHERS FOUND MENTIONS AS FAR BACK AS THE MASSACRE OF THESSALONICA...
YES...

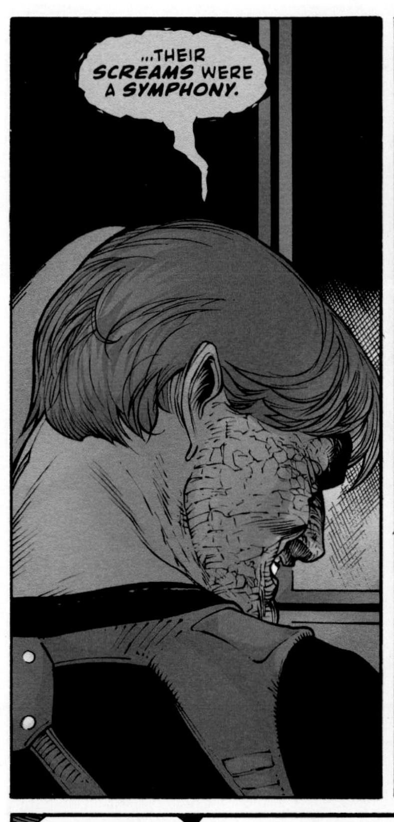
...THEIR SCREAMS WERE A SYMPHONY.

WHAT... WHAT DID YOU JUST SAY?

WHAT... WHAT WAS I SAYING AGAIN...?
OH YES...

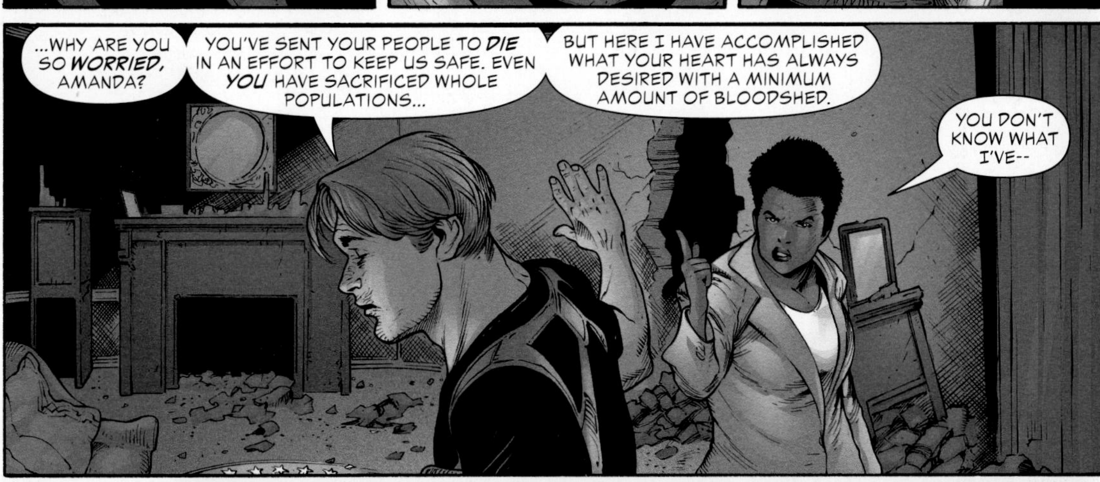
...WHY ARE YOU SO WORRIED, AMANDA?
YOU'VE SENT YOUR PEOPLE TO DIE IN AN EFFORT TO KEEP US SAFE. EVEN YOU HAVE SACRIFICED WHOLE POPULATIONS...
BUT HERE I HAVE ACCOMPLISHED WHAT YOUR HEART HAS ALWAYS DESIRED WITH A MINIMUM AMOUNT OF BLOODSHED.
YOU DON'T KNOW WHAT I'VE--

YOU CAN FINALLY SLEEP AT NIGHT.
KNOWING THAT THE WORLD IS IN GOOD HANDS.
"HE'S STARTING TO LOSE IT..."

...MAX WON'T BE ABLE TO CONTROL THE DIAMOND FOR MUCH LONGER.
THAT'S A GOOD THING, AIN'T IT?
NO.
YOU DON'T UNDERSTAND...THE HEART OF DARKNESS HAS NEVER TOUCHED SOMEONE WITH ABILITIES LIKE MAX'S BEFORE... IT'S ENJOYING IT.
AT FIRST, THE DIAMOND BREEDS CORRUPTION... WHICH CREATES CHAOS...
...AND THEN THE DIAMOND FEEDS ON THE ENTROPY.
WE NEED TO GO. CAN YOU BOOM-TUBE ME TO MAX?
IT WON'T BE EXACT. I CAN GET YOU CLOSE...
...BUT THEN THE DIAMOND WILL KNOW I'M HELPING YOU...IF IT DOESN'T ALREADY.
KATANA AND I CAN KEEP CYBORG CONTAINED HERE.
MAX DOESN'T KNOW THAT WE HAVE ALL THIS INTEL ON HIM AND HIS LOCATION...WE CAN USE THAT.
I'M COMING WITH YOU.
ABSOLUTELY NOT.
AS LONG AS MAX HAS THE JUSTICE LEAGUE UNDER HIS THUMB, IT'S TOO DANGEROUS.
WHY? BECAUSE YOU STILL DON'T TRUST US?

THIS IS THE END OF THE WORLD, BATMAN.

MY OLD LIFE MIGHT HAVE ENDED WHEN I BECAME KILLER FROST, BUT I'M NOT LETTING SOME NUTJOB WITH A PURPLE ROCK TAKE MY NEW ONE.

YOU HAVE TO TRUST US.

BUT I'M GOING TO DO EVERYTHING IN MY POWER TO STOP MAX... WHAT HAVE YOU GOT TO LOSE BY BRINGING ME ALONG?

BRING US ALONG, FROSTY. I STILL HAVE A BONE TO PICK WITH MAX... AND WALLER.

I'M SICK OF BEING TREATED LIKE I AIN'T A THREAT.

THIS DIPSTICK'LL REGRET NOT GIVING ME A BLUE FACE.

THE ONLY WAY WE'RE GOING TO STOP MAX IS TO SEPARATE HIM FROM THE HEART OF DARKNESS DIAMOND.

BUT THAT MEANS HAVING TO GET PAST THE JUSTICE LEAGUE.

DIBS ON AQUAMAN.

THE ODDS ARE AGAINST US. THIS LEAGUE WILL NOT HESITATE TO KILL YOU.
ALL OF US MAY NOT COME BACK.

AND? THAT'S WHAT WE DO, BATS.
HOW'S THIS ANY DIFFERENT?
BECAUSE YOU'RE NOT GOING AS THE SUICIDE SQUAD.

WELCOME TO THE JUSTICE LEAGUE.
"WHAT IS YOUR ENDGAME, MAX?"

CAN YOU TELL ME THAT?
THE UNITED STATES WAS JUST THE START, AMANDA.
I'M GOING TO SHARE THIS GIFT WITH THE WORLD.
FINALLY, ALL OF HUMANITY WILL KNOW SOMETHING THAT MOST THOUGHT WAS NEVER POSSIBLE.
BUT I KNEW... I KNEW THAT IF I HAD MY WAY...
...I COULD GIVE THE WORLD PEACE.
I DID IT.
I DID IT!
ISN'T IT WONDERFUL, AMANDA?
CAN'T YOU HEAR THEM? THEY'RE CHANTING MY NAME.

THE WORLD IS FINALLY FREE.

MAX...
WHAT HAVE YOU DONE?
DOES PEACE SCARE YOU THAT MUCH, AMANDA?
YOU NEED TO GET CONTROL OF YOURSELF.
THAT DIAMOND IS IN YOUR HEAD.
IT'S MAKING YOU SEE THINGS...
...THAT AREN'T REAL.
...WHAT?
LOOK AGAIN, MAX.
THIS IS THE WORLD YOU HAVE CREATED.

NO...
⁞huh⁞ ⁞huh⁞ ⁞huh⁞ ⁞huh⁞
I CAN FEEL THE VOICE...HE'S... CHANGING ME...
KILL THEM!
HELP ME, AMANDA...
...T-TELL ME WH-WHAT TO DO... P-PLEASE...
I...
EEEIIII!!!

DON'T GET HANDSY, YA BUNCHA FREAKS!

EVERYONE FOLLOW ME!
NO KILLING!
THAT'D BE A LOT EASIER IF THESE MANIACS WEREN'T TRYING TO KILL US!
huh huh huh
FOCUS, MAX. YOU CAN DO THIS. LET GO OF THE DIAMOND.
A-AMANDA...
THERE'S MAX!
I...I CAN'T.
SSHHZZTT

YOU DIDN'T LISTEN TO ME, BATMAN.
I'M GLAD.
NOOOO!

KRK
KK
RRRRGGGGG
RIPP
KRAKK
WHAT'S HAPPENING TO THE SUN?!
THAT'S THE SIGN THE DINGO JUST ATE OUR BABY, LUV.
IT'S BEEN FAR TOO LONG SINCE I'VE FELT THE NIGHT'S DARKNESS UPON MY SKIN...

THIS WORLD BELONGS TO ECLIPSO.
AND ONCE I HAVE STRIPPED IT BARE, I WILL CORRUPT ALL OF CREATION.

EATON
FAUCHER
ELTAEB

EATON
FAUCHER
ELTAE

WASHINGTON, D.C.

"SUNRISE TO SUNSET..."

THE PICKET. KIRBY ROAD. VIRGINIA.

...YOU'RE **ALWAYS** HERE. YOU MUST NOT BE A BIG FAN OF THE SUN, **MASTER CHIEF.**

PLANS TONIGHT?

YOU CAN'T GUARANTEE MUCH IN LIFE, BUT AT LEAST YOU KNOW THE SUN ALWAYS RISES.
FUNNY TO HEAR MYSELF SAY THAT. STEVE TREVOR DIDN'T ALWAYS SEE THE WORLD THROUGH ROSE-TINTED GOGGLES.

UH... MASTER CHIEF?
BUT I'VE BEEN LUCKY THE LAST FEW YEARS. AND LUCK AND OPTIMISM ARE FIRST COUSINS.

THROOM
ARE WE UNDER ATTACK?
AH!
NOT US, MASTER CHIEF. IT'S THE *WHITE HOUSE.*
AT 18:35 THE WESTERN WALL WAS STRUCK BY AN EXPLOSIVE PROJECTILE. LIKELY A MISSILE. CONNECTING TO VIDEO NOW.
OH GOD. IT'S NOT A MISSILE.
IT'S **SUPERMAN.**
A FEW YEARS AGO I WAS ASKED TO ACT AS LIAISON TO THE JUSTICE LEAGUE. I WAS TO BE THEIR BRIDGE TO HUMANITY. AND I WAS THERE TO WATCH...

..IN CASE THEY EVER DECIDED TO STOP ACTING AS OUR SAVIORS AND INSTEAD BECOME OUR MASTERS.
REPORTS AND VIDEO COMING IN FROM ALL OVER.
ALERT
SATELLITE CAMERAS SHOW THE GREEN LANTERNS ENCIRCLING THE PLANET IN AN ENERGY SHIELD.
SAT FEED
COAST GUARD REPORTS AQUAMAN AND AN ARMY OF MARINE...ANIMALS RINGING THE SHORES.

AIR FORCE GLOBAL STRIKE COMMAND SAYS THE FLASH HAS DISMANTLED OVER FOUR HUNDRED LGM-MINUTEMAN MISSILES AND COUNTING.
AND CELL PHONE FOOTAGE SHOWS WONDER WOMAN ON THE SENATE FLOOR.
I WAS THERE IN CASE THEY EVER DID THIS.
THAT MARK ON THEIR FACES. SOMEONE'S TAKEN CONTROL OF THE JUSTICE LEAGUE. IF THEY HAVE THE OTHERS, THEY PROBABLY HAVE CYBORG, TOO.
THEY'LL HAVE CONTROL OF THE COMMUNICATIONS AND POWER GRID--
VOOOM
--ANY SECOND.
UHN. HUHN...

LEAH. IT'S OKAY. JUST KEEP CALM. I'LL GET THE REMAINING STAFF AND...
MASTER CHIEF. SOMETIMES WHEN YOU'RE OUT IN THE FIELD, AND I'M ON SUPPORT, I...
I HOPE SOMETHING TERRIBLE HAPPENS TO YOU.

LEAH?
I WANT TO SEE YOU STABBED. OR SHOT. OR BLOWN UP.

I WANT TO WATCH YOU DIE, STEVE.
THAT MARK. THE SAME AS THE ONE ON THE LEAGUE. ON DIANA.
AH!
MY LEG--
SKLCH

I HAVE TO KNOW WHAT HAPPENS.
DOES SOMETHING CHANGE IN YOUR EYES?

DOES A LIGHT GO OUT?

HNH!

SHE'S STRONG. LIKE A METHAMPHETAMINE USER. UNAWARE OF HER LIMITATIONS.

SHE'S RUNNING ON PURE UNFILTERED INSTINCT.

WOK

HNH.
REFLEXIVE IMPULSE.

KLK
SO AM I.

SKLCH
SKLCH
NO. SHE'S A VICTIM. THIS IS SOME KIND OF AIRBORNE INFECTION. WEAPONIZED RABIES.
THE DOOR. BELOW THIS STRUCTURE IS A COMMAND STATION STAFFED BY THE NIGHT SHIFT.
TWENTY COMMUNICATION TECHS.
TWENTY OF THE BRIGHTEST MINDS IN THIS CITY. TWENTY PEOPLE WHO TURNED DOWN JOBS AS LOBBYISTS OR POLITICAL AIDES TO HELP DEFEND THIS COUNTRY.
TWENTY INSANE, BABBLING MONSTERS.

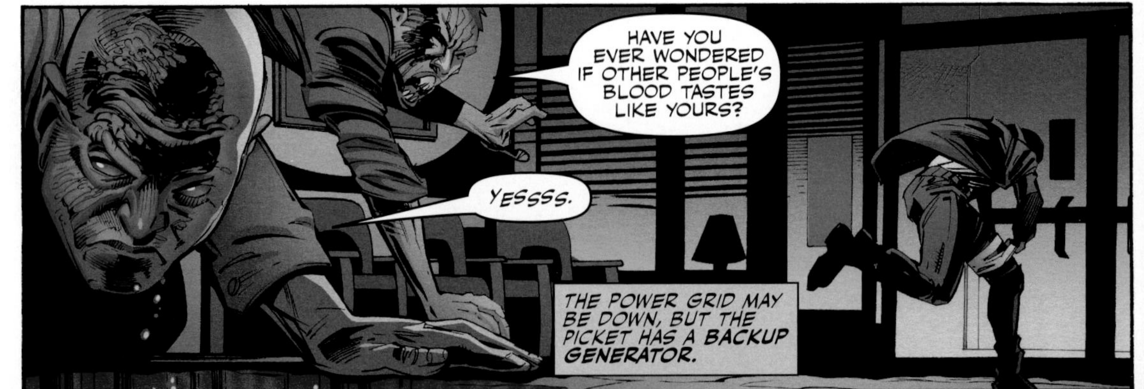
HAVE YOU EVER WONDERED IF OTHER PEOPLE'S BLOOD TASTES LIKE YOURS?
YESSSS.
THE POWER GRID MAY BE DOWN, BUT THE PICKET HAS A BACKUP GENERATOR.

MMM. SALT AND METAL AND PAIN.
LET'S DRINK IT ALL.
IT SHOULD GO ON ANY SECOND...

AS LONG AS THE COMM TECHS DIDN'T DECIDE TO TURN IT OFF.
HNF!
MASTER CHIEF! COME BACK!

WE WANT TO PLAY WITH YOU, STEVEY.
MISTER TREVORRRR.
COME BACK. PLEASE. I'VE ALWAYS WANTED TO TELL YOU... I WANT TO BOIL YOU ALIVE.
I WANT TO TAKE OUT THOSE PRETTY BLUE EYES.
THEY PRATTLE ON, SAYING WHATEVER COMES TO THEIR SICK MINDS, ALL OF THEIR VOICES SLIGHTLY HIGHER PITCHED THAN BEFORE.

LIKE KIDS PLAYING IN THE DARK, EXCITED AND SCARED IN EQUAL MEASURE.

PICKET COMMAND! VOICE I.D.! TREVOR, STEVEN ROCKWELL! CODE WORD: SANDY.
INITIATE EMERGENCY LOCKDOWN!
OPEN ONLY ON MASTER CHIEF'S ORDERS!
SHNK

NO! I WANT TO SEE IT ALL BURNING!
PLEASE, STEVE! TAKE ME WITH! LET ME CRAWL INSIDE YOU!
CELL NETWORKS ARE OUT.
CAN'T CALL TRACY. CAN'T TELL HER TO STAY WHERE SHE IS.

WHEEOOOOO
CAN'T CHECK TO SEE IF IAN AND ALLISON ARE OKAY. CAN'T MAKE SURE THEY AREN'T TORN APART OR WORSE--
STOP.
I'M GOING TO GET TO MY HOUSE. I'M GOING TO FIND MY SISTER AND HER KIDS THERE, SAFE AND SOUND.
I JUST HAVE TO STAY CALM. I HAVE TO LET MY INSTINCTS AND TRAINING TAKE OVER.

I HAVE TO STAY OPTIMISTIC.

DRIVING ACROSS THE FRANCIS SCOTT KEY BRIDGE IN RUSH HOUR CAN BE FRUSTRATING. A FEW MILES BETWEEN "THE OFFICE" AND MY HOUSE CAN TAKE AN HOUR. SOMETIMES YOU WISH YOU COULD BLOW UP THE CARS IN FRONT OF YOU.
WHATEVER HAS HAPPENED TO THESE PEOPLE...
...IT STARTS WITH THOSE DESIRES. THE DEEP-DOWN URGES THAT WE TAMPER WITH CIVILITY.
JUNK! JALOPY! LEMON!
SKRRK
IT'S GOING TO BE DARK AND DANGEROUS ONCE I GET INTO THE NEIGHBORHOODS AND DON'T HAVE THE BENEFIT OF MOONLIGHT.
I'LL LEAVE A TEN SPOT--
NRRGLM
SOUNDS WET. ALMOST DON'T--

--WANT TO KNOW.
MN. MY LOVELY PRINCESS. LOVELY INSIDE.

EIIGHK!
U.V. LIGHT. LOOKS LIKE THAT HURTS THEM. LIKE A VAMPIRE IN THE SUNLIGHT.

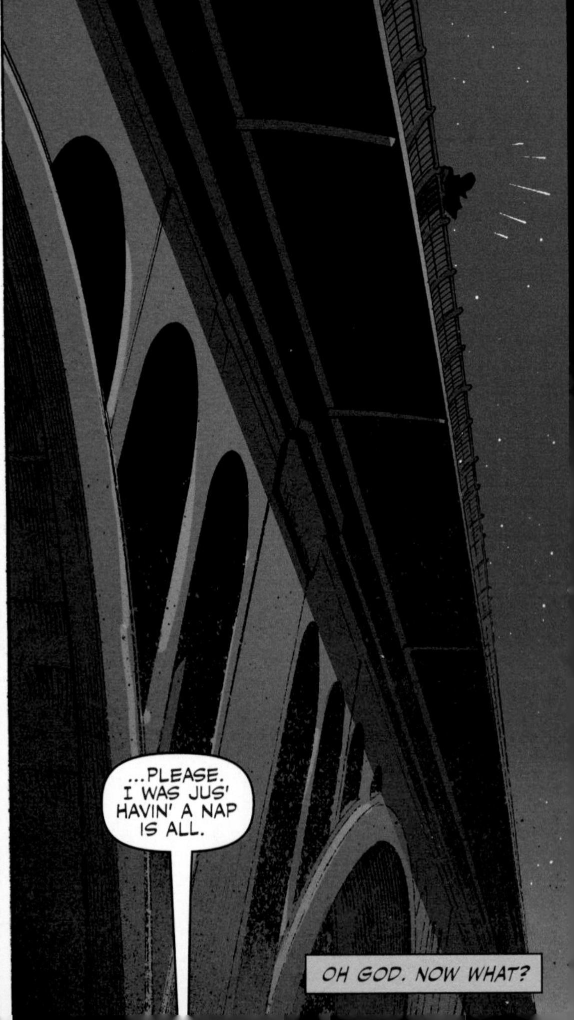

...PLEASE. I WAS JUS' HAVIN' A NAP IS ALL.
OH GOD. NOW WHAT?

THERE IT IS AGAIN. THE WORST, SICKEST, BASEST VILENESS BUBBLING UP.
JUS' TRY AND STAY WARM IS ALL.
DIRTY LOSER. RUINING OUR CITY. BURN FOR WARMTH.

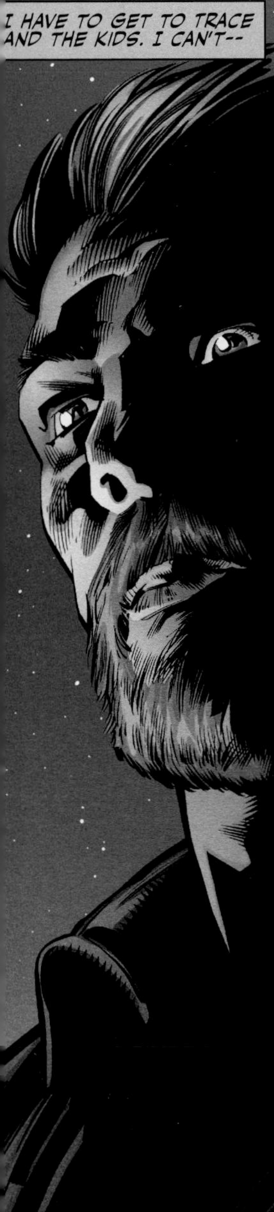

I HAVE TO GET TO TRACE AND THE KIDS. I CAN'T--

NO. WHATEVER'S AFFECTING THEM, IT HASN'T GOTTEN TO ME. I'M STILL MASTER CHIEF TREVOR. AND I DON'T LEAVE ANYONE BEHIND.

GO! HEAD TO THE UNDERPASS. PUT YOUR BACK TO THE CORNER!
UNF!
I WAS IN A PLANE CRASH ONCE. A BAD ONE. COPILOT KILLED. NO IDEA WHERE I LANDED.
AAAAH!

WE'RE CANNED MEAT TO THEM CRAZY MONSTERS!
NO. ROMAN ARMY TACTICS. WE'VE GOT A FORTRESS AT OUR BACKS...
BUT I WAS SAVED. TAKEN IN. HEALED. LIFTED UP BY AN ANGEL.

...AND A WALL OF FLAME IN FRONT OF US.
AIIGH!
IT'S WHAT ELEVATED ME FROM A CYNIC TO A BELIEVER.

NOW WHAT, SMART GUY?
WE MIGHT HAVE JUST HIT THE JACKPOT...

WONDER WOMAN! DOWN HERE!

BECAUSE MY ANGEL IS ALWAYS THERE WHEN I NEED HER.

STEVE. I WAS WONDERING--

--IF YOU WERE DEAD YET.

OH GOD. DIANA.

STUPID SOLDIER BOY.

FIGHTING OFF IN SOME FOREIGN LAND, KILLING PEOPLE--
WHILE WE STARVE IN THE STREETS.

MAYBE WE SHOULD EAT YOU.
NO ONE IS SAFE.

IS IT TOO LATE? AM I THE LAST MAN ON EARTH?

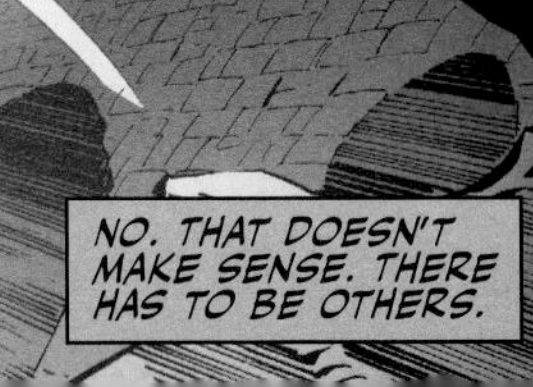

NO. THAT DOESN'T MAKE SENSE. THERE HAS TO BE OTHERS.

BEING AN UNCLE, IT'S NOT QUITE LIKE BEING A DAD. YOU AREN'T THERE FOR EVERYTHING. YOU DON'T HAVE TO DISCIPLINE. YOU STILL GET SLEEP.

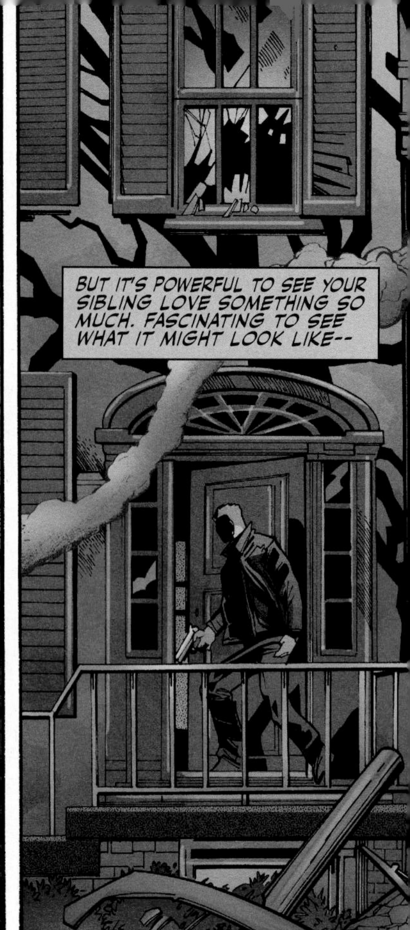
BUT IT'S POWERFUL TO SEE YOUR SIBLING LOVE SOMETHING SO MUCH. FASCINATING TO SEE WHAT IT MIGHT LOOK LIKE--

--IF YOU HAD YOUR OWN KIDS.
WHAT YOUR FUTURE MIGHT LOOK LIKE--

HAHAHA ROUND AND ROUND AND ROUND.
IAN? ALLISON?

RING AROUND THE ROSIE, POCKET FULL OF POSIES...
ASHES. ASHES. BURN MOMMY. BURN.
OH GOD. TRACE. NO NO NO.
THEY'RE GONE. MY SWEET NIECE AND NEPHEW. EVEN IF THEY CAN BE CURED, THEY'LL NEVER...
I'LL NEVER BE ABLE TO LOOK AT THEM AGAIN.
I'LL NEVER BE ABLE TO UNSEE THE DARKNESS.

THE DARKNESS.

STEVEN.

THE DARKNESS SPEAKS.

YOU ASKED. WHY WAS IT JUST YOU?
YOU SEE, STEVEN, IT'S NOT MUCH FUN TO OWN THEM ALL.

IF THEY'RE ALL MINE THEN THERE AREN'T ANY VICTIMS. NO ONE TO SCARE. TO TORMENT.

TO ECLIPSE.

YOU HAVE A STRONG WILL, STEVEN.

FIGHT ME, STEVEN. CHALLENGE ME. FREE YOURSELF FROM THE NIGHT.

NGGHH! GET OUT OF MY HEAD, YOU SPOOKY SONOFA--!

STEVE! YOU DID IT. OH GOD, THANK YOU.

TRACE. I THOUGHT... I THOUGHT YOU WERE--

UNCLE STEVIE!

ALLY. I'M SO GLAD YOU'RE OKAY.

LOOK. IT'S MORNING. I THINK IT'S GOING TO BE OKAY. THE LIGHT CHASES OUT THE DEMONS.

YOU CAN'T GUARANTEE MUCH IN LIFE, BUT AT LEAST YOU KNOW THE SUN ALWAYS RISES.

YOU WERE A CHALLENGE, STEVEN.

BUT SHADOWS FALL ACROSS EVEN THE SUN.

WELCOME TO ECLIPSO, STEVEN.

HA HAHAHA

HA HAHAHA HAH
HA HAHAHA HAH
HA HAHAHA HAH
HA HAHAHA HAH

HAHAHAHAHAHA

WELCOME TO ECLIPSO
TIM SEELEY GUEST WRITER
SCOT EATON PENCILLER
WAYNE FAUCHER INKER
GABE ELTAEB COLORIST
RICHARD STARKINGS & COMICRAFT LETTERER
SCOT EATON, WAYNE FAUCHER & GABE ELTAEB COVER
AMEDEO TURTURRO & DIEGO LOEPZ ASSISTANT EDITORS
BRIAN CUNNINGHAM EDITOR
WELCOME TO MY WORLD.

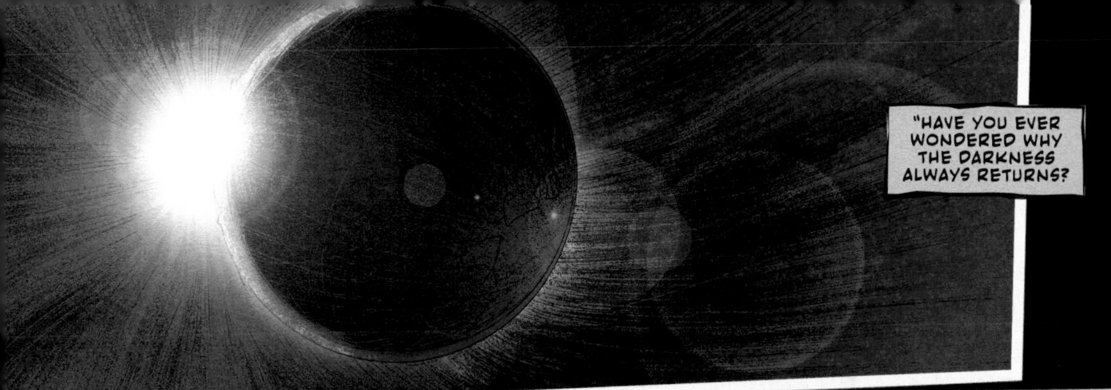
"HAVE YOU EVER WONDERED WHY THE DARKNESS ALWAYS RETURNS?

"BECAUSE IT NEVER LEAVES.

"THE POTENTIAL FOR WICKEDNESS IS ALWAYS PRESENT...
"...INSIDE YOU.

"I DON'T MAKE PEOPLE EVIL..."

...ECLIPSO JUST UNLOCKS THE DARKNESS WITHIN.
JUSTICE LEAGUE VS. SUICIDE SQUAD
CONCLUSION

JOSHUA WILLIAMSON Writer • HOWARD PORTER Artist
ALEX SINCLAIR Color • ROB LEIGH Letterer • HOWARD PORTER & ALEX SINCLAIR Cover
AMEDEO TURTURRO Asst. Editor • JESSICA CHEN & HARVEY RICHARDS Assoc. Editors
ANDY KHOURI Consulting Editor • BRIAN CUNNINGHAM Editor

CAN YOU FEEL THAT? THE ENERGY IN THE AIR...IT'S MORE THAN TERROR OR RAGE...THE CORRUPTION AND CHAOS...
...IT'S EUPHORIC.
BRAKA-BRAKA-BRAKK
SPEAK FOR YOURSELF, UGLY!
DEADSHOT...

DON'T YOU?

WHY DO YOU COVER YOUR FACE FROM THE WORLD?

SHOW ME...WHAT ARE YOU TRYING TO *HIDE?*

KRIKK

I'VE MET MANY KILLERS ON THIS PLANET, AND THE HUNGER TO TAKE LIVES WAS HARDLY THEIR DEEPEST SECRET. THERE IS ALWAYS...
...SOMETHING THEY'D NEVER ADMIT.

"YOUR *DAUGHTER*..."

SHE'S THE ONLY THING THAT KEEPS ME HUMAN. BUT IF I KILLED HER... I WOULDN'T FEEL SHAME OR GUILT ANYMORE.
I COULD JUST KILL WITHOUT REMORSE...

LOVELY.
GO...FIND YOUR WAY, KILLER. WHY STOP WITH YOUR DAUGHTER...?

I'LL KILL EVERYONE.
THAT WAS FUN.
WHO'S NEXT?
AMANDA WALLER.
MAY I HAVE THIS DANCE?
YOUR PRIMITIVE SUN LAMPS COULDN'T CONTAIN MY PRESENCE IN THE HEART OF DARKNESS... AND NEITHER YOU NOR THE SUN CAN HOLD ME BACK FOREVER...
I HAD TO TRY, YOU MONSTER.
MONSTER? ME?
YOU TAKE YOUR WORST THOUGHTS... UNSPEAKABLE ACTS... AND PUT THEM TO GOOD USE.
I LOVE THAT ABOUT YOU.

KILLER ROST...
...WALLER USED... *SUNLIGHT...* TO CONTAIN... THE HEART OF DARKNESS...
IF THAT'S ECLIPSO'S WEAKNESS, WE NEED TO TAKE HIM DOWN FAST.
IT'S BEEN TOO LONG SINCE I HAVE DRAINED SOMEONE'S LIFE FORCE--THEIR BODY HEAT--AND MY POWERS ARE NEARLY OUT!
WE NEED TO HIT HIM WITH A LIGHT AS BRIGHT AS THE SUN.
ECLIPSO ***BLOCKED OUT*** THE SUN, BATMAN. WHERE ARE WE GOING TO GET THAT KIND OF...
SSZZZT
THERE.
SUPERMAN'S CELLS ARE ***SUPERCHARGED*** FROM OUR ***YELLOW SUN.***
CAN YOU CREATE A ***PRISM*** TO TRAP HIS HEAT BLAST AND CONVERT IT INTO ***SUNLIGHT?***
I DON'T KNOW! SUSTAINING COLD ATOMS THAT ***COMPLEX*** WILL TAKE UP ALL THE LIFE FORCE I HAVE LEFT.
WE'D ONLY GET ***ONE SHOT.***
AIN'T ***THAT*** A CRYIN' ***SHAME?***

IF HUMANITY'S LAST HOPE IS YOU, KILLER FROST, WE MIGHT AS WELL GIVE UP NOW.
LOBO, KEEP THE LEAGUE AND SQUAD BUSY WHILE KILLER FROST BUILDS THE PRISM.
FROST?
THEY'RE GONNA WISH THEY TOLD THE MAIN MAN THEIR SAFE WORD, BATS.

HAN JUST A BLOCK OF ICE, BATMAN!

I HAVE TO ENGINEER THE PRISM PROPERLY OR IT WON'T BE ABLE TO DISTRIBUTE THE LIGHT!

AND IT'LL NEED ***CONSTANT*** COLD ATOMS FROM MY POWERS TO KEEP IT STABLE.

FEETAL'S GIZ! S'BETTER'N ROASTING BABY ORCS ON SALEM-9!

YOU'VE LIVED IN THE SHADOWS FOR SO LONG, BATMAN. DON'T YOU THINK IT'S TIME THAT YOU BECAME ***ONE*** WITH THE DARK?
NO MATTER WHAT YOU DO, SUPERMAN, YOU'LL ***NEVER*** BE HUMAN. ***EVER. I*** KNOW IT. ***YOU*** KNOW IT.

AND YOUR ***SON*** KNOWS IT.

BURN.
SSHHHNNT

ZZZZTT

FWASH

RGH!

DON'T LET THE PRISM MELT, FROST!

IT'S-- IT'S NOT HOLDING--!

I...I'M OUT OF HEAT, BATMAN. THAT TOOK EVERYTHING I HAD...
...I...DON'T HAVE ENOUGH... POWER LEFT...

TAKE MY LIFE FORCE.

WHAT... NO.
THAT AMOUNT OF ENERGY WOULD KILL YOU.
I KNOW. *DO IT.*
CAITLIN...

...TAKE THE ENERGY FROM *ALL* OF US.
Uh, WOMEN AND CHILDREN FIRST...
IF I TAKE A LITTLE BIT FROM EACH OF YOU, WE MIGHT HAVE A CHANCE...

FWSSH
IT ...ON'T BE ENOUGH!
LOOK INSIDE YOURSELF, KILLER FROST... WHAT IS YOUR DARKEST DESIRE?
I...
WHAT DO YOU DENY YOURSELF OF? WHAT IS THE THING YOU WILL NEVER ADMIT TO YOURSELF?
...THAT I WANT...
...TO MAKE A DIFFERENCE.
KRRAK
NOW!
SSZZT

RRAAAGH!

M

WE... DID IT...

TOOK... EVERYTHING HAD...ALL THAT NERGY...GONE... I...
...I'M... DYING.

THEN KILL HIM!

WHAT?
KILL MAX NOW.

BUT...
DO YOU WANT TO LIVE OR NOT?!
ABSORB MAX'S LIFE FORCE!

I--I...

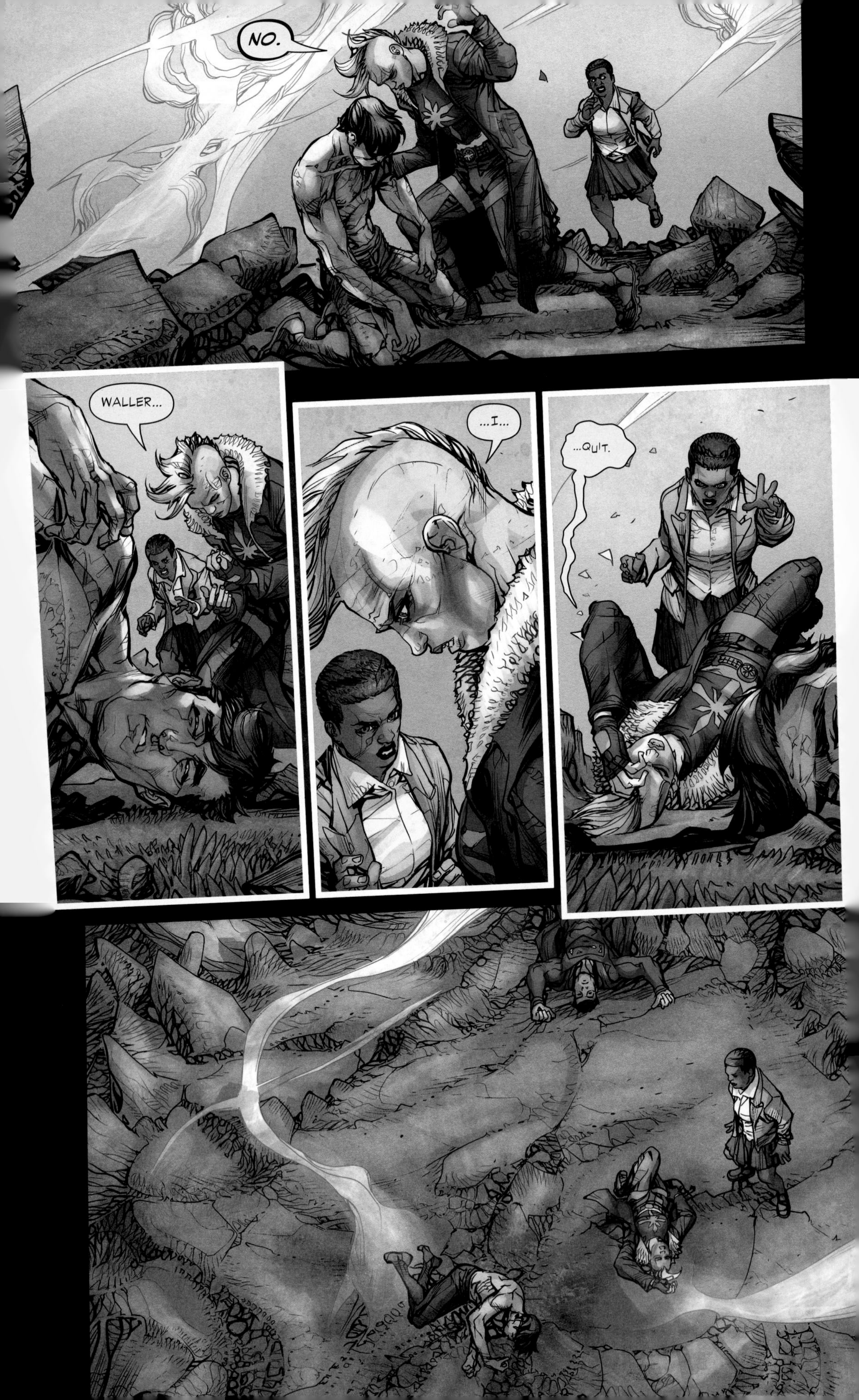
NO.
WALLER...
...I...
...QUIT.

Belle Reve Penitentiary.

I CHANNEL THEM FROM MY EMOTIONS...
SO, WAIT, YOU *CAN* TALK TO FISH, RIGHT?
...SO LEMME GET THIS STRAIGHT--I'D BE THE ONLY MAN ON THE ISLAND?
THERE'D STILL BE NO MEN ON IT.
GOT THIS ONE FROM ATROCITUS.
THAT'S *NOTHING,* TRY BEING IMPALED ON DEATHSTROKE'S SWORD...
IS BATMAN ALWAYS A SOURPUSS?

HOW'RE YOU FEELING?

ALL MY LIFE ALL I EVER WANTED TO DO WAS HELP PEOPLE. IT'S WHY I BECAME A SCIENTIST.
WHEN I TURNED INTO KILLER FROST, I THOUGHT THAT LIFE HAD BEEN STOLEN FROM ME...AND AFTER ALL I'VE DONE, I DIDN'T THINK I DESERVED THAT LIFE ANYMORE.
WHEN ECLIPSO LOOKED INSIDE MY MOST PRIVATE THOUGHTS...
...HE DIDN'T FIND MY FEARS... THAT WASN'T WHAT I WAS HIDING.
HE FOUND *HOPE.*
BUT, SUPERMAN... AFTER I REALIZED THE HOPE WAS THERE, IT DIDN'T MATTER IF I LIVED OR DIED...I JUST WANTED TO STOP ECLIPSO.
MAYBE I'M RIGHT AT HOME WITH THE SUICIDE SQUAD.
WHAT YOU DID WASN'T *SUICIDE,* CAITLIN.
IT WAS *SACRIFICE.*
"KILLER FROST IS COMING WITH ME."

LIKE HELL SHE IS.
YOU ALWAYS CLAIM THAT IF YOUR INMATES COMPLETE THESE MISSIONS FOR YOU, THEY'LL GET A REDUCED PRISON SENTENCE.
KILLER FROST PUT HER LIFE ON THE LINE TO SAVE THE WORLD, WALLER.
THINK OF IT AS EARLY PAROLE FOR GOOD BEHAVIOR.
WITH YOU AS HER PAROLE OFFICER?
WHETHER SHE JOINS ME OR NOT WILL BE UP TO HER, BUT SHE IS NOT STAYING HERE WITH YOU.
SHE'S A KILLER.
YOU SAY THAT AS IF THAT'S ALL SHE IS, WALLER.
FROST SHOWED THE LEAGUE THAT SHE HAS POTENTIAL.
AS MUCH AS I HATE TO ADMIT IT...

...CAITLIN SNOW PROVES THERE IS VALUE IN TASK FORCE X.
I MAY HAVE... MISJUDGED YOUR... SUICIDE SQUAD.
THERE'S ROOM IN THE WORLD FOR BOTH OF OUR TEAMS.
YOU'RE SAYING THAT YOU... BATMAN...WERE WRONG?
YOU CAN HAVE KILLER FROST.
BUT YOU'LL SEE THE BEST PLACE FOR PEOPLE LIKE HER IS WORKING FOR ME.
SHE'LL SHOW YOU.
AND WHEN SHE GETS OUT OF CONTROL...

"...YOU'LL NEED ALL THE HELP YOU CAN GET."
SPACE HOG!
BABY! WHERE YOU BEEN HIDING?!
WE NEED TO TALK.

THEM'S FIGHTING WORDS, BATS.
I'M SURPRISED YOU DIDN'T GO AFTER WALLER.

SHE'S WORTH MORE TO ME ALIVE THAN DEAD.
BUT YOU? I AIN'T DONE WITH YOU BY FAR!

YOU KNOCKED ME OUT OF MAX'S VOODOO MAGIC.
IT'S NOT LIKE MAX WASN'T HAVIN' ME DO THINGS I WOULDN'T NORMALLY DO...BUT THE MAIN MAN AIN'T ANYONE'S SLAVE...

SO...IF YOU EVER NEED A JOB DONE--
--I DON'T GIVE A FRAG HOW MESSY OR CRAZY...

...I'LL GIVE YA ONE FREEBIE.
AND THE MAIN MAN NEVER BREAKS HIS WORD.
I ALREADY HAVE A JOB FOR YOU.

YOU'LL JOIN THE JUSTICE LEAGUE.
SAY WHAT NOW?
WORK ALONGSIDE A NEW KIND OF JUSTICE LEAGUE.
THE MAIN MAN... AIN'T REALLY THE TEAM TYPE...
ARE YOU A MAN OF YOUR WORD...
...OR NOT?
"I'VE BEEN ASKING MYSELF..."

...HOW DID I GET HERE?
WHILE AT CHECK
I DISCOVERED THE
OF THE HEART OF D
IN BELLE REVE. AN I
WOULD HELP ME BRI
AND CONTROL TO T
BUT IF I WERE TO RE
I WOULD NEED
AND THEN I RECEIVED INTEL ABOUT THE VERY FIRST SUICIDE SQUAD LOCKED UP IN THE CATACOMBS. I COULD USE THEIR HATE TO MANIPULATE THEM.
AND I KNEW THE JUSTICE LEAGUE WAS COMING FOR THE SUICIDE SQUAD THAT DISTRACTION CREATED THE PERFECT TIME TO STRIKE.
EVERYTHING FELL INTO PLACE.
"BUT FINDING THE LEAGUE WORKING ALONGSIDE THE SUICIDE SQUAD IN BELLE REVE...THAT WAS A SURPRISE.
"WHY WOULD THE JUSTICE LEAGUE DO THAT WILLINGLY?
HAD I BEEN LESS FOCUSED ON THE DIAMOND, I WOULD HAVE QUESTIONED THEIR PRESENCE MORE. THAT WAS MY MISTAKE.
BUT NOW THAT I'VE HAD SOME TIME TO REFLECT, IT'S CLEAR THAT EVERY SINGLE STEP WAS METICULOUSLY MAPPED OUT BEFORE I EVEN CONCEIVED A PLAN...

...BY YOU, AMANDA.
"LOOK ON HER WORKS, YE MIGHTY AND DESPAIR..."

YOU TOOK CHECKMATE AWAY FROM ME.
YOU TIPPED ME OFF TO THE FIRST SUICIDE SQUAD.
YOU POINTED ME TOWARD THE ECLIPSO DIAMOND.
YOU SET ALL OF THIS IN MOTION BECAUSE BATMAN WAS STARTING TO COME AFTER YOUR PRECIOUS TASK FORCE X.
SO YOU CREATED A COMMON ENEMY.
ME.
BUT YOUR MASTER PLAN WASN'T WITHOUT ITS RISKS, AMANDA.
YOUR STRATEGY WAS EXTRAORDINARILY DANGEROUS. EVEN RECKLESS.
"THERE'S THE SHEER LOSS OF LIFE. THE CATACOMBS AND BELLE REVE ARE NOTHING COMPARED TO WHAT HAPPENED AROUND THE WORLD.
NOT TO MENTION THE LOOSE ENDS...

EMERALD EMPRESS
REE TO FIND WHATEVER
WAS SEARCHING FOR."
THE EYE... IT'S CRUMBLING. IT'S THE ONLY THING KEEPING ME IN THIS TIME.
IF I CAN'T FIND SATURN GIRL ALONE... PERHAPS I CAN DO SO WITH FIVE.
"JOHNNY SORROW'S MASK REMAINED BEHIND...BUT WHAT WOULD HAPPEN IF SOMEONE ELSE WERE TO PUT THAT ON?"
DID YOU HEAR THAT?
HEAR WHAT?
THE MASK--IT'S WHISPERING--ABOUT A LOST SOCIETY...

"DOCTOR POLARIS IS PSYCHOTIC. WHO KNOWS WHAT HE COULD GET UP TO...?"
OH NO... THEY MADE ME BE POLARIS AGAIN...
IS THIS BLOOD?
WHAT... WHAT HAVE I DONE?

"RUSTAM IS NEVER GOING TO FORGIVE YOU, AMANDA. BUT HE'S GOING TO WANT TO SEE YOU HURT.

"AND YOU MAY HAVE FREED ME FROM ECLIPSO, BUT HE IS FAR FROM DEAD...AND HE'S VERY PATIENT. IT'S ONLY A MATTER OF TIME BEFORE HE'LL CORRUPT THE WORLD AGAIN..."
IT JUST FELL FROM THE SKY, DAD!
BE CAREFUL, SON...

...ALL SO THE JUSTICE LEAGUE WOULD *ACCEPT* YOUR LITTLE HOUSE OF *HORRORS.*
I HAVE TO ASK...*WAS IT ALL WORTH IT?*
I DON'T OWE YOU ANY ANSWERS, MAX.
HA! WELL, AT LEAST ALLOW ME TO OFFER MY CONGRATULATIONS ON A GAME WELL PLAYED, AMANDA.

IT'S ALWAYS BEEN MY WISH THAT, IN THE END, MY LEGACY WOULD BE ONE OF HOPE AND INSPIRATION. AND YOU'VE HELPED WITH THAT.
BUT ONCE I USE MY POWERS TO ESCAPE...

I WOULDN'T RECOMMEND THAT.
YOU SEE THOSE TUBES CONNECTED TO YOUR ARMS?

I'M PUMPING YOU FULL OF THE BEST HIGH-GRADE BLOOD THINNERS THAT SCIENCE CAN MAKE.
YOU EVEN ATTEMPT TO USE YOUR POWERS, YOU'LL *BLEED OUT* BEFORE YOU CAN EXIT THE PRISON.

YOU WON'T LET THAT HAPPEN, AMANDA.
IF YOU REALLY WANTED TO BE DONE WITH ME, YOU'D PUT A *BULLET* IN MY HEAD AND CALL IT A *DAY.*
SO IS THIS WHERE YOU SAY, *"WELCOME TO THE SUICIDE SQUAD"?*

NO, MAX.
I HAVE *OTHER* PLANS FOR YOU.

YOUR TALENTS WOULD BE *WASTED* IN *TASK FORCE X.*

BUT YOU'RE PERFECT FOR...
...TASK FORCE XI.

ALASKA.
63°58'2"N,
145°42'33"W.
NOW.

FORT ALUETIA
MISSILE SILO...
CURRENT
ARSENAL: 20
W-87 ICBM
WARHEADS.
S-SIR?

TOTAL COMBINED
PAYLOAD: 9,500
KILOTONS.
S...
SOMEONE...
G-GOT
IN...

ARMAGEDDON
IN A BOX...
INTRUDER
ALERT
OH MY
GOD...

INTRUDER
ALERT
INTRUDER
ALERT
WHICH IS ALL WELL
AND GOOD. BUT...

WHAT IF SOMEONE WITH A GRUDGE LETS IT OUT?
FWAMMM
JUSTICE LEAGUE VS. SUICIDE SQUAD
EPILOGUE: THE COST
ROB WILLIAMS & SI SPURRIER WRITERS GIUSEPPE CAFARO ARTIST HI-FI COLORS PAT BROSSEAU LETTERER
CAFARO & HI-FI COVER BRIAN CUNNINGHAM GROUP EDITOR
AMEDEO TURTURRO ASSISTANT EDITOR HARVEY RICHARDS ASSOCIATE EDITOR ANDY KHOURI EDITOR

BRRATTT
BRRATTT
WHO IS THIS GUY?!
OH MY GOD...THE BODIES...
RRRIPP
TELL HER.
RUSTAM IS COMING.
AND THIS IS A WAR OF HER OWN MAKING.
OH NO...

THIS IS BAD.
CHECK THE WARHEADS!
SIR, LOOK!
A PHOTO-GRAPH!
"HELLUVA TWIST, RIGHT?"
"WHAT? HELL NO! IT SUCKS! WHAT'S THE POINT OF A TWIST IF NOBODY UNDERSTANDS WHAT THEY'RE SEEING?"

...ONE STUPID ORIGAMI UNICORN AND WE'RE ALL SUPPOSED TO ROP OUR JAWS. "CINEMATIC CLASSIC" MY BUTT!
GUYS, C'MON-- NOT NOW.
NUH-UH! JUST BECAUSE YOU DIDN'T UNDERSTAND THE IMPLICATION DOESN'T MEAN--
HEY!
NUMBER ONE: SPOILERS.
YOU'VE NEVER SEEN BLADE RUNNER? HOW ARE YOU EVEN REAL?
AND NUMBER TWO: CAN WE PLEASE SKIP THE COMEDY TWIN NERD SHTICK?
LIKE, SAVE THE CLOWNING FOR WHEN THE LITTLE ONE ARR--
--EXCUSE YOU! DAMN!
BUMP
YO, SON! WATCH WHERE YOU FREAKIN' GOIN'!
UH-HUH! YEAH, LET ME CATCH YOU ON THE STREET AGAIN, SON!
MARTIN, WILL YOU PLEASE CHILL OUT? I'M FINE!
HE'S JUST PLAYIN'! CAN'T LET THESE CATS DISRESPECTIN' YOU!
WE GOT YOU, SIS. WHAT'S THE WORST THAT COULD HAPP--
SCREECH
OH NO.

NATIONAL SECURITY!
GET YOUR HANDS IN THE AIR!
WHAT THE HELL IS THIS?
NO NO NO NO.
CLICK
HELP!!
I'D SAY THAT WENT PRETTY SUPER.

AGREED. COMMENDABLE SUBTLETY, I THOUGHT.
STEALTHIER'N A FART IN A CABBAGE FACTORY, MATE-- THAT'S US.
I WAS WORRIED WE'D HAVE TO CRAM YOU-KNOW-WHO IN A UNIFORM, TOO.
BLOODY RELIEF, LOVE. I THINK HE ATE THE BOOTS ALREADY.
GRRRRR...
AAAAH!!!
HERE--TAKE A LEFT. IT'S RIGHT UP THERE, LOOK. JEEZ-- WHAT A DUNNY.
LOOK LIVELY, BOYS. BOSS IS HERE IN PERSON...
NO COMPLICATIONS? THEY'RE UNHURT? GOOD.
I...I KNOW THAT VOICE.

CORETTA. MARTIN. JESSIE.
YOU'RE SAFE NOW.
M- MOM?
HAPPY FLAMIN' FAMILIES, EH? I'M WELLIN' UP HERE.
AIN'T YOU BOOBY WOO-WOOS GONNA GIVE YOUR MOMSY-WOMSY A BIG OOKY SNOOKEM HUGGAWUGGA, PUDDINS?
GET AWAY FROM THEM, DEVIANTS.
OUTSIDE! SECURE THE PERIMETER!

I IMAGINE YOU'RE WONDERING WHAT THIS PLACE IS.
MOM--WE HAVEN'T SEEN YOU IN TWO YEARS!!
IT WAS EARMARKED AS A BRANCH BASE FOR--FOR AN EARLY VERSION OF MY OPERATION. THERE WERE SOME... TEETHING TROUBLES.
MOM, SERIOUSLY: WE DON'T CARE. WE LIKE OUR FAMILY MEMBERS TO HAVE WARM BLOOD.
WE GOT OUT. WE DON'T NEED YOU.
A REGRETTABLE MISAPPREHENSION, BUT--UNDERSTANDABLE. IT WAS YOUR SAFETY THAT MATTERED MOST, AND BEING NEAR ME? WELL.
ONE MUST BE PREPARED TO MAKE SACRIFICES, ON THE SIDE OF GOOD.
AWWWW--BOSS, I THINK CROC POOPED OUT SOMEONE'S PELVIS IN THE VAN.
I TOLD YOU TO GET OUT, BOOMERANG, OR I WILL DETONATE YOUR WALNUT BRAIN!
"...ON THE SIDE OF GOOD..."
W-WHY NOW?
THE SITUATION HAS CHANGED.
THIS MORNING AN INDIVIDUAL--A TERRORIST, REALLY--STORMED A MILITARY FACILITY IN ALASKA.
HE CAN GET INTO ANYWHERE, DO ANYTHING... THEY ASSUMED HE WAS THERE FOR THE NUKES--THAT'S EXACTLY THE SORT OF THING I'M HERE TO PREVENT--
ROUND OF APPLAUSE.
--BUT... NO, IT WAS A MESSAGE, A THREAT.

WELL, I COULDN'T TRUST THE AUTHORITIES, COULD I? SO I BROUGHT IN MY BEST PEOPLE, MY BEST MONSTERS.
AND I SWEAR TO YOU NOW--I WILL PROTECT YOU. I WILL PROTECT EVERYTHING THAT'S GOOD! YOU DON'T NEED TO BE AFRAID ANYMORE.
YOUR MOMMA'S RESCUED YOU.
...
MOM... SERIOUSLY, I-- I CAN'T BELIEVE I GOTTA SAY THIS OUT LOUD BUT...
WELL, ISN'T THIS ENLIGHTENING...
THIS ISN'T A RESCUE...
...THIS IS WHAT'S CALLED "KIDNAPPING."

COLONEL FLAG HERE, MA'AM. WE'RE IN POSITION.

COPY THAT. I WANT THE EXTERIOR LOCKED DOWN.

FOUR ENTRANCE POINTS TO THIS PLACE, DIRECTOR.

WE HAVE A SNIPER ON EACH OF THEM.

IF YOU SEE IT'S HIM, AND HE COMES IN HEAVY, DON'T HESITATE.

TAKE THE SHOT.

TAKE THE... WHAT THE HELL? IS THIS YOU? IS THIS WHAT YOU DO?

I WORK IN INTELLIGENCE, JESSIE. YOU KNOW THAT.

HOMELAND SECURITY.

FUNNY. HOME NEVER FELT REAL SECURE WITHOUT ANY FUNCTIONING PARENTS IN IT.

...
YOU'VE GOT YOUR DADDY'S EYES.
Y'KNOW, I GENUINELY THOUGHT THE ONLY GOOD ENTERTAINMENT IN LIFE WAS ALCOHOL, STRIP CLUBS AND SUPERGLUING THE FLASH'S FEET TO ARMADILLOS.
BUT THIS IS LIKE WATCHING A BONZER EPISODE OF NEIGHBORS, MATE. HIGH CULTURE! PASS THE FOSTER'S.
HEY, DIGGER...?
SHUT UP.
WHAT DID YOU DO?
EXCUSE ME?
THIS MAN IS COMING AFTER US BECAUSE HE WANTS TO HURT YOU. SO, I'M ASKING YOU, IF OUR LIVES ARE BEING RIPPED APART HERE, IF THERE'S A CHANCE WE MIGHT DIE DUE TO YOUR ACTIONS...
THE LEAST YOU OWE US IS THE REASON WHY.
WHAT'VE YOU BEEN DOING INSTEAD OF BEING HOME WITH US, "MOM"?

THERE WAS A THREAT TO THE WORLD...
...A LOT OF INNOCENT PEOPLE DIED. A LOT MORE WERE GOING TO DIE.
"THE JUSTICE LEAGUE, WORKING WITH SEVERAL OF MY AGENTS, COUNTERED THAT THREAT.
"WE SAVED THE WORLD.
"THE MAN WE THINK MAY BE COMING AFTER YOU. HIS NAME IS RUSTAM. DESPITE OUR BEST EFFORTS, HE ESCAPED...
"ONCE, A LONG TIME AGO, HE WORKED ALONGSIDE ME. HE WAS A GOOD MAN."
HE BETRAYED ME.
NOW HE'S A BAD GUY.
AND THAT'S ALL YOU NEED TO KNOW.
THERE'S SOMETHING ELSE I NEED TO KNOW, MOM.
HAVE YOU VISITED THEIR GRAVES?

"WE DO. WE GET THE BUS OUT THERE EVERY MONTH.
"MAKE SURE THEIR FLOWERS ARE FRESH. CLEAN THEIR HEADSTONES...
JOSEPH WALLER
"YOU BURIED YOURSELF IN YOUR JOB AND WE HARDLY SEE YOU. OKAY, THAT'S YOUR BUSINESS.
JOSEPH WALLER JR.
"BUT THAT WAS YOUR HUSBAND. YOUR SON. YOUR DAUGHTER WHO WERE KILLED."
DAMITA WALLER
BUT I NEVER SEE NO FLOWERS THERE FROM YOU.
WALLER. LONE MALE APPROACHING ON FOOT.
UNCLEAR IF IT'S RUSTAM.
IS HE ARMED?
NOTHING I CAN SEE. ONE RUCKSACK ON HIS SHOULDER.
OKAY...
LET THE MONSTER OUT.

EAT!!!
THINGS!!!
TASTYYYYYY LOOOKINNGGGG FACCCCE...
AAAAHHHHHHH!!!!!
HELP! HELP ME!!! GETITOFF! GETITOFF!
WAY TOO EASY, WALLER. AND YOU HEAR MANY SUPER-ASSASSINS SCREAM LIKE THAT?
IT'S NOT HIM.
CROC! STAND DOWN!
NO.

CEREBRAL IMPLANT 3K-4, LOW-LEVEL PULSE, **ACTIVATE.**

AAAAIIIIEEEEEEEE!!!

FZZZZZZZSSSSS

DEADSHOT. THAT MAN EVEN BREATHES WRONG, DROP HIM.

CEREBRAL IMPLANT? WHAT KIND OF ***HOMELAND SECURITY*** ARE WE ***TALKING*** HERE?

...THIS.
HELLO, AMANDA.

GET HIM OUT OF HERE.
RUSTAM, I SWEAR...YOU COME NEAR MY KIDS...
OH, IF I'D WANTED THEM DEAD THEY WOULD BE, TRUST ME.

I PLACED A TRACER ON THE GIRL EARLIER.
I'VE BEEN LISTENING. I KNOW AN AWFUL LOT ABOUT THEM.

BUT HURTING THEM WAS NEVER MY INTENTION.
I JUST WANTED THEM TO ACTUALLY SEE THEIR MOTHER. FOR ONCE.
I WANT THEM TO **KNOW** YOU.

AMANDA WALLER, THE WOMAN WHO **KNOWS** EVERYTHING...
...WHO DIDN'T EVEN KNOW SHE IS GOING TO BE A **GRAND-MOTHER...**
BECAUSE THAT IS REVENGE.

WHAT...?
CLICK
ONE OF YOU IS GOING TO HAVE A BABY? WHO...
YOU KIDNAP US OFF THE STREETS, TERRIFY US WITH MONSTERS AND KILLERS.
YOU WORK WITH MONSTERS AND KILLERS. THEY OBEY YOUR ORDERS.
I DO IT TO PROTECT PEOPLE. I DO IT TO PROTECT YOU. THAT'S WHAT A MOTHER DOES...
NO! YOU DON'T CALL YOURSELF THAT. YOU DON'T GET TO SAY THAT!
YOU HAVEN'T EARNED THE RIGHT TO SAY THAT THESE LAST FEW YEARS...
CORETTA...

YOU SHUT US OUT!
DADDY DIED, DAMITA AND JOE DIED! YOU NEVER MENTIONED IT! NOT ONCE! ALL YOU CARED ABOUT WAS YOUR JOB! YOU BURIED YOURSELF BECAUSE IT WAS EASIER! BECAUSE YOU'RE A COWARD!
EVERYTHING ELSE IS AN EXCUSE AND YOU KNOW IT!
COME ON, CORETTA. LET'S GO HOME. THEY CAN'T STOP US.
MARTIN...
SHE'S RIGHT. WHAT SHE SAID. YOU'RE JUST PUTTING US IN DANGER BEING HERE. LEAVE US BE NOW.
WE'LL...UH... WE'LL GIVE YOU A MOMENT.
FLAG. TAKE THE SQUAD BACK TO BELLE REVE. I WANT SURVEILLANCE ON THE KIDS FOR THE NEXT 48 HOURS. DISCREET DISTANCE.
...UNDERSTOOD.
...I DON'T UNDERSTAND.
THIS FEELS LIKE LOSING.

BUT I WON.

JUSTICE LEAGUE VS. SUICIDE SQUAD

VARIANT COVER GALLERY

JUSTICE LEAGUE VS. SUICIDE SQUAD #1 variant cover by Amanda Conner and Laura Martin

JUSTICE LEAGUE VS. SUICIDE SQUAD #1 variant cover by Gary Frank and Brad Anderson

JUSTICE LEAGUE VS. SUICIDE SQUAD #2
variant cover by Amanda Conner
and Laura Martin

JUSTICE LEAGUE VS. SUICIDE SQUAD #2 variant cover by Terry and Rachel Dodson

JUSTICE LEAGUE VS. SUICIDE SQUAD #3 variant cover
by Amanda Conner and Laura Martin

JUSTICE LEAGUE VS. SUICIDE SQUAD #3 variant cover by Joe Madureira and Sunny Gho

JUSTICE LEAGUE VS. SUICIDE SQUAD #4 variant cover by Amanda Conner and Laura Martin

JUSTICE LEAGUE VS. SUICIDE SQUAD #4 variant cover by David Finch, Danny Miki and June Chung

JUSTICE LEAGUE VS. SUICIDE SQUAD #5 variant cover by Amanda Conner and Laura Martin

JUSTICE LEAGUE VS. SUICIDE SQUAD #5 variant cover by Andy Kubert and Brad Anderson

JUSTICE LEAGUE VS. SUICIDE SQUAD #6 variant cover
by Amanda Conner and Laura Martin

JUSTICE LEAGUE VS. SUICIDE SQUAD #6 variant cover
by José Luis García-López and Tomeu Morey

JUSTICE LEAGUE #12 variant cover by Yanick Paquette and Nathan Fairbairn

JUSTICE LEAGUE #13 variant cover by Yanick Paquette and Nathan Fairbairn

SUICIDE SQUAD #9 variant cover by Lee Bermejo

SUICIDE SQUAD #10 variant cover by Lee Bermejo

JUSTICE LEAGUE VS. SUICIDE SQUAD #1 variant cover by Lee Bermejo

JUSTICE LEAGUE VS. SUICIDE SQUAD #1
variant cover by Ed Benes and Dinei Ribeiro

JUSTICE LEAGUE VS. SUICIDE SQUAD #1 variant cover by Mark Brooks

JUSTICE LEAGUE VS. SUICIDE SQUAD #1 variant cover by Gabriele Dell'Otto

JUSTICE LEAGUE VS. SUICIDE SQUAD #1 variant cover
by Chad Hardin, Jeremiah Skipper and Alex Sinclair

JUSTICE LEAGUE VS. SUICIDE SQUAD #1 variant cover by Joe Jusko

JUSTICE LEAGUE VS. SUICIDE SQUAD #1
variant cover by Tyler Kirkham
and Tomeu Morey

JUSTICE LEAGUE VS. SUICIDE SQUAD #1 variant cover by Stanley "Artgerm" Lau

JUSTICE LEAGUE VS. SUICIDE SQUAD #1 variant cover by José Luis García-López and Alex Sinclair

JUSTICE LEAGUE VS. SUICIDE SQUAD #1 variant cover by Francis Manapul

JUSTICE LEAGUE VS. SUICIDE SQUAD #1 variant cover by Dawn McTeigue and Sabine Rich

JUSTICE LEAGUE VS. SUICIDE SQUAD #1 variant cover by Francesco Mattina

JUSTICE LEAGUE VS. SUICIDE SQUAD #1 variant cover by Jonboy Meyers

JUSTICE LEAGUE VS. SUICIDE SQUAD #1 variant
cover by Paolo Pantalena and Arif Prianto

JUSTICE LEAGUE VS. SUICIDE SQUAD #1 variant cover by Ashley Witter

JUSTICE LEAGUE VS. SUICIDE SQUAD #1
second printing variant cover by
Jason Fabok and Alex Sinclair

JUSTICE LEAGUE VS. SUICIDE SQUAD
promotional artwork by Jason Fabok and Alex Sinclair

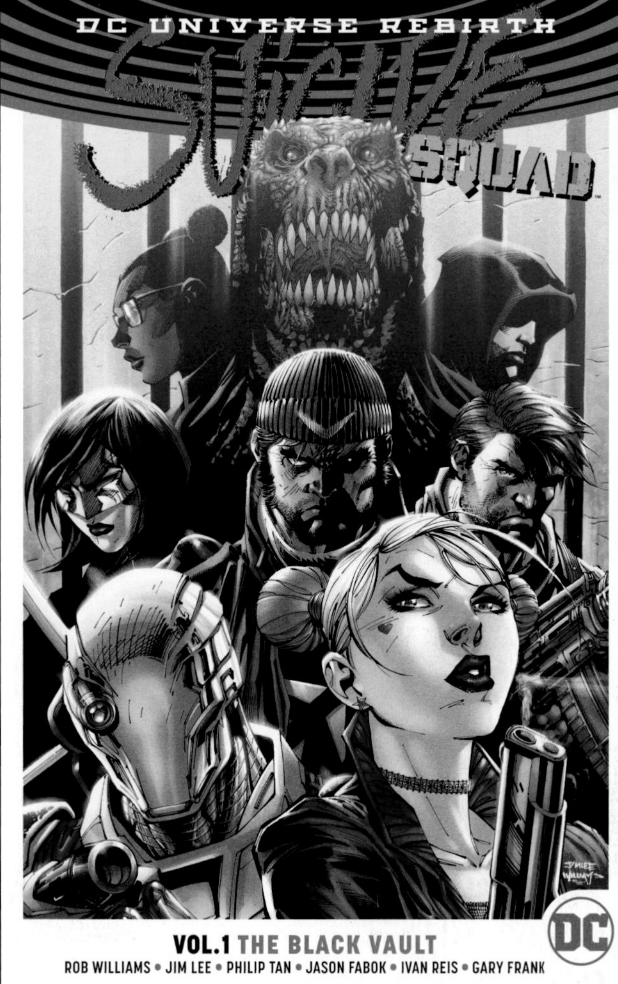

"It's nice to see one of the best comics of the late '80s return so strongly."
– Comic Book Resources

"It's high energy from page one through to the last page." **– BATMAN NEWS**

DC UNIVERSE REBIRTH

SUICIDE SQUAD

VOL. 1: THE BLACK VAULT

ROB WILLIAMS
with JIM LEE and others

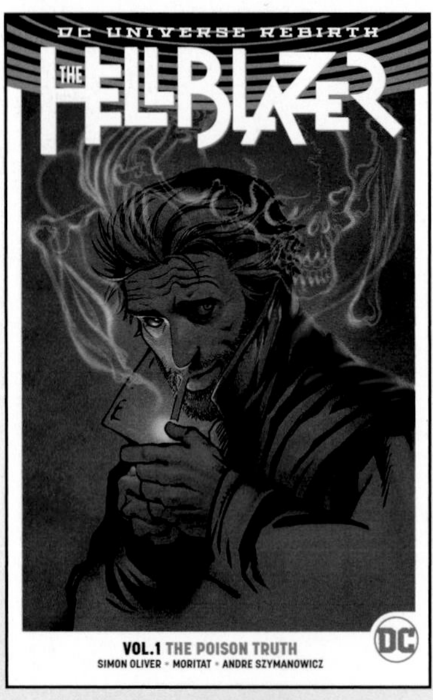

THE HELLBLAZER VOL. 1: THE POISON TRUTH

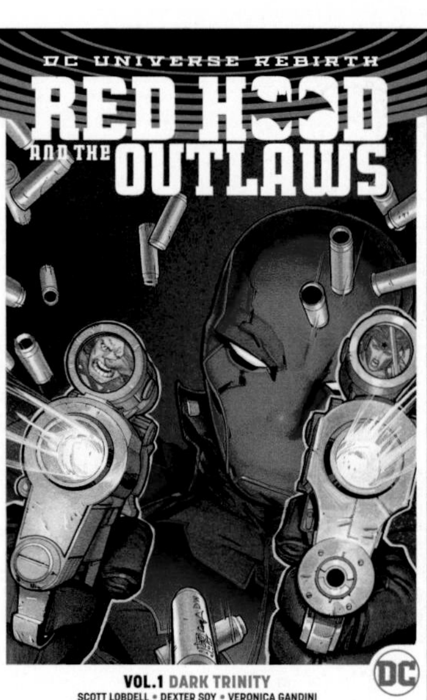

RED HOOD AND THE OUTLAWS VOL. 1: DARK TRINITY

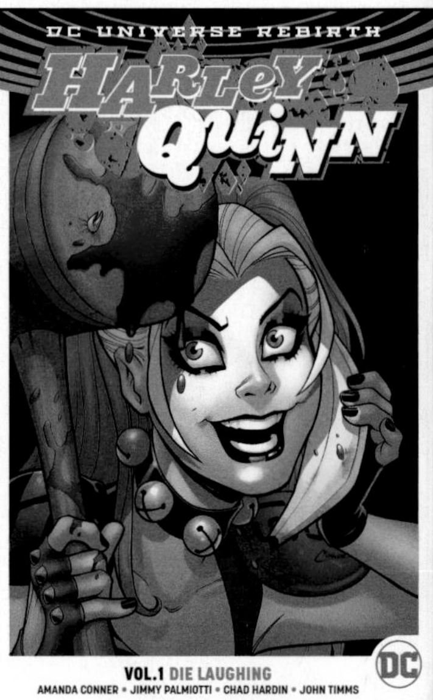

HARLEY QUINN VOL. 1: DIE LAUGHING

Get more DC graphic novels wherever comics and books are sold!